CONCRETENESS IN GENERATIVE PHONOLOGY

CONCRETENESS IN GENERATIVE PHONOLOGY
Evidence from French

by

Bernard Tranel

University of California Press

Berkeley   Los Angeles   London

University of California Press
Berkeley and Los Angeles, California

University of California Press, Ltd.
London, England

Library of Congress Cataloging in Publication Data

Tranel, Bernard.
   Concreteness in generative phonology.

   Bibliography: p. 315
    1. Grammar, Comparative and general—Phonology.
2. Generative grammar.   3. French language—Phonology.
4. French language—Grammar, Generative.   I. Title.
P217.6.T68   415   80-51243
ISBN 0-520-04165-8

Printed in the United States of America

CONTENTS

Preface xi

Part I: The phonology of nasal vowels 1

Introduction 3

I: The standard generative analysis 6
  I.1. Basic claims 6
  I.2. Basic motivations 7
  I.3. Proposed formalizations 9
    I.3.1. Schane (1968*a*) 10
    I.3.2. Schane (1973*b*) 10
    I.3.3. Dell (1970, 1973*c*) 11
    I.3.4. Selkirk (1972) 12
  I.4. Summary 13

II: Critical review of the standard generative analysis 14
  II.1. Introduction 14
  II.2. On the source of nonalternating nasal vowels 15
    II.2.1. Introduction 15
    II.2.2. Critical review of the evidence 16
      II.2.2.1. The simplicity argument 16
      II.2.2.2. The sibilant-voicing argument 20
      II.2.2.3. The slow-speech argument 27
      II.2.2.4. The surface structure constraint arguments 32
    II.2.3. Conclusion 36
  II.3. On artificial difficulties in the abstract generative
    analysis 36
    II.3.1. Introduction 36
    II.3.2. The nonuniqueness of phonological representations . . .37
    II.3.3. The interaction of vowel nasalization and liaison 40
      II.3.3.1. Dell's account 41
      II.3.3.2. Schane's account 51
      II.3.3.3. Vowel nasalization and liaison: conclusion 54
    II.3.4. Conclusion 54

II.4. On the descriptive inadequacy of vowel nasalization 55
  II.4.1. Introduction 55
  II.4.2. The generation of nasal vowels 55
  II.4.3. The generation of [VN] sequences 56
    II.4.3.1. Vowel nasalization within morphemes 57
    II.4.3.2. Vowel nasalization across morphemes
        (within words) 60
      A. The prefix *in-* /in/ 60
      B. The prefix *circum-* /sirkɔm/ 64
      C. The conditional 64
      D. Conclusion 66
    II.4.3.3. Vowel nasalization at the end of words 67
  II.4.4. Conclusion 70
II.5. Summary 70
III: An alternative analysis 71
III.1. Introduction 71
III.2. Nonalternating nasal vowels 71
  III.2.1. Implications 72
  III.2.2. *Mon*-type words, the article *un*, and the
       prefixes *bien-, en-, non-* 73
  III.2.3. Morpheme structure constraints 76
III.3. Nonalternating [VN] sequences 77
  III.3.1. Nonalternating [VN] sequences within morphemes .. 78
  III.3.2. Nonalternating [VN] sequences across morphemes
     (within words) 80
  III.3.3. Nonalternating [VN] sequences at the end of words . 84
III.4. Conclusion 84
III.5. [Ṽ] ~ [VN] alternations 85
  III.5.1. Introduction 85
  III.5.2. Phonological denasalization 87
  III.5.3. Nonuniform treatment 90
    III.5.3.1. Derivational morphology 91
    III.5.3.2. Third-conjugation verbs 97
    III.5.3.3. Gender and liaison alternations 100
      A. Morphophonological vowel nasalization 100
      B. Problems with morphophonological vowel
        nasalization 104
      C. Suggestions 109
      D. The questions of the oral vowel and of the
        nasal consonant 111

  E. A concrete analysis............................117

III.6. Summary..................................121

IV: Nasal vowels and liaison: diachronic and
  dialectal perspectives...............................122

 IV.1. Introduction...............................122

 IV.2. Diachronic and dialectal information.................122

  IV.2.1. Preliminaries.........................122

  IV.2.2. Survey.............................124

   A. Sixteenth century......................124

   B. Seventeenth century.....................125

   C. Eighteenth century......................128

   D. Nineteenth century.....................133

   E. Twentieth century......................140

  IV.2.3. Summary............................146

 IV.3. Explanations and implications....................147

Part II: Final consonants..............................157

Introduction......................................159

V: The standard generative analysis.......................165

 V.1. Basic claims.............................165

 V.2. Basic motivation..........................166

 V.3. Formalizations...........................167

  V.3.1. The formalization of the process of consonant
   deletion...............................167

   V.3.1.1. Schane (1968a)......................167

   V.3.1.2. Schane (1974).......................168

   V.3.1.3. Dell (1970).........................168

   V.3.1.4. Dell (1973b).........................169

   V.3.1.5. Selkirk (1972)......................170

  V.3.2. The role of syntactic structure in liaison...........171

  V.3.3. Pronounced final consonants.....................175

 V.4. Summary...............................178

VI: Plural marking and liaison...........................179

 VI.1. Introduction............................179

 VI.2. Motivations for the systematic plural-suffix hypothesis..180

  VI.2.1. Liaison............................181

  VI.2.2. Singular/plural [al] ~ [o] alternations...........182

  VI.2.3. Singular/plural alternations of the type
   oeuf [œf]/*oeufs* [ø]........................183

VI.2.4. Conclusion 184
VI.3. Arguments against the systematic plural-suffix
    hypothesis 184
VI.3.1. The [al] ~ [o] alternation 185
VI.3.2. Exceptions to final-consonant deletion 191
VI.3.3. Liaison.....................................192
    VI.3.3.1. The restoration of final consonants 192
        A. The cases of *cinq* and other cardinal numbers 192
        B. The cases of *boeufs, oeufs,* and *os* 195
        C. The cases of optional final consonants...........195
        D. Consonantal regressions 196
    VI.3.3.2. New final consonants 197
    VI.3.3.3. New words 197
    VI.3.3.4. Prefixes 199
    VI.3.3.5. The conditional...........................201
    VI.3.3.6. On the determination and treatment of
        exceptions 201
    VI.3.3.7. Summary................................203
    VI.3.3.8. On the generalizations allowed by consonant
        deletion 203
        A. Inflectional morphology 204
        B. Derivational morphology.......................206
        C. Liaison.....................................209
    VI.3.3.9. Conclusion on consonant deletion 209
VI.3.4. Conclusion on the systematic plural-suffix
    hypothesis.....................................210
VI.4. The plural /z/-insertion analysis 210
VI.4.1. Positive evidence 210
    VI.4.1.1. Direct mapping...........................211
    VI.4.1.2. Plural /z/ as a connective morpheme..........211
    VI.4.1.3. On the pronunciation of *oeufs* 212
    VI.4.1.4. Plural marking and cardinal numbers 214
VI.4.2. On the formulation and application of the plural
    /z/-insertion process 217
VII: A treatment of [Ø] ~ [C] alternations 222
VII.1. Introduction 222
VII.2. Liaison 223
VII.2.1. Verb liaison.................................223
    VII.2.1.1. Optional verb liaison with person endings 223
    VII.2.1.2. Obligatory verb liaison with person endings ...230

VII.2.1.3. Generalizing the rules 234
VII.2.1.4. Infinitive liaison 234
VII.2.2. Adjective liaison 235
VII.2.3. Liaison with invariable words 239
VII.2.3.1. Formal proposal 240
VII.2.3.2. Justification of the analysis 241
VII.2.3.3. Apparent exceptions 246
VII.3. Remaining [Ø] ~ [C] alternations 248
VII.3.1. Verb-stem alternations 248
VII.3.2. Masculine/feminine alternations 251
VII.3.2.1. On the predictability of gender consonants 251
VII.3.2.2. Justification of the insertion analysis 266
VII.3.2.3. Summary 272
VII.3.3. Derivational morphology alternations 272
VII.4. Conclusion 275

Part III: Protective schwas and h-aspiré words 277

Introduction 279
1. A note on terminology 279
2. Purpose 280
VIII: Protective schwas 282
VIII.1. Introduction 282
VIII.2. On the phonetic evidence for protective schwas 286
VIII.2.1. Schwa and h-aspiré words 286
VIII.2.2. Schwa and consonant clusters 288
VIII.2.3. Schwa and *rien* 290
VIII.2.4. Schwa and other dialects 291
VIII.2.5. Schwa in songs and poetry 292
VIII.2.6. Schwa and slow speech 292
VIII.2.7. Conclusion 293
VIII.3. On the structural evidence for protective schwas 293
VIII.4. Protective schwas and learnability 293
VIII.5. Conclusion 294
IX: H-aspiré words 295
IX.1. Introduction 295
IX.2. H-aspiré words and elision, liaison, and suppletion 295
IX.3. H-aspiré words and optional schwa deletion 303
IX.4. H-aspiré words and enchaînement 305
IX.5. H-aspiré words and final schwas 306

IX.6. H-aspiré words and liquid deletion 308
IX.7. H-aspiré words and glottal stops 310
IX.8. H-aspiré words and deletable final consonants 311
IX.9. Conclusion 314

References 315

PREFACE

This study deals with four related topics in Modern French phonology and morphology: (i) the status of nasal vowels, (ii) the nature of [Ø] ~ [C] alternations, (iii) the question of final schwas, and (iv) the treatment of h-aspiré words. The theoretical framework is that of generative phonology. These topics have already received considerable attention in the context of generative phonology, most notably in the works of Schane, Dell, and Selkirk, but the analyses proposed here constitute a radical departure from the views advocated by these authors.

The two approaches oppose each other on practically all the main language-specific issues explored in this study. Whereas Schane, Dell, and Selkirk claim that nasal vowels are synchronically derived in much the same way as they arose historically, I argue that they have become lexical. Schane, Dell, and Selkirk treat [V̄] ~ [VN] and [Ø] ~ [C] alternations in a uniform fashion, by means of major phonological processes of vowel nasalization and consonant deletion. I propose the reverse: that these alternations are not of a uniform nature, that they are governed not only by phonological factors but also by grammatical and lexical information, and that phenomena of vowel denasalization and consonant insertion are at work, in particular in the areas of liaison and gender formation. Final schwas are a structural necessity in the type of analysis of nasal vowels and final consonants suggested by Schane, Dell, and Selkirk, but not in the treatment of French phonology and morphology proposed here. Schane, Dell, and Selkirk argue for a treatment of h-aspiré words excluding the use of rule features; I suggest that the data in fact make such a treatment necessary. Within the same broad theoretical framework as that adopted by Schane, Dell, and Selkirk, this study thus offers a drastically different view of central questions of French phonology and morphology.

The analyses proposed by Schane, Dell, and Selkirk may be considered the direct descendants of the type of abstract phonology put forth in Chomsky and Halle's *The Sound Pattern of English*. Broadly characterized, this approach emphasizes formal simplicity; the main

goal is to capture generalizations that are labeled linguistically significant but whose linguistic significance is essentially determined by formal criteria of economy which often ignore elements of a substantive
nature. This kind of treatment typically privileges purely phonological
analyses and results in the postulation of underlying representations
far removed from surface phonetic forms, in derivations of extreme
depth, and in intricate rule ordering. More crucially, the psychological reality of these solutions is usually extremely doubtful. The concrete view of French phonology and morphology which emerges in this
study is more directly connected to a type of generative phonology
which received its impulse in the late sixties and early seventies from
linguists like Kiparsky, Skousen, and Vennemann, and whose goal is
to provide not simply solutions that mechanically crank out data but
analyses that are justified on substantive grounds and demonstrably
have psychological reality. In general, the investigations conducted
along these lines have resulted in descriptions of a more immediately
transparent nature with respect to surface phonetic facts. The relevance of this study thus goes beyond the analysis of French; a contri-
bution is made to the ongoing search for the general theoretical principles that govern the construction of grammars by native speakers.

The organization of the study is as follows: Part I deals with the
phonology of nasal vowels, Part II, with final consonants, and Part
III, with protective schwas and h-aspiré words. The first two parts
have a similar structure. In each one an introduction highlights the
main issues and places them in a historical perspective by considering
briefly and in general terms how these questions have been handled
by generativists as well as by linguists from other schools of thought,
in particular structuralists. Chapters i and v summarize the generative analyses of nasal vowels and final consonants proposed by
Schane, Dell, and Selkirk and specify their main motivations and
basic claims. Chapters ii and vi contain detailed critical reviews of
these generative treatments, with the main focus placed on internal
inconsistencies, the problems created by additional data not previously considered, and the inability to account for external evidence.
Chapters iii and vii offer alternative treatments rendered necessary by
the critical reviews of the preceding chapters; formal proposals are
elaborated on the basis of ample substantive evidence, and their implications are compared with the claims made by the analyses proposed by Schane, Dell, and Selkirk. Chapter iv in Part I considers
nasal vowels in liaison from a diachronic and dialectal perspective.

Part III in essence complements Parts I and II as far as final schwas and h-aspiré words are concerned; Parts I and II show the lack of a structural necessity for the postulation of final schwas; chapter viii demonstrates the lack of a phonological basis. Parts I and II make a rule-feature treatment of h-aspiré words possible; chapter ix justifies such a treatment and points out the weaknesses of other analyses.

In sum, the relevance of this study is threefold: (i) from a descriptive perspective it presents a new integrated account of important aspects of French phonology and morphology and brings to bear data generally omitted from consideration; (ii) from a methodological perspective it demonstrates the revealing and crucial role played by substantive evidence as a tool of investigation, more precisely as a window on psychological reality; (iii) from a theoretical perspective it provides a data-based comparison between two approaches which, within the same broad generative framework, differ in essential respects concerning general principles of grammar construction by native speakers.

Completion of this work was in part made possible by research and travel grants from the School of Humanities at the University of California, Irvine (1975–1978), a summer grant from The Regents of the University of California (1977), and a spring quarter sabbatical (1978).

I wish to thank Charlotte Stringer for her typing and Alice McMurray, Yves-Charles Morin, and Owen Thomas for their comments on both form and content.

PART I
THE PHONOLOGY OF NASAL VOWELS

INTRODUCTION

Nasal and oral vowels exhibit a particularly close relation in natural languages: the nasality feature is usually clearly derived historically, and it often appears temptingly predictable, synchronically (cf. Lightner 1970; Ruhlen 1978). This temptation constitutes the first basic issue concerning the phonology of nasal vowels in Modern French: Are French nasal vowels lexical or derived?

In nongenerative considerations of French phonology, it has generally been assumed that nasal vowels are phonemic. For example, typical of authors of pronunciation treatises and pedagogical manuals, Malmberg (1975:67) writes: "Le français se distingue de la plupart des autres langues de l'Europe en possédant dans son système phonologique une série de voyelles nasales." Representative of linguists examining phonemic inventories in the languages of the world, Trubetzkoy (1967:130–133) cites French as an instance of the feature of nasality on vowels being used for a distinctive opposition. Martinet (1971:143) states the case most forcefully: "Les voyelles nasales sont incontestablement en français normal des phonèmes indépendants, et ne sauraient aucunement être interprétées comme des groupes de phonèmes voyelle orale + consonne nasale."[1]

Certain generative treatments of French phonology, on the other hand, have adopted the view precisely rejected by Martinet, arguing that nasal vowels do not exist lexically but are instead derived from underlying sequences of oral vowel plus nasal consonant (Schane

---

1. By "français normal" Martinet means Standard French. He opposes this type of speech to Southern French, for which he claims no phonemic nasal vowels: "l'inexistence de phonèmes vocaliques nasals est un fait strictement méridional" (1971:143).

1968*a*; Dell 1970). This analysis had precursors in other schools; it was advocated in particular by Trager (1944:131–132; 1955:513), Hjelmslev (1948–49:219), and Togeby (1951:58, 84). The arguments in its favor, however, were mainly developed within the theoretical framework of generative phonology found in *SPE* (Chomsky and Halle 1968). For ease of reference, I call this type of treatment of French nasal vowels the abstract, or standard, generative analysis.[2]

In other generative treatments of French phonology, nasal vowels have been regarded as lexical, but there have been differences on the particular cases where nasal vowels have thus been postulated as (systematic) phonemic. For instance, Selkirk (1972), whose analysis of French nasal vowels may otherwise be considered as standard, posited underlying nasal vowels in a restricted class of words, namely, those that keep their final vowel nasal in liaison (e.g., *mon* 'my', as in *mon ami* [mɔ̃nami] 'my friend'); Tranel (1974*b*) posited underlying nasal vowels when they do not alternate with sequences of oral vowel plus nasal consonant (e.g., *mon* [mɔ̃], *cinq* [sɛ̃k] 'five') and also in a few well-determined alternating cases (e.g., *maison* [mezɔ̃] 'house', cf. *maisonnette* [mezɔnɛt] 'little house'; *bouquin* [bukɛ̃] 'book', cf. *bouquiner* [bukine] 'to read books'); Bibeau (1975) posited underlying nasal vowels whenever they are (classical) phonemic (e.g., *mon, cinq, maison, bouquin, bon* [bɔ̃] 'good' (masc.), *viens* [vjɛ̃] 'come').[3]

In structuralist analyses where phonemic nasal vowels have been posited (e.g., Hall 1948), the morphophonemic representations of alternating nasal vowels seem to be identical with their underlying representations in standard generative analyses (e.g., Hall gives morphophonemic /bɔn/ for *bon* (14), /mən-/ for *main* 'hand' (19), /tən-/ for *tenir* 'to hold' (28), /garsɔn/ for *garçon* 'boy' (46)); in nonalternating cases, however, the phonemic nasal vowels naturally appear morphophonemically.

The assumption that nasal vowels are part of the underlying vocalic system of Modern French thus brings about the second basic

2. The term "abstract" here means that the analysis makes assumptions about the linguistic knowledge of native speakers which are removed from the surface phonetic facts and, as is later shown, are not psychologically real. The word "standard" is used because Schane (1968*a*) and its theoretical framework *SPE* are familiar landmarks. The term is common usage in syntax, where it similarly establishes a convenient reference point (cf. the standard theory [= Chomsky 1965]; the extended standard theory [= Chomsky 1972*b*]; the revised extended standard theory [= Chomsky 1975]).

3. The term "classical phonemic" is borrowed from Schane (1971:503 n. 1).

issue concerning French nasal vowels: Under what conditions should lexical nasal vowels be postulated?

Connected to these issues is an obvious question of crucial importance: How are alternating nasal vowels and sequences of oral vowel plus nasal consonant to be related in Modern French? This central problem may be analyzed into three interrelated points concerning (i) the uniformity of treatment of the alternations, (ii) the directionality of the relation(s), and (iii) the type(s) of relation(s) involved. In other words: (i) Are the alternations between nasal vowels and [VN] sequences to be captured by means of a single relation or by more than one? (ii) Should derivations go from underlying /VN/ sequences to surface nasal vowels or/and from underlying nasal vowels to surface [VN] sequences? (iii) What are the essential characteristics of the relation(s) (e.g., phonological, morphophonological, or lexical; major or minor)?

In the last ten to fifteen years the standard generative analysis, which proposes a uniform treatment whereby a major phonological process of vowel nasalization derives all surface nasal vowels from underlying /VN/ sequences, has been the most widely accepted view, at least among generativists. This particular treatment has drawn its appeal from its unifying account of what other analyses would require to be handled as separate phenomena.

Within the framework of generative grammar, I would like to address myself to the basic issues I have just mentioned, taking as a point of departure the abstract analysis, presenting evidence against it, and offering an alternative to it. Thus, in chapter i, I outline the standard generative treatment of French nasal vowels, with its variations, and I summarize the arguments that have been proposed to justify it. In chapter ii, I provide evidence showing that there is no general phonological process of vowel nasalization in Modern French and that nasal vowels should be considered as lexical in this language. In chapter iii, I propose an alternative analysis, focusing in particular on the question of the treatment of alternating nasal vowels; several conceivable options are discussed. In chapter iv, the behavior of nasal vowels in liaison is examined from a historical and dialectal perspective, providing independent evidence in favor of the concrete view argued for on a synchronic basis in the preceding chapters.

I

THE STANDARD GENERATIVE ANALYSIS

I.1. Basic claims

As noted in the introduction, the abstract generative treatment of French nasal vowels assumes that there are no lexical nasal vowels in Modern French. The nasal vowels that show up phonetically are derived from underlying sequences of oral vowel plus nasal consonant.

The formalization of this view varies among linguists and across time (see sec. I.3.), but the various solutions proposed all share the same essential assumption: there exists in Modern French a general phonological phenomenon of vowel nasalization (i.e., /VN/ → [Ṽ]) which occurs before a consonant (a) morpheme internally, (b) across morpheme boundaries, and (c) across single word boundaries; it also takes place (d) before two word boundaries:[1]

(1) /VN/ → [Ṽ] / — C   (a) e.g., *conte* [kɔ̃t] 'tale'
    / — +C   (b) e.g., *bonté* [bɔ̃te] 'goodness'
    / — #C   (c) e.g., *un bon gars* [ɛ̃bɔ̃ga] 'a good guy'
    / — ##   (d) e.g., *il est bon* [ilɛbɔ̃] 'he is good'

A most important claim made by this analysis is that vowel nasalization in Modern French is purely phonological; it is assumed to take place independently of any available grammatical information

---

1. Other rules are also required: (a) in Schane's (1968*a*) framework, processes of diphthongization and fronting (e.g., *bien* [bjɛ̃] 'good' (noun)/*bénéfique* [benefik] 'beneficial'; *faim* [fɛ̃] 'hunger'/*famine* [famin] 'famine') (for different treatments and suggestions concerning the alternations handled by these rules, see, e.g., Dell and Selkirk (1978), Tranel (1974*b*:124–127; 1977*b*), Walker (1975*b*)); (b) nasal vowel quality adjustments (lowering (e.g., *fin* [fɛ̃]/*fine* [fin] 'thin' (masc./fem.); for certain dialects, unrounding (e.g., *brun* [brɛ̃]/*brune* [bryn] 'brown' (masc./fem.)).

(boundaries excepted).[2] The phenomenon is also considered to be major; the expected behavior for any lexical item meeting the relevant structural description is to undergo vowel nasalization. Another central characteristic of this analysis is that it crucially rests on the postulation of morphological and lexical schwas and on extrinsic rule ordering. Morphological schwas are markers for the feminine of nouns and adjectives, for first-conjugation verbs, and for the present subjunctive. Lexical schwas are part of the lexical representations of words. Morphological and lexical schwas protect the relevant forms from the effect of vowel nasalization (e.g., *bonne* /bɔn + ə/ 'good' (fem.), *paysanne* /peizan + ə/ 'peasant' (fem.), *donne* /dɔn + ə/ 'give', *vienne* /vjɛn + ə/ 'come' (subj.); *homme* /ɔmə/ 'man', *jaune* /žonə/ 'yellow', *samedi* /samədi/ 'Saturday', *omelette* /ɔməlɛtə/ 'omelet'); they are then deleted by late phonological rules ([bɔn], [peizan], [dɔn], [vjɛn], [ɔm], [žon], [samdi], [ɔmlɛt]), which must be extrinsically ordered after vowel nasalization in counterfeeding fashion.

I.2. Basic motivations

At the surface phonetic level, nasal vowels alternate with [VN] sequences in Modern French. The following series of semantically related words exemplify some of these alternations:

(1) (a) *bon* [bɔ̃]
    'good' (masc.)

    bonne [bɔn]
    'good' (fem.)

    bonté [bɔ̃te]
    'goodness'

    bonnement [bɔnmã]
    'simply'

    bonifier [bɔnifje]
    'to improve'

(b) *sain* [sɛ̃]
    'healthy' (masc.)

    saine [sɛn]
    'healthy' (fem.)

    santé [sãte]
    'health'

    sainement [sɛnmã]
    'in a healthy way'

    assainir [asenir]
    'to make healthy'

(c) *fin* [fɛ̃]
    'thin' (masc.)

    fine [fin]
    'thin' (fem.)

    finement [finmã]
    'thinly'

    affiner [afine]
    'to thin'

(d) *paysan* [peizã]
    'peasant' (masc.)

    paysanne [peizan]
    'peasant' (fem.)

    paysannerie [peizanri]
    'peasantry'

2. Implicitly, the claim seems to be that vowel nasalization occurs when the oral vowel and the nasal consonant are tautosyllabic. Cf. Schane (1978c:304–305) and Basbøll (1978:4–5) for explicit formalizations.

Given this initial data-based motivation for relating nasal vowels and sequences of oral vowel plus nasal consonant, the central guiding principle for the standard generative analysis of French nasal vowels is formal simplicity.

The decision to assume that the sequences of oral vowel plus nasal consonant are basic is connected to the argument that one can obtain a simpler grammar if rules are posited which derive nasal vowels from underlying /VN/ sequences rather than the reverse. As illustrated in (3a–b), more than one oral vowel may correspond to a given nasal vowel:

(3) (a) *fine*   [fin]   *fin*   [fɛ̃]   'thin' (fem./masc.)

      brune   [bryn]   *brun*   [brɛ̃]   'brown' (fem./masc.)

      chienne   [šjɛn]   *chien*   [šjɛ̃]   'female/male dog'

      jeûner   [žœne]   *à jeun*   [ažɛ̃]   'to fast'/'on an empty stomach'

    (b) *prenons*   [prənɔ̃]   *prend*   [prã]   '(we) take'/'(he) takes'

      paysanne   [peizan]   *paysan*   [peizã]   'peasant' (fem./masc.)

The derivation of the oral vowels from the nasal vowels would lead to a relatively more complex grammar, since lexical markings and several denasalization rules would be required, instead of a general process of vowel nasalization and nasal vowel quality adjustments of a merging nature.[3] Similarly, as shown in (3c), the nasal consonant in [Ṽ] ~ [VN] alternations varies in place of articulation,

    (3) (c) *craignent* [krɛñ]   *craint*   [krɛ̃]   '(they) fear'/'(he) fears'

---

3. In some cases more than one nasal vowel corresponds to a given sequence of oral vowel plus nasal consonant:

  (i) *vanité*   [vanite]   *vain*   [vɛ̃]   'vanity'/'vain' (masc.)

     paysanne   [peizan]   *paysan*   [peizã]   'peasant' (fem./masc.)

  (ii) *saine*   [sɛn]   *sain*   [sɛ̃]   'healthy' (fem./masc.)

                      santé   [sãte]   'health'

  (iii) *menotte*   [mənɔt]   *main*   [mɛ̃]   'little hand'/'hand'

     prenons   [prənɔ̃]   *prend*   [prã]   '(we) take'/'(he) takes'

Within the framework of the abstract generative analysis of French nasal vowels, Schane (1968*a*) and Dell and Selkirk (1978) advocate different approaches to the treatment of such examples. For instance, in case (i), Schane would posit for *vanité/ vain* an underlying lax /a/ which would be fronted to /ɛ/ under stress in *vain* (hence [vɛ̃]) and which would be tensed to /A/ in *vanité,* because of the learned suffix *-ité;* for *paysanne/paysan,* an underlying tense /A/ would be postulated; in general, the quality of tense vowels remains stable, hence [vanite] and [peizan]/[peizã]. Dell and Selkirk, who do not resort to the tense/lax and stressed/unstressed distinctions used by Schane, would posit an underlying /a/ in *paysanne/paysan* (hence [peizan]/ [peizã]) and an underlying /ɛ/ in *vanité/vain* (hence [vɛ̃]); the [a] of *vanité* [vanite] would be accounted for by a rule called learned backing, which is governed by lexical markings on stems and suffixes.

mesquine [mɛskin] *mesquin* [mɛskẽ] 'mean' (fem./masc.)
famine [famin] *faim* [fẽ] 'famine'/'hunger'
and the insertion treatment needed if nasal vowels were considered basic would be less simple than the deletion account necessary when the sequences of oral vowel plus nasal consonant are assumed to be present underlyingly.

The decision to treat [Ṽ] ~ [VN] alternations in a purely phonological fashion is likewise founded on the simplicity criterion. These alternations cut across various grammatical distinctions:

(4) (a) masculine/feminine (adjectives and nouns):
    bon/bonne   [bɔ̃]/[bɔn]   'good' (masc./fem.)
    baron/baronne   [barɔ̃]/[barɔn]   'baron'/'baroness'
  (b) present indicative singular/plural (third-conjugation verbs):
    vient/viennent   [vjẽ]/[vjɛn]   '(he) comes'/'(they) come'
  (c) present indicative/subjunctive (third-conjugation verbs):
    vient/vienne   [vjẽ]/[vjɛn]   '(he) comes/come'

In order to account for such alternations uniformly, it is necessary to resort to their common denominator, which is phonological. This account is reinforced by the fact that there are alternations between nasal vowels and [VN] sequences for which grammatical distinctions of the above-mentioned kind do not apply:

(5) Derivational morphology:
    maison/maisonnette [mezɔ̃]/[mezɔnɛt] 'house'/'little house'
    bouquin/bouquiner [bukẽ]/[bukine] 'book'/'to read books'
    printemps/printanier [prɛ̃tã]/[prɛ̃tanje] 'spring'/'springlike'

A purely phonological account of vowel nasalization allows for the treatment of these alternations as well.

The generalization of this uniform phonological analysis of alternating nasal vowels to nonalternating nasal vowels is also based on formal simplicity: if nasal vowels do not occur at all underlyingly, then all vowels in the lexicon are redundantly [−nasal]. Arguments of a more substantive nature (discussed in chap. ii) have in addition been proposed to justify this abstract source for nonalternating nasal vowels.

I.3. Proposed formalizations[4]

As indicated earlier, the standard generative view of French nasal vowels has received several formal realizations to express the nasalization of the vowel and the deletion of the nasal consonant in underlying

---

4. I leave aside here the rules referred to in n. 1.

/VN/ sequences. I here present them rapidly, pointing out their essential features.

I.3.1. Schane (1968*a*)

Schane (1968*a*) proposed a two-step analysis with intrinsically ordered rules, vowel nasalization (6) and nasal consonant deletion (7):

(6) $\text{V} \rightarrow [+\text{nasal}] / -\begin{bmatrix} \text{C} \\ +\text{nasal} \end{bmatrix} \begin{Bmatrix} \# \\ \text{C} \end{Bmatrix}$ (a)
(b)

(7) $\begin{bmatrix} \text{C} \\ +\text{nasal} \end{bmatrix} \rightarrow \emptyset / \begin{bmatrix} \text{V} \\ +\text{nasal} \end{bmatrix} -$

As Schane himself pointed out in a footnote, the data require "a more refined statement" (142), since part (a) of rule (6) applies only when the nasal consonant is in phrase-final position, or when the word boundary is followed by a consonant, but not if the next word begins with a vowel, as illustrated in (8):

(8) *il est bon* [ilɛbɔ̃] 'he is good'
un bon gars [ɛ̃bɔ̃ga] 'a good guy'
un bon ami [ɛ̃bɔnami] 'a good friend'

The rule of vowel nasalization actually intended is therefore that given in (9):

(9) $\text{V} \rightarrow [+\text{nasal}] / -\begin{bmatrix} \text{C} \\ +\text{nasal} \end{bmatrix} \begin{Bmatrix} \# & \# \\ (\#) & \text{C} \end{Bmatrix}$ (a)
(b)

I.3.2. Schane (1973*b*)

The formalization intended in Schane (1968*a*) does not account for liaison cases such as *mon ami* [mɔ̃nami] 'my friend', where a nasal vowel is found in an environment when rule (9) cannot generate it, and where a nasal consonant is present in a context where rule (7) should have deleted it. Schane (1973*b*) adopts for vowel nasalization a different formal proposal which addresses itself to this problem.

The new analysis involves a theoretical innovation: Schane rejects one aspect of standard generative phonology, whereby constraints are built directly into rules. He proposes instead that rules be natural phonological rules and that constraints on these rules be listed separately.

Schane's formal treatment of French nasal vowels thus becomes the following: there is in Modern French a natural process of vowel nasalization, rule (10):

(10) $V \rightarrow [+\text{nasal}] / - \begin{bmatrix} C \\ +\text{nasal} \end{bmatrix}$

"Because the nasalization rule does not normally apply when the nasal consonant is followed by a vowel—e.g. *bon ami*—there must be a constraint to this effect" (829–830):

(11) $V \rightarrow [-\text{nasalization rule}] / - \begin{bmatrix} C \\ +\text{nasal} \end{bmatrix} ([-\text{seg}]) V$

The third step of this analysis accounts for the troublesome cases like *mon ami*. "Since the vowels in . . . *un arbre, en été,* etc. exceptionally do undergo nasalization in this environment, they will be marked as exceptions to the constraint. Thus in the lexicon, the relevant vowels of these forms are marked [–constraint [(11)]]. Once the constraint no longer applies, the vowels become nasalized according to the rule" (830). In this system the deletion of nasal consonants is no longer accomplished as a direct consequence of the process of vowel nasalization, but rather through a general natural rule of consonant deletion:[5]

(12) $C \rightarrow \emptyset / - ([-\text{seg}]) \begin{Bmatrix} C \\ \# \end{Bmatrix}$

I.3.3. Dell (1970, 1973c)

Dell (1970, 1973c) proposed a two-step analysis of vowel nasalization comparable to that of Schane (1968a), but he exploited the postulation of two separate rules to account for the contrast offered by data like *bon ami* [bɔnami]/*mon ami* [mɔ̃nami].

Dell's treatment includes the following three rules, vowel nasalization (13), liaison (14), and nasal consonant deletion (15):

(13) $V \rightarrow [+\text{nasal}] / - \begin{bmatrix} C \\ +\text{nasal} \end{bmatrix} \begin{Bmatrix} \# \\ C \end{Bmatrix}$

(14) C # V
    1 2 3 $\Rightarrow$ 2 1 3

(15) $\begin{bmatrix} C \\ +\text{nasal} \end{bmatrix} \rightarrow \emptyset / \begin{bmatrix} V \\ +\text{nasal} \end{bmatrix} -$

In addition, the analysis makes use of "local ordering," a theory of rule application which allows rules to apply in different orders in the derivations of different forms (see Anderson 1969, 1970, 1974).

---

5. Like the natural rule of vowel nasalization (10), rule (12) operates in conjunction with a series of constraints that limit its scope of application (see chap. v).

For words like *mon,* rule (14) applies after rule (13) in unmarked fashion and before rule (15). On the other hand, adjectives like *bon* are lexically marked to undergo rule (14) before rule (13). Sample derivations are given in (16):

(16) (a)

	mon café 'my coffee' /mɔn#kafe/	*mon ami* 'my friend' /mɔn#ami/
Rule (13)	mɔ̃n#kafe	mɔ̃n#ami
Rule (14)	———	mɔ̃#nami
Rule (15)	mɔ̃ #kafe	———
	[mɔ̃kafe]	[mɔ̃nami]

(b)

	bon café 'good coffee' /bɔn#kafe/	*bon ami* 'good friend' /bɔn#ami/
Rule (14)	———	bɔ̃#nami
Rule (13)	bɔ̃n#kafe	———
Rule (15)	bɔ̃ #kafe	———
	[bɔ̃kafe]	[bɔnami]

I.3.4. Selkirk (1972)

As opposed to Schane and Dell, Selkirk (1972) proposed a one-step analysis of vowel nasalization and nasal consonant deletion:[6]

$$(17) \quad \begin{bmatrix} V \\ -nasal \end{bmatrix} \begin{bmatrix} C \\ +nasal \end{bmatrix} \begin{Bmatrix} (\#)C \\ \# \# \end{Bmatrix} \implies \begin{bmatrix} 1 \\ +nasal \end{bmatrix} \emptyset \ 3$$
$$\qquad\qquad 1 \qquad\quad 2 \qquad\quad 3$$

In order to account for liaison cases like *mon ami* [mɔ̃nami], nasal vowels are posited underlyingly in just these instances (/mɔ̃n#ami/).[7] Rule (17) does not apply to words like *mon.* The deletion of the underlying final /n/, which is required when a consonant-initial word follows (e.g., *mon café* /mɔ̃n#kafe/ [mɔ̃kafe]), is performed by a general rule of final consonant deletion which, in particular, accounts for alternations such as *hiver* [ivɛr] 'winter'/*hiverner* [ivɛrne] 'to spend the winter' (see chap. v).

---

6. Dell (1973*b*) collapsed the rules of vowel nasalization and nasal consonant deletion into the following schema:

$$[+syll] \ [+nasal] \ \begin{Bmatrix} C \\ \# \end{Bmatrix} \quad [+nasal] \ \emptyset \ \begin{Bmatrix} C \\ \# \end{Bmatrix}$$
$$\quad 1 \qquad\quad 2 \qquad 3 \implies 1 \quad 2 \quad 3$$

This rule, however, does not cover the range of data to be accounted for.

7. In Dell and Selkirk (1978:2 n. 1), however, the claim is maintained that there are no underlying nasal vowels in Modern French.

I.4. Summary

The standard generative analysis of French nasal vowels assumes that nasal vowels and sequences of oral vowel plus nasal consonant are to be related uniformly by means of a system of purely phonological rules deriving surface nasal vowels from underlying /VN/ sequences. The problem posed by contrasts like *bon ami* [bɔnami]/*mon ami* [mɔ̃nami] is the main cause for the formal variations in the analysis.

II

CRITICAL REVIEW OF
THE STANDARD GENERATIVE ANALYSIS

II.1. Introduction

In this chapter, I provide evidence showing that (i) it is inadequate to assume that nasal vowels are not lexical in Modern French and (ii) it is incorrect to postulate for the language a major phonological process of vowel nasalization.

The evidence is presented in three steps: first, in section II.2., I critically examine the arguments that have been proposed in the generative literature on French phonology in favor of deriving nonalternating nasal vowels from underlying /VN/ sequences. I show that, under close scrutiny, the evidence adduced in support of this abstract source is invalid and even damaging to the analysis itself.

Second, in section II.3., I consider two problems inherent to the standard generative analysis of French nasal vowels: (i) the non-uniqueness of phonological representations, which arises in the determination of the underlying sources for nonalternating nasal vowels, and (ii) the paradoxical interaction between vowel nasalization and the phenomenon of liaison, exemplified in the contrast *bon ami* [bɔnami]/*mon ami* [mɔ̃nami]. It is argued that these problems are artificially caused by the abstractness of the analysis, rather than being attributable to puzzling facts about the language.

Third, in section II.4., I introduce data often omitted from consideration but indicative of the descriptive inadequacy of the phonological rule of vowel nasalization postulated in the standard generative treatment of French nasal vowels.

II.2. On the source of nonalternating nasal vowels[1]
II.2.1. Introduction

The paradigmatic data concerning nasal vowels in Modern French—that is, the surface alternations between [VN] sequences and nasal vowels—leave no doubt that some systematic relation(s) must exist, in the grammar internalized by native speakers, between morphemes exhibiting such allomorphy. The standard generative view of French phonology is that alternating nasal vowels are phonologically derived from underlying /VN/ sequences.

Paradigmatic evidence is the typical kind of proof used in generative phonology to establish and justify underlying representations that differ from some or all of their surface phonetic forms, and to posit rules that relate the two levels of representation. Once the rules relating the underlying and surface phonetic representations of alternating morphemes are discovered, it is not unusual to extend the application of these rules to nonalternating cases. For example, in the synchronic analysis of English phonology proposed in *SPE*, it is argued that alternations such as [aɪ]/[ɪ] (*divine/divinity*) are to be accounted for by postulating an underlying tense /ī/ from which the two surface variants are derived by major phonological rules. It is further claimed that no diphthongs need to be recognized underlyingly, and that a word like *kite* should be lexically represented with an /ī/ too, although it never alternates; the /ī/ of *kite* will simply be turned into [aɪ] at no cost, by the same rules that account for *divine*. Similarly, in the abstract generative treatment of French nasal vowels, it is assumed that nasal vowels need not be postulated lexically, because nonalternating cases can be predicted from underlying /VN/ sequences by the processes independently required to derive alternating nasal vowels.

Schane (1968a) and Dell (1970) made this treatment of nonalternating nasal vowels particularly interesting by adducing in support of their analysis nonparadigmatic arguments of a wide variety. From a theoretical perspective, this abstract phonological representation of nonalternating segments constitutes a challenging counterexample to Kiparsky's (1968a) suggested principle that nonalternating morphemes should have underlying representations identical to their (classical) phonemic representations.

1. This section is a revised version of Tranel (1977a).

The purpose of this section is to show that the evidence provided in favor of the derivation of nonalternating nasal vowels from underlying /VN/ sequences is invalid, and that these segments are therefore not an obstacle to the postulation of the type of constraint on abstractness envisaged by Kiparsky.

II.2.2. Critical review of the evidence

The nonparadigmatic evidence proposed in the literature in support of the abstract analysis of nonalternating nasal vowels in Modern French may be divided into four categories, which I review in turn:
  (i) The simplicity argument (Schane 1968a:142–143);
 (ii) The sibilant-voicing argument (Schane 1968a:48);
(iii) The slow-speech argument (Dell 1970:56–57);
(iv) The surface structure constraint arguments (Dell 1970:57–58).

II.2.2.1. The simplicity argument

The main argument underlying Schane's position concerning the source of nonalternating nasal vowels is that "Once there has been established the necessity for having underlying oral vowels plus nasal consonants instead of underlying nasal vowels [i.e., in the case of morphophonemic alternations], a simpler description follows if all nasalized vowels [i.e., nonalternating nasal vowels included] have as their origin vowel plus nasal consonant" (142). If nasal vowels were posited underlyingly for the words that do not exhibit alternation, nasality would be a required feature for vowels in the lexicon and all vowels should be marked + or − for it. On the other hand, if all nasal vowels are derived in the same way, that is, from underlying /VN/ sequences, then there is no need for such markings, and a generalization can be captured by a morpheme structure constraint stating that, if a segment is a vowel, it is nonnasal.

There are a number of problems in such a reasoning concerned with the formal cost of a description. The problems may be divided into two groups: those characteristic of the French case, and those inherent to the standard notion of simplicity. I first turn to the language-specific problems.

As Chomsky (1957) emphasized, "simplicity is a systematic measure; the only ultimate criterion on evaluation is the simplicity of the whole system . . . by simplifying one part of the grammar, we may complicate other parts" (56). The problem of the treatment of nasal vowels in Modern French illustrates Chomsky's remark very well. The question of the underlying representation of nonalternating nasal vowels is not just a matter of whether the feature [nasal] is or is not redundant for vowels in the lexicon. More than this specific aspect of the lexicon is involved.

Considering nonalternating nasal vowels, I compare, in terms of the standard simplicity metric (Chomsky and Halle 1968), the two possible solutions, the abstract one (/VN/ → [Ṽ]) and the concrete one (/Ṽ/ → [Ṽ]).

Let us take the word *cendre* [sãdr] 'ash' as an example. Within the framework of the abstract analysis, it would informally be represented as /sandr/ in the lexicon, whereas in the concrete analysis it would show up as /sãdr/. For the moment, the feature costs of the segments /s/, /d/, and /r/ can be considered to be the same in the two solutions; the relevant differences concern the /an/ and /ã/ representations. In the abstract solution, there is a morpheme structure constraint which states that a nonconsonantal segment is nonnasal:

(1) [-cons] ⟹ [-nasal]

It follows from (1) that, if a segment is specified as [+nasal], it must automatically be a consonant. In the abstract solution, therefore, the segment that has been written /n/ so far in the lexical representation of *cendre* could simply be marked [+nasal], in distinctive feature terms; it will be automatically specified as a consonant by a redundancy rule. The place of articulation of this segment can similarly be specified by redundancy rules: in general, for a nasalizing nasal consonant, one can assume either that the unmarked coronal nasal consonant /n/ fills the slot, or else that, in case the nasal segment is followed by a consonant, it automatically takes on the same place of articulation as that consonant.

Leaving irrelevant feature notations aside, *cendre* will therefore have the following phonological form in the abstract solution: /sa[+nasal]dr/, where [+nasal] is [Mnasal], in markedness terms. In the concrete solution, the lexical representation of *cendre* will be

$$/s \begin{bmatrix} a \\ +\text{nasal} \end{bmatrix} dr/,$$

where [+nasal] is also [Mnasal], in markedness terms. The only difference between the two representations, then, is where the feature [+nasal] is attached. In one case it is attached to a consonantal segment; in the other it is attached to the vowel. In both cases it is a marked feature; in terms of feature count, therefore, the two representations will cost the same as far as nasality is concerned.

There are some differences between the two solutions, however, when one comes to morpheme structure constraints. It has already been seen that the abstract solution has the morpheme structure constraint (1). The concrete solution would presumably have the following morpheme structure constraint (see sec. III.2.3. for discussion):

(2) If $\begin{bmatrix} V \\ +\text{nasal} \end{bmatrix}$ C   C

     Then   [−nasal]

(2) prohibits sequences of the form /ṼNC/. The concrete solution thus seems somewhat more costly than the abstract one, since (2) is less general than (1).

In another respect, though, that of syllable structure, the abstract solution is more costly than the concrete one. In the abstract solution the /d/ of /sandr/ is a marked consonant, since it is a nonsyllabic segment that follows another nonsyllabic segment. Such a cost does not figure in the concrete solution. In every case of a nonalternating nasal vowel, the abstract solution will thus be more costly than the concrete solution as far as syllable structure is concerned.

What the abstract solution avoids, then, is the relative complexity of (2) as compared with (1). But this is accomplished at the cost of less natural syllable structures at the underlying level. This cost must be superior to the savings obtained by having (1) instead of (2).

Other additional costs in the lexicon must also be considered in the case of the abstract solution. Consider, for instance, words like *amnistie* [amnisti] 'amnesty' or *clamser* [klamse] 'to croak'. In the abstract analysis these items will have to be marked in order to fail to undergo the rule of vowel nasalization. As is shown in section II.4., *amnistie* and *clamser* are far from being isolated examples, and the cost for the required exception features will therefore quickly overrun the savings initially accomplished by avoiding (2) in favor of (1).

Concerning the particular case of the underlying nature of nonalternating French nasal vowels, it is thus not obvious at all that the abstract analysis is to be formally evaluated as less costly than the concrete analysis. I now turn briefly to problems inherent to the standard simplicity metric.

However the respective costs and savings of the abstract and concrete analyses compare, one should take all the accounting with a grain of salt. It has been made abundantly clear in the literature that an evaluation measure based merely on counting symbols, as initially proposed by generative phonologists (e.g., Halle 1961), does not always properly reflect the linguistically significant generalizations that must be captured by a grammar.

Chen (1973) and Fromkin (1971) cite obvious examples where the simplicity metric does not work. The following instance is borrowed from Chen (1973:226). Consider the rules given in (3):

(3) (a) V → [+nasal]

(b) V → [+nasal]/ — $\begin{bmatrix} C \\ +nasal \end{bmatrix}$

(c) V → [+nasal]/ — $\begin{bmatrix} C \\ +nasal \end{bmatrix}$ $

where $ designates a syllable boundary

(3a) states that a vowel becomes nasal unconditionally. (3b) states that a vowel becomes nasal if it is followed by a nasal consonant. (3c) states that a vowel becomes nasal if it is followed by a nasal consonant in the same syllable. The simplicity metric would order these rules from the most highly valued to the least highly valued as (3a) — (3b) — (3c). Chen argues that the reverse order is actually true as far as linguistically significant generalizations are concerned.[2] Fromkin (1971) points out Vennemann's example that, given the standard simplicity metric, (4a) is more highly valued than (4b):

(4) (a) C → [+voiced] / V — V

(b) C → [+voiced] / V (#) — V

Yet, "we know that [(4b)] is the more general" (83). The same point is implicitly made by Schane (1973b) when he writes that (5)

(5) C → Ø / — ([-seg]) $\begin{Bmatrix} C \\ \# \end{Bmatrix}$

"is the most natural rule for consonant deletion that one can write" (825). Yet, according to the standard simplicity metric, (6) is simpler than (5):

(6) C → Ø / — $\begin{Bmatrix} C \\ \# \end{Bmatrix}$

The standard simplicity metric is inadequate from another perspective. Substantive principles such as paradigmatic uniformity (Kiparsky 1971; Harris 1973) or the conservation of functional distinctions (Kiparsky 1972), which play an important role in the acquisition of language by children, simply cannot be taken into account in the evaluation of grammars by a mere symbol-counting automaton.

2. Schane (1973b) posits that (3b) is the most natural rule for vowel nasalization. The argument Chen makes against the simplicity metric remains valid when only (3a) and (3b) are compared.

In closing this section on simplicity, one can say that the simplicity argument used in favor of the abstract analysis of nonalternating nasal vowels in Modern French fails on two grounds: (i) it is not at all certain that a simpler description of Modern French follows if all surface nasal vowels are derived from underlying sequences of oral vowel plus nasal consonant; (ii) it is not at all certain that even if it were the simplest description, it would necessarily be the one that would capture the linguistically significant generalizations.

II.2.2.2. The sibilant-voicing argument

Nonparadigmatic evidence of another kind is also presented by Schane (1968a) in support of the abstract analysis of nonalternating nasal vowels in Modern French. This argument centers on the explanatory role played by a process of sibilant voicing and its interaction with the rules deriving nasal vowels. "In forms such as *persister* [pɛrsiste] 'to persist', *insister* [ɛ̃siste] 'to insist', *résister* [reziste] 'to resist', which contain the morpheme *sist* /sist/, the initial sibilant /s/ is voiced intervocalically: *persister* versus *résister*. Although phonetically, the initial /s/ of /sist/ is intervocalic in *insister* [ɛ̃siste], the sibilant is not voiced. If *insister* is derived from underlying /in + sist + er/, and if sibilant voicing precedes nasalization, then when sibilant voicing occurs, the /s/ is not intervocalic but is still preceded by the nasal consonant" (48). According to Schane, the derivation of all surface nasal vowels from underlying /VN/ sequences and the ordering of sibilant voicing before vowel nasalization (or at least before nasal consonant deletion) thus explain the alternation [s]/[z] undergone by the morpheme /sist/. Such an analysis, however, is not without problems.

Consider in particular the process of intervocalic sibilant voicing which Schane postulates but does not state precisely. Intervocalic sibilant voicing must obviously be restricted to occur at morpheme boundaries between prefixes and stems. Thus it does not take place morpheme-internally (cf. *assez* /ase/ [ase] *[aze] 'enough'), between stems and suffixes (cf. *placer* /plas + e/ [plase] *[plaze] 'to place'), or at word boundaries (cf. *sortir* [sɔrtir] 'to go out'/*resortir* /rə#sɔrt + ir/ [rəsɔrtir] *[rəzɔrtir] 'to go out again').

In the case of *résister* versus *persister,* the sibilant follows the morpheme boundary; in other words, it is the initial segment of the stem. The rule can therefore be written as follows:

(7) $s \rightarrow z$ / V]$_{\text{prefix}}$ + — V

The process of sibilant voicing may appear more general than indicated in (7), since the sibilant can also precede the morpheme boundary; that is, it can be the last segment of the prefix and undergo voicing, as with the prefix *cis-* /sis/:

(8) *cisalpin* 'this side of the Alps'

/sis + alpin/ → [sizalpɛ̃]

cisrhénan 'this side of the Rhine'

/sis + renan/ → [sisrenã]

This can be accounted for by the following rule:

(9) s → z / V —]$_{prefix}$ + V

Using mirror-image conventions, rules (7) and (9) could perhaps be collapsed in to the following schema:

(10) s → z % V —]$_{prefix}$ + V

Consider, however, the prefix *trans-*, which, according to Schane's analysis of nasal vowels, must contain an underlying /VN/ sequence. The underlying final sibilant of /trans/ is voiced to [z] before vowel-initial stems and remains [s] before consonant-initial stems:[3]

(11) *transaction* 'transaction'

/trans + aksion/ → [trãzaksjɔ̃]

transatlantique 'chaise longue'

/trans + atlantik/ → [trãzatlãtik]

transpercer 'to pierce through'

/trans + perse/ → [trãsperse]

transbahuter 'to move from one place to another'

/trans + bayte/ → [trãsbayte]

transmettre 'to transmit'

/trans + metr/ → [trãsmetr]

translucide 'translucent'

/trans + lysid/ → [trãslysid]

If sibilant voicing precedes vowel nasalization, as is claimed by

3. If the underlying form was assumed to be /tranz/, instead of /trans/, then final /z/ would be required to go to /s/, even before voiced consonants, a very unnatural phonological process. The same goes for the prefix *cis-*. Positing an underlying final voiceless sibilant for *trans-* and *cis-* instead of a voiced sibilant thus seems justified. Also, the prefix *trans-* may remain as [trãs] before a vowel-initial word in semantically transparent cases of word formation, where prefix and stem exhibit more independence than in the first two examples of (11), and where the presence of a stronger boundary (#) appears to be possible (see Tranel 1976a) (e.g., *transatlantique* [trãzatlãtik] ~ [trãsatlãtik] 'transatlantic'; *transocéanien* [trãzɔseanjɛ̃] ~ [trãsɔseanjɛ̃] 'transoceanic'). Before stems beginning in a voiced consonant, the final /s/ of these prefixes may undergo partial voicing; this type of phonetic detail need not concern us here.

Schane, the voicing of the sibilant in *transaction* or *transatlantique* cannot be accounted for by schema (10). Another rule of sibilant voicing must be added to the grammar:

(12) s → z / ——]$_{prefix}$ + V

The behavior of *trans-* reveals that when a prefix ends in a sibilant, whether a vowel or a consonant precedes the sibilant is irrelevant to the process of sibilant voicing; what is crucial is the syllabic nature of the initial segment of the following stem. It follows that the alternation undergone by the prefix *cis-* can be more generally accounted for by rule (12). Rule (9) therefore is not necessary, and schema (10) becomes unjustified. We are thus left with rules (7) and (12), which must be considered as separate rules of sibilant voicing. Rule (7) voices *intervocalic stem*-initial sibilants, whereas rule (12) voices *prevocalic prefix*-final sibilants. This distinction between prefix sibilant voicing and stem sibilant voicing must be made in any analysis of nasal vowels, so as to separate out the cases of *transaction* [trãzaksjɔ̃] and *insister* [ɛ̃siste].

Rule (12), prefix sibilant voicing, seems to be adequately motivated. Having isolated rule (7), stem sibilant voicing, I go on to determine how general and well justified this rule really is, since it is the one critical to Schane's argument.

Consider a word such as *assister* [asiste] 'to assist'. The most straightforward underlying representation for this word is /a+sist +e/, with the prefix /a/.[4] Rule (7), however, should apply to this underlying form, yielding the wrong surface phonetic representation *[aziste].

In order to avoid this incorrect output, the devil's advocate suggestion could be made (Sanford Schane, personal communication) that the prefix that shows up as [a] on the surface is not underlying /a/, but underlying /ad/, as it manifests itself phonetically in words like *admettre* [admɛtr] 'to admit' or *adjoindre* [adžwɛ̃dr] 'to adjoin'. It is the /d/ of the prefix /ad/ which prevents the stem sibilant-voicing rule (7) from applying in /ad+sist+e/; it is later eliminated, either through a rule of consonant deletion or through rules of assimilation and degemination.

I will first show that there cannot be a single prefix /ad/ which

---

4. I am not concerned here with the problem of the underlying form of the infinitive ending for first conjugation verbs. Schane (1968a) posits the thematic vowel /e/ plus the infinitive marker /r/. For an alternative, see chap. vii.

shows up on the surface as [ad] and [a], but that it is necessary to postulate two underlying prefixes, /ad/ and /a/.

Assume that there is a single prefix, /ad/, and that [a] is derived from it by a rule of consonant deletion such as the following:

(13) C → Ø / — [-seg] C

The existence of this process has been argued for independently by Schane (1968a:1-6). In addition, it can serve to account for the alternations undergone by other prefixes, as illustrated in (14):

(14) Prefix *des-* /dez/:
   désorganiser 'to disorganize'
      /dez + organize/ → [dezɔrganize]
   démystifier 'to demystify'
      /dez + mistifie/ → [demistifje]
   Prefix *mes-* /mez/:
   mésestimer 'to underestimate'
      /mez + estime/ → [mezestime]
   méconnaître 'to misjudge'
      /mez + kɔnɛtr/ → [mekɔnɛtr]

For the prefix /ad/, the following derivations could be taken to illustrate the same process of consonant deletion at work:

(15) *amener* 'to bring'
      /ad + məne/ → [amne]
   accoler 'to place against'
      /ad + kɔle/ → [akɔle]

Consider the word *admettre* [admɛtr] 'to admit', however. It constitutes an exception to the rule of consonant deletion (13). Since the prefix cannot be considered as an exception to the rule (cf. the examples given in (15)), the verb *mettre* itself must be regarded as an exceptional environment to consonant deletion.[5] But consider the word *démettre* [demɛtr] 'to dislocate', which comes from /dez + mɛtr/. If *mettre* really were an exceptional environment to consonant deletion, one would get *[dezmɛtr] and not [demɛtr], but the reverse is true.

These facts show that it is impossible to predict by rule and/or by exception features whether a given stem is going to take [ad] or [a]. It is therefore necessary to have both /ad/ and /a/ as prefixes in the lexicon. In addition, /ad/ must be marked as an exception to the rule of

5. See Coats (1970), Kenstowicz and Kisseberth (1977), and Kisseberth (1970b) for arguments in favor of allowing rule environment features in the theory of phonology.

consonant deletion. It should be noted that other prefixes also behave exceptionally in this respect:[6]

(16) Prefix *dis-* /dis/:
   disparaître [disparɛtr] 'to disappear'
   Prefix *trans-* /trans/:
   transmuer [trãsmɥe] 'to transmute'

The fact that the two prefixes /ad/ and /a/ are needed underlyingly does not prove that /ad/ is not the prefix in *assister*. I will now demonstrate that the prefix in *assister* is /a/, not /ad/.

Assume that /ad/ is the correct prefix in *assister* (/ad + sist + e/). Note first that, since /ad/ cannot undergo the rule of consonant deletion (13), the /d/ of /ad/ must be eliminated by some other means. The only other somewhat reasonable way to get rid of /d/ is by assimilation to the following /s/ and degemination of the resulting /ss/, after stem sibilant voicing has applied:

(17) /ad + sist + e/
   stem sibilant voicing (7) ———————
   assimilation to /s/ as + sist + e
   degemination a + sist + e
   [asiste]

In order for such a solution not to be ad hoc, it is necessary to find independent evidence for the two processes of assimilation and degemination which are required.

Consider the negative prefix *in-* /in/. When associated with certain stems beginning in a sonorant consonant, the nasal consonant of the prefix assimilates to the initial consonant of the stem, and the geminate consonants thus created may undergo degemination (Tranel 1976a):

(18) *immodéré* 'immoderate'
   /in + mɔdere/ → [immɔdere]/[imɔdere]
   inné 'innate'
   /in + ne/ → [inne]/[ine]
   illégal 'illegal'
   /in + legal/ → [illegal]/[ilegal]
   irrespect 'disrespect'
   /in + rɛspɛct/ → [irrɛspɛ]/[irɛspɛ]

It is important to emphasize that there is free variation between the

---

6. The actual status of the rule of consonant deletion (13) is considered in chapter vi.

forms with a geminate consonant and the forms with a simple consonant.[7] In particular, the gemination does not necessarily depend on emphasis, which may create a geminate consonant out of the first consonant of vowel-initial words (Grammont 1914):

(19) *épouvantable* 'horrible'
[epuvãtábl] (no "accent d'insistance")
[eppúvãtábl] (with "accent d'insistance")

The possibility for the words given in (18) to have geminate consonants under unmarked stress conditions can be directly explained by their underlying representations. Of course, it remains to be explained how the variants with geminate consonants can show up at the surface phonetic level without having undergone vowel nasalization or consonant deletion. In an earlier publication (Tranel 1976a) I discuss and account for the fact that vowel nasalization does not take place. As to consonant deletion, the prefix *in-* may simply be marked as an exception to the process, just as *dis-* and *trans-* were, for example.

Processes of assimilation and degemination are therefore motivated independently of what might be needed to derive [asiste] from /ad + sist + e/. It is easily seen, however, that the rules of assimilation and degemination which apply to the prefix /in/ cannot account for the prefix /ad/.

First, consider the rule of assimilation which takes the /n/ of /in/ to /m/, /n/, /l/, and /r/ before stems beginning in /m/, /n/, /l/, and /r/ respectively:

$$(20) \quad \begin{bmatrix} C \\ +\text{nasal} \end{bmatrix} \rightarrow \begin{bmatrix} \alpha\text{nasal} \\ \beta\text{ant} \\ \gamma\text{cor} \end{bmatrix} / i -]_{\text{prefix}} + \begin{bmatrix} C \\ +\text{son} \\ \alpha\text{nasal} \\ \beta\text{ant} \\ \gamma\text{cor} \end{bmatrix}$$

This rule cannot be generalized so as to take the /d/ of /ad/ to /s/ before stems beginning in /s/, because at the same time it would wrongly change the /d/ of /ad/ to /m/ before stems beginning in /m/ (/d/ does not go to /m/ in *admettre*). Therefore, in order to change the /d/ to /s/ in /ad + sist + e/, a *special* rule of assimilation would be required which is not motivated outside of preventing the application of stem sibilant voicing.

7. Except for *inné*, the geminated forms seem to be preferred in my dialect for the examples given. The pronunciation [inne] is mentioned, for instance, in Martinet (1971).

Even if the change from /d/ to /s/ was independently motivated, the degemination rule that would then be necessary to take /ss/ to /s/ cannot be the same as the one that may take effect with /in/-prefixed words. Note that this rule must be optional to account for the free variation between geminate consonants and simple consonants in the forms given in (18). Note also that the same optional rule explains similar free alternations with other prefixes (e.g., *dis-, trans-*):

(21) *dissemblable* 'dissimilar' [dissãblabl]/[disãblabl]
    transsibérien 'trans-Siberian' [trãssiberjẽ]/[trãsiberjẽ]
    transsaharien 'trans-Saharan' [trãssaarjẽ]/[trãsaarjẽ]

If the same rule of degemination accounted for the required degemination process in the derivation of [asiste] from /ad + sist + e/, it should be possible to get *[assiste] under normal (i.e., nonemphatic) stress conditions, but such is not the case. Therefore, a *special* rule of obligatory degemination would be required which again is not justified outside of preventing the application of stem sibilant voicing.

Thus there is no bona fide synchronic justification to posit that the underlying prefix in *assister* is /ad/; it must actually be /a/. Synchronically, the fact that the /s/ in *insister* [ẽsiste] is not voiced has nothing to do with the underlying representation of the surface segment [ẽ], since there are other cases, like *assister* /a + sist + e/ [asiste], where the postulated rule of stem sibilant voicing does not apply, although the /s/ is intervocalic.

Schane's account of the facts concerning *persister, insister,* and *résister* appears to be a diachronic explanation rather than some synchronic generalization that native speakers of French have captured about the underlying nature of surface nasal vowels. The rule of stem sibilant voicing assumed by Schane and formalized here as (7) cannot be part of a synchronic grammar of Modern French. If any generalization is captured by native speakers, it is perhaps that, with a prefix such as /re/ or /pre/, the following stem-initial sibilant is voiced if separated from the prefix by a morpheme boundary:[8]

(22) *résister* [reziste] 'to resist'
    résurgence [rezyržãs] 'resurgence'

---

8. Even this principle can be questioned, as shown by an instance like *ressusciter* [resysite] *[rezysite] 'to resuscitate'. Examples like those given in (i) would not be counterexamples, however, because the prefix is used productively and may be assumed to be attached with a word boundary (see Tranel 1976*a*):

(i) *présalir* [presalir] *[prezalir] 'to make dirty beforehand'
    présupposer [presypoze] *[prezypoze] 'to presuppose'

(23) *présager* [prezaže] 'to conjecture'

présumer [prezyme] 'to presume'

To return to the main issue under discussion—the status of the stem sibilant-voicing argument with respect to the abstract underlying nature of nonalternating nasal vowels—it seems fairly clear that the segment [ɛ̃] in *insister* [ɛ̃siste] need not be underlying /in/ to explain why the initial /s/ of the morpheme /sist/ does not voice. The alternation [s]/[z] found in the surface realizations of the morpheme /sist/ therefore cannot be construed as an argument in favor of the abstract representation of nonalternating nasal vowels in Modern French.[9]

II.2.2.3. The slow-speech argument

Dell (1970) resorts to slow-speech pronunciation to demonstrate the validity of the claim that vowel nasalization takes place within morphemes. Given the process of vowel nasalization posited by Schane and accepted by Dell, the following must be true, according to Dell: "Dans les représentations phonétiques, une consonne nasale ne peut précéder immédiatement une autre consonne que s'il y a eu effacement d'un schwa intermédiaire" (56). To corroborate this prediction Dell cites as evidence slow-speech pronunciation: "Tout mot prononcé [XNCY] admet aussi une prononciation lente [XNəCY] (N = consonne nasale): *omelette* [ɔmlɛt]/[ɔmələt], de même pour *hanneton, mannequin,* etc. Ce schwa n'apparaît nécessairement dans la diction lente que si la première consonne est une nasale: *gourmette* ([gurmɛt]) ne peut en aucun cas se prononcer *[gurəmɛt]" (56). Dell thus claims that there is a correlation between slow-speech pronunciation and underlying representations and that, in the case under investigation, slow-speech data argue in favor of Schane's abstract analysis of nonalternating nasal vowels.

The relatedness between slow speech and underlying forms has been indirectly assumed in generative phonology. It is well known that in fast speech, numerous phonological processes take place (mostly reduction processes such as unstressed-vowel dropping, consonant assimilation, consonant deletion) which do not necessarily occur in normal speech. The reduced forms of fast speech are invariably derived from the normal speech forms, which are assumed to be closer to the underlying representations. A parallel reasoning can be

9. Schane's sibilant voicing argument is also discussed and criticized in Love and Harris (1974).

applied with respect to slow and normal speech, and it can be argued that slow speech is closer to the underlying level of representation than normal speech.

The problem with Dell's argument is that the correlation he establishes for French may also be interpreted as a correlation between slow-speech pronunciation and knowledge of orthography. Thus he states that, in slow speech, *omelette* is pronounced [ɔmǝlɛt], but *omelette* has an *e* in the orthography; he states that *gourmette* will never be pronounced *[gurǝmɛt], but *gourmette* does not have an *e* in the orthography. In other words, Dell's observation is not revealing because he did not control for the knowledge of spelling which most people have. Dell himself is aware of the role that "la compétence orthographique" (61) may have in pronunciation; it is this orthographic competence, Dell argues, which explains why it is possible in songs for *asile* [azil] 'shelter' to be pronounced with a final schwa ([azilǝ]), but impossible for *avril* [avril] *[avrilǝ] 'April'; parallel observations could be made concerning poetry. Similarly, then, it could be argued that the slow-speech pronunciations of *omelette* and *gourmette* reflect orthographic competence rather than underlying representations with and without an internal schwa, respectively.

The influence of orthography on speech, and not just slow speech or the pronunciation used in songs and poetry, is most dramatically demonstrated with data from a British dialect where initial [h]'s do not show up phonetically (Alec Bamford, personal communication). When a speaker of this [h]-less dialect wants to imitate a speaker of an [h]-dialect, he does it accurately. In order to explain the knowledge of when to pronounce an [h] and when not to, two hypotheses may be put forward: (i) the speakers of the [h]-less dialect have initial /h/'s underlyingly where speakers of the [h]-dialect have them; these /h/'s are normally deleted in all cases, except when an [h]-less speaker wants to imitate an [h]-speaker; (ii) orthography guides the [h]-less speakers when they imitate the [h]-speakers. Crucial evidence is provided by the few words that are written with an *h* but are not pronounced with an [h], even in the [h]-dialects (e.g., *honour, hour, honest*). In these instances, normally [h]-less speakers produce an initial [h] when they imitate [h]-speakers, thus demonstrating the validity of hypothesis (ii). The influence of orthography on speech is thus a very real fact that must be kept in mind. Because of the lack of control on orthographic knowledge, Dell's observations concerning slow-speech pronunciation do not bring any positive evidence in favor of the abstract analysis of nonalternating nasal vowels in Modern French.

In order to be of some interest, an experiment on slow-speech pronunciation must be conducted under one of two conditions:

(i) The first possibility is to use illiterate subjects so as to avoid the possible interference of orthography. This experiment would, of course, be the ideal one, but it is not easy to find adequate subjects. Alternatively, one could perhaps use children before they learn how to read and write.

(ii) The second possibility is to use literate subjects, but to give them a balanced list of words, so that orthographic knowledge is controlled for.

An experiment of type (ii) was informally conducted with six native speakers of French. All were naive insofar as the object of the experiment was concerned. All spoke Standard French (none of them spoke any type of Southern French where schwas are rather pervasive). All were college-educated; although they were not later asked to write down the words used in the experiment, it can safely be assumed that they knew how to spell them. Four orthographic types of words were used in the experiment, as shown in table 1:

Table 1

	Orthography		*Normal pronunciation*	
(a)	*omelette, samedi* 'omelet' 'Saturday'	*XNeCY*	[ɔmlɛt], [samdi]	[XNCY]
(b)	*stencil* 'stencil'	*XNCY*	[stɛnsil]	[XNCY]
(c)	*carrefour, bulletin* 'intersection' 'bulletin'	*XCeCY*	[karfur], [byltɛ̃]	[XCCY]
(d)	*soupçon, dernier* 'suspicion' 'last'	*XCCY*	[supsɔ̃], [dɛrnje]	[XCCY]

Each subject was run separately; no subject attended a session where another subject was being given the test. The experimenter gave the subjects the words in random order, orally, at a normal speech rate and with a normal pronunciation for Standard French, that is, with no schwa pronounced where there was an *e* in the orthography. After each word was given, the subjects repeated the word in slow speech; when they did not pronounce a schwa between the two relevant consonants, they were asked to try to say the word again, even more slowly; after each word was uttered by the experimenter, the subjects could thus be asked to repeat the same word several times in slow speech; if one utterance occurred with a schwa between the two relevant consonants, that was the utterance that was counted.

The results revealed two types of responses:

(i) Four subjects showed an absolutely perfect correlation between slow speech and orthography:

> *XNeCY* was pronounced [XNəCY]
> *XNCY* was pronounced [XNCY]
> *XCeCY* was pronounced [XCəCY]
> *XCCY* was pronounced [XCCY]

(ii) Two subjects never pronounced a schwa, even when there was an *e* in the orthography and however slowly they were asked to say the words:

> $\left.\begin{array}{l} XNeCY \\ XNCY \end{array}\right\}$ were pronounced [XNCY]
>
> $\left.\begin{array}{l} XCeCY \\ XCCY \end{array}\right\}$ were pronounced [XCCY]

Before interpreting the results positively, it is easily seen that they negate all of Dell's assertions quoted earlier:

(a) It is not true that any word pronounced [XNCY] also allows a slow pronunciation [XNəCY] (cf. the pronunciation of *stencil* in both groups and that of *omelette* and *samedi* in group (ii)).

(b) It is not true that the schwa that may show up in slow speech necessarily appears only if the first of the two relevant consonants is nasal (cf. the pronunciation of *carrefour* and *bulletin* in group (i)).

Beyond contradicting Dell's claims, what is the significance of the results of this experiment? I will first try to interpret the results separately for the two groups.

Let us first consider group (ii). From the results obtained with these subjects, it can be concluded that, for them, slow speech does not correlate with orthography. Two possibilities remain:

(a) The hypothesis that slow speech correlates significantly with underlying representations is true. Since the subjects did not pronounce a schwa between the two critical consonants, there must be no schwa there underlyingly. This finding is contrary to the analysis of nasal vowels advocated by Schane and Dell, since it would incorrectly predict that vowel nasalization should take place in cases (a) and (b) of table 1.

(b) There is no reason to believe that slow speech correlates significantly with underlying representations. If it does not, the results obtained from group (ii) say nothing about the underlying representations of the words used, but Dell cannot use slow speech as an argument for his analysis.

Let us now consider group (i). Again, two possible interpretations of the results arise:

(a) The hypothesis that there is a correlation between slow speech and underlying representations is correct. One must conclude that schwas do not necessarily appear in underlying representations between the two critical consonants. This conclusion is contrary to the analysis of nasal vowels proposed by Schane and Dell, because the incorrect prediction is made that vowel nasalization should take place in case (b) of table 1.

(b) There is no reason to assume that slow speech correlates with underlying representations. The results of group (i) can be accounted for by assuming that slow speech is correlated with orthography, and Dell cannot use slow speech as an argument for his analysis.

If we try to account for the behaviors of the two groups together and uniformly, the results can be taken to mean that slow speech does not correlate with orthography, since this hypothesis cannot explain group (ii), but that it correlates with underlying representations (Dell's hypothesis) and that different people have different underlying representations for the same words. This interpretation would show that, at least for some speakers (group (ii)), vowel nasalization within morphemes must not apply at all. If it did apply, there would be absolutely no way to predict when an underlying /VNC/ sequence would yield a surface form with a nasal vowel and when it would not; one would unreasonably have to mark the considerable number of cases that do not undergo vowel nasalization (clamser, omelette, samedi, stencil, etc.) or, alternatively, mark the equally considerable number of cases that would (compter [kɔ̃te] 'to count', enfant [ãfã] 'child', inca [ɛ̃ka] 'Inca', sombre [sɔ̃br] 'dark', etc.). For other speakers (group (i)), it would be demonstrated that vowel nasalization within morphemes must not always apply. Such cases, less numerous than for group (ii), could conceivably be marked as exceptions; it would still not have been shown, however, that the process applies at all morpheme-internally, but only that if it does, there are certainly exceptions to it.[10]

10. See sec. II.4. for arguments against a solution requiring exception features.

In summary, although the slow-speech experiment described here cannot be regarded as absolutely conclusive, it nevertheless makes the following two important points:

(a) If slow-speech pronunciation has nothing to do with the underlying presence/absence of internal schwas, then the data obtained may be interpreted as showing that some speakers correlate slow speech with orthography (group (i)), whereas others do not (group (ii)). At any rate, slow-speech data do not tell us anything in favor of the abstract analysis of nonalternating nasal vowels in Modern French.

(b) If slow speech is taken to reflect the underlying presence/absence of internal schwas, as Dell assumes, then the data obtained are rather detrimental to the abstract analysis advocated by Schane and Dell, since they show that vowel nasalization must not operate morpheme-internally, certainly for some speakers and possibly for all speakers.

Concerning the abstract analysis of nonalternating nasal vowels in Modern French, the evidence from slow-speech pronunciation is therefore at best neutral and, quite conceivably, seriously damaging.

II.2.2.4. The surface structure constraint arguments

In support of the abstract analysis of nonalternating nasal vowels, Dell (1970:56) presents two additional arguments which have to do with the phonetic structure of words. According to Dell, surface phonetic gaps concerning final consonant clusters and vowel sequences are naturally explained if nonalternating nasal vowels are derived by rule instead of being present underlyingly.

Concerning final consonant clusters, Dell observes that, in French, "il existe de nombreux mots dont la représentation phonétique est [XVCC(ə)], où la première consonne de l'amas final n'est pas nasale: *peste* [pɛst(ə)], *larme* [larm(ə)]; mais il ne peut exister de mot de ce genre avec une nasale: *[pant(ə)], etc." (56). Dell states that this gap follows naturally from his analysis: [-nt-] must necessarily come from underlying /-nət-/; thus, a word that would be pronounced [pant(ə)] would have to have an underlying representation /panətə/, but underlying representations of the form /XCəCə/ (with a schwa in the penultimate and ultimate syllables) are impossible (56–57).

Dell's reasoning is sound, but his claim about the data is wrong. In fact, there *are* words whose phonetic representations are of the type [XVNC(ə)]. A few examples are given in (24):

(24) *binse* [bins] 'disorder'
(il) clamse [klams] '(he) is croaking'
hymne [imn] 'hymn'
round [rund] 'round'
suspense [syspɛns] 'suspense'

Since phonetic forms explicitly excluded by the analysis actually exist, it must mean that the analysis is faulty at some point. In order to solve the problem created by such words, three solutions are potentially open to Dell: (i) he must admit the possibility of underlying representations of the form /XVNəCə/ (or /XVNəC/) for [XVNC] surface sequences; (ii) he must say that the words under consideration are exceptions to the process of vowel nasalization; (iii) he must revise his analysis of vowel nasalization in Modern French so as not to allow the rule to apply within morphemes, which is equivalent to admitting the existence of nasal vowels underlyingly. In considering each of these possibilities in turn, I will show that only the adoption of the third one leads to a correct account.

Dell (1970) did not explicitly mention why underlying representations of the form /XCəCə/ are impossible, but it is easy to show that surface forms of the type [XVNC(ə)] cannot come from such underlying sequences. Within the analysis of the French vocalic system which Dell (1970) assumed (namely, that of Schane (1968a); cf. Dell (1970:4 n.3)), the restriction can be related to stress and vowel fronting. In a word with an underlying form of the type /XCəCə/, the second schwa from the right will receive stress. This stressed schwa will then be changed to /ɛ/ by vowel fronting, which follows stress assignment (Schane 1968a:40). After the deletion of the final schwa, underlying /XVNəCə/ will thus ultimately yield [XVNɛC] at the surface phonetic level. In his revised analysis of the French vowel system, Schane (1973a:32) in fact explicitly posits underlying representations of the type /XCəCə/ to derive surface sequences of the form [XCɛC]; thus, *(il) mène* [mɛn] '(he) leads' is derived from /mən + ə/ (whereas in Schane (1968a:35) it is derived from /mɛn + ə/). Dell (1973b:198–212) resorts to similar derivations, except that the rule taking /ə/ to [ɛ] has to precede stress assignment (Dell 1973b:218). Under either analysis it is clear that if the words given in (24) had underlying representations of the shape /XCəCə/, the wrong outputs would be generated:

(25) *binse* *[binɛs]
clamse *[klamɛs]

hymne *[imɛn]

round *[runɛd]

suspense *[syspɛnɛs]

Thus, even when underlying sequences of the type /XVNəCə/ are allowed, they cannot be resorted to in order to represent surface sequences of the form [XVNC(ə)].

In order to avoid the above incorrect derivations, Dell cannot argue either that none of the words under consideration has an underlying final schwa. If, within Dell's (1970) framework, one claimed that nouns such as *binse, hymne, round,* and *suspense* do not have an underlying schwa in final position, one would allow the postulation, between the nasal consonant and the final consonant, of an underlying schwa that would not receive stress and would therefore remain schwa and be deleted after preventing vowel nasalization from applying. One would then, however, have to mark these words as ad hoc exceptions to Dell's major phonological rule of final consonant deletion. In addition, for a verb form like *clamse,* one certainly could not nonarbitrarily proceed to claim no final schwa, since *clamser* is a verb of the first-conjugation class and, in Dell's analysis, the final schwa in such forms is a morphological marker. In Dell's (1973*b*) framework, given the /ə/ to [ɛ] rule postulated (cf. *hôtel* /otəl/ → [otɛl]), the move to have an underlying schwa between the nasal consonant and the final consonant, but none in final position, would immediately result in incorrect outputs of the type illustrated in (25).

For words such as those given in (24), it thus does not seem possible to avoid underlying representations of the type /XVNC(ə)/.[11] Other than marking the forms as exceptions to the rule of vowel nasalization, an ad hoc solution against which arguments are provided in section II.4., the only remaining possibility is to recognize that vowel nasalization does not apply within morphemes, and therefore that nasal vowels must be lexical segments in Modern French. Contrary to what Dell claims, then, surface final consonant clusters in Modern French are far from supporting an analysis where all surface nasal vowels are derived from underlying /VN/ sequences.

Concerning the distribution of vowels, Dell (1970:57) states that, within morphemes, Modern French does not have surface sequences of the type [V_1V_2], where V_1 is nasal, although the other logical possibilities exist:

11. I am not concerned here as to whether the final schwa indicated in parentheses should be present underlyingly or not. See chap. viii for discussion.

(26) (a) *[ṼV] *[nẽa]
     *[ṼṼ] *[nẽã]
 (b) [VV] [kao] *chaos* 'chaos'
 (c) [VṼ] [neã] *néant* 'nothingness'

Dell claims that this phonetic distribution is naturally accounted for in his analysis: since every surface nasal vowel comes from an underlying /VN/ sequence before a consonant, a sequence [ṼV] would have to come from underlying /VNCV/, with /C/ dropping after vowel nasalization and nasal consonant deletion; but this derivation is not possible because consonants do not drop between vowels in Modern French. Dell is aware that the constraint does not hold at the word level (cf. *enhardi* [ãardi] 'emboldened' from the prefix *en-* plus the adjective *hardi*), but his analysis also accounts for such apparent exceptions, since he assumes that /h/ is a systematic phoneme in Modern French, that it is the only consonant that can be dropped intervocalically, and that *hardi* has an initial /h/ underlyingly.

The problem with Dell's argument lies with the data. There is at least one morpheme that does contain a surface phonetic sequence of the type [ṼV]: the word *Panhard* [pãar] (French car make). The existence of such a form shows that Dell's generalization concerning the surface distribution of nasal vowels within morphemes in Modern French is factually wrong, and perhaps that his treatment of nasal vowels accounts for something it should not account for.

The fact that *Panhard* is a proper name and an isolated example of a morpheme-internal [ṼV] sequence in Standard French might lead one to dismiss the word as weak or even irrelevant evidence. However, the word *menhir* [menir] 'menhir' is often pronounced [mãir], especially by children addicted to the reading of the adventures of the comic strip characters Astérix and Obélix (Yves Morin, personal communication). This observation indicates more clearly that morpheme-internal sequences of the form [ṼV] are indeed naturally possible in Modern French. The potential existence of such sequences is the crucial fact, not their extreme rarity, which is simply caused by the lack of the necessary historical processes; consequently, this almost perfect gap in the distribution of nasal vowels in Modern French is better viewed synchronically as accidental rather than systematic.

In order to preserve the abstract analysis of nonalternating nasal vowels, a totally ad hoc underlying representation for the word *Panhard,* for instance, must be posited, namely /panhar/ (Dell

1973*b*:193). Such a representation is ad hoc because of the circularity of the reasoning leading to it. The sole motivation for the presence of the abstract segment /h/ (which is dropped after the application of vowel nasalization and nasal consonant deletion) is the preservation of the claim that nasal vowels do not appear in underlying representations.[12]

II.2.3. Conclusion

In this section I have reviewed the arguments proposed in the literature in support of an analysis of Modern French where nonalternating nasal vowels are derived from underlying /VN/ sequences. I have shown that these arguments are neutral at best and that, more often, a careful examination of the data indicates that vowel nasalization must not apply within morphemes and that the existence of lexical nasal vowels must be recognized.

II.3. On artificial difficulties in the abstract generative analysis
II.3.1. Introduction

One of the main generalizations maintained by the abstract generative analysis is that French nasal vowels are not lexical. This claim creates two difficulties which, taken together, constitute somewhat of a paradox because they reflect antithetic problems concerning phonological representations. On the one hand, since a given nasal vowel may come from several underlying /VN/ sequences, the lexical representation of a nonalternating nasal vowel is not always unique; the grammar therefore requires in such cases *overdetermined* lexical representations. On the other hand, in the same framework, the grammar tolerates *underdetermined* underlying representations when the same canonical underlying form /XVN#VY/ is supposed to yield different phonetic outputs, one with a nasal vowel ([XV̄NVY]), the other with an oral vowel ([XVNVY]) (cf. /mɔn#ami/ → [mɔ̃nami] versus /bɔn#ami/ → [bɔnami]).

In this section I examine and discuss how the advocates of the standard generative analysis of French nasal vowels handle these questions. From a language-specific perspective, I show that their proposals are inadequate and that it is necessary to allow nasal vowels underlyingly. From a general perspective, the consequences are that tighter constraints may be imposed on the theory and that rather powerful theoretical innovations which seem beyond the realm of psychological reality may be excluded.

12. See chap. ix for a discussion and rejection of abstract /h/.

II.3.2. The nonuniqueness of phonological representations

When, at the surface phonetic level, a nasal vowel alternates with a [VN] sequence, the standard generative analysis faces no problem in determining what the underlying /VN/ sequence should be. On the other hand, for a surface nasal vowel that never alternates, some indeterminacy may arise concerning both the quality of the underlying oral vowel and the place of articulation of the underlying nasal consonant.

Taking as an illustration the nonalternating nasal vowel of *vendre* [vãdr] 'to sell', Schane (1968c:714) gives as possible underlying sources for it /an/ (cf. *paysan* [peizã]/*paysanne* [peizan] 'peasant' (masc./fem.)) and /en/ (cf. *genre* [žãr] 'kind'/*générique* [ženerik] 'generic'), observing in addition that /ɛn/ is not a possible candidate (cf. *américain* [amerikẽ]/*américaine* [amerikɛn] 'American' (masc. /fem.)). Since no archiphoneme can specify both /a/ and /e/ without also including /ɛ/, "in the case of *vendre* one is forced to make a choice between /an/ and /en/, the choice being completely arbitrary. Within the framework of generative phonology, *vendre* thus requires a non-unique underlying representation" (714). In order to solve this problem, Schane suggests that appeal be made to the theory of markedness. Since /a/ is less marked than /e/, the underlying representation of the nasal vowel of *vendre* must be /an/.[13]

As Hyman (1970) and Vennemann (1972b) point out, however, it is not always true that markedness will allow a unique solution in indeterminate cases. Consider, for example, the French nasal vowel

---

13. One might question the validity of the particular case discussed by Schane. For instance, the relation claimed between *genre* and *générique* is particularly doubtful. More generally, the postulation of /en/ as a source for stressed [ã] is puzzling, since in Schane's (1968a) analysis of the French vocalic system, the rules provide no such correspondence. In fact, in this framework, only tense /A/ and tense /ɛ/ would actually be able to serve as underlying sources for a nonalternating stressed [ã], and an archiphoneme solution could then resolve the nonuniqueness problem.

Schane's intent, however, is preserved in the context of his (1973b) revised analysis of the French vocalic system, where the competing underlying oral vowels for a nonalternating stressed [ã] are no longer /A/ and /ɛ/, but /A/ and /ə/. Under this analysis an archiphoneme solution is not available, since one cannot specify the class /A,ə/ without also including lax /a/ (which, when stressed, underlies [ẽ]; cf. *humanité* [ymanite] 'humanity'/*humain* [ymẽ] 'human' (masc.)). Markedness would therefore presumably have to enter this picture to pick a unique underlying representation.

Perhaps also worth noting is the fact that in an abstract analysis one might actually want to relate *vendre* and *vénal* [venal] 'venal', which would suggest that /An/ is not, after all, the underlying representation of the nasal vowel of *vendre*, albeit markedness. Rather implausibly, this would also suggest that the speakers who know the (learned) word *vénal* have a different lexical representation for *vendre* than those who do not.

[ɛ̃]. In the dialects where [œ̃] has merged with [ɛ̃], there are, following Schane (1968a), five possible underlying sources for this nasal vowel (not taking into consideration variations of the nasal consonant) (uppercase vowels are tense, lowercase vowels are lax):

(i) /I + nasal consonant/ (cf. *fin* [fɛ̃]/*finesse* [finɛs])

(ii) /U + nasal consonant/ (cf. *brun* [brɛ̃]/*brunette* [brynɛt])

(iii) /E + nasal consonant/ (cf. *plein* [plɛ̃]/*plénitude* [plenityd])

(iv) /o + nasal consonant/ (cf. *à jeun* [aʒɛ̃]/*jeuner* [ʒœne])

(v) /a + nasal consonant/ (cf. *humain* [ymɛ̃]/*humanité* [ymanite])

In words such as *thym* [tɛ̃] 'thyme' or *lundi* [lɛ̃di] 'Monday', for which no related morphological alternates exist which exhibit a [VN] sequence, what should the underlying representations of the surface nasal vowels be? Let us examine each possible vowel candidate in turn. Throughout, I will use Schane's (1968a) analysis of the French vowel system as a working framework. Thus it should be kept in mind that vowel nasalization and stress assignment apply before the various vowel-shift rules; stress assignment will stress the only syllable of *thym* and the last syllable of *lundi*. In one case, therefore, the nasal vowel under consideration is stressed (*thym*); in the other case it is not (*lundi*).

(i) Let us first consider /a/. When /a/ is stressed, it undergoes fronting to /ɛ/ (cf. *clarté* [klarte] 'clarity' versus *clair* [klɛr] 'clear'). With vowel nasalization also applying, the output is [ɛ̃]. /a/ could therefore be the underlying vowel of *thym*, but it could not be the underlying vowel for the unstressed nasal vowel of *lundi*, because if it were, the output would be the incorrect *[lãdi].

(ii) Let us now consider /o/. When /o/ is stressed, it is fronted to /ø/. With vowel nasalization, nasal-vowel lowering, and front nasal-vowel unrounding applying too, the output is [ɛ̃]. /o/ could therefore be the underlying vowel of *thym*, but not that of the unstressed nasal vowel of *lundi*, because if it were, the output would be the incorrect *[lõdi].

(iii) The remaining three vowels /I/, /U/, and /E/ are all possible candidates for *thym* and *lundi*. Whether stressed or not, the tense vowels /I/ and /E/ do not undergo changes in their quality, as lax vowels do, and /U/ shifts to /Y/. So, after the application of vowel nasalization, nasal-vowel lowering, and front nasal-vowel unrounding, /I/, /U/, and /E/ all ultimately become [ɛ̃] and can therefore be used in the underlying representations of the surface nasal vowels of *thym* and *lundi*.

The possible candidates are thus /a/, /o/, /I/, /U/, and /E/ for *thym*, and /I/, /U/, and /E/ for *lundi*. Let us consider to what decisions markedness theory and the simplicity metric will lead. Of the two lax vowels /a/ and /o/, /o/ can be eliminated immediately since it is more marked than /a/. Of the three tense vowels /I/, /U/, and /E/, /E/ can be eliminated too, since it is more marked than /I/ and /U/. Three vowels remain, which are of equal complexity: lax /a/ is unmarked for all its features, except tenseness (Chomsky and Halle 1968:405); its complexity can thus be evaluated as 1. The tense vowels /I/ and /U/ are equally marked (Chomsky and Halle 1968:409), and their complexity is also 1. We are thus left with nonuniqueness problems unresolved by the present theory of markedness: for a word such as *thym*, no choice can be made among /a/, /I/, and /U/; for a word such as *lundi*, the indeterminacy lies between /I/ and /U/.

Such indeterminacy problems could probably be solved through refinements of the theory of markedness; for example, one might propose that /i/ should in fact be less marked than /u/. Markedness could also turn out to eliminate nonuniqueness in a different analysis of the vocalic system of Modern French; for instance, in a more traditional and less abstract underlying inventory than that of Schane (1968*a*) (e.g., the one assumed by Dell and Selkirk 1978), it would seem that [ɛ̃] could come only from the oral vowels /i/, /y/, and /ɛ/; in such an analysis, markedness would uniquely resolve the indeterminacy problem (namely, in favor of /i/).

The true question, however, is not whether a more discriminating theory of markedness will remove all indeterminacies, for there is little doubt that it will always be possible to propose some new principle that will take care of whatever indeterminacy remains. Nor is the true question whether an alternative analysis of the language will in fact allow markedness to operate and make a choice. Rather, the real question is whether it is legitimate at all to use markedness to get rid of indeterminacies. In other words, one must ask whether the choices made by markedness are the ones made by native speakers, whether there is empirical evidence internal to the language which demonstrates that the solution picked by markedness on a purely formal basis is the one with psychological reality. It is in fact difficult to see how synchronic data could actually bear on these questions, since, as pointed out by Malone (1970:330), Schane's proposal is precisely designed to cover the cases where the language does not provide any information.

Quite justifiably, therefore, another way of looking at the non-uniqueness of phonological representations is to suggest that this issue, when it arises, is simply an indication of the incorrectness of the analysis. This stance is taken by Vennemann (1972*b*), who argues more generally that the problem develops "only in theories of grammar which lack proper constraints on lexical representation" (113). In the abstract analysis of nasal vowels in Modern French, the sole reason for indeterminacy is that nasal vowels are not recognized underlyingly. In a theory that would require nonalternating segments to appear as such lexically, the nonuniqueness issue would be avoided.

In the absence of positive evidence to the contrary, one can therefore hold that the nonuniqueness difficulties that arise in the abstract treatment of nasal vowels in Modern French are in fact linguistically irrelevant problems. It is the analysis that artificially creates them by being too much removed from surface phonetic facts and by requiring nonpertinent information about the linguistic knowledge of native speakers.

II.3.3. The interaction of vowel nasalization and liaison

The abstract analysis of nasal vowels in Modern French is also the cause of problems in the treatment of liaison. The question is how to account for the following facts. When the correct conditions for liaison are met, words that end, according to the abstract analysis, in underlying /VN/ sequences behave in one of two ways (see table 2): for some forms, the surface vowel is nasal (list 1); for others, the surface vowel is oral (list 2).

Table 2

List 1	List 2
on arrive [ɔ̃nariv] 'we are coming'	*un bon enfant* [ɛ̃bɔnãfã] 'a good child'
mon ami [mɔ̃nami] 'my friend'	*un certain auteur* [ɛ̃sɛrtɛnotœr] 'a certain author'
en avant [ãnavã] 'forward'	*un sain exercice* [ɛ̃sɛnɛgzɛrsis] 'a healthy exercise'
bien entendu [bjɛ̃nãtãdy] 'of course'	*en plein air* [ãplɛnɛr] 'outdoors'
rien à faire [rjɛ̃nafɛr] 'nothing to do'	*le divin enfant* [lədivinãfã] 'the divine child'
un ami [ɛ̃nami] 'a friend'	*un vain espoir* [ɛ̃vɛnɛspwar] 'a vain hope'

In this section I critically examine how Schane and Dell account for the fact that, in their analyses of French nasal vowels, identical underlying representations of the form /XVN#VY/ can yield two different phonetic outputs, [XṼNVY] and [XVNVY].

II.3.3.1. Dell's account

The treatment of the phenomenon of liaison in Dell (1970, 1973c) is characterized by the postulation of a rule that permutes the final consonant of a word and the following word boundary when the next word begins in a vowel:

(27) [-syll] # [-cons]

$$\quad 1 \quad 2 \quad 3 \implies 2 \quad 1 \quad 3$$

According to Dell, this rule of liaison (27) allows the simplification of a number of rules ordered after it. Thus, Schane's (1968a) rules of consonant truncation and final-consonant deletion can be merged, and the rules of final-schwa deletion, schwa epenthesis, and liquid deletion see their environments significantly reduced. I return to these points later.

First, let us recall (cf. chap. i) how the rule of liaison (27) can interact with the process of vowel nasalization, formalized by Dell as (28),

$$(28)\quad V \rightarrow [+\text{nasal}]/ - \begin{bmatrix} C \\ +\text{nasal} \end{bmatrix} \begin{Bmatrix} C \\ \# \end{Bmatrix}$$

and how the interaction solves the problem created by the forms given in table 2. The data given in list 1 require the rule of vowel nasalization (28) to apply before the rule of liaison (27):

(29) (a)　　/ɔn#ariv/　　　(b)　　　/ɔn#ariv/
　　　(28)　ɔ̃n#ariv　　　　　(27)　ɔ#nariv
　　　(27)　ɔ̃#nariv　　　　　(28)　──────
　　　　　[ɔ̃nariv]　　　　　　　*[ɔnariv]

But the data given in list 2 require the rule of liaison (27) to apply before the rule of vowel nasalization (28):

(30) (a)　　/bɔn#ami/　　　(b)　　　/bɔn#ami/
　　　(27)　bɔ#nami/　　　　　(28)　bɔ̃n#ami
　　　(28)　──────　　　　　　(27)　bɔ̃#nami
　　　　　[bɔnami]　　　　　　　*[bɔ̃nami]

Dell claims that the ordering paradox that thus arises is a problem only in a theory of phonology which requires linear ordering (Chomsky and Halle 1968). Following Anderson's proposal that, within the same grammar, some derivations may require a rule X to precede another rule Y, while other derivations may require X to follow Y (local ordering), Dell considers that the two required orders of vowel nasalization (28) and liaison (27) actually exist in the grammar. He regards the counterbleeding ordering of (28) before (27) as the normal unmarked sequence of application and the reverse order as the marked sequence of application. List 2 items (e.g., *bon, certain, plein*) are therefore lexically marked as requiring the rule of liaison (27) to apply before the rule of vowel nasalization (28), and list 1 items (e.g., *mon, en, rien*) are left unmarked in this respect. Dell's rule of nasal consonant deletion, which operates in the context of an immediately preceding nasal vowel, will not affect list 1 cases because it is ordered after the rule of liaison (see chap. ī). Dell's choice of which words are marked and which words are unmarked is supported by substantive evidence he provided against an alternative solution making *"bon ami* la règle, et . . . *on arrive* l'exception": "Il n'est pas rare d'entendre parler du [plɛ̃nãplwa] *plein emploi* ou d'un [ãsjɛ̃nami] *ancien ami,* alors qu'on attend [plɛnãplwa] et [ãsjɛnami]; par contre [ɔnariv] pour *on arrive* ou [anɛspañ] pour *en Espagne* 'font provincial' " (Dell 1970:76).

Whether local ordering should be introduced into the theory of phonology is a controversial question. It certainly is a powerful theoretical innovation. But if languages indeed change through rule reordering (Kiparsky 1968*b*; King 1969), and if language changes are indeed diffused through the lexicon (Wang 1969; Chen and Wang 1975), then it should be logically possible that lexical diffusion affects rule reordering, hence giving rise to synchronic phenomena requiring rules to be ordered in different ways, depending on the lexical items.

A number of facts, however, show clearly that Dell's solution for the French case presented in table 2 is incorrect. Most of the arguments against Dell's local-ordering analysis center on the adequacy of the rule of liaison (27). I will provide evidence showing that (27) does not exist,[14] and I will demonstrate that the bona fide generalizations which (27) allows can be captured independently of its existence.

(i) The homophony argument

Dell (1970:68), following other linguists (e.g., Delattre 1966), observes that native speakers do not perceive any phonetic difference between instances when a consonant is to the left of a word boundary

---

14. Some of the arguments presented here against Dell's rule of liaison have been independently arrived at by Selkirk (1972). See also Cornulier (1977, 1978) for relevant observations.

and links with the following vowel-initial word, and those when a consonant is to the right of a word boundary. The following pairs, for instance, are homophonous:

Table 3

C is to the left of the word boundary	C is to the right of the word boundary	Pronunciation
petit ami 'little friend'	petit tamis 'small sieve'	[ptitami]
petit homme 'little man'	petit tome 'small tome'	[ptitɔm]
les aunes 'the ells'	les zones 'the zones'	[lɛzon]
un invalide 'an invalid'	un nain valide 'a valid dwarf'	[ɛ̃nɛ̃valid]

Dell argues that his rule of liaison accounts for the homophony of such pairs. His reasoning seems to imply that homophonous sequences of words should have the same segment/word-boundary structure. But using this argument is to interpret phonological or phonetic adjustments as word restructuring. The following two observations show that word restructuring is not involved at all here:

(a) Assume first that Dell's hypothesis is correct, that is, that homophonous sequences of words should have the same word-boundary structures. It is then completely arbitrary whether the rule of liaison takes a sequence /XC#VY/ to /X#CVY/ or a sequence /X#CVY/ to /XC#VY/. Yet it is intuitively right to claim that in liaison the final consonant of a word is somehow attached to the initial vowel of the following word. This intuition can be captured in a motivated way only if the homophony phenomenon is characterized by being related to syllabification. In other words, the grammar must reflect the fact that the homophony phenomenon is phonological in nature and not to be conflated with morphological information, which is in part captured through word and morpheme boundaries.

(b) Consider next the phrase petite amie [ptitami] 'little friend' (fem.). In Standard French it is homophonous with the phrase petit ami [ptitami] 'little friend' (masc.). According to Dell's hypothesis, these two phrases should have the same structure [pti#tami]. In order to obtain this structure for *petite amie,* which, in Dell's analysis, comes from underlying /pətit + ə#ami + ə/, it is necessary to have the rule of liaison (27) apply after the rule of final-schwa deletion. But since final-schwa deletion follows final-consonant deletion, which it-self follows liaison (see chap. v), it is necessary to duplicate liaison in the ordered list of rules. Such duplication is generally not permitted in generative phonology, except under two conditions: either the rule that must be duplicated is cyclic or it is an anywhere rule. Cyclicity cannot be invoked here, because even if a cycle were needed to ac-count for the phonology of Modern French, the rules under consid-eration would all be involved on the same cycle. The remaining solu-tion then is that the rule of liaison is an anywhere rule; but this is im-possible because, in Dell's analysis, this rule is crucially ordered with respect to the rule of vowel nasalization.

In summary, the homophony noted by Dell and others offers no support for the rule of liaison (27). This phenomenon is to be ex-plained through syllable restructuring, not word boundary/segment permutations.

(ii) The case of consonant deletion

In an analysis where the rule of liaison (27) is not postulated (e.g., Schane 1973*b*), a schema such as (31) is necessary in order to account for the process of consonant deletion in Modern French.[15]

$$(31) \quad \begin{bmatrix} + \text{cons} \\ \alpha \text{nas} \\ \alpha \text{son} \end{bmatrix} \rightarrow \emptyset \; / \; — \; [-\text{seg}] \begin{Bmatrix} C \\ \# \end{Bmatrix} \begin{matrix} (a) \\ (b) \end{matrix}$$

(31) states that a nonliquid consonant is deleted before a [−segment] unit followed by a consonant (consonant truncation (31a)) or at the pause (final-consonant deletion (31b)). This schema will explain the following data, for example:

(32) *le petit garçon* 'the little boy'
    /##lə#pətit#garsɔ̃##/ → [ləpətigarsɔ̃] (by 31a)
    il est petit 'he is small'
    /##il#ɛ#pətit##/ → [ilɛpəti] (by 31b)
    ils sont petits 'they are small'
    (ils sont)/pətit + z##/ → [pəti] (by 31a and 31b)
    le petit ami 'the little friend'
    /##lə#pətit#ami##/ → [ləpətitami] ((31) inapplicable)

---

15. The discussion on consonant deletion contained in this section assumes, as Dell and others do, that the process is to be accounted for by major phonological rules. See Part II for a different analysis of [Ø] ~ [C] alternations.

By positing the rule of liaison (27), and by ordering it before the process of consonant deletion, Dell can considerably simplify (31) and account for the same basic facts as those given in (32):

(33) $\begin{bmatrix} +\text{cons} \\ \alpha\text{nas} \\ \alpha\text{son} \end{bmatrix} \rightarrow \emptyset \ / - [-\text{son}]_\circ \ \#$

(33) states that any number of nonliquid consonants before a word boundary are deleted. From a purely formal point of view, (33) is less complex than (31) and therefore is assumed to be preferable. From a substantive point of view, (33) eliminates the distinction made in (31) between consonant truncation (31a) and final-consonant deletion (31b): with (33), the final /t/ of /pətit/ is dropped by the same rule in *le petit garçon* and *il est petit;* similarly, the /t/ and the /z/ of /pətit + z/ in *ils sont petits* are deleted by the same rule. The /t/ of /pətit/ in *le petit ami* does not drop because, before the application of (33), it has been moved onto the other side of the following word boundary by the rule of liaison (27). Note also that (33) can account for a number of words which are assumed to end in /kt/ underlyingly but which lose these two consonants before a word boundary:

(34) *instinct* [ɛ̃stɛ̃]/*instinctif* [ɛ̃stɛ̃ktif]
    'instinct'   'instinctive'
    respect [rɛspɛ]/*respectable* [rɛspɛktabl]
    'respect'   'respectable'

To account for these data, Schane (1968a:87) had to posit an additional rule, a rule of prefinal-consonant deletion (35), ordered between truncation and final-consonant deletion (see chap. v):

(35) $C \rightarrow \emptyset \ / - C \ \#$

Dell's solution for consonant deletion in Modern French thus appears more general than a solution that does not include his rule of liaison (27). Two facts, however, show that his analysis of consonant deletion is incorrect:

(a) Notice first that (33) does not provide for the deletion of consonants at morpheme boundaries. Yet the following two cases demonstrate that the process must apply in that environment:

— Prefixes such as /dez/ and /mez/ keep the final consonant before stems beginning in a vowel (cf. (36a) and (37a)) but they lose it before stems beginning in a consonant (cf. (36b) and (37b)).

(36) (a) *déshabiller* [dezabije] 'to undress'
       désarmer [dezarme] 'to disarm'
       désorganiser [dezɔrganize] 'to disorganize'

    (b) *déboucher* [debuše] 'to uncork'
        déterrer [detere] 'to unearth'
        défaire [defɛr] 'to undo'
(37) (a) *mésentente* [mezãtãt] 'discord'
        mésestimer [mezestime] 'to underestimate'
        mésalliance [mezaljãs] 'misalliance'
    (b) *mécontenter* [mekɔ̃tãte] 'to displease'
        médire [medir] 'to slander'
        méconnaître [mekɔnɛtr] 'to misjudge'

— In the formation of a small class of adverbs, the masculine form of the adjective is required instead of the customary feminine form; the regular suffix *-ment* [mã] is added:

(38) *brillamment* [brijamã] 'brilliantly'
    savamment [savamã] 'learnedly'
    éloquemment [elɔkamã] 'eloquently'
    indépendamment [ẽdepãdamã] 'independently'
    apparemment [aparamã] 'apparently'
    (Compare *lentement* [lãtmã] 'slowly'
            grandement [grãdmã['greatly'
            adroitement [adrwatmã] 'skillfully')

Let us take *savamment* as an example. If the feminine form of the adjective were used to derive the adverb, the incorrect form **savantement* *[savãtmã] would obtain. The masculine form of the adjective is needed: /savãt+mã/. The surface phonetic form [savamã] is derivable through consonant deletion at a morpheme boundary and then vowel denasalization. In these two cases where consonant deletion must take place before morpheme boundaries, a schema like (31) can handle the process, but Dell's rule (33) cannot.

    In order to account for these facts of consonant deletion at morpheme boundaries, it could be suggested that the word-boundary symbols in Dell's rules of liaison and consonant deletion be replaced by [–segment], thus including morpheme boundaries. The problem with this amendment is that the /k/ in words such as *instinctif* or *respectable* would then be wrongly deleted, as shown in (39):

(39) *instinctif* /ẽstɛkt+if/
               ẽstẽk+tif (by amended rule of liaison)
               ẽstẽ+tif   (by amended rule of consonant
                             deletion)
     *[ẽstẽtif]

Dell's solution concerning the process of consonant deletion in

Modern French thus cannot account for the deletion of consonants at morpheme boundaries.

(b) Another damaging argument is the fact that, with respect to the process of consonant deletion, some words behave differently at the pause and before a consonant-initial morpheme:

(40) (a) *ils sont six* [ilsɔ̃sis] 'there are six of them'
ils sont huit [ilsɔ̃ɥit] 'there are eight of them'
ils sont dix [ilsɔ̃dis] 'there are ten of them'
(b) *six tables* [sitabl] 'six tables'
huit tables [ɥitable] 'eight tables'
dix tables [ditabl] 'ten tables'
(c) *un os* [ɛ̃nɔs] 'a bone' (from /ɔs/)
un œuf [ɛ̃nœf] 'an egg' (from /œf/)
(d) *des os* [dezo] 'bones' (from /ɔs+z/)
des œufs [dezø] 'eggs' (from /œf+z/)

Words like *six, huit, os,* behave regularly with respect to consonant deletion before a word or morpheme boundary and a consonant (cf. (40b) and (40d), but exceptionally with respect to consonant deletion at the pause (cf. (40a) and (40c)). This exceptionality can be captured in Schane's analysis by marking *six, huit, os* as [−rule (31b)], but it cannot be conveyed within Dell's framework, since there is only one rule of consonant deletion.[16]

The postulation of the rule of liaison (27) thus allows Dell to simplify the consonant-deletion treatment otherwise required, but the simplifications are specious, since the resulting grammar cannot handle all the data explained under the other analysis.

(iii) The raising of /ɔ/ before a word boundary

There is in Modern French a rule that changes /ɔ/ to /o/ at the end of words:

(41) ɔ → o / — #

The existence of this process is evidenced in the masculine/feminine forms of certain adjectives,

(42) *sot* [so]/*sotte* [sɔt] 'stupid' (masc.)/(fem.)
idiot [idjo]/*idiote* [idjɔt] 'idiotic' (masc.)/(fem.)
(Compare *gros* [gro]/*grosse* [gros] 'fat' (masc.)/(fem.)
faux [fo]/*fausse* [fos] 'false' (masc.)/(fem.))

in abbreviations and reduplications,

---

16. Unless environments are allowed on exception features. For instance, *six* could be marked [−rule (33) / — ##]). See n. 19 below for such a proposal by Schane.

(43) (a) *métro* [metro]/*métropolitain* [metrɔpɔlitɛ̃] 'subway'
    chrono [krono]/*chronomètre* [krɔnɔmɛtr] 'chronometer'
  (b) *coco* [koko]/*communiste* [kɔmynist] 'communist'
    (faire) dodo [dodo]/*dormir* [dɔrmir] 'to sleep'
and in various other derivational processes,

(44) *héros* [ero]/*héroïne* [erɔin] 'hero'/'heroine'
    cahot [kao]/*cahotique* [kaɔtik] 'jerk'/'jerky'
    rot [ro]/*roter* [rɔte] 'a belch'/'to belch'
    numéro [nymero]/*numéroter* [nymerɔte]
    'a number'/'to number'
    piano [pjano]/*pianoter* [pjanɔte]
    'piano'/'to strum on the piano'

Let us consider the interaction of rule (41) with Dell's rules of consonant deletion (33) and liaison (27):

— (27) must precede (33):

(45)   *petit ami* 'little friend'
    /##pətit#ami##/   /##pətit#ami##/
  (27) ##pəti#tami##   (33) ##pəti #ami##
  (33) ——————   (27) ——————
    [pətitami]   *[pətiami]

— (33) must precede (41):

(46)   *il est sot* 'he is silly'
    /##il#ɛ#sɔt##/   /##il#ɛ#sɔt##/
  (33) ##il#ɛ#sɔ ##   (41) ——————
  (41) ##il#ɛ#so ##   (33) ##il#ɛ#sɔ ##
    [ileso]   *[ilesɔ]
    un bien sot garçon 'a very silly boy'
    /##ɛ̃#bjɛ̃#sɔt#garsɔ̃##/   /##ɛ̃#bjɛ̃#sɔt#garsɔ̃##/
  (33) ##ɛ̃#bjɛ̃#sɔ #garsɔ̃## (41) ——————
  (41) ##ɛ̃#bjɛ̃#so #garsɔ̃## (33) ##ɛ̃#bjɛ̃#sɔ #garsɔ̃##
    [ɛ̃bjɛ̃sogarsɔ̃]   *[ɛ̃bjɛ̃sɔgarsɔ̃]

— (41) must precede (27):

(47)   *bon ami* 'good friend'
    /##bɔn#ami##/   /##bɔn#ami##/
  (41) ——————   (27) ##bɔ#nami##
  (27) ##bɔ#nami##   (41) ##bo#nami##
    [bɔnami]   *[bonami]
    sot ami 'silly friend'
    /##sɔt#ami##/   /##sɔt#ami##/
  (41) ——————   (27) ##sɔ#tami##

(27) ##sɔ#tami## [sɔtami]   (41) ##so#tami## *[sotami][17]

The first and second sets of derivations—(45) and (46)—show that we must have the order (27)-(33)-(41); the first and third sets—(45) and (47)—require the ordering (41)-(27)-(33). Within Dell's framework, it is thus impossible to get the correct derivations for (46) and (47) at the same time.

The problem is with the rule of liaison (27). The data show that, when the final consonant of a word is not deleted, the preceding /ɔ/ does not change to /o/; in other words, contrary to what (27) asserts, the final consonant of a word cannot "leave" the word it lexically belongs to and be attached to the next vowel-initial word through a permutation with the intervening word boundary.

The arguments presented so far against Dell's rule of liaison show that the postulation of this rule leads to an incorrect grammar of Modern French. Dell's solution, however, allows genuine generalizations concerning other rules. I now demonstrate that the same generalizations can be captured without (27).

(iv) The simplification of the rules of final-schwa deletion, schwa epenthesis, and liquid deletion

In Dell's analysis, the rules of final-schwa deletion, schwa epenthesis, and liquid deletion, which are ordered after the rules of liaison (27) and consonant deletion (33), have the following forms:

(48) Final-schwa deletion (obligatory):
ə → Ø / VC_0 — #
e.g., *petite fille* 'little girl'
/pətit+ə#fij/ → [pətitfij]

(49) Schwa epenthesis (optional; ordered after (48)):
Ø → ə / CC — # C
e.g., *il parle fort* 'he speaks loudly'
/il#parl+ə#fɔr/ → il#parl#fɔr (48) → [ilparləfɔr]

(50) Liquid deletion (obligatory; ordered after (48) and (49)):
L → Ø / [-son] — # C
e.g., *pauvre garçon* 'poor boy'
/povrə#garsɔ̃/ → povr#garsɔ̃ (48) → [povgarsɔ̃]
([povrəgarsɔ̃] would obtain if (49) were applied)

In an analysis where the rule of liaison (27) is not posited, the

17. Some speakers, however, seem to prefer [sotami] (or even [soami]) over [sɔtami]. See chap. vii for a discussion of these facts.

three rules given above must be seriously complicated in order to account for the effects of the plural morpheme /z/ (Dell 1970:71):

(48') Final-schwa deletion:

$$\text{ə} \rightarrow \emptyset \ / \ VC_\circ - (C) \ \#$$

e.g., *petites étoiles* 'small stars'

/pətit+ə+z#etwalə+z/ → [pətitzetwal]

(49') Schwa epenthesis:

$$\emptyset \rightarrow \text{ə} \ / \ CC - \begin{cases} C \ \# \ [+seg] & \text{(a)} \\ \# \ C & \text{(b)} \end{cases}$$

e.g., *autres amis* 'other friends'

/otrə+z#ami+z/ → otr+z#ami+z (48') →
[otrəzami] (49'a)

autre zéro 'other zero'

/otrə#zero/ → otr#zero (48') → [otrəzero] (49'b)

(50') Liquid deletion:

$$L \rightarrow \emptyset \ / \ [-son] - \begin{cases} C \ \# \ [+seg] & \text{(a)} \\ \# \ C & \text{(b)} \end{cases}$$

e.g., *autres amis* 'other friends'

/otrə+z#ami+z/ → otr+z#ami+z (48') →
[otzami] (50'a)

autre zéro 'other zero'

/otrə#zero/ → otr#zero (48') → [otzero] (50'b)

Dell's rules are simpler than the rules that have to be posited in an analysis without the rule of liaison (27) because, in Dell's solution, the plural morpheme /z/ has been moved onto the other side of the following word boundary by (27) prior to the application of the rules under consideration. Note, however, that Dell assumes that a morpheme boundary is what links a word to the plural morpheme. If it were assumed that a word boundary is what links a word to the plural morpheme, then the generalizations in Dell's analysis would also be captured in the other analysis.[18] There is in fact independent motivation to assume that the plural morpheme is preceded by a word boundary. For example, consider the pronunciation of the phrase *de sots amis* 'stupid friends': [dəsozami] *[dəsɔzami]. The /t/ of /sɔt/ has undergone deletion because of the presence of the plural morpheme /z/, and then the change from /ɔ/ to /o/ has taken place. This change can easily be explained in the context of rule (41) if /z/ is as-

---

18. Dell (1973*b*:243) mentions this possibility but does not pursue it.

sumed to be preceded by a word boundary (see sec. VI.3.1. and Tranel 1977c for additional arguments).

In summary of the discussion of Dell's rule of liaison (27), it is clear that this rule should not be part of the grammar of Modern French, since its postulation leads to the generation of incorrect outputs, and since the genuine generalizations it allows can be captured independently of its existence. Consequently, Dell's account of the data exemplified in table 2 simply collapses, as the existence of (27) is necessary to his use of local ordering.

Dell's solution is not the only analysis that has been suggested within the framework of the abstract analysis of French nasal vowels to solve the problem of the interaction between vowel nasalization and the phenomenon of liaison. Schane (1973b) has also made some proposals, and I now turn to them.

II.3.3.2. Schane's account

Schane (1973b:828–830) presents two possible treatments to account for the paradox illustrated in table 2. I will show that neither of them correctly accounts for the data. The first solution, which Schane ultimately rejects, involves the use of a minor rule that would affect the words of list 1 in table 2. I will come back to this proposal later. The treatment that Schane finally adopts is the one already presented in chapter i and summarized here for convenience: there is in French a natural process of vowel nasalization, rule (51),

$$(51) \quad V \rightarrow [+\text{nasal}] \,/\, - \begin{bmatrix} C \\ +\text{nasal} \end{bmatrix}$$

and a constraint, (52), which will "normally" prevent rule (51) from applying (cf. *bon ami* [bɔnami]):

$$(52) \quad V \rightarrow [-\text{nasalization rule}] \,/\, - \begin{bmatrix} C \\ +\text{nasal} \end{bmatrix} ([-\text{seg}]) \, V$$

Words such as *mon,* which "exceptionally do undergo nasalization" in the environment specified in (52) (cf. *mon ami* [mɔ̃nami]), will be marked as "exceptions to the constraint."

The view that Schane proposes concerning the organization of the phonological component is interesting because it reflects directly part of Stampe's (1969, 1973) theory of language acquisition: that one of the general steps through which children go during the acquisition of their native language is the learning of language-specific restrictions on natural phonological processes. A debatable point in Schane's solution, however, is his concept of a natural rule for vowel nasalization.

Chen (1973), for instance, claims that rule (53) expresses a linguistically more significant generalization than rule (51):

(53) $V \rightarrow [+\text{nasal}] / - \begin{bmatrix} C \\ +\text{nasal} \end{bmatrix} \$$

     where $ designates a syllable boundary

An even more general, and perhaps more accurate, statement would be that given in (53'):

(53') "a vowel is nasalized if followed by a tautosyllabic nasal consonant" (Lightner 1970:197).

There is no doubt that (51) and (53') are both natural. (51), which is less restricted than (53'), expresses the fact that, in any language, a vowel followed by a nasal consonant will most probably acquire a touch of nasalization, even if the nasal consonant is followed by a vowel. In an environment such as that of (53'), on the other hand, it is very likely that the vowel will be phonetically more nasalized than in the context of a nasal consonant followed by a vowel, and that subsequently the nasal consonant will be dropped (cf., for instance, English *can't* [kæ̃t]), with the possible consequence that the nasalized vowel will be phonemicized. Both rules thus capture well-known universal phonetic processes, but their phonological implications are clearly different. It is therefore difficult to decide which of the two natural rules should be referred to in the type of phonological component suggested by Schane.

Note that, if (53') were taken as the basic vowel-nasalization rule in Schane's treatment of French, then constraint (52) would not be needed anymore, but words like *mon* could not be accounted for, since phrases such as *mon ami* [mɔ̃nami] are of the form /XV$N#VY/ (e.g., /mɔ$n#ami/). Schane's solution seems to work only because he picked rule (51) over (53').

The following criticism of Schane's solution is directly relevant to the problem of the relation between liaison and vowel nasalization. Given Schane's analysis, consider the masculine indefinite article *un*. In the lexicon, the vowel of *un* will be marked as [–constraint (52)]. Hence the following derivation for *un arbre* 'a tree':

(54)   /yn#arbr/

      constraint (52)   ————

      rule (51)   ỹn#arbr

      nasal-vowel lowering   œ̃n#arbr

      nasal-vowel unrounding   ɛ̃n#arbr

                       [ɛ̃narbr]

Consider now the feminine indefinite article *une,* which Schane relates to the masculine form: /yn + ə/ (/ə/ is the feminine marker).
Since the /y/ of the morpheme /yn/ is marked [–constraint (52)], it
will always undergo the rule of vowel nasalization (51). As a result,
une will incorrectly show up at the surface phonetic level with a nasal
vowel. Similarly, all the words that one might want, in an abstract
analysis, to relate to *un* (e.g., *unique* [ynik] 'unique', *unanime*
[ynanim] 'unanimous') will incorrectly be derived with a nasal vowel.[19]
The minor-rule treatment briefly contemplated by Schane in the same
article (829) will identically give the wrong results, since the minor
rule suggested to account for troublesome words like *mon* is the same
as (51).

Given the abstract analysis of French nasal vowels, the minor rule
of vowel nasalization actually needed to account for words like *mon* is
the following:

$$(55) \quad V \rightarrow [+\text{nasal}]/ - \begin{bmatrix} C \\ +\text{nasal} \end{bmatrix} \#$$

The words that contain a nasal vowel in liaison where other words
show an oral vowel must be marked [+rule (55)]. The word boundary
in the rule is necessary to ensure that vowel nasalization takes place in
un without affecting *une.* In an analysis where nasal-consonant deletion is performed in the context of a preceding nasal vowel (Schane
1968*a*, Dell 1970), rule (55) must apply in counterfeeding fashion
after the rule of nasal-consonant deletion; if rule (55) were applied
before nasal-consonant deletion, the nasal consonant of the words
marked to undergo (55) would incorrectly delete (e.g., *on arrive* 'we
are coming' /ɔn#ariv/ [ɔ̃nariv] *[ɔ̃ariv]).

I will now point out some undesirable substantive characteristics
shared by a minor-rule treatment such as (55) and the feature [–constraint (52)] of Schane's analysis. Note first that the latter is really an
exception feature, since Schane assumes that constraint (52) *normally*
prevents rule (51) from applying and that some words *exceptionally*
undergo rule (51) in the environment specified in constraint (52).
Both minor rule (55) and Schane's treatment therefore consider that
words like *mon* exhibit an unexpected behavior in liaison, whereas

19. It has been pointed out by Sanford Schane (personal communication) that his
(1973*b*) analysis can still generate the correct phonetic outputs if *un* is lexically
marked as [–constraint (52) / — #], instead of just [–constraint (52)]. This amend-
ment increases the power of the theory of exceptions considerably by allowing environments on exceptional lexical markings. It remains to be demonstrated that such a
move is justified on a basis wider than this one French example.

words like *bon* are regular. But as briefly mentioned earlier and as explained in detail in chapters iii and iv, the substantive evidence available does not support this classification, but rather the reverse. Such observations constitute an important argument against both the minor-rule treatment and Schane's analysis.

A minor rule like (55) and the exception feature [−constraint (52)] have in fact no independent motivation beyond preservation of the claim that French nasal vowels do not appear underlyingly. In both analyses, the exception features simply ensure that words like *mon* will always contain a nasal vowel, no matter what environment they are in.

II.3.3.3. Vowel nasalization and liaison: conclusion

Given the abstract analysis of French nasal vowels, it has been shown that no adequate solution is available to account for the behavior of words that always show up with a final nasal vowel, even in liaison contexts. In particular, treatments that may be formally possible (e.g., Schane 1973*b*) have no independent motivation and make incorrect substantive claims.

The data summarized in table 2 constitute a paradox only for the proponents of the standard generative treatment of French nasal vowels. The paradox is a consequence of the fundamental claim of the abstract analysis that French nasal vowels are not (systematic) phonemic.

II.3.4. Conclusion

In this section I have demonstrated that the abstract analysis of French nasal vowels creates descriptive difficulties which are only pseudoproblems. By being unduly removed from surface phonetic facts, the underlying representations posited for nonalternating nasal vowels are indeterminate or ambiguous. They are indeterminate when the language provides no evidence making it possible to decide what underlying /VN/ sequences should be picked as the source of nonalternating nasal vowels. They are ambiguous when the same canonical underlying representation /XVN#VY/ is supposed to give different phonetic outputs, [XṼNVY] and [XVNVY]. To eliminate the indeterminacy and ambiguity problems, additional theoretical mechanisms (markedness, local ordering, exception features, minor rules) need to be brought in, which, independently justified or not in the theory, appear to make unsubstantiable or incorrect claims about the native speakers' knowledge of French.

In summary, it has been shown that the abstract analysis of French nasal vowels asks linguistically nonsignificant questions and provides psychologically nonreal answers. A logical alternative is to admit that nonalternating nasal vowels appear as such in lexical representations.

II.4. On the descriptive inadequacy of vowel nasalization
II.4.1. Introduction

In the preceding two sections I have hinted at the descriptive inadequacy of the major phonological process of vowel nasalization postulated in the standard generative analysis of French nasal vowels. In this section I consider this question in detail.

The rule of vowel nasalization under investigation is repeated for convenience, in its expanded form, in (56):

$$(56) \quad V \rightarrow [+\text{nasal}]/ - \begin{bmatrix} C \\ +\text{nasal} \end{bmatrix} \begin{cases} C & \text{(a)} \\ +C & \text{(b)} \\ \# \ C & \text{(c)} \\ \# \ \# & \text{(d)} \end{cases}$$

Rule (56) must apply in the generation of all surface nasal vowels but not in the derivation of surface [VN] sequences. I will show that the analysis fails in both respects: (i) it cannot generate all cases of surface nasal vowels; (ii) it cannot account for all cases where vowel nasalization does not take place.[20]

II.4.2. The generation of nasal vowels

The behavior in liaison of words like *mon* constitutes the major illustration of the fact that not all surface nasal vowels can be reasonably derived from underlying /VN/ sequences (see sec. II.3.3.). There are other similar examples. The prefixes *bien-, en-,* and *non-* exhibit the same pattern as words like *mon*; that is, they contain a nasal vowel not only before consonant-initial stems but also before vowel-initial stems:

(57) (a) *bien-fondé* [bjɛ̃fɔ̃de] 'well-foundedness'
bienvenu [bjɛ̃vny] 'welcome'
empaqueter [ãpakte] 'to pack'
enlaidir [ãledir] 'to make ugly'

20. Taken together, the rule of vowel nasalization and the constraint on its application proposed in Schane (1973b) have the effect produced by rule (56), and the evidence showing inadequacy (ii) of rule (56) therefore applies equally to that particular treatment.

       non-paiement [nɔ̃pɛmã] 'nonpayment'
       non-lieu [nɔ̃ljø] 'dismissal'

(b) *bien-aimé* [bjẽneme] 'beloved'
      bienheureux [bjẽnørø] 'happy'
      enherber [ãnɛrbe] 'to lay grass'
      s'enivrer [sãnivre] 'to get drunk'
      non-inscrit [nɔ̃nẽskri] 'not registered'
      non-urbain [nɔ̃nyrbẽ] 'not urban'

Certain proper names (perhaps isolated, but nevertheless existing words) also point to the inadequacy of the rule of vowel nasalization:

(58) *Van Impe* [vãnimp] (surname)

(59) *Panhard* [pãar] (French car make)

In order for the process of vowel nasalization formalized in (56) to apply in cases like *mon,* (57b), and (58), there would have to be two word boundaries separating the underlying /VN/ sequences from the following vowel. For morphological reasons, the postulation of such boundaries is clearly impossible. In addition, even if two word boundaries could actually be motivated in these positions, one would then incorrectly expect the nasal consonant to be deleted. These data thus provide counterexamples to the claim that nasal vowels otherwise come from underlying /VN/ sequences followed by an optional boundary and a consonant.[21] As to the word *Panhard,* it was seen in section II.2. that its nasal vowel could be generated only by the ad hoc postulation of an internal abstract consonant between the underlying /VN/ sequence and the following vowel.

The cases presented in this section illustrate the occurrence of nasal vowels whose derivations from underlying /VN/ sequences create serious problems in the abstract generative treatment of French nasal vowels, but which are straightforwardly analyzable as lexical nasal vowels.

II.4.3. The generation of [VN] sequences

The preceding section indicates only that certain instances of surface nasal vowels cannot legitimately be derived from underlying /VN/ sequences. It can therefore be argued that lexical nasal vowels should be recognized in such cases, but that otherwise the standard

---

21. Schane's (1973b) analysis can formally account for this type of data, but it fails on substantive grounds (see sec. II.3.3.2.).

generative analysis of French nasal vowels should be preserved. An illustration of this type of position is the treatment advocated by Selkirk (1972), who postulates lexical nasal vowels for words like *mon* but maintains that all other nasal vowels are phonologically derived from underlying /VN/ sequences (see sec. I.3.4.).

Such an analysis is not very plausible because of the resulting strangely defective distribution of (systematic) phonemic nasal vowels. I now provide evidence that any such intermediate position is in fact untenable, because the postulation of a phonological process of vowel nasalization fails to explain the occurrence of surface [VN] sequences in environments where vowel nasalization "should" take place. I consider incorrect applications of the process first within morphemes, then across morphemes, and finally at the end of words.

II.4.3.1. Vowel nasalization within morphemes

Morphemes whose surface phonetic shapes are of the form [XVNCY], and whose most straightforward underlying representations are of the same type /XVNCY/, exist in Modern French. Examples are given in (60).

(60) (a) *Agamemnon* [agamɛmnɔ̃] 'Agamemnon'
amnésie [amnezi] 'amnesia'
amnistie [amnisti] 'amnesty'
gymnase [žimnaz] 'gymnasium'
hymne [imn] 'hymn'
indemnité [ɛ̃dɛmnite] 'indemnity'
insomnie [ɛ̃sɔmni] 'insomnia'
omnibus [ɔmnibys] 'omnibus'

(b) *binse* [bins] 'disorder'
(il) clamse [klams] '(he) is croaking'
décemvir [desɛmvir] 'decemvir'
INSEE [inse] (French statistics institute)
Kremlin [krɛmlɛ̃] 'Kremlin'
SIMCA [simka] (French car make)
sprint [sprint] 'sprint'
week-end [wikɛnd] 'weekend'

According to the standard generative analysis of French nasal vowels, vowel nasalization should apply to such morpheme-internal /VNC/ sequences, but it does not.

In order to explain this absence of vowel nasalization, one could conceivably assume that there is an underlying schwa separating the

nasal consonant from the following consonant in the troublesome sequences, as illustrated in (61):

(61) *amnistie* /amənisti/

   décemvir /desɛməvir/

The presence of the schwa would render the vowels ineligible for
nasalization, since the structural description of the rule would not be
met. The schwa would later be deleted by the rule of internal-schwa
deletion which obligatorily eliminates internal schwas when they are
preceded by a single non-word-initial consonant (Dell 1973*b*:229).
Note that a similar solution is adopted by Schane (1968*b*) and Dell
(1970, 1973*b*) to account for the absence of vowel nasalization in
words with orthographic *e* between a nasal consonant and another
consonant:

(62) *Danemark* /danəmark/ [danmark] 'Denmark'

   ennemi /ɛnəmi/ [ɛnmi] 'enemy'

   Fontainebleau /fɔntɛnəblo/ [fɔ̃tɛnblo] (name of town)

   hanneton /anətɔn/ [antɔ̃] 'cockchafer'

   mannequin /manəkin/ [mankɛ̃] 'model'

   samedi /samədi/ [samdi] 'Saturday'

As shown in section II.2.2.4., however, this solution cannot account for cases where the [VNC] sequences are in the last syllable of a
word, since the internal schwa would then incorrectly turn to [ɛ] (e.g.,
hymne [imn] *[imɛn]; *clamse* [klams] *[klamɛs]; *sprint* [sprint]
*[sprinɛt]). Second, it would make very little sense to postulate an in-
ternal schwa in the case of acronyms (e.g., *SIMCA* [simka]), where
each phoneme usually represents the initial letter of a word. Finally, if
the argument is accepted that the pronunciation of word-internal
schwas in slow speech is, at least for some speakers, an indication of
an underlying presence (cf. Dell 1970 and sec. II.2.2.3.), then a word
like *amnistie*, which gives [amnisti] in slow speech, rather than
*[amənisti], cannot have an internal schwa.

The only way to maintain the existence of a phonological process
of vowel nasalization within morphemes is to claim that words such as
those given in (60) are exceptional. In order to minimize the ad hoc
character of such a treatment, it might be proposed that the words in
question are immune to vowel nasalization because they are foreign or
learned. Some foreign and learned words, however, do contain nasal
vowels:

(63) *dandy* [dãdi] 'dandy'

   farniente [farnjãt] 'pleasant idleness'

handicap [ãdikap] 'handicap'
impressario [ɛ̃prɛsarjo] 'manager'
interview [ɛ̃tɛrvju] 'interview'
sandwich [sãdwitš] 'sandwich'
Santiago [sãtjago] 'Santiago'
Vancouver [vãkuvɛr] 'Vancouver'

Moreover, there are even some foreign and learned words that contain both a nasal vowel and a [VN] sequence that "should" nasalize:

(64) *Agamemnon* [agamɛmnɔ̃]
insomnie [ɛ̃sɔmni]
Kremlin [krɛmlɛ̃]

Foreignness and learnedness therefore do not seem pertinent in considering whether or not a word undergoes vowel nasalization. In addition, the data under scrutiny include colloquial words that are considered native:[22]

(65) *binse* [bins]
clamse [klams]

Any exception treatment therefore would clearly be ad hoc.

An exception treatment would also create a difficulty whose resolution would lead to indeterminacy. Note that the assignment of an exception feature such as [–vowel nasalization] poses a problem when a word contains both a nasal vowel and a [VN] sequence that "should" nasalize. It is generally assumed that morphemes constitute the smallest domain that can be an exception to a rule. If this assumption is correct, however, it is impossible to account for both the nasal vowel and the [VN] sequence in a word like *insomnie* [ɛ̃sɔmni]. To solve this problem, Schane (1973*b*) proposed that individual segments rather than whole formatives should be marked as exceptions to a rule. This increase in the power of the theory of exceptions remains to be justified across a wide variety of languages. At any rate, it clearly offers the disadvantage of indeterminacy. Since exceptional environments seem to be necessary in the theory (Coats 1970; Kenstowicz and Kisseberth 1977; Kisseberth 1970*b*), the question is to know which segment is to be marked as exceptional to vowel nasalization: Is

---

22. As suggested by Yves Morin, *binse* may come from *business* and *clamser,* from German *Klaps,* but this etymology is not generally recognized by native speakers. Historically, *clamser* may be one of the verbs that have completely lost their internal schwa (e.g., *cacheter* [kašte] 'to seal', *je cach'te* [žəkašt] 'I seal'; *déchiqueter* [dešikte] 'to tear apart', *il déchiqu'te* [ildešikt] 'he tears apart'). Dauzat (1919:254) gives the spelling *clamecer;* Bauche (1951:181) gives both *clamecer* and *clamcer.*

it the vowel that does not nasalize, the nasal consonant, or the following consonant? The choice is arbitrary.

To this indeterminacy problem must finally be added an incorrect substantive claim made by the exception treatment. As exceptions, the [VN] sequences under consideration should tend to nasalize, for example, in popular French or in the speech of children; to my knowledge, they do not do so, and in fact the phonotactics of these words offers nothing strange to the native ear.

The only explanation for the existence of [VNC] sequences in words like those of (60) is that vowel nasalization does not apply within morphemes in Modern French. This of course constitutes the strongest argument for the necessity to postulate lexical nasal vowels in nonalternating morpheme-internal cases.

II.4.3.2. Vowel nasalization across morphemes (within words)

Within words, but across morphemes, there are also instances where phonological vowel nasalization "should" apply, but does not. I consider three such cases, which have to do with the prefixes *in-* and *circum-* and the conditional of first-conjugation verbs.

A. The prefix *in-* /in/

Consider the following adjectives, built from the concatenation of the prefix /in/ and certain morphemes beginning in a nasal consonant:

(66) *immaculé* [immakyle] 'immaculate'
    immodéré [immɔdere] 'immoderate'
    immoral [immɔral] 'immoral'
    immortel [immɔrtɛl] 'immortal'
    innombrable [innɔ̃brabl] 'innumerable'
    innommable [innɔmabl] 'horrible'

As noted in section II.2., these words can also be pronounced with a single nasal consonant, but this pronunciation results from the application of an optional rule of consonant degemination which affects prefixes (Tranel 1976*a*). It is impossible to explain the absence of vowel nasalization in examples like (66) by claiming that either the vowel /i/ or the consonnat /n/ of the prefix is exceptional with respect to the rule, since the process applies to /in/ in other words:

(67) *imberbe* [ɛ̃bɛrb] 'beardless'
    impossible [ɛ̃pɔsibl] 'impossible'
    incohérent [ɛ̃kɔerã] 'incoherent'
    indifférent [ɛ̃diferã] 'indifferent'

insincère [ɛ̃sɛ̃sɛr] 'insincere'
intolérant [ɛ̃tɔlerã] 'intolerant'

One could conceivably propose, as an alternative explanation, that vowel nasalization does not apply when the underlying /VN/ sequence occurs before a nasal consonant. Such a move would not only account for the words given in (66); it would also explain those given in (60a). Other problems would arise, however. First, consider the prefix *en-*. In the abstract generative analysis of French nasal vowels, its underlying representation would be /an/. Contrary to the restriction just imposed on the process of vowel nasalization, this prefix shows up on the surface as a nasal vowel before stems beginning in a nasal consonant:

(68) *emmagasiner* [ãmagazine] 'to store'
    emmancher [ãmãše] 'to joint together'
    emmener [ãmne] 'to take away'
    emmerder [ãmɛrde] 'to bother'
    emmurer [ãmyre] 'to wall in'
    ennoblir [ãnɔblir] 'to dignify'

Second, consider the prefix *in-* itself. When added to consonant-initial deverbal adjectives in *-able,* it surfaces as a nasal vowel, even if the stems begin in a nasal consonant (Tranel 1976*a*):

(69) *immaîtrisable* [ɛ̃mɛtrizabl] 'which cannot be controlled'
    immémorisable [ɛ̃memɔrizabl] 'which cannot be
        memorized'
    immesurable [ɛ̃məzyrabl] 'which cannot be measured'
    immettable [ɛ̃mɛtabl] 'which cannot be put on' (clothes)
    immodelable [ɛ̃mɔdlabl] 'which cannot be molded'
    immodernisable [ɛ̃mɔdɛrnizabl] 'which cannot be
        modernized'
    immontrable [ɛ̃mɔ̃trabl] 'which cannot be shown'
    innégociable [ɛ̃negɔsjabl] 'which cannot be negotiated'
    inneutralisable [ɛ̃nøtralizabl] 'which cannot be neutralized'
    innominalisable [ɛ̃nɔminalizabl] 'which cannot be
        nominalized'

Incidentally, words like those of (69) also provide a counterargument to the potential claim that the stems illustrated in (66) are exceptional environments to the general rule of vowel nasalization, since a given stem may take both the nasalized and nonnasalized surface versions of underlying /in/:

(70) stem /mɔdɛr/

    immodérable [ɛ̃mɔderabl] 'which cannot be moderated'

    immodéré [immɔdere] 'immoderate'

In another attempt to preserve the validity of a phonological process of vowel nasalization, it could be proposed that, in the data illustrated in (68) and (69), a word boundary, rather than a morpheme boundary, separates the prefixes from the stems, and that the rule of vowel nasalization given in (56) should be restricted to operating in the context of a nonnasal consonant only in cases (56a) and (56b), that is, morpheme-internally and across morpheme boundaries.

It is in fact argued in Tranel (1976*a*) that the prefix /in/ is separated from the following stem by a word boundary in its productive combination with deverbal adjectives in *-able,* but by a morpheme boundary elsewhere. This boundary distinction accounts in particular for the different behaviors exhibited by *in-* in (66) and (71), where assimilation occurs, versus (69) and (72), where nasalization takes place:

(71) *illettré* [illetre] 'illiterate'

    illogique [illɔžik] 'illogical'

    irrational [irrasjɔnɛl] 'irrational'

    irréel [irreɛl] 'unreal'

(72) *inlavable* [ɛ̃lavabl] 'which cannot be washed'

    inliquéfiable [ɛ̃likefjabl] 'which cannot be liquefied'

    inracontable [ɛ̃rakɔ̃tabl] 'which cannot be told'

    inratifiable [ɛ̃ratifjabl] 'which cannot be ratified'

Since the prefix *en-* exhibits the same behavior as the prefix *in-* in (69) and (72), with no case parallel to (66) and (71), that is, *en-* never assimilates, but always nasalizes, even before sonorant consonants,

(73) *emménager* [ãmenaže] 'to move in'

    emmieller [ãmjele] 'to bother'

    enlacer [ãlase] 'to embrace'

    enluminer [ãlymine] 'to color'

    enrouler [ãrule] 'to roll'

    enrubanner [ãrybane] 'to put ribbons around'

one could conceivably argue that /an/ is always attached with a word boundary. Even if the argument that the prefix *en-* is always attached with a word boundary could indeed be defended,[23] the restriction that

---

23. The case for the word boundary attachment of *en-* in all instances is in fact very weak. In particular, *en-*prefixation is not always as productive as *in-*prefixation

would thereby be made possible on rule (56) would be ad hoc. Although Chomsky and Halle's (1968) convention that phonological rules which apply morpheme-internally also apply across morpheme boundaries would in a sense explain why cases (56a) and (56b) go together, it would remain a mystery why the restriction should apply in these two instances rather than in case (56c), or why it should not affect all three parts of the rule. The ad hoc character of such a modified rule of vowel nasalization would be compounded by the following problem.

Consider words such as *ennui* [ãnɥi] 'boredom' and its derivatives (e.g., *ennuyer* [ãnɥije] 'to bore', *ennuyant* [ãnɥijã] 'boring') and *néanmoins* [neãmwɛ̃] 'nevertheless'. With the general rule of vowel nasalization (56), the following underlying representations were needed to derive these forms:

(74) *ennui* /annɥi/

     néanmoins /neanmwɛn/

These underlying representations were already unjustified, except as a means for supplying the correct phonetic outputs within the hypothesis that French nasal vowels do not appear underlyingly. With the restricted rule, however, such underlying representations are no longer adequate to allow the generation of the correct phonetic forms, since vowel nasalization within morphemes or across morpheme boundaries is not supposed to take place before nasal consonants. Words like *ennui* and *néanmoins* cannot be handled even with exception features, since a vowel must undergo nasalization, although it does not meet the structural description of the rule. In order to make these vowels nasalize anyway, it would be necessary to assume that (56c) or (56d) applies; one would therefore have to postulate one or two word boundaries between the two nasal consonants posited in the underlying representations given in (74):

(75) (a) /an#nɥi/

        /nean#mwɛn/

    (b) /an##nɥi/

        /nean##mwɛn/

If one could find some justification, synchronically, for the existence

---

with deverbal adjectives in *-able,* and the meanings resulting from the combinations are not always predictable. Most *en*-prefixed words cannot be derived by an active word-formation rule and must be entered as such in the lexicon, probably with a simple morpheme boundary between prefix and stem. See chapter iii for further discussion of this prefix.

of an internal boundary in *néanmoins* (cf. the independent existence of the words *néant* [neã] 'nothingness' and *moins* [mwɛ̃] 'less'), it is difficult to imagine how a word boundary, rather than a morpheme boundary, could be motivated on general grounds. As to *ennui,* there is absolutely no independent reason to assume the existence of internal boundaries of any kind in a synchronic consideration of the word.

The behavior of the prefix /in/ exemplified in (66) thus creates genuine problems for an analysis assuming the existence of a general phonological process of vowel nasalization across morphemes (within words). As I have shown (Tranel 1976*a*), the prefix /in/ nasalizes before any consonant when attached by means of a word boundary but only before nonsonorant consonants when attached with a morpheme boundary; this difference can be neatly captured in the context of a rule of nasalization limited to the prefix /in/ (see sec. III.3.2. for further discussion of this limitation).

B. The prefix *circum-* /sirkɔm/
The prefix *circum-,* which does not nasalize at all and exhibits no tendency to do so, provides another indication of the absence of a general phonological process of vowel nasalization across morphemes:

    (76) *circumnavigation* [sirkɔmnavigasjɔ̃]
        circumpolaire [sirkɔmpɔlɛr]
        circumsolaire [sirkɔmsɔlɛr]
        circumzénithal [sirkɔmzenital]

C. The conditional
In the conditional first and second person plural of first-group verbs (e.g., *demander* 'to ask'), the standard pronunciation contains an obligatory schwa between stems and endings:

    (77) *nous demanderions* [nudəmãdərjɔ̃] 'we would ask'
        vous demanderiez [vudəmãdərje] 'you would ask'

Some speakers, however, may sometimes pronounce these forms without a schwa and say the following (see Pernot 1929:111; Bauche 1951:108; Martinet 1969:217; Sauvageot 1972:132):

    (78) [nudəmãdrijɔ̃]
        [vudəmãdrije]

As will be seen directly, whereas the pronunciations illustrated in (77) are probably derived from underlying representations containing a thematic schwa which must show up on the surface, those given in (78) must be derived from underlying representations without a thematic schwa.

There is in Modern French a constraint that prohibits sequences of the form [CLjV] (consonant-liquid-yod-vowel) in the same syllable[24] (Morin 1971, Tranel 1972). This constraint explains why, for example, the rule of schwa deletion which obligatorily deletes a word-internal schwa when it is preceded by a single non–word-initial consonant (Dell 1973b:229) fails to apply when its application would yield such sequences:

(79) (a) *ennemi* [εnmi] 'enemy'
           samedi [samdi] 'Saturday'
     (b) *appeler* [aple] 'to call'
           (cf. *j'appelle* [žapεl] 'I call')
           acheter [ašte] 'to buy'
           (cf. *j'achète* [žašεt] 'I buy')
(80) (a) *atelier* [atəlje] *[atlje] *[atlije] 'workshop'
           Richelieu [rišəljø] *[rišljø] *[rišlijø] (French statesman)
     (b) *coutelier* [kutəlje] *[kutlje] *[kutlije] 'knife maker'
           (cf. *coutellerie* [kutεlri] 'knife-making')
           hôtelier [otəlje] *[otlje] *[otlije] 'innkeeper'
           (cf. *hôtel* [otεl] 'hotel')

The constraint also accounts for the complementary distribution of the sequences [jV] and [ijV] after consonants: [ijV] occurs after consonant-liquid sequences, [jV] elsewhere.

(81) (a) *pioche* [pjɔš] 'axe'
           papier [papje] 'paper'
           piaule [pjol] 'pad'
     (b) *banquier* [bãkje] 'banker'
           (cf. *banque* [bãk] 'bank')
           rentier [rãtje] 'retired person'
           (cf. *rente* [rãt] 'revenue of retired person')
           figuier [figje] 'fig tree'
           (cf. *figue* [fig] 'fig')
     (c) *amplifier* [ãplifje] 'to amplify'
           (cf. *amplifie* [ãplifi] 'amplify' (imperative))
           scier [sje] 'to saw'
           (cf. *scie* [si] 'saw')
           étudier [etydje] 'to study'
           (cf. *étudie* [etydi] 'study' (imperative))

24. *Parlions* [parljõ] and *parliez* [parlje] '(we, you) were talking' are thus possible because the syllable boundary falls between the [r] and the [l].

(82) (a) *brioche* [brijɔš] *[brjɔš] *[bərjɔš] (type of cake)
  peuplier [pœplije] *[pœplje] *[pœpəlje] 'willow tree'
  trio [trijo] *[trjo] *[tərjo] 'trio'
 (b) *encrier* [ãkrije] *[ãkrje] *[ãkərje] 'inkwell'
  (cf. *encre* [ãkr] 'ink')
  gaufrier [gofrije] *[gofrje] *[gofərje] 'waffle iron'
  (cf. *gaufre* [gofr] 'waffle')
  sablier [sablije] *[sablje] *[sabəlje] 'hourglass'
  (cf. *sable* [sabl] 'sand')
 (c) *crier* [krije] *[krje] *[kərje] 'to shout'
  (cf. *cri* [kri] 'shout')
  plier [plije] *[plje] *[pəlje] 'to fold'
  (cf. *pli* [pli] 'fold')
  trier [trije] *[trje] *[tərje] 'to sort'
  (cf. *tri* [tri] 'sorting')

(80) shows that when a schwa is present underlyingly between the consonant and the liquid, the sequence [CLjV] is never avoided through the application of schwa deletion and the adjustment of [jV] to [ijV]; rather, the schwa must remain. (82) shows that when no schwa is present underlyingly between the consonant and the liquid, one always finds [CLijV] on the surface, never, through schwa insertion, [CəLjV]. For the verb forms under consideration in (77) and (78), it is therefore clear that cases such as (77) are parallel to (80) and thus they are most generally accounted for by assuming the underlying presence of a thematic schwa, whereas cases such as (78) are parallel to (82) and thus there must be no thematic schwa present underlyingly for these pronunciations.

When the thematic schwa is absent and when the verb stem ends in a vowel followed by a nasal consonant (e.g., *aimer* 'to like'), the standard generative analysis of French nasal vowels predicts that vowel nasalization should occur. The fact is that it does not, as illustrated in (83):

(83) *nous aimerions* [nuzɛmrijɔ̃] *[nuzɛ̃r(i)jɔ̃] 'we would like'
  (standard pronunciation: [nuzɛmərjɔ̃])

If no general phonological process of vowel nasalization is postulated across morphemes, data like (83) are automatically explained.

D. Conclusion

The facts concerning the conditional and the prefixes *in-* and *circum-* show that there is in Modern French no general phonological process of vowel nasalization which applies across morphemes (within words).

II.4.3.3. Vowel nasalization at the end of words

At the surface phonetic level, sequences of oral vowel plus nasal consonant appear in word-final position, whether in the context of a single word boundary followed by a consonant or before two word boundaries.

(84) *certaine* [sɛrtɛn] 'certain' (fem.)
      divine [divin] 'divine' (fem.)
      baronne [barɔn] 'baroness'
      paysanne [peizan] 'peasant' (fem.)
      donne [dɔn] 'give' (present indicative and subjunctive)
      vienne [vjɛn] 'come' (present subjunctive)

(85) (a) *frime* [frim] 'fake'
           bitume [bitym] 'tar'
           homme [ɔm] 'man'
           femme [fam] 'woman'
           peine [pɛn] 'pain'
           jeune [žœn] 'young'
      (b) *abdomen* [abdɔmɛn] 'abdomen'
           album [albɔm] 'album'
           cyclamen [siklamɛn] 'cyclamen'
           ohm [om] 'ohm'
           clown [klun] 'clown'
           quidam [kidam] 'person'

In the course of their derivations, such sequences must have been protected from the effect of the process of vowel nasalization posited in the standard generative treatment of French nasal vowels. Two protective devices have been postulated by all the advocates of this analysis: morphological and lexical schwas. Some have in addition resorted to a third protective device, exception features.

Morphological final schwas have been posited for the kind of data illustrated in (84). In these cases the underlying final schwa which prevents vowel nasalization from applying is a grammatical morpheme, the feminine marker or some verb conjugation marker (see Schane 1968*a, b*; Selkirk 1972; Dell 1970, 1973*b*).

For the instances given in (85), the treatments differ. For example, Dell (1970) assumes that, whenever a schwa cannot be grammatically justified, one is present as part of the lexical representations of the words and prevents the application of the rule. In such an analysis there are thus no words that are exceptions to the process of vowel nasalization at the end of words. Schane, on the contrary, considers that there are words that are exceptional in this respect. The examples selected by Schane (1973*b*), for instance, show clearly that words with a final *e* in the orthography are supposed to have a lexical final schwa, as in the data given in (85a), whereas words without one are presumed to be exceptions to vowel nasalization, as in the data given in (85b).

The issue of word-final schwas is discussed in chapter viii. Here I simply wish to show that, within the standard generative analysis of French nasal vowels, exception features are formally necessary (thus invalidating Dell's position)[25] but substantively inadequate (thus invalidating Schane's position).

Consider first noun/verb pairs such as *téléphone* [telefɔn] 'telephone'/*téléphoner* [telefɔne] 'to phone'. For the verb stem, there is no reason to postulate any underlying representation other than /telefɔn/ (e.g., the verb stem of *arriver* [arive] 'to arrive' has usually been assumed to be /ariv/). For an adequate expression of the relatedness between the verb and the noun, it would clearly make more sense if the two items had identical phonological representations, namely /telefɔn/. This of course entails that the noun is an exception to vowel nasalization. The same is true of many other nouns:

(86) *peigne* [pɛñ] 'comb' (cf. *peigner*)

     peine [pɛn] 'pain' (cf. *peiner*)

     trône [tron] 'throne' (cf. *trôner*)

     rime [rim] 'rime' (cf. *rimer*)

The problem with characterizing these nouns as exceptions is, first, that they are quite numerous and, second, that they do not behave like exceptions (i.e., they do not tend to undergo vowel nasalization).[26] On the other hand, all these nouns are straightforwardly accounted for if no general phonological rule of vowel nasalization is assumed to operate at the end of words.

Consider next the following type of data:

(87) *la FEN* [fɛn] (teachers' union)

     la SACEM [sasɛm] (authors' and composers' association)

---

25. Dell's (1970) proposal with respect to final consonant deletion is similar to his handling of vowel nasalization: the systematic postulation of lexical final schwas when needed leads to an exceptionless rule. Selkirk (1972) demonstrates the incorrectness of this approach. See chap. v.

26. As pointed out by Schane at a conference on French phonology (Indiana University, September 1977), if /telefɔnə/ is postulated instead of /telefɔn/, the problem is solved. But the only reason for positing a final schwa in the verb stem is that the corresponding noun does not nasalize. This evidence is rather indirect and weak, with no motivation except for preservation of the claim that /VN/ sequences phonologically nasalize in word-final position.

la SAVIEM [savjɛm] (truck and bus make)
le procédé SECAM [sekam] (color television technique)
la SOFIM [sɔfim] (French and Italian engine company)
l'UQUAM [yk(w)am] (University of Quebec in Montreal)

These words are acronyms for which the postulation of underlying lexical final schwas makes no sense. If a phonological process of vowel nasalization at the end of words did exist in Modern French, these words would need to be marked as exceptions to the rule. But there is no substantive evidence that such words are exceptional: there is no tendency by native speakers to nasalize them.[27] Words like those of (87) are adequately accounted for if no general phonological process of vowel nasalization at the end of words is postulated.

Consider, third, the abbreviatory process whereby the initial /C₀VC/ sequence of a word is retained and the rest of the word dropped:

(88) *baccalauréat* [bakalɔrea] (high school diploma)
  → *bac* [bak]
faculté [fakylte] 'university'
  → *fac* [fak]
putain [putɛ̃] 'whore'
  → *pute* [pyt][28]
café concert [kafekɔ̃sɛr] (type of restaurant with entertainment)
  → *caf' conc'* [kafkɔ̃s]

The same process can apply when the last consonant of the initial /C₀VC/ sequence is a nasal consonant; reduplication occurs in certain cases. Contrary to expectations in the framework where a phonological rule of vowel nasalization is posited word-finally, the resulting abbreviations do not undergo nasalization:

(89) *camelote* [kamlɔt] 'bad merchandise'
  → *came* [kam] *[kã]
premier [prœmje] 'first'
  → *prem* [prœm] *[prɛ̃]
piano [pjano] 'slowly'
  → [pjanpjan] *[pjãpjã]
promenade [prɔmnad] 'walk'
  → [prɔmprɔm] *[prɔ̃prɔ̃]

---

27. *Otan* [ɔtã] (NATO) is probably a spelling pronunciation, lexicalized as /ɔtã/.
28. This is a synchronic reanalysis of the pair *putain/pute*. Historically, *pute* was the subject case, *putain* the oblique case. Fouché (1966:805) claims, however, that Modern French *pute* was actually borrowed from Provençal *puto*.

Such forms do not contain a final schwa and must therefore be assumed to be exceptions to vowel nasalization. Like the cases cited earlier, however, they do not behave like exceptions, since native speakers do not in the slightest tend to nasalize them. These abbreviations are easily accounted for in the absence of a general process of vowel nasalization at the end of words.

The view that phonological vowel nasalization does not occur word-finally also accounts for the data illustrated in (84) and (85) directly. In the latter case, there is in addition no indeterminacy as to whether a word should have a lexical final schwa or be an exception or, if it is considered as an exception, whether the vowel or the nasal consonant should be the exceptional segment.

II.4.4. Conclusion

The evidence provided in this section shows that the abstract generative treatment of French nasal vowels cannot account for all occurrences of nasal vowels and that it cannot account for all cases where vowel nasalization does not take place. These problems are eliminated in an analysis that recognizes that vowel nasalization is not a general phonological process characteristic of Modern French and that French nasal vowels can be lexical.

II.5. Summary

This chapter has been essentially concerned with arguments against the standard generative analysis of French nasal vowels. In sum, I have shown (i) the invalidity of the nonparadigmatic evidence adduced in support of the abstract source of nonalternating nasal vowels, (ii) the artificiality of certain problems that arise in such a framework, and (iii) the descriptive inadequacy of the postulated major phonological rule of vowel nasalization.

The implications of these negative results are far-reaching. All three lines of investigation indicate the necessity to recognize lexical nasal vowels in Modern French, and therefore they point to the existence of a closer match between underlying and phonetic representations. In particular, they provide detailed language-specific support for a theoretical principle such as the strong alternation condition (Kiparsky 1968a). In addition, since a phonological process of vowel nasalization cannot be what accounts for alternating nasal vowels, the crucial question arises as to the nature of the generalizations that native speakers make concerning these [Ṽ]/[VN] alternations.

III

AN ALTERNATIVE ANALYSIS

III.1. Introduction

Following the critical review of the standard generative treatment of French nasal vowels in chapter ii, I now adopt a more constructive perspective and build an analysis that avoids the pitfalls of the abstract solution. For ease of reference I label the new treatment "concrete."

The most obvious and straightforward features of the alternative proposals essentially concern nonalternating nasal vowels and [VN] sequences. The full ramifications of the postulation of lexical nasal vowels and of the absence of a phonological rule of vowel nasalization are explored in these nonalternating cases. I then get to the crux of the matter, namely, [Ṽ] ~ [VN] alternations. Several conceivable solutions are examined and discussed in detail in the light of substantive evidence.

III.2. Nonalternating nasal vowels

One of the basic claims made by the abstract generative analysis of French nasal vowels is that nasal vowels do not exist underlyingly. I propose, on the contrary, that nasal vowels be allowed lexically, in particular whenever there is no surface alternation between nasal vowels and [VN] sequences. The nasality feature on vowels, at the underlying level of representation, is thus not redundant, but it contributes to meaning distinctions:

(1) *entre* [ãtr] /ãtr/ 'between' vs *âtre* [atr] /atr/ 'fireplace'
    cinq [sɛ̃k] /sɛ̃k/ 'five' vs *sec* [sɛk] /sɛk/ 'dry'
    conte [kɔ̃t] /kɔ̃t/ 'tale' vs *cote* [kɔt] /kɔt/ 'price'

III.2.1. Implications

One of the consequences of recognizing (systematic) phonemic nasal vowels in Modern French is a much more direct mapping between the underlying and surface phonetic levels.

Concerning linguistic description, the question of the nonuniqueness of phonological representations no longer exists. In nonalternating cases, the surface nasal vowels are automatically posited lexically, thereby avoiding the problems that arose in the abstract analysis in determining the nature of the underlying /VN/ sequences. Not raising these questions does not mean that the concrete analysis is eschewing an important theoretical issue; rather, it claims that there is simply no psychological reality to it. Words such as *vendre* [vãdr] 'to sell', *thym* [tɛ̃] 'thyme', *lundi* [lɛ̃di] 'Monday', which always show up on the surface with a nasal vowel, are thus represented as /vãdr/, /tɛ̃/, /lɛ̃di/ at the underlying level. Nasal vowels whose very derivations were problematic in the standard generative analysis (cf. words like *Panhard* [pãar] (French car make), *Van Impe* [vãnimp] (surname), *ennui* [ãnɥi] 'boredom'), are also handled straightforwardly and directly, without recourse to any ad hoc internal underlying segment or boundary marker (/pãar/, /vãnimp/, /ãnɥi/).

In the domain of language acquisition, no lexical restructuring has to be assumed on the part of children in the learning of words with nonalternating nasal vowels. In the abstract analysis, the restructuring of nonalternating nasal vowels had to be a necessary step in the child's acquisition of his language. The abstract analysis in effect claimed that, when learning a word such as *conte* [kɔ̃t] 'tale', children, after having in all likelihood lexicalized /kɔ̃t/ at first, then restructured the word into something like /kɔnt/, when they had enough evidence to do so. Since it has been shown that, for Modern French, no general rule of vowel nasalization within morphemes could explain the distribution of all nasal vowels and all sequences of oral vowel plus nasal consonant, there is in fact no way for the child learning the language actually to recover underlying /VN/ sequences for nonalternating nasal vowels.

From a diachronic perspective, the fact that nasal vowels are recognized as phonemic in Modern French makes the claim that, in the history of the language, lexical restructuring has taken place. Nasal vowels have been lexicalized in at least all cases where these segments did not alternate on the surface with sequences of oral vowel plus nasal consonant. This point is considered in more detail in chapter iv.

III.2.2. *Mon*-type words, the article *un*, and the prefixes *bien-*, *en-*, *non-*

Words like *mon* (i.e., the possessive adjectives *mon, ton, son,* the adverbs *bien* 'well' and *rien* 'nothing', the clitic pronoun *on,* the preposition and pronoun *en*) created problems in the abstract analysis of French nasal vowels because their vowels are always phonetically nasal, even when they occur in a liaison context with a following vowel-initial word:

(2) (a) *mon café* [mɔ̃kafe] 'my coffee'
      le mot 'mon' [ləmomɔ̃] 'the word 'mon' '
      mon écureuil [mɔ̃nekyrœj] 'my squirrel'
   (b) *bien dit* [bjɛ̃di] 'well said'
      c'est bien [sɛbjɛ̃] 'it's good'
      bien annoncé [bjɛ̃nanɔ̃se] 'well announced'
   (c) *on pense* [ɔ̃pãs] 'we think'
      existe-t-on? [egzistətɔ̃] 'do we exist?'
      on oublie [ɔ̃nubli] 'we forget'
   (d) *il en parle* [ilãparl] 'he talks about it'
      parles-en [parləzã] 'talk about it'
      il en a [ilãna] 'he has some'

Since these words contain nonalternating nasal vowels, they are assumed to contain a nasal vowel underlyingly.

The masculine indefinite article *un* presents a particular, but interesting, behavior. Like words such as *mon,* it does not exhibit an alternation between a nasal and an oral vowel, and it always shows up phonetically with a nasal vowel:

(3) *un café* [ɛ̃kafe] 'a cup of coffee'
    j'en veux un [žãvøɛ̃] 'I want one'
    un écureuil [ɛ̃nekyrœj] 'a squirrel'

By the alternation condition adopted above, *un* is therefore assumed to contain a nasal vowel underlyingly. It does, however, display a [Ṽ] ~ [VN] alternation when gender is taken into consideration:

(4) (a) *un tabouret* [ɛ̃taburɛ] 'a stool'
      un ami [ɛ̃nami] 'a friend' (masc.)
   (b) *une table* [yntabl] 'a table'
      une amie [ynami] 'a friend' (fem.)

This alternation is exactly parallel to that found in adjectives like *bon* [bɔ̃]/*bonne* [bɔn] 'good', *certain* [sɛrtɛ̃]/*certaine* [sɛrtɛn] 'certain', *fin* [fɛ̃]/*fine* [fin] 'thin', which have been widely assumed to have underlying representations of the form /XVN/ (e.g., Bloomfield 1933:217; Schane 1968*a*; Tranel 1947*b*; see sec. III.5.3.3. for discussion). Liaison and gender data thus seem to offer contradictory evidence concerning the underlying representation of the morpheme *un*. The paradox can be eliminated, and the alternation condition strictly maintained, by assuming that *un* and *une* have separate lexical entries, and that, as warranted by the liaison data, the masculine form contains an underlying nasal vowel. This solution was in fact adopted by Selkirk (1972) and Tranel (1974*b*), and it is the one provisionally retained here. Since it turns out that the case of *un* is neither unique nor marginal, the treatment of its gender alternation is reconsidered when [Ṽ] ∼ [VN] alternations are fully discussed (see sec. III.5.3.3.).

The prefixes *bien-*, *en-*, and *non-* normally show up on the surface with a nasal vowel, no matter what type of segment follows:

(5) (a) *bien-aimé* [bjɛ̃neme] 'beloved'
     bienheureux [bjɛ̃nørø] 'happy'
     bien-fondé [bjɛ̃fɔ̃de] 'cogency'
     bienvenu [bjɛ̃vny] 'welcome'

  (b) *s'enivrer* [sãnivre] 'to get drunk'
     embarquer [ãbarke] 'to embark'
     emmener [ãmne] 'to take away'
     enlaidir [ãledir] 'to make ugly'
     enrager [ãraže] 'to enrage'

  (c) *non-inscrit* [nɔ̃nɛ̃skri] 'not registered'
     non-paiement [nɔ̃pɛmã] 'nonpayment'
     non-moi [nɔ̃mwa] 'nonego'
     non-lieu [nɔ̃ljø] 'dismissal'
     non-réussite [nɔ̃reysit] 'failure'

These prefixes are therefore assumed to contain nasal vowels (namely, /ɛ̃/, /ã/, and /ɔ̃/) in their phonological representations.

For the words considered in this section, there arises the question of the linking [n] that shows up before vowel-initial stems. This [n] can be accounted for in one of two ways: (i) the [n] is present underlyingly (e.g., *mon* /mɔ̃n/; *rien* /rjɛ̃n/; *en* /ãn/), and a rule of consonant truncation is required to delete it before consonant-initial stems and at the pause; (ii) the [n] is not present underlyingly (e.g., *mon*

/mɔ̃/; *rien* /rjɛ̃/; *en* /ɑ̃/), but it is inserted as a linking consonant before vowel-initial stems.

I would like to argue in favor of the insertion solution. As is shown in Part II, just as there is no reason to postulate an across-the-board phonological rule of vowel nasalization, there is no motivation for major phonological processes of final-consonant deletion such as the ones posited by Schane (1968*a*, 1973*b*), Dell (1970, 1973*b*), or Selkirk (1972). Given underlying representations of the type /XṼn/, then, the deletion of the /n/ before consonant-initial stems and at the pause would require a special rule. (For additional arguments against a final underlying /n/, see also part D of sec. III.5.3.3.).

Note, on the other hand, that the linking consonant is predictable: it is the nasal consonant [n], and it shows up between a nasal vowel and a vowel which are separated by a single boundary. A fairly general rule of /n/-insertion can therefore be proposed. I write the rule transformationally as follows:

$$(6) \quad \begin{bmatrix} V \\ +\text{nasal} \end{bmatrix} \quad [-\text{seg}] \quad V$$

$$1 \qquad\quad 2 \quad 3 \quad \Longrightarrow \quad 1 \quad 2 \quad n \quad 2 \quad 3$$

(6) states that /n/ is inserted between a nasal vowel and a vowel separated by a boundary. In addition, it indicates that the boundary that links the two vowels in the structural description is copied on each side of the inserted element in the structural change. This particular formalization avoids the problem of knowing on which side of the boundary the nasal consonant should be inserted. More precisely, it makes the claim that the inserted element does not belong to either the preceding or the following word, but that it is a connective element. A sample derivation is given in (7):

(7) *mon ami* /mɔ̃#ami/

mɔ̃#n#ami

[mɔ̃nami]

The behavior of the prefix *en-* in itself seems to favor the insertion analysis over the deletion treatment. As opposed to the prefix *in-*, *en-* shows no pattern of nasal-consonant assimilation before stems beginning in a sonorant consonant (see chap. ii). This can be straightforwardly explained if *en-* is assumed to have the phonological representation /ɑ̃/, with no nasal consonant present. If an underlying nasal consonant were posited, it would not be impossible to account for the absence of assimilation, but it would not follow as naturally.

III.2.3. Morpheme structure constraints

The solution just proposed to account for the linking consonant [n] allows for a more general and more natural statement concerning the apparent distribution of nasal vowels in the lexical representation of morphemes. Within the present analysis, it may have to be stated that lexical sequences of the form /ṼNC/ do not exist (see sec. II.2.2.1.). If words such as *mon* have lexical representations of the form /XṼ/, as opposed to /XṼn/, then it is possible to state that morpheme-final sequences of the form /ṼN-/ do not exist either (see also sec. III.5.). The two restrictions can be combined into a negative sequence structure condition which states that lexical sequences of the form /ṼN/ do not exist within the same syllable.

This analysis of lexical restrictions on phoneme combinations presupposes that the notion of syllable is meaningful at the level of lexical representations. It therefore claims, in keeping with the rest of the proposals made here, that lexical representations are much more concrete than generally assumed in standard generative phonology.

This constraint on the occurrence of nasal vowels is clearly not true, however, of surface phonetic representations. There are thus numerous examples of derived [ṼN] sequences in the same syllable; for instance, schwa deletion gives [āmne] from /ā + mən + e/ (*emmener* 'to take away'), [ɔ̃nsɛpa] from /ɔ̃#nə#sɛ#pa/ (*on ne sait pas* 'we don't know'), and the optional nasalization of stops after a nasal vowel (Morin 1971:48-52) gives [sɔ̃mtɥø] from /sɔ̃ptɥø/ (*somptueux* 'sumptuous'), [tɔ̃m] from /tɔ̃b/ (*il tombe* 'he is falling'), [vɛ̃ndø] from /vɛ̃t + dø/ (*vingt-deux* 'twenty-two'), [yngrānfam] from /yn#grād# fam/ (*une grande femme* 'a tall woman'). There are also the two (uncommonly used) passé simple forms *nous vînmes* [nuvɛ̃m] 'we came' and *nous tînmes* [nutɛ̃m] 'we held', which I take to be formed by the concatenation of the special verb stems /vɛ̃/ and /tɛ̃/ and the ending /m/ (/vɛ̃ + m/, /tɛ̃ + m/). The existence of phonetic [ṼN] sequences in the same syllable naturally leads one to question the psychological reality of the lexical syllable structure constraint proposed above (see Shibatani 1973; Hooper 1975, 1976:179-184; Clayton 1976). Could it be that the apparent absence of lexical /ṼN/ sequences in the same syllable is synchronically an accidental gap? A few relatively recent monomorphemic borrowings brought to my attention by Yves Morin (personal communication)—*bamba* [bāmba] 'bamba', *samba* [sāmba] 'samba', *Honda* [ɔ̃nda] (Japanese car make), which must be lexically entered as /bãmba/, /sãmba/, /ɔ̃nda/—do seem to indicate that this gap can be filled and that there is therefore no special sequential restriction on the lexical occurrence of nasal vowels. An interesting point is that, if it were not for these borrowings, the standard theory of generative phonology would dictate a (clearly artificial and incorrect) distinction between lexical and phonetic sequential constraints. On the other hand, a theory that does not claim the *independent* existence of lexical constraints predicts the possibility of the kinds of borrowings that have actually occurred. (Cf. Kaye 1974, 1975, and Walker 1975*a* for a view of the other side of the coin, and see Clayton 1976:310-311 for a brief discussion of Kaye's arguments.)

Not all vowels may be nasal in French (e.g., *[ĩ], *[ẽ], *[ũ], *[ỹ]). The present analysis must therefore include segment structure conditions stating which vowel features may co-occur with the feature [+nasal]. These constraints are true of lexical as well as phonetic representations (see also sec. III.5.). They indicate that the only existing nasal vowels are /ẽ/, /œ̃/ (not in all dialects), /ɔ̃/, and /ã/. The fact that the articulations of the nasal vowels do not exactly match any of those of the oral vowels (see Straka 1950:178, Delattre 1965:97-98, and part A of both sec. III.5.3.1. and sec. III.5.3.3.) can be accounted for automatically by the presence of the nasality feature. The defective distribution of the feature [nasal] is not an unusual characteristic of vowel systems. In languages with phonemic nasal vowels, there are often fewer (and never more) nasal vowels than oral vowels (Trubetzkoy 1967:132; Ferguson 1977:277; Ruhlen 1978:217-223). More generally, it is relatively rare, in fact, that the features necessary to describe systematically all the vowels of a language can combine absolutely freely. For example, English vowels require the postulation of the features [back] and [round] (among others), but do not include the combination [-back, +round]; French vowels require the postulation of the features [low], [back], and [round] (among others), but do not include the combination [-low, +back, -round].

III.3. Nonalternating [VN] sequences

Another claim made by the abstract generative treatment of French nasal vowels is that there exists a general phonological process of vowel nasalization affecting /VN/ sequences. In the analysis proposed here, no such rule is assumed to exist. This view has explanatory value for a number of nonalternating /VN/ sequences which are expected to nasalize in the abstract solution but which do not in fact turn into surface phonetic nasal vowels.

III.3.1. Nonalternating [VN] sequences within morphemes

The absence of vowel nasalization within morphemes accounts for the existence of words with morpheme-internal sequences of the form /VNC/ at both the underlying and surface phonetic levels. All these words, which were odd in the framework of the abstract treatment, offer nothing strange at all in the context of the new analysis; this is in keeping with native speakers' intuitions (cf. chap. ii).

Rather learned words such as *amnésie* [amnezi] 'amnesia' and *hymne* [imn] 'hymn', borrowings like *Linda* [linda] 'Linda', *stencil* [stɛnsil] 'stencil', and *week-end* [wikɛnd] 'weekend', colloquialisms such as *binse* [bins] 'disorder' and *clamser* [klamse] 'to croak' (see chap. ii), can all have very straightforward underlying representations of the form /XVNCY/, and they do not have to be considered as exceptional in any way.

At a conference on French phonology (Indiana University, September 1977), François Dell remarked that these words constitute a statistical minority, and that therefore a generalization is lost concerning the distribution of nasal vowels and sequences of oral vowel plus nasal consonant if one rejects vowel nasalization as a process taking place within morphemes. But whether such words are in fact a statistical minority or not is not the point. What is important is their emergence in the language, which is evidence of the relaxation of a particular constraint on sound sequences in French. The possibly correct fact that these words are a statistical minority is not a consequence of the assumption that the constraint still operates; rather, it is the result of the fact that words do not usually enter a language at a rate allowing for a rapid statistical reversal of pattern distributions.

The absence of a phonological process of vowel nasalization within morphemes also straightforwardly explains the absence of vowel nasalization in words containing geminate nasal consonants:

(8) *commentaire* [kɔmmãtɛr] 'commentary'
   grammaire [grammɛr] 'grammar'
   sommaire [sɔmmɛr] 'summary'
   sommet [sɔmmɛ] 'summit'
   summum [sɔmmɔm] 'peak'

It is probably controversial whether these geminate consonants are lexical or derived. If at least some of them are lexical (as the [mm] of *grammaire* probably is for many speakers, since [grammɛr] is their only pronunciation), then there is an additional set of problem words for the abstract generative analysis of French nasal vowels. If the geminate consonants are derived, then the absence of vowel nasalization would require extrinsic ordering between the rules of vowel nasalization and sonorant consonant gemination.[1] The concrete analysis avoids both complications.

The absence of a phonological process of vowel nasalization within morphemes also allows for a unified explanation of the facts concerning slow-speech pronunciation, even if the production of internal schwas in slow speech is to be attributed to an underlying presence (cf. sec. II.2.2.3.). For some speakers, words like *samedi* [samdi] 'Saturday' and *omelette* [ɔmlɛt] 'omelet' can be considered to contain an underlying internal schwa (/samədi/, /ɔmələt/) which, though normally deleted, does show up in slow-speech pronunciation. For other speakers, these words can be considered not to contain an underlying internal schwa (/samdi/, /ɔmlɛt/), which accounts for the absence of a schwa in slow-speech pronunciation. That vowel nasalization does not take place in the first instance does not have to be explained by the ordering of vowel nasalization before internal-schwa deletion, as had to be the case in the abstract analysis; that vowel nasalization does not take place in any event simply follows from the proposal that vowel nasalization does not operate within morphemes.[2] If the production of internal schwas in slow-speech pronunciation is to be attributed to orthographic knowledge, which some speakers, but not all, put into practice under such a condition, then there is no

---

1. The existence of geminate consonants morpheme-internally is particularly characteristic of sonorant consonants in general, especially /m/ (cf. (8)) and /l/ (cf. (i)).
  (i) (a) *Hollande* [ɔllād] 'Holland'
       illusion [illyzjō] 'illusion'
       villa [villa] 'villa'
      (b) *installation* [ɛ̃stallasjō] 'installation'
       pollution [pɔllysjō] 'pollution'
The pronunciations given in (ia) are common, and for the speakers who use them practically exclusively, the geminates may be assumed to be present underlyingly. The pronunciations given in (ib) can be observed sporadically in some speakers and under special oratory circumstances; the geminates are probably derived by a stylistic rule which operates in elevated speech.
2. The possible variation from speaker to speaker regarding the presence or absence of underlying internal schwas would not seem to be unique to French. Ohala (1974) apparently registered similar differences among speakers of Hindi, although in her schwa-eliciting experiments she did not use slow speech, but the creation of non-existing words through the concatenation by subjects of existing words and suffixes.

reason not to assume that words like *samedi* and *omelette* have under-lying representations such as /samdi/ and /ɔmlɛt/, without internal schwas; for all speakers, then, the nonnasalized surface forms must necessarily be explained by the fact that there is no process of vowel nasalization within morphemes.

III.3.2. Nonalternating [VN] sequences across morphemes (within words)

It is claimed in the abstract analysis of French nasal vowels that the process of vowel nasalization applies across morphemes (within words) without any restrictions. It is shown in chapter ii that vowel nasalization cannot in fact be assumed to be such an unconstrained rule of Modern French. The analysis proposed here claims that there is no general rule of vowel nasalization taking place across mor-phemes (within words), but that vowel nasalization is in fact limited to the prefix *in-*.

In the consideration of the phonetic evidence for this view, I exam-ine the restrictions on the process of vowel nasalization across mor-phemes (within words) first between stem and suffix, and then be-tween prefix and stem.

(i) Between stem and suffix:

As seen in chapter ii, certain pronunciations of the conditional present first and second person plural of first-conjugation verbs demonstrated that vowel nasalization could not be assumed to operate between a verb stem and the following irrealis marker /r/ (cf. *nous aimerions* [nuzɛmrijɔ̃] 'we would like'). In addition, since final schwas are not generally postulated in the analysis presented here (see chap. viii), further examples can be adduced to show the nonapplicability of the process between stem and suffix.[3]

Consider, for instance, adverbs formed with a feminine adjective ending in a sequence of oral vowel plus nasal consonant. When the adverbial suffix *-ment* [mã] is added to such stems, vowel nasalization does not take place:

(9) *certainement* [sɛrtɛnmã] *[sɛrtɛ̃mã] 'certainly'
    (from /sɛrtɛn + mã/; cf. *certaine* [sɛrtɛn] 'certain' (fem.))
    finement [finmã] *[fɛ̃mã] 'thinly'
    (from /fin + mã/; cf. *fine* [fin] 'thin' (fem.))

---

3. If final schwas are generally postulated, then the following data illustrate that rule ordering need not be resorted to in order to explain the absence of vowel nasalization.

suprêmement [syprɛmmã] *[syprɛ̃mã] 'supremely'
(from /syprɛm+mã/; cf. *suprême* [syprɛm] 'supreme')
indignement [ɛ̃diñmã] *[ɛ̃dɛ̃mã] 'infamously'
(from /ɛ̃diñ+mã/; cf. *indigne* [ɛ̃diñ] 'infamous')

Consider also deverbal nouns formed by adding the suffix *-ment* [mã] to verb stems. When the verb stems end in a sequence of oral vowel plus nasal consonant, vowel nasalization similarly does not take place:

(10) *rayonnement* [rɛjɔnmã] *[rɛjɔ̃mã] 'radiance'
(from /rɛjɔn+mã/; cf. *rayonner* [rɛjɔne] 'to radiate')
alluvionnement [alyvjɔnmã] *[alyvjɔ̃mã] 'production of alluvions'
(from /alyvjɔn+mã/; cf. *alluvionner* [alyvjɔne] 'to alluvionate')
raffinement [rafinmã] *[rafɛ̃mã] 'refinement'
(from /rafin+mã/; cf. *raffiner* [rafine] 'to refine')
déchaînement [dešɛnmã] *[dešɛ̃mã] 'outburst'
(from /dešɛn+mã/; cf. *déchaîner* [dešɛne] 'to let loose')

At the conference on French phonology mentioned earlier, Yves Morin pointed out that in the argot of l'Ecole des Arts et Métiers, a suffix /s/ may be added to any noun; for example, *Tabagne* [tabañ], the name given to the school by the students, becomes [tabañs]. This is a productive process which can potentially apply to all nouns ending in a [VN] sequence. No vowel nasalization results from the suffixation.[4]

The process of vowel nasalization across morphemes (within words) can thus be regarded as inoperative between stem and suffix.[5]

(ii) Between prefix and stem:

The relevant prefixes are the following: *bien-*, *circon-*, *circum-*, *con-*, *en-*, *in-*, and *non-* (Nyrop 1936:213–252).

The prefixes *bien-*, *en-*, and *non-* were shown earlier to contain a nasal vowel underlyingly. There can therefore be no question of wanting to apply the process of vowel nasalization to them.

---

4. Note that if, as claimed by Dell (1970), word-final sequences of the form [-VNC] were really against the phonotactics of Modern French, it is doubtful that such a productive suffixation process would have entered the language.

5. A form like *bonté* [bɔ̃te] 'goodness' (from the adjective *bon* and the nominalizing suffix *-té*) does not infirm this statement, since in any analysis it must be specified that the masculine form of the adjective is required in this case (cf. also *beauté* [bote] 'beauty'). See Guillet (1971).

The prefix *circon-* is rather rare; it never appears before a vowel-initial stem. Its surface form is always the same: [sirkɔ̃].

(11) *circonférence* [sirkɔ̃ferãs] 'circumference'
     circonlocution [sirkɔ̃lɔkysjɔ̃] 'circumlocution'

Since this prefix does not exhibit any alternation, its surface form is also considered as its underlying form. Here again, there can be no question of having the process of vowel nasalization apply.

The prefix *circum-,* mentioned in chapter ii, is historically related to *circon-,* but it is best considered as separate, from a synchronic point of view. It is very rare, and it never appears before a vowel-initial stem, but, as already pointed out, it never shows up nasalized:

(12) *circumpolaire* [sirkɔmpɔlɛr] 'circumpolar'
     circumnavigation [sirkɔmnavigasjɔ̃] 'circumnavigation'

The underlying representation of this prefix is therefore posited to be /sirkɔm/ and, obviously, vowel nasalization must not apply to it.

The prefix *con-,* like some of the prefixes already considered, never occurs before vowel-initial stems. Before obstruent-initial stems it shows up as [kɔ̃]:

(13) *combattre* [kɔ̃batr] 'to fight'
     compatriote [kɔ̃patrijɔt] 'fellow citizen'
     concourir [kɔ̃kurir] 'to compete'

From a historical point of view *con-* can be said to occur before sonorant consonant-initial stems, but it then shows up as [kɔ]:

(14) *commettre* [kɔmɛtr] 'to commit'
     connaître [kɔnɛtr] 'to know'
     collateral [kɔlateral] 'collateral'
     correspondre [kɔrɛspɔ̃dr] 'to correspond'

Synchronically, however, this surface [kɔ] can also be interpreted as the manifestation of the prefix *co-,* which shows up as [kɔ] before vowel-initial stems as well as before consonant-initial stems:[6]

---

6. The prefix *co-* can actually show up as either [kɔ] or [ko], depending on the tightness of the connection between the prefix and the stem. When *co-* is very tightly linked to the following stem, in which case a morpheme boundary can be assumed to be the connection, *co-* shows up as [kɔ]; if *co-* is more independent of the stem, in which case a word boundary can be assumed to be the connection, then *co-* shows up as [ko]:

(i) *coexistence* [koɛgzistãs] 'coexistence'
    coaccusé [koakyze] 'codefendant'
    corédacteur [koredaktœr] 'coeditor'
    corégent [korežã] 'coregent'
    copropriétaire [koprɔprijetɛr] 'condominium apartment owner'

In this case, given the underlying representation /kɔ/, the /ɔ/ of /kɔ/ is taken to undergo the rule that raises /ɔ/ to /o/ before a word boundary (see sec. II.3.3.1.).

(15) *coïncidence* [kɔɛ̃sidɑ̃s] 'coincidence'
     cosignataire [kɔsiɲatɛr] 'cosignatory'

The facts then are the following: there are two prefixes, *con-* and *co-*. The first, *con-*, has a defective distribution, in that it never occurs before vowel-initial stems; the second, *co-*, has a regular distribution, in that it occurs before any stem, whatever the initial segment is. The problem is to determine which of these two prefixes should be identified with the prefix that shows up as [kɔ] before stems with initial sonorant consonants, synchronically speaking. If the historical evolution were recapitulated synchronically, then *con-* would be set up as underlying /kɔn/, and nasalization would have to apply when the prefix is followed by an obstruent-initial stem. To account for the form of the prefix before sonorant consonant-initial stems, a special rule of nasal-consonant deletion would have to be postulated. It would also have to be stated in the grammar that /kɔn/ can occur only before consonant-initial stems.

The alternative solution seems more attractive: the underlying form of *con-* is assumed to be /kɔ̃/, and this prefix is restricted to occurring only before obstruent-initial stems. The prefix *co-* is underlying /kɔ/, with no co-occurrence restrictions. The prefix that shows up as [kɔ] before stems with initial sonorant consonant, but which is historical /kɔn/, is simply assumed to be a surface manifestation of /kɔ/. The advantage of this solution is that it does not call for the postulation of the very limited rule of /n/-deletion before sonorant consonants. In addition, note that the historical solution has no motivation except the presence in the orthography of two *m*'s, two *n*'s, two *l*'s, two *r*'s. These double consonants in the spelling do not normally show up as geminates in speech.

The adoption of the latter analysis for *con-* makes it unnecessary for the process of vowel nasalization to have to apply to this prefix.

The remaining prefix to examine is *in-*. As opposed to the other prefixes considered, *in-* has a regular distribution, and it exhibits a number of surface allomorphs, as illustrated in the following examples:

(16) *inassouvi* [inasuvi] 'unsatisfied'
     inattention [inatɑ̃sjɔ̃] 'carelessness'
     incohérent [ɛ̃kɔerɑ̃] 'incoherent'
     impertinent [ɛ̃pɛrtinɑ̃] 'impertinent'
     immoral [i(m)mɔral] 'immoral'
     inné [i(n)ne] 'innate'

illégitime [i(l)ležitim] 'illegitimate'
irrespect [i(r)rɛspɛ] 'disrespect'

The data given in (16) strongly suggest that the underlying representation of this prefix be /in/, and that processes of nasalization and assimilation be postulated. For a comprehensive treatment along these lines see Tranel (1976*a*).

Of the prefixes relevant to the discussion, only *in-* requires vowel nasalization to take place.

In this section I have shown that the data do not warrant an all-encompassing rule of vowel nasalization across morphemes (within words), but that, on the contrary, a process of vowel nasalization with a very restricted scope is needed.

III.3.3. Nonalternating [VN] sequences at the end of words

[VN] sequences are commonly found in word-final position in Modern French (cf. feminine adjectives and nouns such as *bonne* [bɔn] 'good', *paysanne* [peizan] 'peasant'; verb forms like *donne* [dɔn] 'give', *vienne* [vjɛn] 'come'; invariable adjectives and nouns like *jaune* [žon] 'yellow', *homme* [ɔm] 'man', *album* [albɔm] 'album'; acronyms such as *FEN* [fɛn] (teachers' union); abbreviations like *prem* [prœm] 'first'). Their occurrence renders opaque the major phonological rule of vowel nasalization claimed in the abstract analysis to apply in such a context. The absence of the rule, advocated in the concrete analysis, accounts for the existence of these word-final [VN] sequences directly. It makes unnecessary the postulation of final schwas, or at least avoids the resort to extrinsic rule ordering; it eliminates exception features; it avoids indeterminacy and incorrect substantive claims (cf. chap. ii).

III.4. Conclusion

The postulation of lexical nasal vowels in nonalternating cases and the rejection of a phonological process of vowel nasalization applying across the board lead to a very direct account of the relevant parts of French phonology. The recognition of the phonemic nature of nasal vowels in French is nothing startlingly new or intuitively surprising, but its reaffirmation and clear demonstration appeared necessary in the face of the coherently argued-for position found in abstract generative treatments of French phonology. The rejection of phonological vowel nasalization has great explanatory value from a French-specific perspective, and it eliminates the need to resort to extrinsic rule ordering, which is of interest from a theoretical perspective.

III.5. [Ṽ] ~ [VN] alternations
III.5.1. Introduction

It now remains to account for alternating nasal vowels and [VN] sequences. As traditionally described, these alternations fall into the following categories:
   (i) Gender distinctions:
   (17) (a) Adjectives:
   bon [bɔ̃]/*bonne* [bɔn] 'good' (masc./fem.)
   plein [plɛ̃]/*pleine* [plɛn] 'full' (masc./fem.)
   fin [fɛ̃]/*fine* [fin] 'thin' (masc./fem.)
   brun [brɛ̃]/*brune* [bryn] 'brown' (masc./fem.)
   (b) Nouns:
   baron [barɔ̃]/*baronne* [barɔn] 'baron'/'baroness'
   paysan [peizɑ̃]/*paysanne* [peizan] 'peasant' (masc./fem.)
   voisin [vwazɛ̃]/*voisine* [vwazin] 'neighbor' (masc./fem.)
   souverain [suvrɛ̃]/*souveraine* [suvrɛn] 'king'/'queen'
Often considered in connection with these masculine/feminine alternations are the cases of liaison which occur when a masculine singular adjective precedes a vowel-initial noun:
   (ii) Liaison with masculine singular adjectives:
   (18) *un bon amiral* [ɛ̃bɔnamiral] 'a good admiral'
   (cf. *un bon vaisseau* [ɛ̃bɔ̃veso] 'a good ship')
   le plein air [ləplɛnɛr] 'the open air'
   (cf. *un plein verre* [ɛ̃plɛ̃vɛr] 'a full glass')
   un certain âge [ɛ̃sɛrtɛnaž] 'a certain age'
   (cf. *un certain livre* [ɛ̃sɛrtɛ̃livr] 'a certain book')
   (iii) Third-conjugation verbs:
   (The examples are given in the third person)
   (19) Present indicative singular/plural:
   vient [vjɛ̃]/*viennent* [vjɛn] 'come'
   joint [žwɛ̃]/*joignent* [žwañ] 'join'
   craint [krɛ̃]/*craignent* [krɛñ] 'fear'
   prend [prɑ̃]/*prennent* [prɛn] 'take'
   (20) Present indicative/subjunctive:
   vient [vjɛ̃]/*vienne* [vjɛn]
   joint [žwɛ̃]/*joigne* [žwañ]
   craint [krɛ̃]/*craigne* [krɛñ]
   prend [prɑ̃]/*prenne* [prɛn]
   (iv) Derivational morphology:
   (21) Nouns/First conjugation verbs (zero suffixation):

béton [betɔ̃]/*bétonner* [betɔne] 'concrete'/'to build with concrete'

don [dɔ̃]/*donner* [dɔne] 'gift'/'to give'

gueuleton [gœltɔ̃]/*gueuletonner* [gœltɔne] 'banquet'/'to have a banquet'

jalon [žalɔ̃]/*jalonner* [žalɔne] 'landmark'/'to place landmarks'

question [kɛstjɔ̃]/*questionner* [kɛstjɔne] 'question'/'to ask questions'

talon [talɔ̃]/talonner [talɔne] 'heel'/'to follow closely, to urge'

cancan [kãkã]/*cancaner* [kãkane] 'gossip'/'to gossip'

ruban [rybã]/*rubaner* [rybane] 'ribbon'/'to trim with ribbons'

assassin [asasɛ̃]/*assassiner* [asasine] 'murderer'/'to murder'

bouquin [bukɛ̃]/*bouquiner* [bukine] 'book'/'to read books'

chemin [šəmɛ̃]/*cheminer* [šəmine] 'path'/'to walk along'

dessin [desɛ̃]/*dessiner* [desine] 'drawing'/'to draw'

examen [ɛgzamɛ̃]/*examiner* [ɛgzamine] 'exam'/'to examine'

patin [patɛ̃]/*patiner* [patine] 'skate'/'to skate'

tambourin [tãburɛ̃]/*tambouriner* [tãburine] 'drum'/'to beat the drum'

vaccin [vaksɛ̃]/*vacciner* [vaksine] 'vaccine'/'to vaccinate'

(22) Word derivation by nonzero suffixation:

garçon [garsɔ̃]/*garçonnet* [garsɔnɛ] 'boy'/'little boy'

maison [mezɔ̃]/*maisonnette* [mezɔnɛt] 'house'/'little house'

canon [kanɔ̃]/*canonique* [kanɔnik] 'canon'/'canonical'

ion [jɔ̃]/*ionique* [jɔnik] 'ion'/'ionic'

citron [sitrɔ̃]/*citronnier* [sitrɔnje] 'lemon'/'lemon tree'

marron [marɔ̃]/*marronnier* [marɔnje] 'chestnut'/'chestnut tree'

intervention [ɛ̃tɛrvãsjɔ̃]/*interventionnisme* [ɛ̃tɛrvãsjɔnism] 'intervention'/'interventionism'

protection [prɔtɛksjɔ̃]/*protectionnisme* [prɔtɛksjɔnism] 'protection'/'protectionism'

Chalon [šalɔ̃]/*chalonnais* [šalɔnɛ] (name of town/ corresponding adjective)

Gabon [gabɔ̃]/*gabonais* [gabɔnɛ] 'Gabon'/'Gabonese'

coussin [kusɛ̃]/*coussinet* [kusinɛ] 'cushion'/'little cushion'

jardin [žardɛ̃]/*jardinet* [žardinɛ] 'garden'/'little garden'

jardin [žardɛ̃]/*jardinier* [žardinje] 'garden'/'gardener'

magasin [magazɛ̃]/*magasinier* [magazinje] 'warehouse'/
   'warehouse-keeper'
Berlin [bɛrlɛ̃]/*Berlinois* [bɛrlinwa] 'Berlin'/'Berliner'
Pékin [pekɛ̃]/*Pékinois* [pekinwa] 'Peking'/'Pekinese'
intestin [ɛ̃tɛstɛ̃]/*intestinal* [ɛ̃tɛstinal] 'intestine'/'intestinal'
matin [matɛ̃]/*matinal* [matinal] 'morning'/'morning'
   (adjective)
océan [ɔseã]/*océanique* [ɔseanik] 'ocean'/'oceanic'
volcan [vɔlkã]/*volcanique* [vɔlkanik] 'volcano'/'volcanic'
cancan [kãkã]/*cancanier* [kãkanje] 'gossip'/'gossipy'
printemps [prɛ̃tã]/*printanier* [prɛ̃tanje] 'spring'/'springlike'
Chaban [šabã]/*chabaniste* [šabanist] (French politician/
   partisan of Chaban)
Otan [ɔtã]/*otaniste* [ɔtanist] 'NATO'/(partisan of NATO)
Sedan [sədã]/*sedanais* [sədanɛ] (name of town/
   corresponding adjective)
Soudan [sudã]/*Soudanais* [sudanɛ] 'Sudan'/'Sudanese'

III.5.2. Phonological denasalization

In chapter ii it is demonstrated that phonological nasalization cannot be an adequate uniform account of [Ṽ] ~ [VN] alternations. Since
it has also been established, however, that nasal vowels need to be
recognized as lexical, it might be suggested that a uniform solution is
still possible if one builds an analysis based instead on a general
phonological process of vowel denasalization. I now explore this
hypothesis in some detail, but ultimately it will be rejected.

Concerning the phonological representations of alternating nasal
vowels, the only difference between such an analysis and the standard
generative treatment would be the presence of the feature [+nasal]
on the relevant vowels (e.g., /bɔ̃n/, /plɛ̃n/, /fĩn/, /brỹn/). The morpheme structure constraints discussed in section III.2.3. would clearly
be invalid, since underlying nasal vowels could occur, immediately
followed by nasal consonants in the same syllable (at least morpheme-
finally), and more than the existing surface nasal vowels would be
possible underlyingly (e.g., /ĩ/, /ỹ/).

Like the standard generative treatment, this analysis would require the postulation of morphological schwas for the feminine of
nouns and adjectives and in the conjugation of verbs. For example,
/bɔ̃n+ə/, /plɛ̃n+ə/, /fĩn+ə/, /brỹn+ə/, would be the feminine
underlying representations of the adjectives given above.

Concerning the phonological component, a phonological rule of vowel denasalization (23) would be needed instead of a phonological rule of vowel nasalization:

(23) $\begin{bmatrix} V \\ +\text{nasal} \end{bmatrix} \rightarrow [-\text{nasal}]/ - \begin{bmatrix} C \\ +\text{nasal} \end{bmatrix} [-\text{seg}]\ V$

Otherwise, the same processes would have to be posited: a rule of nasal-consonant deletion, which could be formalized as (24a) or perhaps (24b) (see part B of sec. III.5.3.3. for problems with a type of formalization such as (24b)),

(24) (a) $\begin{bmatrix} C \\ +\text{nasal} \end{bmatrix} \rightarrow \emptyset / \begin{bmatrix} V \\ +\text{nasal} \end{bmatrix} - [-\text{seg}] \begin{Bmatrix} C \\ [-\text{seg}] \end{Bmatrix}$

(b) $\begin{bmatrix} C \\ +\text{nasal} \end{bmatrix} \rightarrow \emptyset / \begin{bmatrix} V \\ +\text{nasal} \end{bmatrix} - \$$

where $ designates a syllable boundary

rules of nasal vowel quality adjustment (Schane 1968*a*), and rules of schwa deletion (Dell 1970, 1973*b*).

Sample derivations are provided in (25):

(25)

	bon	*bon ami*	*bon café*	*bonne*
	/bɔ̃n/	/bɔ̃n#ami/	/bɔ̃n#kafe/	/bɔ̃n+ə/
relevant syllabification	bɔ̃n$	bɔ̃$n#ami	bɔ̃n#kafe$	bɔ̃$n+ə
rule (23)	——	bɔ$n#ami	———	bɔ$n+ə
rule (24)	bɔ̃	———	bɔ̃ #kafe$	———
other rules	——	———	———	bɔn
	[bɔ̃]	[bɔnami]	[bɔ̃kafe]	[bɔn]

The rest of the data illustrated in section III.5.1. would be similarly accounted for. The feminine nouns of (17) would undergo derivations identical to that of *bonne,* and the masculine nouns, derivations identical to that of *bon* or *bon café.* The underlying forms of the third-conjugation verb stems illustrated in (19) and (20) would undergo rule (24) when no vowel follows the verb stems (e.g., in the present indicative singular), and rule (23) when a vowel does follow the verb stems (e.g., in the subjunctive). For nouns and first-conjugation verbs of the type given in (21), rule (24) would derive the surface phonetic forms of the nouns ([XṼ]) and rule (23) would derive the surface phonetic forms of the verb stems ([XVN]), since these do not occur independently but are normally always followed by some vowel-initial morpheme. The alternations illustrated in (22) would be straightforwardly derived by rules (23) and (24) as well.

Concerning *mon*-type words and prefixes like *bien-*, note that the [n] that shows up phonetically before vowel-initial stems follows the distribution pattern described by rule (24). It would therefore be postulated underlyingly (e.g., /mɔ̃n/, /bjɛ̃n/), and rule (24) would delete it in the correct contexts. These morphemes would be marked as exceptions to the rule of vowel denasalization, since their nasal vowels remain nasal in all environments. The masculine indefinite article *un* would be treated like *mon,* and its feminine counterpart *une* [yn] would be entered in the lexicon separately.

Extrinsic rule ordering would also be required in this analysis. Thus, rule (23) would have to be ordered before the nasal vowel quality adjustments and before schwa deletion. Given this ordering of rule (23) and schwa deletion, rule (24) would not need to be ordered.

I now examine some of the problems faced by this analysis, leaving aside the important, but controversial, issues concerning morphological schwas and extrinsic rule ordering. Independently of these questions, I will show, mostly on the basis of substantive evidence, that this alternative phonological treatment of alternating nasal vowels fails to capture the facts correctly.

Recall first the fact mentioned in chapter ii that, with linking adjectives, there is an innovative trend not to have denasalization (see part B of sec. III.5.3.3. and chap. iv for more detail). This tendency does not exist in the case of feminine adjectives, in the area of verb conjugation, or in derivational morphology. The phonological process of vowel denasalization (23), which accounts for all these surface phonetic forms uniformly, thus not only fails to predict the change affecting masculine singular linking adjectives; it also fails to explain that there should be a split occurring between the forms it derives. Along the same lines, recall that words like *mon,* prefixes such as *bien-,* and the masculine indefinite article *un* would be marked as exceptions to rule (23), since the nasal vowels of these morphemes remain nasal in all environments. But it is quite incorrect to view such forms as exceptional, since they do not tend to denasalize and actually represent a spreading pattern.

Consider, second, the noun/verb pairs illustrated in (21). It has been seen that the correct derivation of the phonetic forms of the verb stems results from the assumption that a vowel normally follows in all their underlying occurrences. There is, however, a clear case where a consonant rather than a vowel actually follows. As evidenced in certain pronunciations of the first and second person plural of the conditional present of first-conjugation verbs, a thematic schwa may not be present underlyingly after verb stems (see sec. II.4.3.2.); in such instances, the grammar will yield incorrect phonetic outputs, since the structural description of vowel denasalization will fail to be met, whereas that of nasal consonant deletion will be met (e.g., *nous jalonnerions* /nu#žalɔ̃n+r+jɔ̃/ [nužalɔnrijɔ̃] *[nužalɔ̃r(i)jɔ̃] 'we would place landmarks').

Third, observe the distribution of the nasal consonant handled by rule (24). It is in fact governed by the more general phonological process of final-consonant deletion (Schane 1968*a*, 1974; Dell 1970, 1973*b*; Selkirk 1972) which would be required in the context of the analysis suggested in this section in order to account for [Ø] ~ [C] alternations. There is, however, much evidence against the existence of such a rule (see Part II). This treatment of alternating nasal vowels would therefore be based on an unjustified phonological process of consonant deletion. If rule (24) were maintained independently to account for the distribution of nasal consonants after nasal vowels, then the alternations between [VN] sequences and nasal vowels on the one hand, and the alternations between final consonants and zero on the other hand, would be implausibly accounted for by widely different operations.

Finally, consider the prefix *in-*. Its underlying form would presumably be /ĩn/, and it would be difficult to derive its surface allomorphs in adjectives such as *immoral* [i(m)mɔral], *inné* [i(n)ne], *illégal* [i(l)legal], *irréel* [i(r)reɛl]. In addition, a vowel nasalization treatment of this prefix is well motivated (Tranel 1976*a*) and thus clearly undermines the uniform treatment sought in the analysis outlined in this section.

For a variety of reasons, vowel denasalization as a major phonological process thus cannot be retained as a viable analysis of [Ṽ] ~ [VN] alternations.

III.5.3. Nonuniform treatment

As chapter ii and the preceding section show, neither phonological nasalization nor phonological denasalization can adequately account for [Ṽ] ~ [VN] alternations. Since only a phonological solution can explain these alternations in a uniform fashion, and since nasalization and denasalization are the only logical phonological possibilities, it follows that [Ṽ] ~ [VN] alternations must involve separate phenomena, to be handled in a nonunified way. My exploration of this line of investigation follows the grammatical divisions according to which [Ṽ] ~ [VN] alternations have been traditionally described (see (17)–(22)).

III.5.3.1. Derivational morphology

A. The alternations between nouns and verbs illustrated in (21) are considered to constitute a particular type of relation between nasal vowels and [VN] sequences.

Observe first that, in all such cases, the verbs are denominal: from a semantic point of view, the nouns are basic, and the meanings of the verbs are built upon them. It would therefore be counterintuitive to derive the nouns from the verb stems by means of a rule of vowel nasalization. From a phonological point of view, the nouns cannot in fact be derived from the verbs by vowel nasalization, because from a verb stem ending in a [VN] sequence it is impossible to predict whether the sequence is going to remain the same in the noun (as in *téléphoner* [telefɔne]/*téléphone* [telefɔn] 'to phone'/'a phone') or switch to a nasal vowel (as in *bétonner* [betɔne]/*béton* [betɔ̃] 'to build with concrete'/'concrete').

Note, second, that the creation of verbs directly from nouns[7] is a productive word-formation process characteristic of Modern French (cf. the relatively recent verbs *s'émotionner* [semɔsjɔne] 'to panic' from *émotion* [emɔsjɔ̃] 'emotion'; *impressionner* [ɛ̃prɛsjɔne] 'to impress' from *impression* [ɛ̃prɛsjɔ̃] 'impression'; *ovationner* [ɔvasjɔne] 'to give an ovation' from *ovation* [ɔvasjɔ̃] 'ovation'; *solutionner* [sɔlysjɔne] 'to solve' from *solution* [sɔlysjɔ̃] 'solution').

I therefore propose that there exists in Modern French a word-formation rule which creates, out of nouns ending in a nasal vowel, first-conjugation verbs whose stems end in an oral vowel plus the nasal consonant /n/. For this word-formation process, as well as others to be considered later, the correspondences between nasal and oral vowels are governed by the following table:

Table 1

(a) ɔ̃ → ɔ
(b) ã → a
(c) ɛ̃ → i

---

7. By "directly" I mean without the addition of a meaningful verbal suffix, e.g., *-is-*, as in *fossiliser* [fosilize] 'to fossilize', from *fossile* [fosil] 'fossil'; *-ifi-*, as in *momifier* [mɔmifje] 'to mummify', from *momie* [mɔmi] 'mummy'.

For the nasal vowels /ɔ̃/ and /ã/, the matching oral vowels are /ɔ/ and /a/. These two correspondences are one-to-one correspondences throughout the language. For the nasal vowel /ɛ̃/, the matching oral vowel is /i/; this is the productive correspondence, as opposed to /ɛ̃/ ~ /y/ (cf. *un* [ɛ̃]/*une* [yn]) or /ɛ̃/ ~ /ɛ/ (cf. *plein* [plɛ̃]/*pleine* [plɛn]). It is worth noting again that the articulation of a nasal vowel never exactly matches that of a phonologically corresponding oral vowel; in particular, [ã] is a back rather than a front vowel, and [ɔ̃] is higher than [ɔ] (also, [ɛ̃] is lower than [ɛ]) (cf. Straka 1950:178; Delattre 1965:97–98).

Since the correspondences of table 1 are also valid for other productive word-formation processes, they will not be incorporated into each of the rules. They will remain as a separate look-up table, and duplication will thus be avoided. The word-formation rule under consideration is therefore written as follows:

$$(26) \quad \begin{bmatrix} X & \begin{bmatrix} V \\ +\text{nasal} \end{bmatrix} \end{bmatrix}_{\text{Noun}} \implies \begin{bmatrix} X & \begin{bmatrix} V \\ -\text{nasal} \end{bmatrix} n \end{bmatrix}_{\text{Verb}}$$

The application of (26) automatically triggers the correspondences of table 1.

Rule (26) captures the ability of native speakers of French to create new verbs. It is therefore clearly part of their competence. The problem remains, however, to determine the type of relation which exists between these nouns and verbs, once the verb has been coined from the noun by rule (26). Is the verb generatively derived from the noun, that is, do nouns and verbs share the same phonological representation /XṼ/, or is the verb lexically entered with its final [Vn] sequence, and related to the noun within the lexicon, by means of a redundancy rule?

A case might be made in favor of deriving the noun and the verb from a common underlying form (namely /XṼ/), if it could be shown that each noun/verb pair would be best accounted for, syntactically and semantically, by having the same lexical entry (as proposed in Chomsky 1972*a* for English verbs and derived nominals). If, however, distinct lexical entries are required independently of the phonology (as proposed in Jackendoff 1975 for English), then the option of having different phonological representations for the nouns and verbs (/XṼ/ and /XVn/, respectively) would become open. The latter solution is in fact phonologically attractive, since the phonological representations would directly correspond to the surface phonetic forms. In addition, if it were assumed that nouns and verbs had distinct lexical entries but shared the same phonological representation /XV̄/, some encoding indicating that the verb is derived from the noun would be required in the lexicon, and nothing would be gained over a solution adopting different phonological representations related within the lexicon. Arguments in favor of distinct lexical entries can thus be interpreted as arguments in favor of different phonological representations.

In the case at hand, it seems clear that distinct lexical entries ought to be posited. One reason for such a view is semantic and stands out most clearly when the noun/verb pairs are contrasted with alternating adjectives like *bon/bonne*. Such variable adjectives have the same meaning whether they are in the masculine or the feminine; it therefore makes sense to postulate for them a single lexical entry and to derive the two surface forms generatively from a common phonological representation. On the other hand, in the noun/verb pairs under consideration, although the meanings of the verbs are built upon the meanings of the nouns, no exact prediction can be made as to what the meanings of the verbs will actually be. Consider for instance the noun *brouillon* [brujɔ̃] 'rough draft'. To my knowledge there is no existing corresponding verb; however, using the word-formation rule (26), I can make one up: *brouillonner* [brujɔne]. Note that this verb could perfectly well have one of a variety of meanings: for example, 'to write a rough draft', 'to read rough drafts', 'to act in a confused manner'. *Bouquiner,* which does exist, and which means 'to read books', could have equally well meant 'to sell books' or 'to write books'. *Cochonner,* which also happens to exist, and which means 'to do something in a slovenly manner, to botch', could have meant 'to sell pigs' or 'to herd pigs'. The meanings of the verbs are obviously constrained by the meanings of the nouns (one does not write pigs or herd books), but the semantic relations between nouns and verbs within pairs are not totally predictable. Some semantic information concerning the meanings of the verbs is thus idiosyncratic, that is, properly lexical, and native speakers must learn it independently of the meanings of the corresponding nouns. From this lack of complete semantic predictability, the postulation of distinct lexical entries for the nouns and verbs under consideration appears necessary.

Further evidence comes from semantic drift. Consider the fact that, for a number of noun/verb pairs, the meaning of the noun and the meaning of the verb have drifted so far apart that it is not evident that the two should any longer be related at all in the grammar. For example, it is likely that very few native speakers ever make the connection between *don* [dɔ̃] 'gift, talent' and *donner* [dɔne] 'to give', or *son* [sɔ̃] 'sound' and *sonner* [sɔne] 'to ring' (a bell). The separate lexical listings advocated here actually account—or at least allow—for the possibility of a semantic drift. Such a drift could not occur if the two forms had a single lexical entry in the minds of native speakers. Note in contrast that semantic drifts do not ordinarily take place between the masculine and feminine forms of adjectives like *bon/bonne*; but such pairs have a single lexical entry postulated (see part D of sec. III.5.3.3.).

It therefore seems reasonable to assume that the noun/verb pairs in question have distinct lexical entries and that /XVN/ is the canonical phonological representation of the verbs. As a word-formation rule, (26) is thus viewed as a once-only rule, which serves the purpose of actually creating a word from another (Aronoff 1976). Once the verb has been coined, it is entered in the lexicon with its final /Vn/ sequence and particular meaning. The members of the noun/verb pairs under consideration are thus not generatively related.

Nevertheless, there are obvious phonological and semantic relations between the members of such pairs, and it would surely be underrepresenting the knowledge of native speakers to have completely separate lexical entries. I therefore propose distinct, but related, lexical entries, as exemplified below with the pair *bouquin/bouquiner*:

(27) (a) Lexical entry i for *bouquin* [bukɛ̃] 'book':

$$\begin{bmatrix} \text{(Phonological representation P}_i: /buk\tilde{\epsilon}/) \\ \text{(Syntactic features)} \\ \text{(Semantic features S}_i) \end{bmatrix}$$

(b) Lexical entry j for *bouquiner* [bukine] 'to read books':

$$\begin{bmatrix} \text{(Phonological representation P}_j: /bukin/ \\ \text{related to P}_i \text{ via (26))} \\ \text{(Syntactic features)} \\ \text{(Semantic representation S}_j: \text{'to read S}_i\text{')} \end{bmatrix}$$

Rule (26) thus performs a dual function: the creative function of a word-formation rule and the analyzing function of a lexical rule of correspondence (or via rule) (cf. Vennemann 1972c:224–232; Hooper 1976:17, 47–48, 63).

A via rule capturing a more encompassing correspondence than the one provided by (26) is necessary in order to account for fairly rare noun/verb pairs which represent past formations that are no longer phonologically productive, but whose members native speakers still relate (e.g., *parfum* [parfɛ̃]/*parfumer* [parfyme] 'perfume'/'to perfume'; *étain* [etɛ̃]/*étamer* [etame] 'tin'/'to tin'; *dédain* [dedɛ̃]/*dédaigner* [dedɛñe] 'disdain'/'to disdain'). This via rule establishes a very general relation between nasal vowels and sequences of oral vowel plus nasal consonant (namely /Ṽ/⟺/VN/).

The members of pairs like *solution/solutionner* and *parfum/parfumer* are thus related by via rules, but in the first case the operating via rule, that is, (26), is also a word-formation rule, whereas in the second case the via rule used has no existence outside its lexical function. This distinction in the treatment of *solution/solutionner* and *parfum/parfumer* captures the psychologically real difference between, on the one hand, alternations that are productive and, on the other hand, alternations that are historical relics. Native speakers are clearly aware of this dichotomy: nobody would question the use of verbs like *parfumer, donner,* or *sonner,* but verbs like *solutionner, s'émotionner, ovationner* are felt as neologisms, and their use is commonly frowned upon by normative speakers.

B. The second type of [Ṽ] ~ [VN] alternations found in derivational morphology (cf. (22)) is obtained by the addition of a vowel-initial suffix to a word ending in a nasal vowel, and the ensuing triggering of /n/-insertion and vowel denasalization.

The process of /n/-insertion which thus occurs at the morpheme boundary separating a stem from a suffix is comparable to the one motivated earlier to account for phrases such as *mon ami* [mɔ̃nami] 'my friend' or sequences of prefix plus stem like *bienheureux* [bjɛ̃nørø] 'happy'. In the latter cases, however, vowel denasalization does not normally take place, whereas in the former case vowel denasalization always occurs. In fact, one can state very generally that vowel denasalization always occurs in a word when the stem-final nasal vowel is followed by a nasal consonant and a vowel. Earlier, this was found to be true in a class of adverbs in *-ment* which are formed with masculine instead of feminine adjectives (e.g., *savant* [savã]/*savante* [savãt] 'learned' (masc./fem.); *savamment* [savamã], **savantement* 'learnedly'; cf. sec. II.3.3.1.).

The following rules thus appear to operate:

(28) $\begin{bmatrix} V \\ +\text{nasal} \end{bmatrix}$ + V

$\qquad$ 1 $\qquad$ 2 $\quad$ 3 $\implies$ 1 $\quad$ 2 $\quad$ n $\quad$ 2 $\quad$ 3

(29) $\begin{bmatrix} V \\ +\text{nasal} \end{bmatrix} \rightarrow [-\text{nasal}]/\overline{}_{\text{stem}} + \begin{bmatrix} C \\ +\text{nasal} \end{bmatrix} V$

As with the productive word-formation process (26), which derives first-conjugation verbs from nouns, the correspondence established by rule (29) between nasal and oral vowels is automatically governed, in the active cases, by table 1.

The derivation for *maisonnette* 'little house' exemplifies how the rules work. The underlying form of *maison* [mezɔ̃] is /mezɔ̃/; when the diminutive suffix /ɛt/ is added, (28) and (29)—in conjunction with table 1—apply:

(30)   /mezɔ̃ + ɛt/

    (28)   mezɔ̃ + n + ɛt

    (29)   mezɔ + n + ɛt

        [mezɔnɛt]

Martinet (1965:22) provides substantive evidence in support of the claim that /i/ is the oral vowel that productively corresponds to /ɛ̃/: "lorsqu'en 1940, les prisonniers français du camp de Weinsberg, en Würtemberg, ont appris par voie orale (la radio allemande en langue française) la prise du pouvoir par le maréchal Pétain, ils ont désigné ceux d'entre eux qui approuvaient cette action, non comme des *pétainistes*, mais comme des *pétinistes*."

A few nouns ending in [ɛ̃] have derivatives containing a corresponding oral vowel other than [i]. Two examples with the oral vowel [e] are *rein* [rɛ̃]/*rénal* [renal] 'kidney'/'renal', and *Rhin* [rɛ̃]/*rhénan* [renã] 'Rhine'/'Rhenish'. There are also the cases of *parfum* [parfɛ̃]/ *parfumerie* [parfymri] 'perfume'/'perfumery' and *faim* [fɛ̃]/*famine* [famin] 'hunger'/'famine'. I believe such pairs to be isolated cases. *Rénal* and *rhénan* are the only two examples of noun plus suffix combinations I was able to find where [ɛ̃] alternates with [e]; note in addition that *rénal* is not a common word, but a rather technical one. As for the pair *Rhin/rhénan*, it is not certain that the two words are related in the minds of all native speakers; I personally had not made the connection until looking for such alternations. This absence of relation may also be owing in part to the fact that the suffix *-an* is not productively used and enters into the formation of very few words (Dubois 1962:17, 85). The case of *parfum/parfumerie* is, phonologically speaking, doubly unusual: first, it exhibits the oral vowel [y] corresponding to the nasal vowel [ɛ̃]; second, an [m] instead of an [n] shows up in the suffixed word. The pair *faim/famine* constitutes a semantic, as well as a phonological, oddity: first, [ɛ̃] alternates with [a], and [m] is the connecting nasal consonant; second, the suffix *-ine* is of rather restricted use (except in a technical usage, as in *albumine* [albymin] 'albumin', *caféine* [kafein] 'caffeine', *nicotine* [nikɔtin] 'nicotine'; cf. Nyrop 1936:137–138), and its meaning in *famine* may be somewhat obscure from a synchronic point of view; the way it affects the semantics of the stem is certainly not commonly perceived as being of general validity in the language. These derivatives then can be best handled by being entered in the lexicon in their (classical) phonemic forms and by being phonologically related to their respective historical parents, perhaps only in the grammars of some speakers, with the general via rule /Ṽ/⟺/VN/ suggested earlier.

In the case of the noun/verb pairs illustrated in (21), the question was raised as to whether the members of each pair were related to each other generatively or lexically. The same question can be legitimately asked of the pairs illustrated in (22). In other words, one can wonder whether rules (28) and (29) are not once-only processes taking place at the creation of a new word, and then whether they do not simply function in an analyzing fashion within the lexicon.

It is clear again that the derived words have a lexical existence of their own. Take, for example, the word *chalandonette* [šalādɔnɛt]; it refers to a type of house built in a project created under the auspices of a minister named *Chalandon* [šalādɔ̃]. Obviously, the meaning of *chalandonette* is quite idiosyncratic; it cannot be derived from the person to whom *Chalandon* refers and from the meaning of the suffix *-ette*. It would consequently not make much sense to assume that in every instance of the word, *chalandonette* is generatively derived from an underlying form /šalādɔ̃ + ɛt/, itself created by a word-formation process of *-ette* suffixation. On the other hand, the phonological relation between *Chalandon* and *chalandonette* is clearly reflective of a general pattern in the language; this general pattern can be lexically captured by means of rules (28) and (29), functioning either as via rules or in a manner reminiscent of upside-down phonology (Leben and Robinson 1977).

The fact that rule (29) is a word-internal process conditioned by morphological information (cf. the feature [stem]) may actually be an additional cue to the lexical function of this rule (and of rule (28) by consequence). Dell and Selkirk (1978) hypothesize that such "morpholexical" rules could either be part of a prephonological component or operate in the lexicon.

III.5.3.2. Third-conjugation verbs

Several alternative treatments seem possible for the [Ṽ]∼[VN] alternations found in the conjugation of third-conjugation verbs (cf.

(19)–(20)). They all share the necessary features of crucially referring to grammatical information.

The few verbs involved in these alternations are part of a closed set. The four types of alternations involved are given in (31) with sample verbs:[8]

$$
\begin{array}{llll}
(31) & \text{(i)} & [\text{j}\tilde{\epsilon}] \sim [\text{j}\epsilon\text{n}] & \text{(e.g., } venir, tenir) \\
& \text{(ii)} & [\text{w}\tilde{\epsilon}] \sim [\text{wañ}] & \text{(e.g., } joindre) \\
& \text{(iii)} & [\tilde{\epsilon}] \sim [\epsilon\text{ñ}] & \text{(e.g., } craindre, peindre) \\
& \text{(iv)} & [\tilde{a}] \sim [\epsilon\text{n}] & \text{(e.g., } prendre)
\end{array}
$$

From the above phonetic correspondences it is obvious that one can predict either column from the other. One could therefore equally well postulate that the /VN/ sequences are basic and that the nasal vowels are derived by means of a morphophonological rule of vowel nasalization and nasal-consonant deletion which would apply in the indicative and imperative present singular (Tranel 1974*b*, 1978*b*), or consider that the nasal vowels are basic and that the [VN] sequences are obtained by a morphophonological rule of nasal-consonant insertion and vowel denasalization which would operate in the complement environment of the preceding solution's context (as suggested in Tranel 1978*b*:66–67). A third alternative would be to assume that both sets of allomorphs are listed in the lexicon and that rules distribute them in the correct grammatical contexts.

The last-mentioned suggestion may have the most psychological reality and hence may be preferable. Substantive evidence in the area of language acquisition suggests that for such complex but nonproductive conjugations, speakers have actually memorized several lexical roots for a given verb, and that rules of distribution govern their use. For example, children will often one time say the correct *je viendrai* [žvjɛ̃drɛ] 'I'll come', but the next time they will produce the incorrect *je venirai* [žvənirɛ]; similarly, for the infinitive *tenir* [tənir]

---

8. A more complete list, drawn from Bescherelle (1959), follows:
Type (i) (*tenir* and *venir* and their derivatives)
    (a) appartenir, contenir, détenir, entretenir, maintenir, retenir, soutenir, tenir
    (b) advenir, circonvenir, contrevenir, convenir, devenir, disconvenir, intervenir, prévenir, provenir, revenir, souvenir, subvenir, survenir, venir
Type (ii) (*oindre,* and *joindre* and its derivatives)
    adjoindre, conjoindre, disjoindre, joindre, oindre, rejoindre
Type (iii) (the most varied group)
    astreindre, ceindre, craindre, dépeindre, empreindre, enfreindre, épreindre, éteindre, étreindre, feindre, geindre, peindre, plaindre, repeindre, teindre
Type (iv) (*prendre* and its derivatives)
    apprendre, comprendre, méprendre, prendre, rapprendre, reprendre, surprendre

'to hold', they may produce the correct form one time, but they may say *tiendre* [tjẽdr] the next time (Guillaume 1927). It is difficult to account for these random alternations if the surface forms are assumed to be derived from a single underlying representation. On the other hand, if several roots are postulated in the lexicon, then the alternations can very plausibly be explained by the hypothesis that the children have imperfectly learned the rules of distribution which normally account for the surface occurrences of the various roots.

It ought to be stated in the grammar, however, that exactly the types of alternations given in (31) occur, and no other combination. To this end, the correspondences of (31) could be included in the lexicon as via rules relating the various verb roots listed in each relevant lexical entry.

The essential argument presented in this section on the conjugation of third-conjugation verbs is that the surface alternations between nasal vowels and [VN] sequences are morphophonologically determined. This view contrasts with that of the standard generative analysis, where the alternations are deemed to be phonologically governed. It is of interest to compare the two claims in the light of data on the acquisition of verb forms. Cohen (1962:24) relates the story of a four-and-a-half-year-old boy who said *Je veux que tu viens* [žvøktyvjẽ] (indicative of *venir*), but who was corrected by an adult who told him that one should say *Je veux que tu viennes* [žvøktyvjɛn] (subjunctive) 'I want you to come'. The child, however, immediately replied that such a sentence was for girls: *"Je veux que tu viennes est fait pour les filles."* Although one could hypothesize that this statement is sociolinguistically explainable by the belief that girls are supposed to speak more correctly and more daintily than boys, there is also a linguistic explanation which may be more plausible. This child's behavior could indicate that he had not yet acquired the rules that govern the use and formation of the subjunctive, but that he was aware that gender distinctions can manifest themselves by alternations of the form [Ṽ] ~ [VN] at the end of words. To him, the sentence he produced was no doubt perfectly correct; but since he could not account for the sentence given by the adult through his as yet incomplete grammar, the only way for him to explain it away was to assume that the adult had applied another rule which he knew could create alternations of the type [Ṽ] ~ [VN], namely, the one that accounts for gender alternations. The postulation of the existence of grammatically governed rules to account for certain [Ṽ] ~ [VN] alternations seems to capture the child's knowledge of French as reflected in Cohen's story in a much more direct and plausible way than the abstract phonological analysis could.

III.5.3.3. Gender and liaison alternations

A. Morphophonological vowel nasalization

As was true of the [Ṽ] ~ [VN] alternations found in third-conjugation verbs, grammatical information (namely gender) correlates with the [Ṽ] ~ [VN] alternations exemplified in the adjectives and nouns given in (17).

The morphophonological solutions generally proposed to account for these gender alternations have assumed the [VN] sequences to be basic and the nasal vowels to be derived, as briefly suggested, for example, in Bloomfield (1933:217), Picard (1974), and Churma (1977), and considered in detail in Tranel (1974*b*). This type of treatment seems to constitute the next logical and least drastic step following the impossibility of a purely phonological vowel nasalization account, since at least the lexical representations and the idea that vowel nasalization occurs are carried over. As a starting point for the discussion, I use the analysis actually formalized in Tranel (1947*b*).

In Tranel (1974*b*:178–182), the masculine/feminine [Ṽ] ~ [VN] alternations are accounted for by a morphophonological rule of vowel nasalization of the following form:

$$(32) \quad \begin{bmatrix} \# & X & V & \begin{bmatrix} C \\ +\text{nasal} \end{bmatrix} & \# \end{bmatrix}_{\text{masc.}}$$

$$1 \quad 2 \quad 3 \quad 4 \quad 5 \implies 1 \quad 2 \quad \begin{bmatrix} 3 \\ +\text{nasal} \end{bmatrix} \quad \varnothing \quad 5$$

Condition: 3 and 4 must be tautosyllabic

(32) states that a sequence of an oral vowel plus a nasal consonant at the end of a masculine word turns into a nasal vowel if the oral vowel and the nasal consonant belong to the same syllable.

Words such as *bon* and *baron* are entered in the lexicon with a final sequence of oral vowel plus nasal consonant: /bɔn/, /barɔn/. In addition, they are marked to undergo rule (32). Words such as *jaune* [žon] 'yellow', which never alternate with morphemes exhibiting a final nasal vowel, lexically end in sequences of oral vowel plus nasal consonant too (/žon/), but they are not marked as being able to undergo rule (32). Rule (32) is thus considered to be a minor rule. As explicitly stated in Bloomfield (1933:217), the type of gender alternation accounted for by the rule is therefore deemed irregular.

Let us take the adjective *bon* as an example to illustrate concretely the functioning of the grammar. If /bɔn/ is marked as [+feminine] in the course of the syntactic derivation, nothing will happen to the form; in particular, rule (32) will not be applicable and [bɔn] will correctly show up in all cases at the surface phonetic level. If /bɔn/ becomes marked [+masculine], then rule (32) will be eligible to apply. Note, however, the particular phonological constraint on the rule, namely, that the vowel and the nasal consonant must be tautosyllabic. This phonological constraint is destined to account for the liaison phenomenon. It is assumed that there exist in French rules of syllabification which apply any time their structural descriptions are met (cf. Hooper 1972 for such rules in Spanish). Two of these are the following:

(33) (a)   C   [−seg]   V
          1   2   3 $\Longrightarrow$ $ 1   2   3

(b)   C   [−seg]   C
     1   2   3 $\Longrightarrow$ 1   2   3
                                              $

where $ designates a syllable boundary

(33a) accounts for the fact that the final consonant of a word gets phonetically attached to the initial vowel of the next word (cf. homophonous phrases such as *petit ami* 'little friend' (masc.), *petite amie* 'little friend' (fem.), *petit tamis* 'little sieve': [pti$tami]). (33b) accounts for the fact that the final consonant of a word does not get phonetically attached to the next word if it begins with a consonant (e.g., *honnête garçon* [ɔnɛt$garsɔ̃] 'honest boy'; *petite fille* [ptit$fij] 'little girl'; *même chose* [mɛm$šoz] 'same thing'). It is also assumed that a syllable boundary automatically occurs with two word boundaries, as at the end of a phonological phrase (e.g., *il est bon* [ilɛbɔ̃$]; *elle est bonne* [ɛlɛbɔn$]).

The following three sample derivations are now self-explanatory; they illustrate how /bɔn/ [+masculine] shows up as [bɔn] before vowel-initial words and as [bɔ̃] before consonant-initial words and at the end of a phonological phrase:

(34)

	bon ami	*bon garçon*	*c'est bon*
	/bɔn#ami/	/bɔn#garsɔ̃/	/sɛ#bɔn##/
relevant	bɔ$n#ami	bɔn#garsɔ̃	sɛ#bɔn##
syllabification		$	$
(32)	——	bɔ̃ #garsɔ̃	sɛ#bɔ̃ ##
		$	$
	[bɔnami]	[bɔ̃garsɔ̃]	[sɛbɔ̃]

For nouns such as *baron* /barɔn/, the vowel and the nasal consonant will always be tautosyllabic: in the singular, nouns are always followed by two word boundaries, since they never link; in the plural, they are always followed by a boundary and the plural morpheme /z/ (Selkirk 1972). As a result, the masculine of /barɔn/ will always correctly show up as [barɔ̃] on the surface.

In the abstract generative analysis of French nasal vowels, the nasalization in *bon* and *baron* is a purely phonological process. The claim made in the solution just presented is that the historically phonological process of vowel nasalization has been morphologized, although there remains an interesting phonological constraint having to do with syllable boundaries.

This morphophonological treatment handles inherently masculine nouns such as *album* [albɔm] 'album', *abdomen* [abdɔmɛn] 'abdomen', *homme* [ɔm] 'man', through the postulation of straightforward underlying forms of the type /XVN/: /albɔm/, /abdɔmɛn/, /ɔm/. There is no reason for vowel nasalization to apply to such items, since the rule is a minor rule. Consequently, there is no indeterminacy in the grammar as to whether these words contain a final lexical schwa, or are exceptional with respect to vowel nasalization (and then, which segment is exceptional).

Morphophonological vowel nasalization shares with the abstract generative analysis the property of allowing for a merging correspondence between the oral vowels of the underlying /VN/ sequences and the surface nasal vowels. The facts concerning the quality of French nasal vowels are, however, more complex than is usually assumed. For example, Schane (1968a:49) considers that the four surface nasal vowels of French are phonetically low, and he therefore posits a general lowering rule which accounts for (35),

(35) /in/ → /ɛ̃/
     /yn/ → /œ̃/

and which applies vacuously to /ɛ̃/ from /ɛn/ and in the cases of the two back nasal vowels. But this rule is too general: the nasal vowel commonly written [ɔ̃] is in fact not phonetically low, but more accurately intermediate between low mid and high mid (Delattre 1965:98). Schane's lowering rule therefore needs to be restricted to front nasal vowels. In addition, [ã] is clearly a back nasal vowel, and since it comes from underlying /an/ (where /a/ is a front vowel), a backing rule is required for this vowel. Finally, [œ̃] is unrounded in the speech of many speakers, and an unrounding process is thus also necessary.

It will be useful at this point, for the sake of the discussion, to present the extension of this analysis of [Ṽ] ~ [VN] gender and liaison alternations to adjectives like *petit* 'little', which exhibit parallel [Ø] ~ [C] alternations (cf. *petit* [pəti]/*petite* [pətit]/*petit ami* [pətit-ami]).

Corresponding to rule (32), the following minor morphophonological rule of final-consonant deletion can be proposed (Tranel 1974*b*: 193–196):

(36) $[\#\quad X\quad C\quad \#]_{masc.}$

    1   2   3   4 ⟹ 1 2 Ø 4

Condition: 3 must be in syllable coda

(36) states that the final consonant of a masculine word is deleted if it closes the syllable.

Adjectives and nouns that exhibit an alternation of the type [Ø] ~ [C] in final position between their masculine and feminine forms contain the final consonant underlyingly and are marked for rule (36) (cf. (37a)). Adjectives and masculine nouns that are invariable, and always show a final consonant phonetically, have similar underlying representations, but they are not marked to undergo rule (36) (cf. (37b)).

(37) (a) *petit* [pəti]/*petite* [pətit] 'little' (masc./fem.)
        bavard [bavar]/*bavarde* [bavard] 'talkative'
          (masc./fem.)
        grivois [grivwa]/*grivoise* [grivwaz] 'obscene'
          (masc./fem.)
        blanc [blã]/*blanche* [blãš] 'white' (masc./fem.)
        Anglais [ãglɛ]/*Anglaise* [ãglɛz] 'Englishman'/
          'Englishwoman'
        éléphant [elefã]/*éléphante* [elefãt] 'male/female
          elephant'
        président [prezidã]/*présidente* [prezidãt] 'man/woman
          president'
        avocat [avɔka]/*avocate* [avɔkat] 'man/woman lawyer'
   (b) *honnête* [ɔnɛt] 'honest' (masc. and fem.)
        rude [ryd] 'tough' (masc. and fem.)
        rose [roz] 'pink' (masc. and fem.)
        rouge [ruž] 'red' (masc. and fem.)
        pilote [pilɔt] 'pilot' (masc.)
        garde [gard] 'warden' (masc.)
        mec [mɛk] 'guy' (masc.)
        siège [sjɛž] 'seat' (masc.)

The derivations given in (38), which illustrate how the correct outputs are obtained, are very similar to those of (34):

		petit ami	*petit garçon*	*c'est petit*
(38)		/pətit#ami/	/pətit#garsɔ̃/	/sɛ#pətit##/
	relevant	pəti$t#ami	pətit#garsɔ̃	sɛ#pətit##
	syllabification		$	$
	(36)	———	pəti #garsɔ̃	sɛ#pəti ##
			$	$
		[pətitami]	[pətigarsɔ̃]	[sɛpəti]

The morphophonological rules of vowel nasalization and final-consonant deletion can be collapsed by means of angled brackets, thus formally capturing the functional unity of the processes involved:

$$(39) \quad \begin{bmatrix} \# & X & \langle V\rangle & \begin{bmatrix} C \\ \langle +\text{nasal}\rangle \end{bmatrix} & \# \end{bmatrix}_{\text{masc.}}$$

$$1 \quad 2 \quad 3 \quad\quad 4 \quad\quad 5 \implies 1 \; 2 \left\langle \begin{bmatrix} 3 \\ +\text{nasal} \end{bmatrix} \right\rangle \; \emptyset \; 5$$

Condition: 4 must be in syllable coda

B. Problems with morphophonological vowel nasalization

Morphophonological vowel nasalization and final-consonant deletion allow for a superficially reasonable account of the facts, but, looked at more closely, they are also the source of several problems, to which I now turn.

Consider first the opposition between variable and invariable adjectives. Variable adjectives like *bon* and *petit* are taken to have the same canonical underlying representation as invariable adjectives like *jaune* and *honnête* (i.e., /bɔn/, /žon/; /pətit/, /ɔnɛt/). Still, the two types of adjectives have to be distinguished, since the morphophonological rules of vowel nasalization and final-consonant deletion must apply to *bon* and *petit* but not to *jaune* and *honnête*. To implement this necessary distinction, it has been assumed that these rules were minor rules, therefore that adjectives like *bon* and *petit* were lexically marked to undergo the rules, whereas adjectives like *jaune* and *honnête* were not. The formal consequence of this move is that *bon*-type and *petit*-type adjectives are more complex than *jaune*-type and *honnête*-type adjectives. This distinction corresponds to the intuition that adjectives with a single form for the two genders should somehow be simpler than those with two forms.

If the notion of "minor rule" is taken seriously, however, then, from a historical perspective and barring other changes, one expects these minor rules eventually to drop out of the language. If they did, the surface forms of the presently alternating adjectives would be the underlying representations now postulated, in effect the feminine allomorphs. The prediction that these forms would take over, if a change from an alternating system to a nonalternating system were to occur, does not, however, seem intuitively correct; thus it calls into question the validity of the analysis. Reinforcing this point is the fact that mistakes do not occur wherein the morphophonological processes (32) and (36) fail to apply. Thus, outside of liaison, one does not find, for example, [bɔn] or [pətit] for the masculine. Such mistakes would be expected in the speech of children or in popular speech if the morphophonological rules of vowel nasalization and final-consonant deletion were really minor rules. In fact, it would appear that the only tendency might be toward generalizing gender alternations rather than toward eliminating them (cf., in popular speech, *tiède* 'tepid': [tjɛ]/ [tjɛd], *bleu* 'blue': [blø]/[bløz], *bizarre* 'strange': [bizar]/[bizard] (from Bauche 1951); the alternation concerning the adjective *pécuniaire* 'monetary' ([pekynje]/[pekynjɛr] instead of invariable [pekynjɛr]), also mentioned by Bauche (1951), seems to be well anchored at present in the speech of numerous speakers).

A conceivable alternative would be to consider these morphophonological rules as major rules, thus treating *bon*-type and *petit*-type adjectives as regular, and *jaune*-type and *honnête*-type adjectives as exceptional. But this solution does not seem appropriate either, since invariable adjectives would then be counterintuitively treated as more complex than variable adjectives. In addition, it seems very unlikely that adjectives like *jaune* will develop a [Ṽ] ~ [Vn] gender alternation; to my knowledge, no such trend has been observed. Similarly, unjustified complications would result in the treatment of masculine words such as *abdomen* [abdɔmɛn] 'abdomen', *homme* [ɔm] 'man', and *cep* [sɛp] (type of mushroom), *granit* [granit] 'granite', since these items show no tendency to nasalize or lose the final consonant. Note finally the instance of the invariable adjective *marron* [marɔ̃] 'brown' (masc. and fem.), whose phonological representation must be /marɔ̃/. Children tend to say [marɔn] for the feminine, an indication that alternations such as *bon/bonne* are the rule rather than the exception, and that the invariability, in standard speech, of the adjective *marron* is to be regarded as an irregularity. But even if rule (32) is considered to be major, the irregular *marron* still cannot be accounted for directly; its underlying representation ends in a nasal vowel, and the adjective therefore bears no formal relation to the structural description of rule (32).

Whether rules (32) and (36) are major or minor, they claim that the feminine forms are more basic than the masculine forms, since the feminine forms are derived directly from the underlying level of representation, whereas the masculine forms are derived through the application of morphophonological rules. This treatment contradicts the common assumption that the masculine is unmarked and the feminine marked.

As a second major problem, consider the phenomenon of liaison. The derivation of liaison data (e.g., *bon ami* [bɔnami]; *petit ami* [pətitami]) is based in part on principles of syllabification which state that, across single boundaries, the final consonant of a word gets phonetically attached to the initial vowel of the following word but remains in syllable coda if the next word begins in a consonant. The morphophonological rules of vowel nasalization and final-consonant deletion are thus not applicable in (40a), but they apply in (40b).

(40) (a) *bon écureuil* 'good squirrel'
/bɔn#ekyrœj/ → /bɔ$n#ekyrœj/ → [bɔnekyrœj]
petit écureuil 'little squirrel'
/pətit#ekyrœj/ → /pəti$t#ekyrœj/ → [pətitekyrœj]

(b) *bon tamanoir* 'good anteater'
/bɔn#tamanwar/ → /bɔn#tamanwar/ → [bɔ̃tamanwar]
$
petit tamanoir 'little anteater'
/pətit#tamanwar/ →
/pətit#tamanwar/ → [pətitamanwar]
$

When the initial consonant of a word is a liquid, however, the final consonant of the preceding word usually becomes tautosyllabic with the liquid (cf. *petite roue* [pti$tru] 'little wheel', homophonous with *petit trou* 'little hole'). The correct derivation of phrases like *bon rami* [bɔ̃rami] 'good gin' or *petit rami* [pitrami] 'little gin' may thus be prevented, since intermediate forms like /bɔ$n#rami/ and /pəti$t#rami/ might necessarily be the input to the morphophonological rules of vowel nasalization and final-consonant deletion and ultimately yield the ungrammatical *[bɔnrami] and *[ptitrami] (cf. Walker 1973).

It might be possible to resolve these difficulties formally. For example, it might be argued that, across single word boundaries, the process of syllabification attaching a word-final consonant to a following word-initial liquid is a late rule (perhaps optional, if a phrase like *petite roue* can be syllabified as [ptit$ru] as well as [pti$tru] in non-artificial speech), and that rules (32) and (36) apply before it. Hooper (1976:194, 200) mentions cases where the presence of a word boundary crucially influences syllabification and the application of rules. On a more general level, however, there seems to be something fundamentally suspicious about having morphophonological rules dependent upon syllable structure for their application. The syllabification question could be eliminated altogether by writing schema (39), that is, the collapsed rules (32) and (36), as follows:

$$(41) \quad \begin{bmatrix} \# & X & \langle V \rangle & \begin{bmatrix} C \\ \langle +\text{nasal} \rangle \end{bmatrix}\# \end{bmatrix}_{\text{masc.}} \quad \begin{Bmatrix} [-\text{seg}] \; C \\ \# \quad \# \end{Bmatrix}$$

$$\quad 1 \quad 2 \quad 3 \quad\quad 4 \quad 5 \quad\quad\quad 6 \quad \Longrightarrow$$

$$\quad\quad 1 \quad 2 \quad \left\langle \begin{bmatrix} 3 \\ +\text{nasal} \end{bmatrix} \right\rangle \quad \emptyset \quad 5 \quad 6$$

No matter what is done to preserve the morphophonological analysis of vowel nasalization and final-consonant deletion, it is important to point out that morphophonological final-consonant deletion does not explain liaison data like the following:

(42) *un court instant* [ɛ̃kurɛ̃sta] *[ɛ̃kurtɛ̃stā] 'a short time'
    (cf. fem. *courte* [kurt])
    un lourd objet [ɛ̃lurɔbžɛ] *[ɛ̃lurtɔbžɛ] 'a heavy object'
    (cf. fem. *lourde* [lurd])

More generally, no proposed analysis that postulates adjectives with lexical representations including latent final consonants, and rules of final-consonant deletion (whether phonological or morphophonological), derives the correct outputs in examples like those of (42). Treating adjectives such as *court* and *lourd* as exceptional in that they lose their final consonants /t/ and /d/ in all cases in the masculine, even in liaison contexts, does not seem correct, because there is to my knowledge no tendency to eliminate this purported irregularity and say *[ɛ̃kurtɛ̃stā] or *[ɛ̃lurtɔbžɛ] instead of [ɛ̃kurɛ̃stā] and [ɛ̃lurɔbžɛ]. In a purely phonological analysis, one might be tempted to make final-consonant deletion more general in the presence of a preceding /r/. But such a decision would pose a problem, as, for instance, when a masculine plural adjective whose stem ends in /r/ precedes a vowel-initial noun; in such instances the plural marker /z/ is present on the surface (e.g., *de rares objets* [dərarzɔbžɛ] 'rare objects').

A third set of difficulties arises when one compares adjectives like *bon* and the indefinite article *un*. As already established, words whose final vowels are always nasal, even in liaison contexts with vowel-initial morphemes, must contain underlying nasal vowels (Selkirk 1972; Tranel 1974*b*; sec. III.2.2.). Although most of these words have non-alternating nasal vowels, a few of them do exhibit an alternation, which is governed by gender:

(43) *un* (*un ami* [ɛ̃nami] 'a friend')/*une* [yn] 'a' (masc./fem.)
aucun (*aucun ami* [okɛ̃nami] 'no friend')/*aucune* [okyn] 'no' (masc./fem.)
commun (*d'un commun accord* [dɛ̃kɔmɛ̃nakɔr] 'in common agreement')/*commune* [kɔmyn] 'common' (masc./fem.)
chacun (*chacun un* [šakɛ̃nɛ̃] 'one each')/*chacune* [šakyn] 'each' (masc./fem.)

This entails that separate lexical entries must be set up for the masculine and feminine forms of these words.[9]

One problem with this approach is that one is led to treat lexically the gender alternations given in (43) because the behavior in liaison of the masculine forms does not agree with that of adjectives like *bon*. But the gender alternations given in (43) are really of the same general type as those of adjectives like *bon,* which are considered rule-governed. The difference in liaison behavior between the two groups of words is thus not captured directly, and the formal treatment given in fact reflects a difference in gender alternation where there is none.

Another problem is the following: since the liaison behavior of items like *un* is in a sense captured through a complication in their treatment, the substantive assumption seems to be that these words are special or irregular as compared with adjectives like *bon*. The fact is that the reverse appears to be true. Thus there seems to be an innovating tendency to have a nasal vowel in liaison cases with adjectives like *bon,* as illustrated in (44).[10]

---

9. As mentioned earlier, this solution is adopted in Selkirk (1972) and Tranel (1974*b*), at least for the pair *un/une* (*aucun/aucune, commun/commune, chacun/ chacune* are not mentioned in these studies).

10. The nasal vowels that occur in liaison in the examples given should not be attributed to a phonetic phenomenon of assimilation. In parallel phrases with feminine adjectives and nouns, the vowels under consideration remain oral. Some expressions sound quite impossible with a nasal vowel in liaison, e.g., *le divin enfant* [lədivinãfã] *[lədivɛ̃nãfã] 'the divine child', *le Moyen Age* [ləmwajɛnaž] *[ləmwajɛ̃naž] 'the Middle Ages'. This is because they are fixed phrases, comparable in a sense to a word like *vinaigre* [vinɛgr] *[vɛ̃nɛgr] 'vinegar' (historically derived from *vin aigre* 'sour wine').

(44) *mon prochain invité* [mɔ̃prɔšɛ̃nɛ̃vite] 'my next guest'
l'ancien ambassadeur [lãsjɛ̃nãbasadœr] 'the former ambassador'
un bon exemple [ɛ̃bɔ̃nɛgzãpl] 'a good example'
un certain assouplissement [ɛ̃sɛrtɛ̃nasuplismã] 'a certain relaxation'

This trend is also mentioned by Dell (1970:76) (cf. sec. II.3.3.1.; see chap. iv for more detail). In the same vein, pronunciations like [ynarbr] instead of [ɛ̃narbr] for *un arbre* 'a tree' are almost never heard any longer, and they are at any rate decidedly conservative (see Martinon 1913:299; Tranel 1974*b*:128, 207; chap. iv). These observations indicate that the liaison behavior of *un* (as in *un ami* [ɛ̃nami]) rather than that of *bon* (as in *bon ami* [bɔnami]) probably represents the generalization rather than the exception. This supposition is confirmed by the behavior of adjectives not normally placed before nouns (e.g., *enfantin* [ãfãtɛ̃] 'childish', *éléphantin* [elefãtɛ̃] 'elephantlike', *chevalin* [šəvalɛ̃] 'horselike', *mesquin* [mɛskɛ̃] 'mean'). When such adjectives are given in prenominal position, the final nasal vowel remains nasal in liaison:

(45) *un enfantin exemple* [ɛ̃nãfãtɛ̃nɛgzãpl] 'a childish example'
un mesquin adversaire [ɛ̃mɛskɛ̃nadvɛrsɛr] 'a mean adversary'

Similarly, I have heard the phrase *du matin au soir* 'from morning till evening', where liaison does not normally take place between *matin* and *au*, occur with a linking [n] and a nasal vowel (rather than an oral vowel) ([dymatɛ̃noswar], *[dymatinoswar], normally [dymatɛ̃oswar]).

C. Suggestions

The problems mentioned in the preceding section are mostly connected with the setting up, for adjectives like *bon*, of lexical representations with oral vowels rather than nasal vowels. In order to see this more clearly, let us assume, as a working hypothesis, that these adjectives contain a nasal vowel underlyingly, and that a morphophonological process of vowel denasalization derives the oral vowel of the feminine. I will come back later to the issue of the underlying presence of the nasal consonant and to the question of the quality of the derived vowel.

The postulation of underlying nasal vowels in adjectives like *bon* solves a number of problems and explains a number of phenomena. First, a distinction can be made between *bon*-type adjectives and *jaune*-type adjectives at the level of lexical representation (/bɔ̃(n)/[11] versus /žon/). As a result, adjectives such as *jaune* do not meet the structural description of the morphophonological rule deriving feminines, and the prediction of a possible confusion between the two types of adjectives is correctly eliminated. The feminine of *marron* used by children, [marɔn], is straightforwardly explained. The underlying representation of *marron* contains a nasal vowel, like that of *bon,* but the word is, in standard speech, an exception to the morphophonological rule of vowel denasalization which normally derives feminines. Children tend to regularize this adjective by ignoring the exception feature that is part of the standard adult grammar.

Second, the words *un, aucun, commun,* and *chacun* no longer need to be entered in the lexicon in both their masculine and feminine forms. The feminine forms can now be derived by the morphophonological rule of vowel denasalization from lexical representations with nasal vowels, which are independently required to account for liaison. As far as the alternations governed by gender are concerned, *un, aucun, commun,* and *chacun* can thus receive a treatment parallel to that of *bon* and other similar adjectives.

Third, for liaison data, the occurrence of oral and nasal vowels is explained in revealing fashion. The presence of an oral vowel in instances like *bon écureuil* [bɔnekyrœj] 'good squirrel' can be accounted for by a phonological rule of vowel denasalization. The problem is to distinguish between *mon* and *bon,* for example, since denasalization does not take place with *mon* (e.g., *mon écureuil* [mɔ̃nekyrœj] 'my squirrel'). But assume that the phonological rule of vowel denasalization is a minor rule; adjectives like *bon* are marked to undergo it and words like *mon* are not. This treatment makes the claim that words like *mon* are regular, and that adjectives like *bon* are irregular. The innovative tendency illustrated in (44) and (45) is naturally explained as the absence of the lexical rule feature commanding phonological vowel denasalization. Similarly explained are the practically complete disappearance of pronunciations such as [ynarbr] for *un arbre* [ɛ̃narbr] and the strong regression of pronunciations like [mɔnami] for *mon ami* [mɔ̃nami] (Martinet 1971: 145–146). The occurrence of the prefix *non-* as [nɔn] before a vowel-initial adjective or noun, which seems to be possible, in addition to [nɔ̃n],

11. Until the question of the underlying presence of the nasal consonant is resolved, I simply write this segment in parentheses.

(46) *non-humain* [nɔ̃nymɛ̃] ~ [nɔnymɛ̃] 'nonhuman'
 non-inscrit [nɔ̃nɛ̃skri] ~ [nɔnɛ̃skri] 'not registered'
 non-économique [nɔ̃nekɔnɔmik] ~ [nɔnekɔnɔmik]
 'noneconomic'

can also be accounted for by means of this minor rule. Fouché (1959:465) indicated only the pronunciation [nɔn] in liaison. The apparent spread of the variant [nɔ̃n] between the fifties and now is in keeping with the postulated minor character of this denasalization process. It remains to explain the particular order in which these lexical markings have been apparently removed from the lexicon. This historical issue is considered in chapter iv.

D. The questions of the oral vowel and of the nasal consonant

The standard generative treatment of French nasal vowels (see chap. i) and the morphophonological vowel nasalization analysis of *bon*-type adjectives presented earlier both assumed derivations whose directionality was from underlying /VN/ sequences to surface nasal vowels. The solution just suggested assumes the reverse directionality and must deal with the questions of the predictability of the nasal consonant and of the oral vowel. In the following discussion of these issues, I outline and compare various conceivable answers.

The setting up of underlying nasal vowels in adjectives like *bon* resolves many substantive difficulties, but it faces the problem of predicting the quality of the oral vowel in the feminine and in linking masculine singular adjectives, since several oral vowels can correspond to a single nasal vowel (see table 2).

Table 2

(a) $\tilde{ɔ} \rightarrow ɔ$
(b) $\tilde{a} \rightarrow a$
(c) $\tilde{ɛ} \rightarrow i$
(d) $\tilde{ɛ} \rightarrow y$
(e) $\tilde{ɛ} \rightarrow ɛ$

Earlier, a similar problem was easily resolved in the domain of derivational morphology because the productive correspondences between nasal and oral vowels are one-to-one correspondences (see table 1). For inflectional morphology, the problem is not as straightforwardly solvable, since one could not reasonably claim, for example, different treatments for the pairs of adjectives *fin* [fɛ̃]/*fine* [fin] and *plein* [plɛ̃]/*pleine* [plɛn].

One conceivable solution, which would not be anomalous within the abstract framework of the standard theory of generative phonology, would be to postulate underlying representations with the nasality feature of the masculine on the vowel found in the feminine (e.g., *fin/fine:* /fĩ(n)/; *plein/pleine:* /plɛ̃(n)/; *brun/brune:* /brỹ(n)/). Such mixed lexical representations are abstract in the sense that they do not necessarily correspond to any of the surface allomorphs, but at least the vowel features included all occur in one surface phonetic form or another. Concerning rule interaction, this solution would require the application of the morphophonological rule of vowel denasalization deriving the feminine before that of the necessary rules of nasal vowel quality adjustment. This ordering could be predicted on the basis of the primacy of application of morphophonological rules over phonological rules, if such a principle can be maintained.

Another solution, more compatible with a strictly concrete theory such as natural generative phonology (Vennemann 1971; Hooper 1976), would be to have the surface nasal vowels underlyingly and to mark the relevant words for the appropriate denasalization (see sec. VII.3.2.1. for evidence of some predictability). In addition to a general morphophonological denasalization process, this treatment would therefore include several subrules establishing the needed correspondences between alternating nasal and oral vowels (see table 2).

The differences between the two solutions just mentioned may not be so large as might appear at first. The information captured by means of the lexical markings and the subrules in the more concrete analysis is incorporated, in the more abstract treatment, in the phonological representations of the words and in the rules of nasal vowel quality adjustment.

The following question arises concerning the nasal consonant that appears in surface [VN] sequences where the oral vowel is derived from an underlying nasal vowel: Should the nasal consonant be included or not in the phonological representations of adjectives like *bon*? The inclusion of the final nasal consonant would be acceptable within the framework of the standard theory of phonology. One would again have mixed underlying representations (e.g., /bɔ̃n/), that is, representations that are a composite picture of the various surface forms. Given such phonological representations, several logically possible sets of rules could account for the surface phonetic facts.

Morphophonological vowel denasalization could derive the feminine forms, and the masculine could be obtained by the application of a phonological rule of nasal-consonant deletion such as (47):

$$(47) \quad \begin{bmatrix} C \\ +\text{nasal} \end{bmatrix} \rightarrow \emptyset \, / \, \begin{bmatrix} V \\ +\text{nasal} \end{bmatrix} - \left\{ \begin{matrix} [-\text{seg}] \, C \\ \# \quad \# \end{matrix} \right\}$$

Rule (47) would have to apply after the morphophonological rule of vowel denasalization. This ordering might also be predicted by the suggested general principle that morphophonological rules precede phonological rules.

Given the existence of rule (47), it might be argued that for words like *mon*, or prefixes such as *bien-*, a final underlying /n/ should be postulated, since its surface distribution would be accounted for by rule (47), and the otherwise necessary rule of /n/-insertion posited earlier (see sec. III.2.2.) could be eliminated. When the possessive adjectives *mon, ton, son*, are used with (vowel-initial) feminine nouns, however, they are presumably marked [+feminine]; similarly for the pronoun *on* when it refers to females (cf. the agreement in, e.g., *on est cuites* [ɔ̃nɛkɥit] 'we (fem.) are cooked'). But morphophonological vowel denasalization does not apply in such cases (e.g., *mon arrivée* [mɔ̃narive] *[monarive] 'my arrival'; *on est cuites* *[ɔnɛkɥit]). It therefore appears that words like *mon* should preserve their underlying representations without a final /n/, and that the rule of /n/-insertion is motivated, even if rule (47) is posited.

The problem with the solution that includes rule (47) is its implication that there must be a parallel phonological process that deletes final consonants in words like *petit*. (If the lexical representation of *bon/bonne* is /bɔ̃n/, with a final /n/, the lexical representation of *petit/petite* must surely be /pətit/, with a final /t/.) But no such phonological process can be assumed to exist, as is later shown in Part II. An additional disadvantage of this analysis is that it would capture no parallelism between the generation of feminine forms like *bonne*, which would be obtained morphophonologically, and feminine forms like *petite*, which would be derived directly from the lexical representations. Finally, rule (47) would incorrectly not allow the forms *vînmes* [vɛ̃m] '(we) came' and *tînmes* [tɛ̃m] '(we) held'.

Given phonological representations such as /bɔ̃n/, an alternative account of the surface phonetic facts would be to postulate a morphophonological rule of final-consonant deletion which would apply in the masculine in the environment

$$\left\{ \begin{matrix} [-\text{seg}] \, C \\ \# \quad \# \end{matrix} \right\}.$$

This rule would be similar to that posited in the morphophonological analysis considered at the beginning of section III.5.3.3., the only differences being that now nasal vowels would be posited underlyingly, and the feminine forms would be obtained by rule instead of directly. Two possibilities would in fact be open to derive the feminine forms. One would be to posit a morphophonological process of vowel denasalization; the other would be to postulate a phonological rule of vowel denasalization such as (48), applying after the morphophonological rule deriving the masculine.

$$(48) \quad \begin{bmatrix} V \\ +\text{nasal} \end{bmatrix} \rightarrow [-\text{nasal}] \: / \: — \begin{bmatrix} C \\ +\text{nasal} \end{bmatrix} \#$$

The latter solution is reminiscent of the treatment actually proposed in Bibeau (1975:128–130).

Note that morphemes like *mon*, under either treatment, are still best accounted for with underlying representations of the form /XṼ/ and a rule of /n/-insertion. If the underlying representations were of the form /XṼn/, adverbs like *bien* and *rien* and the preposition *en* could not eliminate their final /n/ in front of consonant-initial words, since they are not marked for gender; neither could the pronoun *on* when marked [+feminine]. Morphophonological vowel denasalization would incorrectly apply to the possessive adjectives *mon, ton*, and *son* before vowel-initial feminine words, and to the pronoun *on* when marked [+feminine]. Rule (48) would incorrectly denasalize the same items whenever they are found before vowel-initial words.

The problem with obtaining the feminine forms by morphophonological vowel denasalization is that, as mentioned above, the parallelism between the formations of words like *bonne,* on the one hand, and *petite,* on the other hand, would not be captured. The problem with rule (48) is that, since it must apply only to feminine nouns and adjectives, it is a formalization that can be considered as a mere phonological disguise for what is really a morphophonological process; rule (48) would incorrectly not allow the forms *nous vînmes* [nuvẽm] and *nous tînmes* [nutẽm]. As to the morphophonological consonant-deletion rule deriving the masculine forms, it of course would not solve the problem of the derivation of phrases like *un court instant* (cf. (42)).

The inclusion of the nasal consonant in the phonological representations of words such as *bon* thus leads to a number of difficulties. I now consider the alternative: the assumption that the nasal consonant is not present in the phonological representations of these forms.

A strictly concrete theory of phonology would reject the underlying presence of a final nasal consonant, since the lexical representations would not correspond to the basic unmarked allomorphs (e.g., [bɔ̃]) (Vennemann 1971). On a more substantive note, it is worth pointing out that, with two exceptions, the nasal consonant in question is always [n]; it might therefore be appropriate to derive it by rule. The two adjectives that are exceptions to this regularity are *malin* and *bénin*; the feminine of *bénin* [benɛ̃] is *bénigne* [beniñ], and in grammars and dictionaries, the feminine of *malin* [malɛ̃] is usually given as *maligne* [maliñ]. Interestingly, *malin* and *maligne* have semantically drifted apart: for most speakers, *malin* has kept the sense of 'cunning', but *maligne* has lost it, and it means only 'cancerous' (as in *une tumeur maligne*); with this meaning, *malin* sounds somewhat strange (??*un kyste malin*). In revealing fashion, for the sense of 'cunning', a new feminine adjective has been formed with a final [n]: *maline* [malin].

If the phonological representations of adjectives like *bon* contain a nasal vowel without the nasal consonant (e.g., /bɔ̃/), then the morphophonological rule deriving the feminine can insert the /n/ in addition to performing vowel denasalization. Under this analysis, the feminine *maligne* cannot be predicted, and *malin* and *maligne* both have to be in the lexicon; but the existence of two separate lexical entries actually explains, or at least constitutes a necessary condition for, the semantic drift that occurred. In addition, the morphophonological rule that derives feminines accounts for the new feminine with a final [n], *maline*.[12]

Under this treatment a separate phonological rule of /n/-insertion is required to account for liaison, but this rule is independently needed for phrases like *mon ami* [mɔ̃nami] (from /mɔ̃#ami/) (see sec. III.2.2.). The minor rule of phonological vowel denasalization applies to the output of this phonological rule of /n/-insertion to derive phrases like *bon ami* [bɔnami].

---

12. Both *bénin* and *bénigne* also have to be in the lexicon. To my knowledge, these two words have not semantically drifted apart, and no new feminine form [benin] has appeared. The absence of the predicted feminine form [benin] may be attributable to the fact that the adjective in question is a rather learned word which is used relatively rarely, and which is not normally part of the vocabulary of children. When the adjective is used at all, its lexicalized masculine and feminine forms can therefore be expected to be known. In other words, it may be surmised that, since semantic drift has not taken place, the formation of [benin] is blocked by the existence of [beniñ] (see Aronoff's (1976) notion of blocking).

This analysis offers an advantage over the preceding one in that it can treat feminine forms like *bonne* and *petite* in parallel fashion, namely, through consonant insertion. It also claims, in accord with widely held principles, that masculine forms are unmarked and feminine forms are marked, since the short masculine forms are in effect the bases from which the long feminine forms are derived. This allows for a more unified account of the relations between masculine and feminine forms, as examples like *tigre* [tigr]/*tigresse* [tigrɛs] 'tiger' (male/female), *ogre* [ɔgr]/*ogresse* [ɔgrɛs] 'oger' (male/female) show clearly that the long feminine forms are obtained from the short masculine forms. Also, by generating gender and liaison consonants along different derivational paths, this analysis opens the door to an account of data such as (42) (see chap. vii).

On the other hand, the consonant-insertion treatment presents some obvious difficulties concerning the predictability of the inserted consonant. In particular, it is not always true that the feminine forms of masculine adjectives or nouns ending in a nasal vowel undergo /n/-insertion and vowel denasalization:

(49) *décent* [desã]/*décente* [desãt] 'decent' (masc./fem.)

fécond [fekɔ̃]/*féconde* [fekɔ̃d] 'fertile' (masc./fem.)

saint [sɛ̃]/*sainte* [sɛ̃t] 'holy' (masc./fem.)

A certain amount of information must therefore be lexically encoded in order for the correct gender consonants to be inserted. *Paysan* must thus be distinguished from *décent, bon* from *fécond,* and *plein* from *saint,* by being marked for taking a nasal consonant rather than /t/ or /d/. These lexical markings correspond to the underlying presence of final consonants in other analyses. These different lexical formalizations are not merely notational variants, however, since it was just argued that consonant insertion is preferable over consonant deletion. Further evidence in favor of consonant insertion is provided in Part II. Note simply in addition here that the variations found in numerous feminine forms across social and regional dialects favor the lexical marking solution over the claim that the gender consonants are actually part of the phonological representations (e.g., *pourri* [puri] 'rotten' is invariable in Standard French, but it has a feminine [purit] in some regional dialects; *géant* [žeã] 'giant' (masc.) has the feminine *géante* [žeãt] in contemporary French, but there used to be a feminine [žean] (Nyrop 1968:288); corresponding to the masculine *partisan* [partizã], there used to be two competing feminines, *partisane* [partizan] and *partisante* [partizãt], which have both subsisted in the language, but with different meanings, 'partisan' and 'favorable to', respectively; see Pichon 1942:33–34).

E. A concrete analysis

In this section an explicit set of rules for a concrete treatment of *bon*-type adjectives is suggested and further discussed. Some revisions are introduced in chapter vii in the light of a detailed consideration of [Ø] ~ [C] alternations.

The grammar contains a morphophonological rule of vowel denasalization and /n/-insertion,

$$(50) \quad \begin{bmatrix} \# & X & \begin{bmatrix} V \\ +\text{nasal} \end{bmatrix} & \# \\ & & & \text{fem.} \end{bmatrix}$$

$$1 \quad 2 \qquad 3 \qquad 4 \implies 1 \quad 2 \quad \begin{bmatrix} 3 \\ -\text{nasal} \end{bmatrix} \quad n \quad 4$$

a phonological rule of /n/-insertion,

$$(51) \quad \begin{bmatrix} V \\ +\text{nasal} \end{bmatrix} \quad \# \quad V$$

$$1 \qquad 2 \quad 3 \implies 1 \quad 2 \quad n \quad 2 \quad 3$$

and a minor phonological rule of vowel denasalization,

$$(52) \quad \begin{bmatrix} V \\ +\text{nasal} \end{bmatrix} \rightarrow [-\text{nasal}] \; / \; — \; \# \quad n \quad \# \quad V$$

In addition, the grammar includes the following table of correspondences between nasal and oral vowels:

Table 2

(a) ɔ̃ → ɔ
(b) ã → a
(c) ɛ̃ → i
(d) ɛ̃ → y
(e) ɛ̃ → ɛ

This table is different from and more complex than table 1. Table 1, which is of relevance only in productive cases of word formation, is thus applied in conjunction with processes such as (26). Table 2 is of relevance only for the morphophonological and phonological rules of vowel denasalization (50) and (52).

Rule (50) derives the feminine forms of adjectives and nouns such as *bon* and *baron,* which are marked to undergo this rule. (50) and this lexical marking (see chap. vii) express the fact that there is a masculine/feminine alternation of the type $[\tilde{V}] \sim [VN]$ and that words like *bon* and *baron* fall into such a morphophonological pattern. It is far from obvious that (50) should be part of the phonological component; it actually creates words, and no rule needs to apply before it; it might therefore be more adequately considered to operate in the lexicon or in a prephonological component of the type hinted at by Dell and Selkirk (1978). Rule (51) inserts the [n] that is found in liaison cases such as *mon ami* and *bon ami*. Rule (52) denasalizes the vowel of masculine singular adjectives like *bon*. Both (51) and (52) are clearly part of the phonological component.

These rules need not be extrinsically ordered. For rule (50), the question is automatically resolved if it operates prephonologically: it then necessarily applies before rules (51) and (52). The same order of application also follows intrinsically if rule (50) is part of the phonological component: when the structural descriptions of both rules (50) and (51) are met (i.e., in sequences of the form

$$/X\tilde{V}]_{\text{fem.}} \# VY/,$$

as in *bonne étendue* /bɔ̃#etãdy/ [bɔnetãdy] 'good stretch'), rule (50) automatically applies first since it is more specific than rule (51) (see Kiparsky 1973a; Koutsoudas, Sanders, and Noll 1974:8–10). The fact that it is a morphophonological rule, whereas the other is phonological, may also account for the primacy of application. Rules (50) and (52) do not interact. Rule (51) necessarily applies before rule (52), since it feeds it, and rule (52) would never apply if it were not for the existence of rule (51).

In rule (51), a boundary on both sides of the inserted element captures its connective character. Rule (52) is formalized accordingly. For rule (50), the /n/ is inserted to the left of the word boundary, since the feminine adjectives and nouns thus derived form rather tight units.

It might appear to be an important loss of generalization that the processes of vowel denasalization and /n/-insertion required in this concrete approach are each split into separate rules of morphophonological and phonological natures. The fact that adjectives with a masculine/feminine $[\tilde{V}] \sim [Vn]$ alternation link with /n/ in the masculine singular can be explicitly captured in the lexicon (see chap. vii, where similar redundancies between gender and linking consonants are expressed in the case of $[\emptyset] \sim [C]$ alternations such as *petit/petit ami/petite*). It is also shown in chapter vii that gender consonants and liaison consonants are interpreted by native speakers as different in status and that they therefore warrant distinct insertion processes.

Concerning vowel denasalization, the following points argue in favor of the dual role assigned to this process. The sandhi rule of vowel denasalization, rule (52), affects with any regularity only a very limited number of adjectives: the adjective *bon* (/õ/ becomes /ɔ/; e.g., *un bon hiver* [ɛ̃bɔnivɛr] 'a good winter') and a few adjectives like *plein* (/ɛ̃/ becomes /ɛ/; e.g., *le plein emploi* [ləplɛnãplwa] 'full employment'); the two adjectives *fin* and *divin* are also affected, but somewhat marginally (/ɛ̃/ becomes /i/; e.g., *un très fin enfant* [ɛ̃trɛfinãfã] 'a very refined child'; *le divin apparat* [lədivinapara] 'the divine pomp'). As already pointed out (see also chap. iv), the effect of this rule tends to vanish, and it has therefore been characterized as minor.[13] On the other hand, when morphologically anchored, that is, when serving the purpose of directly marking grammatical distinctions, vowel denasalization is not a process moving toward extinction. The extension, in the speech of children, of the masculine/feminine [Ṽ] ~ [Vn] alternation to the invariable adjective *marron* bears witness to this. In addition, the postulation of the morphophonological rule (50) is consistent with the existence of the word-formation rule that creates feminine nouns from nouns ending in a nasal vowel by vowel denasalization and /n/-insertion:

(53) *Berlin* [bɛrlɛ̃] → *berline* [bɛrlin] 'berlin'
     Guillotin [gijɔtɛ̃] → *guillotine* [gijɔtin] 'guillotine'
     Pralin [pralɛ̃] → *praline* [pralin] (type of candy)

This word-formation rule can also be used facetiously, but in revealing fashion, in the creation of feminine forms from normally invariable masculine nouns (e.g., *témoin* [temwɛ̃] 'witness' → [temwin]).[14]

---

13. For some speakers, *bon* is the only adjective exhibiting this alternation, and it might be appropriate to treat it suppletively, on a par with alternations such as *vieux* [vjø]/*vieil* [vjɛj] 'old', *nouveau* [nuvo]/*nouvel* [nuvɛl] 'new', *beau* [bo]/*bel* [bɛl] 'beautiful', *mou* [mu]/*mol* [mɔl] 'soft', *fou* [fu]/*fol* [fɔl] 'mad' (see chap. iv).

14. This example is particularly interesting and significant: the feminine counterpart of the masculine noun *témoin* [temwɛ̃] is [temwin], despite the verb *témoigner* [temwañe] and the noun *témoignage* [temwañaž]. In Schane's (1968a) treatment of the French vowel system, the [ɛ̃] of *témoin* would presumably be derived from /añ/; the expected feminine of *témoin* would therefore be *[temwɛñ] (because of the application of vowel fronting). Dell and Selkirk (1978) would probably derive this [ɛ̃] from /ɛñ/ and also incorrectly predict *[temwɛn]. Cases like this seem to confirm the necessity to treat phonological relations in derivational morphology by means of lexical rules of correspondence rather than generatively (Vennemann 1972c; Hooper 1976; Tranel 1977c).

The grammatical use of vowel denasalization exemplified in rule (50) is also consistent with the existence of the word-formation rule that creates first-conjugation verbs from nouns (e.g., *bouquin* [bukɛ̃] → *bouquiner* [bukine]; see sec. III.5.3.1.). The distinction made in the grammar between phonological and morphophonological vowel denasalization thus appears justified.

As opposed to rules (50) and (52), however, the word-formation rules just mentioned have only [i] as the oral vowel corresponding to the nasal vowel [ɛ̃]. As indicated earlier (sec. III.5.3.1.), this is the productive correspondence in contemporary French (as opposed to [ɛ̃] ~ [ɛ] or [ɛ̃] ~ [y]). The following anecdote provides further evidence. As a naive native speaker of French was using the word *chamberlain* [šãbɛrlɛ̃] for *parapluie* 'umbrella', I asked her what she would say if *parapluie* were feminine instead of masculine. The answer she gave was "une [šãbɛrlin]." After I pointed out the spelling of *chamberlain,* the answer was changed to "une [šãbɛrlɛn]." These data reveal the influence of orthography on pronunciation (*ai* is common for [ɛ]), but they also clearly indicate that, when spelling is not interfering, the active oral vowel corresponding to the nasal vowel [ɛ̃] is [i].

A residual problem with the solution just presented concerns the formalization of the phonological rules of /n/-insertion (51) and vowel denasalization (52), where a word boundary has been postulated before the inserted /n/. If the denasalized /ɔ/ of *bon* in a phrase like *bon ami* is immediately followed by a word boundary, then one incorrectly expects *[bonami] instead of [bɔnami], since /ɔ/ has been generally assumed to go to [o] before a word boundary (see Schane 1968*a*, 1978*b*; Selkirk 1972; Tranel 1974*b*, 1977*c*; and secs. II.3.3.1. and VI.3.1.). In order to avoid this difficulty in the analysis, rules (51) and (52) could be revised so that /n/ would be inserted to the left of the word boundary found in the structural description. The disadvantage of this adjustment is that it loses the concept of linking consonants as connective elements and places gender and linking consonants in identical phonological positions when a difference in this respect is rather well motivated (see chap. vii). A more attractive alternative is to consider that masculine [bɔn] is a suppletive form, on a par with *bel* [bɛl], for instance (cf. *un beau tapis* [ɛ̃botapi] 'a beautiful carpet'/ *un bel athlète* [ɛ̃bɛlatlɛt] 'a beautiful athlete'). This assumption would explain why, in dialects where rule (52) has apparently ceased to function, the adjective *bon* may still retain its masculine linking form [bɔn] (see n. 13 and chap. iv).[15]

III.6. Summary

This chapter provides evidence in support of the following statements concerning French phonology:

(i) Nasal vowels must not only be postulated as lexical in nonalternating cases; lexical nasal vowels are also required in alternating cases.[16]

(ii) Alternations between nasal vowels and [VN] sequences are not the reflection of a uniform phonological process of vowel nasalization or denasalization. The phonologically determined relations between [Ṽ] and [VN] are limited to a minor rule of vowel denasalization (in liaison) and to a restricted rule of vowel nasalization (for the prefix *in-*). Most of the alternations are of a purely grammatical or lexical nature (inflectional and derivational morphology).

(iii) The phonetic occurrence of nasal vowels and [VN] sequences is not dependent on the postulation of lexical or morphological schwas, and extrinsic rule ordering plays no part in their derivation.

15. The problem mentioned here is perhaps indicative of a state of transition even better illustrated with the following pronunciations I elicited for the phrase *(un bien) sot ami* '(a really) silly friend' (masc.): [sɔtami], [sotami], [soami] (see chap. vii for discussion).

16. The only exception is the prefix *in-* (see Tranel 1976a).

IV

NASAL VOWELS AND LIAISON: DIACHRONIC AND DIALECTAL PERSPECTIVES

IV.1. Introduction

Diachronic accounts of French nasal vowels, in manuals on the history of the language (e.g., E. and J. Bourciez 1967; Ewert 1933; Fouché 1969; Pope 1934) or in specialized studies (e.g., Rochet 1976; Straka 1955), usually concentrate on the formation of these segments and the evolution of their timbre. Vowel denasalization generally receives partial coverage, the emphasis being placed on the application of the process word-internally. In this chapter I investigate the diachronic phenomenon of vowel denasalization across words, that is, the historical evolution of nasal vowels in liaison. I also examine the pronunciation of nasal vowels in liaison in various contemporary dialects of French.

The relevance of the information gathered in this chapter goes beyond filling an apparent gap in the systematic description of the French language. Viewed as representative of the outputs of successive grammars in the course of time, the data show that the nasal or oral quality of nasal vowels in liaison has for several centuries been governed by grammatical factors rather than being purely phonologically determined, and that, in agreement with the traditional view rejected by the standard generative analysis, nasal vowels have long been lexical in French.

IV.2. Diachronic and dialectal information
IV.2.1. Preliminaries

In Old French, vowels became nasalized when they were followed by a nasal consonant and subsequently underwent a number of changes in their quality. In Middle French, two new processes set in: nasal consonants which were in the same syllable as a preceding nasalized vowel were deleted, and nasalized vowels followed by a nasal consonant in a separate syllable lost their nasality. Within words, the effects of this process of vowel denasalization have been general and persistent. Thus, few words have filtered down to standard Modern French with internal sequences of the form [V̄NV] (e.g., *ennui* [ãnɥi] 'boredom'). Across words (i.e., in liaison), the effects of vowel denasalization have been less sweeping and definitive. Thus, in standard Modern French, some words do denasalize in liaison (e.g., *bon* 'good': *un bon ami* [ɛ̃bɔnami] 'a good friend'; *plein* 'full': *le plein emploi* [ləplɛnãplwa] 'full employment'), but others do not (e.g., *un* 'a': *un ami* [ɛ̃nami] 'a friend'; *mon* 'my': *mon ami* [mɔ̃nami] 'my friend'; *on* 'one': *on arrive* [ɔ̃nariv] 'one arrives'). Among the purposes of this chapter are to trace the diachronic evolution of this phenomenon from the sixteenth century to the present and to find explanations for the splits that occurred among words phonetically susceptible to undergo vowel denasalization in liaison.

For data on nasal vowels and liaison in the sixteenth, seventeenth, and eighteenth centuries, I have relied for the most part on Thurot's *De la prononciation française depuis le commencement du XVIᵉ siècle d'après les témoignages des grammairiens* (1881–1883) (Vol. II, Bk. IV, chap. vii, pp. 550–559). Thurot's monumental work has been widely praised for its thoroughness and accuracy (see, e.g., Gaston Paris's preface to the index (Thurot II:xi) and Rosset (1911:8)). In a few instances I have consulted the original texts for more detailed information than is provided by Thurot. An important additional source I have taken into consideration is Vaudelin (1713, 1715), as analyzed in Cohen (1946).[1] For the nineteenth and twentieth centuries I have relied on a number of dictionaries, grammars, and pronunciation treatises that appeared during the period.

The phonetic transcriptions of past pronunciations given in this chapter are in general based on the essentially orthographic systems and/or the explanations used by the various authors to convey how words were pronounced. The claimed accuracy of these transcriptions is limited to the nasal or oral quality of the vowel preceding the linking [n]. The orthography of the illustrative phrases and quotations has been modernized, but the punctuation has been preserved.

1. In his annotated bibliography Thurot mentions Vaudelin's second book (Thurot I:lxxvi), but he did not actually use it in his text as a source of information.

The type of survey undertaken in this chapter faces several limitations which can potentially vitiate its value. The first problem concerns the comprehensiveness of the information gathered. There are no doubt many additional documents that could have been used, but either I did not have access to them or they simply escaped my notice. I believe, however, that I have taken into consideration enough representative sources to have minimized this problem. Second, the question of interpretation of the documents arises. The notations and descriptions used in the past to convey pronunciation cannot always be interpreted with absolute certainty, especially when the author's emphasis is not exactly on the matter at hand. Third, there is the question of the reliability of the sources. In at least a few instances, they probably do not accurately reflect the contemporary usage. The course I follow with respect to these two problems is to mention explicitly the uncertainty of some interpretations and the questionable reliability of some authors.

I am concerned only with the pronunciation of the nasal vowels in liaison, specifically whether they remain nasal or become oral. I do not consider the syntactic or stylistic conditions under which liaison occurs. These conditions have actually changed very little since the seventeenth century (Thurot II:550–555). The main difference from present usage seems to be that, up to the beginning of the eighteenth century, some speakers linked a noun ending in a nasal vowel with a following vowel-initial word "dans le discours soutenu" (Thurot II:551); such pronunciations are completely extinct today. It also appears that, at least up to the beginning of the twentieth century, liaison was possible with the interrogative word *combien* [kɔ̃bjɛ̃] 'how much' (Martinon 1913:390); this is contrary to the contemporary pronunciation.

IV.2.2. Survey

A. Sixteenth century

Little information is available on the pronunciation of nasal vowels in liaison in the sixteenth century (Thurot II:555–556). Thurot's hypothesis is that "la voyelle finale restait nasale et la syllabe suivante commençait par une *n*." He found this pronunciation actually attested for three words: *en, bon,* and *on.* According to Meigret (1550), "n finale ayant ensuite un vocable commençant par voyelle . . . double sa puissance: comme *en allant, en étant,* que nous prononçons comme *en nallant, en nétant*: tellement qu'autant sonne l'un que l'autre: et n'y trouvons aucune différence" (i.e., *en allant* [ãnalã]; *en étant* [ãnetã]). Saint-Liens's (1580) representation of the pronunciation of *bon or* and *bon argent* (*bon nor, bon narjant*) also indicates the absence of vowel denasalization ([bɔ̃nɔr], [bɔ̃naržã]). Similarly, Bèze (1584) stated that *on a dit* was pronounced as if it were written *on na dit* (i.e., [ɔ̃nadi]).

Vowel denasalization across words probably began, however, toward the end of the sixteenth century, at least in popular French. Thus Bèze (1584) "reproche au peuple de Paris de prononcer" *il s'en est allé* and *on m'en a parlé il se nest allé* (i.e., [ilsɑ̃netale]) and *on me na parlé* (i.e., [ɔ̃mənaparle]) instead of *il s'en n'est allé* (i.e., [il-sãnetale]) and *on m'en na parlé* (i.e., [ɔ̃mãnaparle]), and Serreius (1598) represents the pronunciation of *bon esprit* as *bo-nesprit* (i.e., [bɔnɛspri]).

In sum, nasal vowels were probably not denasalized in liaison in the first half of the sixteenth century, but the effects of the process were beginning to be felt, at least in popular French, toward the end of the century.

B. Seventeenth century

The vowel denasalization trend across words emerged more noticeably in the seventeenth century. Some grammarians still seem to report nasal pronunciations, but others explicitly attest to the existence of oral pronunciations.

The following sources suggest the existence, throughout the century, of a dialect characterized by the absence of vowel denasalization. Oudin (1640:25) states that "*fin* substantif ne s'attachera pas avec une voyelle suivante: v.g. *la fin en sera mauvaise,* gardez-vous de prononcer, *la finnen sera,* etc. mais retenez la langue en l'air: au contraire, *fin* adjectif se doit attacher au mot suivant, *vous êtes un fin-nhomme.*" Oudin adds that the *n* is pronounced in a few words "comme *un, bon, mon, ton, son, en, bien,* adverbe, *combien, non, rien.* Item aux adjectifs, comme *fin, ancien, certain, malin.* Ajoutez-y, *amen, examen, hymen*: v.g. *un autre,* lisez *unnautre*: *mon âme,* dites *monnâme,* etc." The main focus of this passage is on where [n] is pronounced, not on the oral or nasal quality of the vowel preceding [n]. Nevertheless, the orthographic system used to symbolize the pronunciations of the examples given would seem to indicate a nasal pronunciation, that is, *un fin homme* [œ̃fɛ̃nɔm], *un autre* [œ̃notr], *mon âme* [mɔ̃nam].[2] Testimonies of a similar nature are listed in Thurot

2. The testimony of Vaugelas (1647) and Dangeau (1694) suggests the exercise of caution in this interpretation (see text below and nn. 3 and 4).

(II:556–557): Chifflet (1659) (*en allant* [ãnalã], *on a* [ɔ̃na], *bon ami* [bɔ̃nami], *fin homme* [fɛ̃nɔm], *divin amour* [divẽnamur], *commun accord* [kɔmœ̃nakɔr], *un enfant* [œ̃nãfã], *aucun homme* [okœ̃nɔm]); T. Corneille (1687) (*en affaire* [ãnafɛr], *on observe* [ɔ̃nɔpsɛrv], *malin esprit* [malɛ̃nɛspri], *un commun accord* [œ̃kɔmœ̃nakɔr], *un certain aventurier* [œ̃sɛrtɛ̃navãtyrje]; Hindret (1696) (*rien à faire* [rjɛ̃nafɛr], *divin amour* [divẽnamur]); and de Soule (1698) (*bon homme* [bɔ̃nɔm], *certain ivrogne* [sɛrtɛ̃nivrɔ̃ɲ], *divin amour* [divẽnamur]).

Notations in the next two sources unambiguously indicate the existence of oral pronunciations: Anonyme (1624) (*mon âme: mo-name*, i.e., [mɔnam]; *ton esprit: to-nesprit*, i.e., [tɔnɛspri]; *bon homme: bo-nhomme*, i.e., [bɔnɔm]); Roux (1694) (*bien obligeant: bie-n-obligeant*, i.e., [bjɛnɔbližã]) (Thurot II:556–557).

In a third group of sources, the authors refer more or less directly to the two types of pronunciation. In a remark on h-aspiré words, Vaugelas (1647) wrote: ". . . ceux qui parlent mal, prononceront *en haut,* comme ils prononcent *en affaire*; et cependant il y faut mettre une grande différence, car l'*n* qui finit un mot, et en précède un autre qui commence par une voyelle, se prononce comme s'il y avait deux *n*. On prononce *en affaire*, tout de même que si l'on écrivait *en naffaire,* comme beaucoup de femmes ont accoutumé d'orthographier. *En honneur,* comme si on écrivait *en nonneur*; mais *en haut, en hasard,* se doit prononcer comme n'y ayant qu'une *n*, et après l'*n*, il faut aspirer l'*h*, à quoi ceux des Provinces qui parlent mal, surtout de la Loire, ne songent point" (196). Criticizing those who pronounced *"on-za,* pour dire *on a, on-zouvre,* pour dire *on ouvre, on-zordonne* pour dire *on ordonne,"* Vaugelas stated in another remark: "Ce vice est d'autant moins excusable, que la lettre *n*, qui finit *on,* n'a pas besoin du secours d'une autre consonne pour ôter la cacophonie de la voyelle suivante, puisqu'elle-même y suffit en se redoublant, comme nous avons dit en la Remarque de la lettre *h* [see above excerpt], car on prononce *on a, on ouvre, on ordonne,* comme si l'on écrivait *on-n-a, on-n-ouvre, on-n-ordonne,* qui est la plus douce prononciation que l'on saurait trouver en ces mots-là, sans en chercher une autre" (436–437). Thus, for *en* and *on,* Vaugelas's observation that the *n* is doubled in liaison explicitly indicates a nasal pronunciation, for example, *en affaire* [ãnafɛr], *on a* [ɔ̃na]. For the masculine indefinite article *un,* Vaugelas's testimony may be interpreted as indicating an oral pronunciation in liaison: "quand on prononce ou qu'on écrit *l'épigramme* ou *une épigramme,* l'oreille ne saurait juger du genre" (preface). This quotation shows that *un* and *une* had the same pronunciation before vowel-initial words; assuming that *une* was pronounced with an oral vowel, *un* presumably underwent vowel denasalization in liaison.[3]

Dangeau's (1694) "lettres d'un académicien à un autre" provide particularly valuable information, because the author's attention was specifically directed to the question of the nasal or oral quality of the vowels in question. In a first report, Dangeau indicated pronunciations with nasal vowels: *on appelle* [ɔ̃napɛl], *bon enfant* [bɔ̃nãfã], *mon ami* [mɔ̃nami], *en Allemagne* [ãnalmañ], *bien appris* [bjɛ̃napri], *pour bien écrire* [purbjɛ̃nekrir]. In a subsequent communication, however, he wrote: "on m'a fait remarquer que, dans mon premier discours . . . j'ai dit trop généralement que, quand un mot terminé par une de nos lettres nasales précède immédiatement un mot qui commence par une voyelle et auquel il est intimement uni, alors le premier mot garde sa prononciation nasale et fait de plus entendre une véritable *n* . . . il valait mieux dire que dans ces cas il ne reste plus rien de la prononciation nasale, et qu'on lit . . . *certai-nome,* . . . *mo-nami*" (i.e., *certain homme* [sɛrtɛnɔm], *mon ami* [mɔnami]) (Thurot II:557). Dangeau's retraction from a report where he claimed that nasal vowels remain nasal in liaison to one where he stated that they become oral clearly establishes that, at least for some speakers, vowel denasalization across words was occurring at the end of the seventeenth century.[4]

The information found in de la Touche (1696) (Thurot II:557) is also of particular interest because it attests to the existence of nasal pronunciations and indicates that both phonetic characteristics and lexical traits influenced the application of vowel denasalization. De la

3. This interpretation may not be the correct one, as Vaugelas elsewhere symbolized the pronunciation of *un homme* and *un obstacle* as *un nomme* and *un nobstacle.* This notation, however, was used in a remark where a contrast is established between words like *homme* or *obstacle,* with which linking with [n] occurs, and the word *oui,* with which it does not, and where nothing explicit is said about the pronunciation of the vowel preceding the linking [n]: "On prononce donc *un oui,* et non pas *un noui,* comme l'on prononce *un nomme, un nobstacle,* quoique l'on écrive *un homme,* et *un obstacle*" (243). Nevertheless, it cannot be ruled out that both *un* and *une* had a nasal pronunciation, in which case Vaugelas's testimony would reflect only nasal pronunciations for nasal vowels in liaison.

4. Dangeau's testimony also tends to cast some doubt on the accuracy of the interpretation given to the orthographic notations of authors like Oudin (1640) (see above), especially when these grammarians were concentrating on the question of the presence of a linking [n], rather than on the question of the nasal or oral quality of the preceding vowel.

Touche reported nasal pronunciations for *en, on, bon, mon, ton, son, bien, rien, certain, un, aucun: en avez-vous* [ãnavevu], *on aime* [ɔ̃nɛm], *bon ami* [bɔ̃nami], *ton épée* [tɔ̃nepe], *bien heureux* [bjɛ̃nørø], *rien à faire* [rjɛ̃nafɛr], *certain homme* [sɛrtɛ̃nɔm], *un éternel adieu* [œ̃netɛrnɛladjø], *aucun effet* [okœ̃nefɛ]. In addition, he stated: "Pour les adjectifs qui finissent en *in,* comme *fin, divin,* etc., on n'y prononce qu'une *n,* qui se joint à la voyelle suivante, . . . *de fi-nor, un divi-namour"* [i.e., [dəfinɔr], [œ̃divinamur]). This description can be interpreted to capture the stage of a dialect where vowel denasalization across words had just begun to be felt and had affected one particular class of adjectives. De la Touche also mentioned, however, that the adjectives *divin* and *malin* did not always undergo vowel denasalization: "Pour *divin* et *malin,* il me semble qu'on ne prononce pas par example *divi-nesprit, mali-nesprit* [i.e., [divinɛspri], [malinɛspri]], comme on prononce *fi-nor* [i.e., [finɔr]], mais plutôt *divain-nesprit, malain-nesprit* [i.e., [divɛ̃nɛspri], [malɛ̃nɛspri]], d'une manière douce." The exceptional absence of vowel denasalization in these phrases can be interpreted as the mark of conservative pronunciations; if one assumes, quite reasonably, that 'the divine spirit' and 'the evil spirit' were expressions frequently and almost exclusively used in religious circumstances (e.g., sermons), and that the type of speech characteristic of these occasions did not tend to be linguistically innovative, one can easily explain how phrases like *le divin esprit* and *le malin esprit* became frozen with conservative nasal pronunciations.

It is clear that in the seventeenth century vowel denasalization across words was operating, but with wide variation. There appeared to be at least a three-way dialect split: (i) complete absence of denasalization, (ii) denasalization in some words, and (iii) across-the-board denasalization. The sources indicating that denasalization affected only some words suggest that vowel denasalization across words began with noun modifiers.

C. Eighteenth century

The statements of many grammarians explicitly indicate the existence of dialectal variations in the eighteenth century. In the second half of the century the pronunciation of nasal vowels in liaison became the subject of a controversy among authors.

Vaudelin's testimony (1713, 1715), analyzed by Cohen (1946), is particularly interesting and valuable because it provides in the author's own phonetic alphabet a description of the pronunciation characteristic of "le bon usage de la Cour et des Salons" (Cohen

1946:3). *On, en, rien,* and *bien* did not undergo vowel denasalization in liaison. *On*: "õ devant consonne, õn devant voyelle (sans dénasalisation)" (Cohen 1946:21); for example, *on est* [õnɛ], *on y supplée* [õnisyple]. *En* (pronoun): "Pas de dénasalisation devant voyelle" (Cohen 1946:52); for example, *combien y en a-t-il?* [kõbjẽjãnati]. Examples with the preposition *en* also show the absence of denasalization; for example, *en allemand et en anglais* [ãnalmãeãnãglɛ] (Cohen 1946:47). *Rien*: "La liaison en *n* se fait, sans dénasalisation de la voyelle" (Cohen 1946:58); for example, *plus rien à désirer* [plyrjẽnadzire]. *Bien*: "La liaison, sans dénasalisation de la voyelle, paraît habituelle devant un adjectif" (Cohen 1946:61); for example, *bien assuré* [bjẽnasyre]. As to adjectives, in front of a noun "la liaison est faite, avec dénasalisation" (Cohen 1946:47), but only *bon* is given as an illustration: *bon enfant* [bɔnãfã].[5] For the possessive adjectives *mon, ton, son,* "la grande majorité des exemples montre la dénasalisation de la voyelle nasale devant une voyelle" (Cohen 1946:52); for example, *mon âme* [mɔnam], *mon esprit* [mɔnɛspri], *ton escient* [tɔnesjã], *son amour* [sɔnamur]; but Cohen also noted *son histoire* [sõnistwer] (53), which would indicate some variability in the application of vowel denasalization to possessive adjectives. For the indefinite article *un,* vowel denasalization generally occurred before vowel-initial words: for example, *un esprit* [œnɛspri], *un abus* [œnaby];[6] Cohen (1946:38) added that "le fait est marqué expressément à propos des noms de nombre." Cohen also noted, however, that "à propos des liaisons, on lit *œn ami* [un ami], avec voyelle nasale" (39); thus, there also appears to have been variation concerning the application of vowel denasalization to *un.* Vaudelin's testimony thus shows that toward the beginning of the eighteenth century, at least in one dialect, vowel denasalization across words operated selectively: the process applied to noun modifiers (with some variability in the cases of *mon, ton, son,* and *un*) but not to pronouns, prepositions, and adverbs.

Other testimonies in the first half of the eighteenth century leave no doubt as to the existence of a dialect split. De Longue (1725) noticed that some speakers "ne distinguent point en parlant le masculin du féminin: ils prononcent *bo-n-home* [i.e., [bɔnɔm]], comme *bon-âme* [i.e., [bɔnam]] . . . ils ne veulent point entendre *eun n'home*

5. For the word *bonheur* 'happiness', however, Vaudelin provided two different phonetic transcriptions, one with a nasal vowel ([bõnœr]) and one with an oral vowel ([bɔnœr]) (Cohen 1946:47).
6. Since Vaudelin's phonetic alphabet did not provide for a distinction between [ø] and [œ], we actually know for certain only that the timbre of the vowel in *un* was that of a mid front rounded vowel (Cohen 1946:8, 9).

[i.e., [œ̃nɔm]], mais *u-n'home* [i.e., [ynɔm]]" (Thurot II:557). This statement indicates that some speakers denasalized *bon* and *un* in liaison, and that others (including de Longue) kept the vowel nasal and said [bɔ̃nɔm] and [œ̃nɔm] for *bon homme* and *un homme*. Dumas (1733) made similar remarks. His notation reflects the following pronunciations: *on appelle* [ɔ̃napɛl], *bon enfant* [bɔ̃nãfã], *mon ami* [mɔ̃nami], *bien appris* [bjɛ̃napri], *un arbre* [œ̃narbr]; but he also noted that "la nasale *on* selon quelques personnes perd la nasalité devant une voyelle et devient par exemple l'*o* pur dans . . . *mo-nâme* [i.e., [mɔnam]]; selon d'autres, il faut redoubler le *n* et dire *mon-nâme* [i.e., [mɔ̃nam]]" (Thurot II:557).

In the second half of the eighteenth century grammarians began to split into two groups: those who recommended vowel denasalization in liaison, and those who did not.

The following sources advocated oral pronunciations in liaison (Thurot II:558): Antonini (1753) (*en aimant* [anɛmã], *on aspire* [ɔnaspir], *bon enfant* [bɔnãfã], *mon ami* [mɔnami], *bien entendu* [bjɛnãtãdy], *divin esprit* [divinɛspri]); Mauvillon (1754) (*mon âme* [mɔnam], *ton argent* [tɔnaržã]); Galmace (1767) (*en Italie* [anitali], *j'en achèterai* [žanašɛtrɛ]); Cherrier (1766); Roche (1777); and the Syllabaire de Bouillon (1777) (*il en a* [ilana]). According to the biographical information provided by Thurot (I:xxii–lxxxvii), at least some of the grammarians were originally from Italy (Antonini), Spain (Galmace), and Provence (Mauvillon); their recommendations may therefore have reflected the pronunciation used in southern France.[7]

Lévizac (1797) appears to indicate across-the-board vowel denasalization also. He states that "*N,* in the monosyllable *en,* both when a preposition and when a pronoun, in *on, mon, ton, son* pronouns, and in *bon, bien, rien,* ceases to be nasal when these words are immediately followed by a vowel or an h mute, as *en Italie, on en aura, mon ami, c'est un bon homme, on a bien essayé, je suis bien aise qu'il n'ait rien oublié.* But *en* and *on* remain nasal, when they are placed after the verbs; as *donnez-en à votre sœur. A-t-on essayé? Va-t'en au logis*" (9). The interpretation of this excerpt is made somewhat clearer by the following: "*M* final is nasal and not sounded in *faim, daim, nom, renom, parfum*; it is not nasal, and is sounded in *Amsterdam, Rotterdam, Sem, Cham, item, Jérusalem, Sédim, Ibrahim,* and most proper names, except *Joachim*" (20). When he writes

---

7. Note, however, that Dumarsais (1751), though born in Marseille, advocated a nasal pronunciation (see below).

that a nasal consonant is not nasal (or ceases to be nasal), Lévizac thus seems to mean that it is pronounced, but that the preceding vowel is oral. If this interpretation is accurate, then Lévizac indeed indicated vowel denasalization in liaison for *en, on, mon, ton, son, bon, bien,* and *rien.* Lévizac less obscurely reported an oral pronunciation for *un, aucun,* and *commun*: "*Un* has the sound of *u* close, as in *une, unième, unanime,* when followed by a word beginning with a vowel or an h mute, as *un homme, un esprit, aucun ami, commun accord*" (9).

Other authors advocated pronunciations with no vowel denasalization in liaison. Thus, in the *Encyclopédie* of Diderot and d'Alembert, under the entry *Baillement,* Dumarsais (1751:17) wrote: "Lorsque l'adjectif qui finit par un son nasal est suivi d'un substantif qui commence par une voyelle, alors on met l'*n* euphonique entre les deux, du moins dans la prononciation; par example *un-n-enfant, bon-n-homme, commun-n-accord, mon-n-ami.* La particule *on* est aussi suivie de l'*n* euphonique, *on-n-a.* Mais si le substantif précède, il y a ordinairement un *baillement; un écran illuminé, un tyran odieux, un entretien honnête, une citation équivoque, un parfum incommode*; on ne dira pas *un tyran-n-odieux, un entretien-n-honnête,* etc. On dit aussi *un bassin à barbe,* et non *un bassin-n-à barbe.* Je sais bien que ceux qui déclament des vers où le poète n'a pas connu ces voyelles nasales, ajoutent l'*n* euphonique, croyant que cette *n* est la consonne du mot précédent: un peu d'attention les détromperait; car, prenez-y garde, quand vous dites, *il est bon-n-homme, bon-n-ami,* vous prononcez *bon* et ensuite *n-homme, n-ami.*" Dumarsais's notation and especially his last statement clearly indicate nasal pronunciations.

Also in the *Encyclopédie,* but under the entry for *N,* Beauzée (1765:1–2) similarly noted that "dans plusieurs mots terminés par la lettre *n,* comme signe de nasalité, il arrive souvent que l'on fait entendre l'articulation *ne,* si le mot suivant commence par une voyelle ou par un *h* muet." His examples cover adjectives (*bon, ancien, certain, vilain, vain*), the indefinite article *un,* the possessive adjectives *mon, ton, son,* the adverbs *bien* and *rien,* the preposition and pronoun *en,* and the pronoun *on.* Beauzée wondered about the nature of this linking [n], and his answer seems to indicate that the preceding vowel was pronounced nasal: "Est-ce le *n* final qui se prononce dans les occasions que l'on vient de voir, ou bien est-ce un *n* euphonique que la prononciation insère entre deux? Je suis d'avis que c'est un *n* euphonique, différent du *n* orthographique; parce que si l'on avait introduit dans l'alphabet une lettre, ou dans l'orthographe un signe quelconque, pour en représenter le son nasal, l'euphonie n'aurait pas moins amené le *n* entre-deux, et on ne l'aurait assurément pas pris dans la voyelle nasale; or on n'est pas plus autorisé à l'y prendre, quoique par accident la lettre *n* soit le signe de la nasalité, parce que la différence du signe n'en met aucune dans le son représenté. On peut demander encore pourquoi l'articulation insérée ici est *ne*, plutôt que *te*, comme dans *a-t-il reçu?* c'est que l'articulation *ne* est nasale, que par là elle est plus analogue au son nasal qui précède, et conséquemment plus propre à le lier avec le son suivant que tout autre articulation, qui par la raison contraire ferait moins euphonique."

Boulliette (1760) reported nasal pronunciations in phrases such as *en étudiant* [ãnetydjã], *on aime* [ɔ̃nɛm], *mon âme* [mɔ̃nam], *bon ami* [bɔ̃nami], *ancien historien* [ãsjɛ̃nistɔrjɛ̃], but an oral pronunciation in *divin amour* [divinamur]. He explicitly condemned the denasalized pronunciations advocated by others: "On prononce *mon-nâme, bon-nami, bien-nobligeant, un-nécu*. Plusieurs très habiles grammairiens se sont imaginés que, dans ces occasions, les voyelles nasales perdent leur nasalité, et qu'on doit prononcer *mo-nâme, bo-nami* ou *u-nécu*. Mais il n'y a qu'à bien écouter et sans prévention ceux qui parlent, et même les meilleurs parleurs, on s'apercevra que naturellement tous, et soi-même saussi lorsqu'on n'y pense pas, prononcent *mon nâme, bon nami*, etc… il n'y a que ces mots *divin amour* que l'usage fait prononcer *divi-namour*… mais ce changement et cette prononciation ne se font point en d'autres mots terminés en *in*… on dit toujours le *malin-nesprit*" (Thurot II:558).

Thurot added that Demandre (1769) and de Wailly (1770) "donnent le même précepte que Boulliette, sans parler des adjectifs en *in*" (Thurot II:558). De Wailly's explanations are actually not so explicit as those of Boulliette, but his notation would indeed seem to reflect the absence of vowel denasalization in liaison between a noun modifier and a noun: "*N* finale sonne dans *abdomen, Amen, examen, hymen*. Acad. et dans l'adjectif suivi de son substantif, qui commence par une voyelle ou une *h* muette. *Mon ami, un ancien étui, un bon historien, un homme*: prononcez *mon nami, ancien nétui, bon nhistorien, un nhomme*" (de Wailly 1770:460). Restaut (1763:488) provided similar indications: "on prononce, *mon âme, un bon ami, un ancien historien*, comme s'il y avait, *mon nâme, un bon nami, un ancien nistorien*."

In conclusion, it may be instructive to compare Boulliette's (1760) remarks concerning the adjectives *divin* and *malin* with those of de la Touche (1696). In the dialect described by de la Touche, vowel denasalization applied to adjectives in *in* (e.g., *fin or* [finɔr], *divin amour* [divinamur]), except in frozen expressions such as *malin esprit* [malɛ̃nɛspri]. In the dialect described by Boulliette, the pronunciation [malɛ̃nɛspri] is considered regular, whereas [divinamur] is taken to be exceptional. These differences across a time span of about sixty years can be interpreted to show that, at least for some speakers living in the mid-eighteenth century, vowel denasalization across words had actually regressed and was no longer an actively operating phonetic process. Vaudelin's testimony, which indicates that vowel denasalization affected different categories of words differently in "le bon usage" at the beginning of the century, demonstrates that, for this dialect at least, the process had much earlier ceased to be a purely phonetically motivated sandhi rule. It is also apparent that in the eighteenth century there were speakers who, in liaison contexts, applied vowel denasalization across the board, and yet others who kept the vowels nasal in all cases.

D. Nineteenth century

The types of dialectal variations found in the eighteenth century in the pronunciation of nasal vowels in liaison continued to be reported in the nineteenth century, but the information given by many grammarians advocating either nasal or oral pronunciations became more clearly prescriptive and often relied on past pronunciation treatises or on a priori principles.

Across-the-board vowel denasalization was advocated mainly in the first part of the nineteenth century. Domergue (1805), cited in Thurot (II:558–559), attempted to formulate a "natural" reason justifying the oral pronunciation: "Toute syllabe se termine naturellement par une voyelle: *hi-la-ri-té.*... Il résulte de là que la consonne quitte naturellement la syllabe consommée pour s'unir à la voyelle qui suit. Or dans *un ami, divin Homère,* je prononce *u, divi,* et la syllabe est consommée, le *n* appartient à la voyelle qui suit.... Il en est ainsi de *mon ami, certain auteur, bien aimable.*... Ce sont encore les Normands qui ont tâché d'accréditer cette prononciation *mon nami, on nignore, certain nauteur, bien nélevé."*

Dubroca (1824) also favored vowel denasalization: "Mon opinion est que, lorsqu'il s'agit de lier les voyelles nasales, leur propriété grammaticale disparaît entièrement; que la voyelle qui précède le *n* final reprend sa prononciation naturelle; qu'on l'énonce dégagée de toute espèce de nasalité, et que le *n* va s'attacher comme une consonne pure à la voyelle initiale du mot suivant avec laquelle il forme une syllabe" (38). Lesaint (1871), who argued in favor of the absence of vowel denasalization (see below), provided numerous examples of the oral pronunciation advocated by Dubroca and others (367): *un ami* [ynami] ~ [œnami]; *j'en ai* [žanɛ]; *en outre* [anutr]; *on a* [ɔna]; *non interrompu* [nɔnɛ̃terɔ̃py]; *mon enfant* [mɔnãfã]; *ton histoire* [tɔnistwar]; *son image* [sɔnimaž]; *bien à plaindre* [bjɛnaplɛ̃dr]; *rien appris* [rjɛnapri]; *chacun un* [šakynœ̃]; *aucun ami* [okynami]; *un bon élève* [œ̃bɔnelɛv]; *ancien auteur* [ãsjɛnotœr]; *divin amour* [divinamur]; *vain espoir* [vɛnɛspwar].

Landais (1850) similarly indicated vowel denasalization for *on, mon, ton, son,* and adjectives: "on fera sonner la consonne *n* dans *on,* avant son verbe. *On arrive* et *on est arrivé* se prononcent: *o-narrive,* et *o-nest arrivé....* On la fera également sonner dans les pronoms possessifs *mon, ton, son,* et dans tous les adjectifs placés avant les substantifs, comme *ton esprit, bon ange, son âme, certain auteur,* qu'on prononcera *to-nesprit, bo-nange, so-nâme, certai-nauteur"* (37). Even more explicitly, in answer to one of J.-M. Ragon's criticisms directed at his *Dictionnaire des Dictionnaires,* Landais wrote: "Sans craindre qu'on vienne nous démentir, nous prétendons qu'on prononce *on a dit,* comme s'il y avait *o-na-dit,* et non point *on-na-dit"* (206). The disagreement between Ragon and Landais concerning the pronunciation of *on a dit* clearly shows the existence of dialectal variations in the pronunciation of nasal vowels in liaison.

Other grammarians indicated, throughout the nineteenth century, that nasal vowels were to remain nasal in liaison. Thus, according to Girault-Duvivier (1843:7–8), "dans plusieurs mots terminés par la lettre *n* comme signe nasal, il arrive souvent que cette consonne est sonore, sans que cependant la nasalité cesse d'avoir lieu; c'est-à-dire que l'on fait entendre un *n* intercalaire qui s'unit avec la voyelle suivante, comme dans *bon ami,* que l'on prononce *bon-nami....* On fera donc sonner la consonne *n* finale, dans tous les adjectifs suivis immédiatement d'un nom qui commence par une voyelle ou par un *h* non aspiré: ainsi, dans *ancien ami, certain auteur, vilain homme, en plein air,* tout en conservant la nasalité des syllabes en *in,* on liera la consonne finale *n* avec la voyelle ou le *h* non aspiré qui suit; de sorte qu'on prononcera comme s'il y avait *ancien-nami, vilain-nhomme,* etc." Girault-Duvivier opposed Dubroca's view: "M. Dubroca, l'un des collaborateurs du *Manuel des amateurs de la langue française,* . . . veut qu'on prononce: *vain espoir, on est ici bien heureux,* comme s'il y avait *vai-nespoir, o-nest ici bie-nheureux.*

"Cette manière, dit M. Dubroca, de lier les voyelles sauve les principes, et ne jette pas dans l'insoutenable contradiction du double emploi de ce son, qui est simple et indivisible par essence. Le caractère grammatical de ces sons est renversé, à la vérité, dans leur liaison; mais c'est pour en faire résulter un ordre naturel de prononciation, un ordre qui est tellement dans le génie de notre langue, que nous l'exécutons dans un très grand nombre de mots, par un principe de prononciation universel et reconnu. En effet, ajoute-t-il, que l'on observe notre manière de prononcer les mots *inattentif, inabordable, inhumain,* etc., quelqu'un s'avise-t-il de dire *in-nattentif, in-nabordable, in-nhumain?* non sans doute: et cependant qui ignore que ces mots sont composés de la particule *in,* qui répond à la préposition latine *non,* particule que l'on rend toujours nasale dans les mots où elle est suivie d'une consonne, comme dans *in-décent, in-tempérant?* Que fait-on donc dans le premier cas? on prononce l'*i* pur, dont on forme la première syllabe du mot, tandis que le *n,* qui lui appartient naturellement, va se réunir, comme une consonne pure, à la voyelle suivante, et l'on dit *i-nattentif, i-nabordable, i-nhumain.* C'est d'après ce même principe que nous prononçons encore *bo-nheur,* formé de *bon* et de *heur; no-nobstant,* qui résulte de *non* et de *obstant; vi-naigre,* évidemment formé des mots *vin* et *aigre,* etc."

"Nous n'examinerons pas jusqu'à quel point l'opinion de M. Dubroca est fondée: cette discussion n'entre pas dans le plan que nous nous sommes proposé. Seulement nous dirons que la prononciation que ce Grammairien veut faire admettre a contre elle l'usage universel, et que ce motif seul suffit pour faire donner la préférence au sentiment de Beauzée, de Dumarsais, de Dangeau, de D'Olivet, etc., etc." (7).[8]

The information given by Laveaux (1847) is identical with that found in Girault-Duvivier. The following examples and comments are provided (727–728): *ancien ami* [ãsjẽnami], *vilain homme* [vilẽnɔm], *certain auteur* [sɛrtẽnotœr], *en plein air* [ãplẽɛr], *bon ami* [bõnami], *un homme* [œ̃nɔm], *un arbre* [œ̃narbr], *on a dit* [õnadi], *en Allemagne* [ãnalmañ], *en Espagne* [ãnɛspañ]. "Dans les exemples que nous venons de donner, où la voyelle nasale se fait sentir, on laisse à cette syllabe sa nasalité entière, et on en prolonge le son par l'addition d'un *n* euphonique, que l'on prononce au commencement du second mot: *certain nauteur.* Quelques grammairiens, s'élevant contre cet usage général dont les meilleurs grammairiens ont fait une règle, veulent que l'on retranche le *n* de la voyelle nasale, qu'on le

---

8. As noted earlier, Dangeau (1694) had actually changed his report and indicated that nasal vowels became oral in liaison.

transporte au commencement du mot suivant, et qu'on prononce, par exemple, *certai nauteur,* au lieu de *certain nauteur*; *o na dit,* au lieu de *on na dit.* Cette innovation est d'autant plus absurde qu'elle dénaturerait le premier mot de chacune de ces phrases, pour en faire des mots barbares." Laveaux's conclusion about "cette singulière innovation" is simply that "Il n'y a point d'erreur qui ne trouve quelques partisans, surtout dans les questions où l'on est porté à suivre sans examen les opinions des autres."

Lesaint (1871) followed in the same footsteps as Girault-Duvivier and Laveaux, arguing that "malgré la liaison de la lettre *n* avec la voyelle suivante, le son nasal final doit être conservé; on s'exprimerait mal en prononçant *anciè-nami, vè-nesspoar, óku-nakcidan, cèrtè-nóteur, mali-nèsspri, ce divi-namour, u-naimpòrtu-nami,* etc.; car, outre qu'on se mettrait en opposition avec l'usage général en faisant disparaître le son nasal, on n'établirait plus, dans la prononciation, aucune distinction entre les adjectifs masculins et les adjectifs féminins" (356–357). The long lists of examples provided by Lesaint include the following (356–366): liaison with adjectives: *ancien ami* [ɑ̃sjɛ̃nami], *vain espoir* [vɛ̃nɛspwar], *aucun accident* [okœ̃naksidɑ̃], *certain auteur* [sɛrtɛ̃notœr], *vilain homme* [vilɛ̃nɔm], *en plein air* [ɑ̃plɛ̃nɛr], *ce divin amour* [sədivɛ̃namur], *le malin esprit* [ləmalɛ̃nɛspri], *au moyen âge* [omwajɛ̃naž], *aucun ouvrage* [okœ̃nuvraž], *d'un commun accord* [œ̃kɔmœ̃nakɔr], *un importun ami* [œ̃nɛ̃portœ̃nami]; liaison with possessive adjectives: *mon enfant* [mɔ̃nɑ̃fɑ̃], *ton intéressant ouvrage* [tɔ̃nɛterɛsɑ̃tuvraž], *son entière liberté* [sɔ̃nɑ̃tjɛrlibɛrte]; liaison with *un*: *un arbre* [œ̃narbr]; liaison with *on: on aime* [ɔ̃nɛm]; liaison with *chacun*: *chacun un* [šakœ̃nœ̃]; liaison with *en* (preposition and pronoun): *il en a acheté* [ilɑ̃naašte], *en Italie* [ɑ̃nitali]; liaison with *non*: *non encore revu* [nɔ̃nɑ̃kɔrrəvy]; liaison with *bien*: *enfant bien élevé* [ɑ̃fɑ̃bjɛ̃nelve]; liaison with *rien*: *rien à perdre* [rjɛ̃naperdr]. Like Girault-Duvivier and Laveaux, Lesaint found justification for his position in the writings of other grammarians (especially past grammarians): "quand l'*n* finale nasale doit se lier, l'usage est de conserver le son nasal et d'ajouter, dans la prononciation, une *n* devant la voyelle initiale du mot suivant. . . . Tel est l'avis de Dangeau, Beauzée, Dumarsais, Th. Corneille, d'Olivet, Restaut, Bouillette, Régnier-Desmarais, de Wailly, Lévizac, et de quelques autres auteurs modernes" (366).[9] Lesaint criticized Dubroca's recom-

9. Dangeau (1694) and Lévizac (1797) actually reported oral pronunciations (see above).

mendation on the basis of a certain usage: "Cette innovation, car c'en est une, a trouvé des partisans, gens de cabinet, mais non gens du monde, qui, sans consulter l'usage, ont, de leur propre autorité, lancé des décrets, sans même se donner la peine de se mettre d'accord entre eux. . . . Mais demandez à un capitaine, à un colonel, à un général si, parlant à leur troupes, ils disent *a-navant* ou *an-navant*. Allez au Théâtre-Français, l'académie du bon langage, des bonnes manières, du bon ton; allez écouter, au Palais de l'Institut, les premiers savants de France; interrogez enfin cette société choisie de la capitale qui parle le français tout naturellement, sans aucune teinte d'affectation, et vous n'hésiterez pas à condamner la réforme de M. Dubroca" (367–368). To reinforce his position Lesaint also quoted J. Duquesnois, "professeur d'éloquence parlée, auteur d'une *Nouvelle Prosodie* et d'un *Manuel de l'orateur et du lecteur*": "Nous avons été bien des fois consulté pour savoir si l'on devait, en faisant la liaison de l'*n*, conserver au son nasal sa sonorité, ou bien la changer et dire: *u-nhomme, le divi-namour,* etc. Nous avons toujours répondu que, les sons nasaux étant pour marquer le masculin, il fallait leur conserver leur sonorité, sans quoi ils perdraient leurs véritables significations, et, au lieu de mettre de la clarté dans la pensée, ils y jetteraient la confusion. . . . Prononcez donc *mon-nami, un-nami, divin-namour,* etc., et non *mo-nami, u-nami, divi-namour*" (368–369). Lesaint's testimony gives the overall impression that at least the high and educated society of Paris used the nasal pronunciation, and that therefore the nineteenth-century controversy concerning the pronunciation of nasal vowels in liaison may have reflected the existence of different social dialects.

Duperré de Lisle (1883) also advocated the absence of vowel denasalization: "Quand on fait la liaison, il faut conserver le son nasal au mot qui a l'*n* et dire: *un n'ami* et non pas *u nami. Un certain_auteur* et non pas: *un certai nauteur. Le divin_amour* et non pas: *le divi namour. Un ancien_ennemi* et non pas *ancie nennemi.* Il n'y aurait, pour l'oreille, aucune différence avec la forme féminine: *une amie, une certaine amie, une ancienne ennemie.* Cette opinion est celle de tous les grammairiens contemporains" (129–130).

In the nineteenth century two groups of grammarians thus opposed each other on the question of the pronunciation of nasal vowels in liaison. The value of their testimonies is diminished by their obvious desire to have a uniform set of facts explainable by a single "logical" principle. The reliance of those who advocated nasal pronunciations on the writings of past grammarians further strains their credibility as faithful reporters of contemporary usage.[10] In sum, it is difficult to determine with any certainty whether the controversy really indicated the existence of two sharply distinguished dialects, one with oral and the other with nasal pronunciations, or whether the debate was caused by the selective application of vowel denasalization across words and the inability or unwillingness of some grammarians to recognize such variation.

A third group of nineteenth-century grammarians actually reported variations among words in the pronunciation of nasal vowels in liaison. Malvin-Cazal (1846) gave as a general rule that nasal vowels lost their nasality (233-234), but his detailed observations in fact reveal subtle distinctions. For example, he indicated that for the words *en* (52), *on* (76), *un* (80), and *combien, bien, rien* (238), the vowels were actually pronounced slightly nasalized in liaison ("légèrement nasalé"). This touch of nasality cannot be assumed to be caused by phonetic assimilation because, within words, vowels followed by a nasal consonant and a vowel are clearly described as oral. In addition, for adjectives in *-ain* and *-ein* (*certain, lointain, prochain, soudain, souverain, vain, vilain, plein*) (242-243), and for the adjective *bon* (245-246), Malvin-Cazal specified that the nasality of the vowels was lost in liaison; he also explicitly contrasted the liaison pronunciation of *combien, bien,* and *rien* with that of the adjective *ancien*: "la finale *ien* de *combien, bien* et *rien*, conserve un peu de sa nasalité, malgré la liaison de l'*n* avec la voyelle suivante; au lieu que dans *ancien*, la nasalité disparaît entièrement à la liaison" (238). For *mon, ton, son,* there is no indication as to whether the vowels lost their nasality completely or not.

Malvin-Cazal also observed dialectal variations. The two adjectives *divin* and *malin* are given nasal pronunciations in liaison (*divin amour* [divɛ̃namur], *malin esprit* [malɛ̃nɛspri], *malin aspect* [malɛ̃naspɛ]), but it is noted that an "assez grand nombre de per-

10. At the end of his detailed study of the *Grammaire des Grammaires,* Levitt (1968:301) states that "[Girault-Duvivier's] description of the language is highly conservative, based too exclusively on literature, and distorted by the principles on which he believes his rules must be based . . . he is aware of the usage of his time and tries to describe it insofar as his principles permit him to do so . . . . Above all, Girault-Duvivier reflects a somewhat idealized and rationalized picture of the language, a picture that evolved during the eighteenth century and continued well into the nineteenth."

sonnes font perdre la nasalité à *divin* quand cet adjectif est devant le substantif *amour,* et prononcent *divi-n'amour''*(240). Concerning the liaison pronunciation of the vowel in the masculine indefinite article *un,* Malvin-Cazal indicated that it was a slightly nasalized mid front rounded vowel (written *eu*), but he acknowledged the existence of pronunciations with [y] instead: "Quelques personnes, étrangères au bon usage, prononcent le mot *un* placé devant un mot commençant par une voyelle ou une *h* muette, en donnant à l'*u* sa valeur propre, au lieu de celui *eu* légèrement nasalé, que nous indiquons dans les exemples de cette règle. En disant *u-n'in-bé-si-l', u-n'i-po-cri-t'* (*un imbécile, un hypocrite*), on donne à penser qu'il est question d'une femme; tandis qu'en prononçant *eu-n'in-bé-si-l', eu-n'i-po-cri-t',* on voit tout de suite que c'est d'un homme que l'on parle" (80–81). *Aucun, commun, importun,* and *opportun* are also given with the vowel *eu* in liaison (251–253).

Féline (1851) indicated vowel denasalization with the adjective *bon* and the possessive adjectives *mon, ton, son*:[11] "le substantif *bon* ne se lie jamais. On dit *le b̥o et le beau.* Mais *b̥on,* adjectif, se lie quand il est suivi de son substantif. Au moyen de cette liaison, le son nasal est remplacé par celui dont il dérive. On dit: *Un bon homme*" (i.e., [œ̃bɔnɔm]) (91). For *mon,* "lorsqu'on fait la liaison, la voyelle *o̥* perd sa nasalité et se prononce o. On dit *Mon ami, mon espoir,* et non pas *M̥on ami, m̥on espoir*" (i.e., (mɔnami], *[mɔ̃nami]; [mɔnɛspwar], *[mɔ̃nɛspwar]) (259).[12] Féline attributed to *certain* both a nasalized and a denasalized pronunciation in liaison, depending on specific phonetic properties of the following noun: "Nous croyons pouvoir indiquer comme règle que, lorsque la voyelle initiale du substantif est suivie d'une consonne nasale ou mouillée (m, n, l̥ [=j], g̥ [=ñ]), le son final *i* perd sa nasalité et reprend celui de la voyelle primitive. . . . On dit: *serten homme, serten animal, serten agneau, serten œillet* [i.e., [sɛrtɛnɔm], [sɛrtɛnanimal], [sɛrtɛnaño], [sɛrtɛnœjɛ]]. Dans les autres cas, on maintient la nasalité et l'on dit: *sertin accoutrement, sertin auditeur, sertin utopiste*" (i.e., [sɛrtɛ̃nakutrəmã], [sɛrtɛ̃noditœr], [sɛrtɛ̃nytɔpist]) (108–109). I have not found this subtle distinction attested anywhere else.

Toward the end of the nineteenth century Littré (1881) also de-

11. In Féline's notation, nasal vowels are underlined (thus o̥ = [ɔ̃] and o = [ɔ]).
12. Similar statements are provided under the entries for *ton* and *son:* "lorsqu'on fait la liaison, o̥ se transforme en o."

scribed a dialect where vowel denasalization in liaison occurred only in certain words; in addition, he recognized the existence of other pronunciations in other speakers. In Littré's dialect, vowel denasalization applied in *un* (*un homme* [ynɔm]), *aucun* (*aucun ami* [okynami]), *bien, mon, ton, son,* and *bon,* but not in *commun* (*un commun intérêt* [œ̃kɔmœ̃nɛ̃terɛ]), *on,* and *en.* Littré referred to the existence of a nasal pronunciation for *un* and *bien,* but he attributed it, for the latter word, to "mauvais usage." He did not mention the existence of nasal pronunciations for *mon, ton, son,* and *bon.* Littré neutrally remarked that some speakers denasalized in *commun* and *on.* No information is provided for the liaison pronunciation of adjectives such as *ancien, certain, plein.* Under *malin,* Littré gives *malin esprit* as [malɛ̃nɛspri]; under *divin,* he gives *divin amour* as [divɛ̃namur], but he recognized that others denasalized ([divinamur]). In contrast with Littré's dialect, Passy (1899) gives nasal pronunciations for *un, bien,* and *mon, ton, son,* as well as for *on* and *en.*

In addition to the two clans of grammarians arguing for and against across-the-board vowel denasalization in liaison, a third nineteenth-century group thus reported that vowel denasalization could affect different words differently. Within this group, further dialectal variations are apparent, for example, with respect to the word *un.*

E. Twentieth century

In the twentieth century, testimonies generally become less divergent, more detailed, and more easily interpretable. The reports usually indicate selective vowel denasalization in liaison, with variations in the range of words affected. This relative uniformity may be due to the growing dominance of a type of French spoken in Paris and to the fact that grammarians were mostly concerned with describing this particular dialect. First considering the testimonies of a group of grammarians who wrote during the first thirty years of the century, I next examine mid-century reports. Finally I describe the types of pronunciation of nasal vowels in liaison which have come to my attention in contemporary French.

Rousselot and Laclotte (1902:179) state that the nasal vowel of *bon* is always denasalized, except in Normandy, where speakers say [bɔ̃nami] for *bon ami. Divin* is also denasalized (*divin enfant* [divinãfã], *divin Homère* [divinɔmɛr]), but *malin,* at least in *malin esprit,* is not ([malɛ̃nɛspri]). For adjectives like *ancien* and *certain,* denasalization occurs (*ancien ami* [ãsjɛnami]; *certain auteur* [sɛrtɛnotœr]). *Mon, ton,* and *son* offer the two options (e.g., *mon ami*: [mɔ̃nami] ~ [mɔnami]). For *un,* these authors mention the existence of three pronunciations in liaison: *un ami* [ynami], [œ̃nami], and [œnami]; the first pronunciation is considered old: "Littré, comme font encore plusieurs à Paris, surtout parmi les personnes âgées, disait *u-n-ami*"; the other two forms "tendent à prévaloir à Paris"; interestingly, the same speaker may not always use the same form. *En, on,* and *bien* are characterized by the absence of vowel denasalization (*en allant* [ãnalã], *on aime* [ɔ̃nɛm], *bien aimable* [bjɛ̃nemabl]).

Rosset's (1905) phonetic transcriptions indicate nasal pronunciations not only for *en* (e.g., *en arrière* [ãnarjɛr]; *s'en écarter* [sãnekarte]), *on* (e.g., *on aperçoit* [ɔ̃napɛrswa]), and *rien* (e.g., *sans rien entendre* [sãrjɛ̃nãtãdr]), but also for *un* (e.g., *un abri* [œ̃nabri], *un homme* [œ̃nɔm]), *aucun* (*aucun être* [okœ̃nɛtr]), *mon, ton, son* (e.g., *mon oreille* [mɔ̃nɔrɛj], *ton étendue* [tɔ̃netãdy], *son âge* [sɔ̃naž]),[13] and *ancien* (*l'ancien état* [lãsjɛ̃neta]).[14]

Martinon (1913:386–391) provides one of the most detailed descriptions of the pronunciation of nasal vowels in liaison: "La plupart des adjectifs qui peuvent se lier sont en *-ain*: *certain, hautain, lointain, humain, prochain, soudain, souverain, vain* et *vilain,* avec *plein, ancien* et *moyen*. Mais la liaison offre ici un phénomène très remarquable, car la nasale se décompose, et c'est le son du féminin qu'on entend: *certai-nauteur, un vai-nespoir, un vilai-nenfant, en plei-nair, le moye-nâge, un ancie-nami,* et même *au prochai-navertissement.*" Martinon adds that "quelques personnes lient sans décomposer: *plein nair*; mais c'est encore une erreur, qui provient uniquement du fétichisme de l'orthographe, et du besoin de prononcer les mots comme ils sont écrits. Ou peut-être est-ce un respect scrupuleux d'anciennes traditions: l'abbé Rousselot a remarqué que cette prononciation se rencontre de préférence dans certains milieux traditionnalistes et réactionnaires." For *bon,* "le phénomène est exactement le même: *un bo-nélève,* et non *un bon nélève.*" "L'exemple de *bon* est suivi par *mon, ton, son...*: *mo-nhabit, to-namour, so-nesprit.*" "Le cas des adjectifs en *-in* est plus délicat... la grande diffusion des cantiques

13. *Son* is given an oral pronunciation in one instance (*son appréhension* [sɔnapreãsjɔ̃]), but the omission of the nasality marker is probably a typographical error.

14. In the fixed expression *moyen âge* 'Middle Ages', the pronunciation given is oral: [mwajenaž].

de Noël a répandu et imposé l'expression *divi-nenfant*. Par analogie, on dira très correctement *divi-nAchille, divi-nUlysse, divi-nHomère*; mais la décomposition de la nasale s'impose moins absolument, quoique la liaison soit également indispensable. C'est d'ailleurs le seul adjectif en *-in* qui puisse se décomposer: *malin esprit* ou *fin esprit* se lieront donc *au besoin* sans décomposition; mais je pense qu'*esprit malin* et surtout *esprit fin* vaudraient beaucoup mieux." "L'adjectif *un* s'est longtemps décomposé comme les autres, et Littré disait encore *u-nhomme*. Cette prononciation a disparu à peu près complètement, à Paris du moins, chez les personnes instruites... l'usage s'est établi de faire la liaison sans décomposer: *un nhomme, un nami, un nun.*" In a footnote, however, Martinon indirectly indicates that at least some speakers denasalized *un* with a mid vowel: "Mais si l'on ne dit pas *u-nami*, ce n'est pas une raison pour dire *eu-nami.*" "*Aucun* a fait exactement comme *un*, dont il est le composé, et conserve aujourd'hui le son nasal devant un substantif: *aucun nhomme*. On dit aussi *d'un commun naccord*, ou encore *chacun nun*, qui évite un hiatus désagréable, et même, en géométrie, *chacun na chacun.*" Martinon finally notes the absence of denasalization for *en, on, rien, bien,* and *combien* (e.g., *s'en aller* [sãnale], *en Asie* [ãnazi]; *on a dit* [ɔ̃nadi]; *rien à dire* [rjɛ̃nadir]; *bien aimable* [bjɛ̃nemabl]; *combien avez-vous de...* [kɔ̃bjɛ̃navevudə]), but in a footnote he mentions that "Dans le midi, on pousse la dénasalisation jusqu'au bout: par exemple, on fait rimer de deux syllabes, *les savants en us* avec *anus!* On y dit de même *a-neffet, a-noutre*, et *o-nest venu*, que préconisait Domergue."

Nyrop (1914:131) gives examples with no vowel denasalization for *mon* (*mon enfant* [mɔ̃nãfã]), *en* (*en avant* [ãnavã]; "*en agent* se prononcera comme *en nageant*"), *aucun* (*aucun autre* [okœ̃notr]). But he also adds: "Il peut se faire qu'en cas de liaison, la voyelle perde son timbre nasal et passe à la voyelle orale correspondante. Ce phénomène de dénasalisation est surtout fréquent dans le midi de la France; mais on peut entendre un peu partout [mɔnami] (*mon ami*), [bɔnami] (*bon ami*)." Nyrop also notes some variation concernant *un*: "Il y a aussi des gens qui ne font pas de différence entre *un ami* et *une amie*, et qui prononce *une homme*, tout comme si les hommes portaient des jupons. Cependant la tendance moderne est, semble-t-il, de dénasaliser le moins possible, sans doute, par suite de l'influence croissante de la langue écrite, et aussi, pour éviter des confusions perpétuelles entre le masculin et le féminin. La prononciation *une homme* est considérée comme provinciale et affectée."[15]

Grammont (1914:133–134) states that "Certaines voyelles nasales peuvent se dénasaliser quand leur *n* se lie. C'est la voyelle ẽ qui est le plus sujette à ce phénomène." Grammont gives the following examples: *certain auteur* [sɛrtɛnotœr], *un vain espoir* [œ̃vɛnɛspwar], *un vilain enfant* [œ̃vilɛnãfã], *en plein air* [ãplɛnɛr], *le moyen-âge* [ləmwajɛnaž], *ancien ami* [ãsjɛnami], *bien aimable* [bjɛnemabl]; for *bien aimable*, however, he adds that the nasal pronunciation [bjẽnemabl] is possible. With the vowel [ɔ̃], Grammont gives an oral pronunciation for *bon*: *un bon ami* [œ̃bɔnami], *un bon élève* [œ̃bɔnelɛv], and explicitly excludes [œ̃bɔ̃nami], [œ̃bɔ̃nelɛv]; for *mon, ton, son,* he notes that "on peut dire" [mɔnami], [tɔnami], [sɔnami], "mais on dit plutôt" [mɔ̃nami], [tɔ̃nami], [sɔ̃nami]; for the pronoun *on,* he indicates that the nasal vowel must remain nasal: *on a vu* [ɔ̃navy], *[ɔnavy]. Finally, Grammont states that "Les autres voyelles nasales ne se dénasalisent pas: *un n homme, s'en n aller*" ([œ̃nɔm], [sãnale]).

Langlard (1928) indicated denasalization with adjectives like *bon, divin, certain, ancien,* but no denasalization with *on, en, bien, rien, mon, ton, son.* He also noted that the absence of denasalization in *un* was a recent phenomenon.

Bruneau (1931:64–65) indicated no vowel denasalization for *en, on,* and *un;* concerning *un,* he observed that "il a été distingué, dans les dernières années du XIXe siècle, de prononcer *u-n-homme,* et c'est sans doute l'ancienne prononciation." Vowel denasalization is reported to occur with adjectives like *bon* (*un bon élève* [œ̃bɔnelɛv]), *vain* (*un vain espoir* [œ̃vɛnɛspwar]), *certain* (*certain auteur* [sɛrtɛnotœr]), *plein* (*le plein air* [ləplɛnɛr]), *ancien* (*un ancien ambassadeur* [œ̃nãsjɛnãbasadœr]); Bruneau also indicated vowel denasalization in the expressions *d'un commun accord* and *chacun un,* but with the oral vowel [œ] rather then [y]: [dœ̃kɔmœnakɔr], [šakœnœ̃]. Finally, he reported both oral and nasal pronunciations for *bien* and *rien* (*bien aimable*: [bjɛnemabl] ~ [bjẽnemabl]; *rien à faire*: [rjɛnafɛr] ~ [rjẽnafɛr]), and also for the possessive adjectives: "On hésite entre les deux prononciations pour: *mon ami, ton ami, son ami.*"

15. According to Bauche (1951:41 n. 1), "On entend quelques Parisiens dire *une* pour 'un' devant voyelle: *une homme.* C'est une habitude prise dans les maisons religieuses d'éducation. (Cf. Proust, *Le Temps retrouvé: Je ne suis pas une ange.* Dit par un prêtre sortant d'un mauvais lieu.)"

For the first thirty years of the twentieth century the pronunciation of nasal vowels in liaison may be summarized as follows, at least for northern France and more specifically for Paris. Adjectives were generally denasalized. *Bon* in fact had to exhibit an oral vowel in liaison. For adjectives like *ancien,* some speakers kept the vowel nasal. *Divin* denasalized, but *malin* retained its nasal vowel in the stock phrase *malin esprit.* The possessive adjectives *mon, ton,* and *son* showed the most variability, with the beginning of a preference for the nasal pronunciation noticeable. *On* and *en* kept their vowel nasal. *Bien* and *rien* also did, for most speakers. *Un, aucun,* and *commun* generally kept their vowel nasal as well but, especially for *un,* there were speakers who denasalized, either as [yn] (the most conservative pronunciation) or as [œn]. The few reports on the pronunciation of nasal vowels in liaison in southern France indicate that vowel denasalization was general in this dialect.

Around the middle of the twentieth century the reports are all very similar (cf. the pedagogical manuals by Peyrollaz (1954), Kammans (1956), Fouché (1959), Léon (1966)). Fouché's description is representative. Fouché (1959:435–436) reported vowel denasalization for adjectives like *certain, vain, vilain, plein, ancien, moyen, divin, bon.* He noted that "*Malin* conserve sa voyelle nasale dans l'expression ecclésiastique *le malin esprit* [malɛ̃nɛspri]" and that the conservation of the nasal vowel in expressions like *le divin Achille, le divin Homère, le divin Ulysse,* and *le divin amour* was "surannée." Fouché reported nasal pronunciations for *un* (*un ami* [œ̃nami]), *aucun* (*aucun homme* [okœ̃nɔm]), *commun* (*d'un commun accord* [dœ̃kɔmœ̃nakɔr]), and also for *bien* (*bien aimable* [bjɛ̃nemabl]), *rien* (*rien à faire* [rjɛ̃nafɛr]), *en* (*en avant* [ãnavã], *j'en ai* [žãnɛ]), and *on* (*on a dit* [ɔ̃nadi]). For *mon, ton, son,* Fouché stated that the nasal vowel "conserve sa nasalité ou devient orale": *mon ami* [mɔ̃nami] ~ [mɔnami], *ton épaule* [tɔ̃nepol] ~ [tɔnepol]; however, he added that the "prononciation avec voyelle nasale est considérée pour le moment comme la meilleure," and Kammans (1956) described the oral pronunciation as "vieillie." Martinet's (1945 [1971]) statistical study confirms these impressions about the decline of the oral pronunciation and the spreading of the nasal pronunciation in possessive adjectives, both from a geographical point of view and across generations: "La prononciation nasale paraît être une innovation. Elle est presque générale à Paris. Les régions périphériques de l'Ouest et du Sud-Est sont celles qui maintiennent le mieux la prononciation orale traditionnelle. Les deux régions partiellement allogènes de la Bretagne et du Nord semblent n'avoir jamais réellement adopté cette prononciation qui complique la flexion des adjectifs possessifs" (145). Across generations, Martinet provided the following percentages of speakers pronouncing [mɔ̃nami] for *mon ami*:

Table 1

	Northern France	Paris
Born before 1900	71%	88%
Born between 1900 and 1910	73%	85%
Born between 1910 and 1921	78%	96%

"La tendance générale est bien à l'élimination de la prononciation à voyelle orale. Cette tendance est surtout nette dans le passage de la génération moyenne aux classes d'âge plus jeune. A une exception près, les jeunes Parisiens ne connaissent que *mon n-ami*" (146).

Compared with the first thirty years of the century, the middle of the twentieth century thus shows the following characteristics: (i) A stabilization of the pronunciations of *un, aucun, chacun, commun, bien,* and *rien,* which no longer denasalize and have thus joined the group formed by *on* and *en.* (ii) A push toward the absence of vowel denasalization in the possessive adjectives *mon, ton, son.* (iii) Aside from the phrase *malin esprit,* which remains frozen with a nasal pronunciation, vowel denasalization is general in adjectives; no mention is made of adjectives like *ancien* or *plein* keeping their nasal vowel in liaison.[16]

In contemporary French, five types of pronunciation of nasal vowels in liaison have come to my attention:

Dialect I: In the dialect that is usually considered standard, one finds the following: vowel denasalization with adjectives such as *bon, plein, certain, prochain, ancien,* and *divin,* and no denasalization with *un, aucun, chacun, commun, mon, ton, son, on, en, bien,* and *rien.* Speakers of this dialect usually come from northern France, Paris in particular.

16. It is likely that the nasal pronunciation of adjectives in liaison existed (see below), but characterized a type of speech which fell outside the descriptive scope of the pronunciation treatises written in the middle of the twentieth century. (The object of these manuals was essentially to present for pedagogical purposes the pronunciation of educated Parisians.)

Dialect II: Another type of pronunciation is similar to that of Dialect I, except that *mon, ton,* and *son* are denasalized. I have observed this type of pronunciation in speakers coming from the area of Lyons.

Dialect III: In a third dialect, across-the-board vowel denasalization is typical. This pronunciation is found in southern France.

With respect to Dialect I, Dialects II and III can thus be characterized by an increasing use of oral pronunciations. Dialect III appears to be stable, but the trend for Dialect II seems to be one of regression: the testimony of Vaudelin at the beginning of the eighteenth century, those of the first thirty years of the twentieth century, and those of the middle of the twentieth century show that the type of pronunciation characteristic of Dialect II used to have a much wider distribution than it does at present and that it has been gradually declining in favor of the type of pronunciation found in Dialect I.

Still considering Dialect I as a reference point, one finds two other dialects exhibiting a decreasing use of oral pronunciations:

Dialect IV: In this dialect, nasal vowels remain nasal in liaison, except for the adjective *bon.* This type of pronunciation is found in Quebec French, and it also seems to be an innovative trend in the area where Dialect I is spoken (see chap. iii).

Dialect V: Finally, there is a type of pronunciation where all nasal vowels remain nasal in liaison, even in the adjective *bon.* I have met native speakers of French from North Africa with this particular pronunciation; some Parisian speakers also seem to have it (see chap. iii).

Except for Dialect III, it thus seems that the tendency in contemporary French is for the nasal pronunciation of nasal vowels in liaison to take over.

IV.2.3. Summary

Variation has characterized the pronunciation of nasal vowels in liaison since the timid inception of vowel denasalization across words in the second half of the sixteenth century. This process operated in more general fashion in the seventeenth century, but apparently not for all speakers. From that time on, dialects with completely nasal and completely oral pronunciations seem to have coexisted, but the effects of vowel denasalization had probably ceased to spread by the eighteenth century. The selective application of vowel denasalization is definitely attested at the beginning of the eighteenth century; the existence of this type of dialect is also reported in the middle and at the end of the nineteenth century and in the twentieth century, with nasal pronunciations gradually tending to take over.

IV.3. Explanations and implications

The behavior of nasal vowels in liaison is not particularly puzzling in the dialects with completely oral or completely nasal pronunciations: the process of vowel denasalization applies across the board or not at all. The perplexing questions lie in the dialects where vowel denasalization takes place selectively, affecting certain words but not others: Are the various distributions of oral and nasal pronunciations due to random lexical diffusion, or is there some rationale behind the splits which occurred historically and which manifest themselves in contemporary dialects? My goals in this section are to present the regularities that characterize the selective application of vowel denasalization in liaison, to determine the linguistic correlates of these regularities, to account for the relations among the various dialects, and to examine the implications of the proposed explanations.

It is often argued that, diachronically, vowel quality was a governing factor in the application of both vowel nasalization and vowel denasalization. For example, Pope (1934) considered that vowel nasalization first affected low vowels and progressively spread to less open vowels until it reached high vowels, and that, at least word-internally, vowel denasalization took place in the reverse order. For nasal vowels in liaison, it might be similarly hypothesized that the quality of the vowels is a determining factor in the selective application of vowel denasalization. Whatever the merits of this phonetic wave hypothesis may be,[17] obviously it is not sufficient to account for the facts, since variations may occur within the domain of a given nasal vowel (cf. the vowel /ɔ̃/ in Dialects I and II). There must therefore be factors at work which are other than purely phonological. In order to study these factors independently of the phonetic dimension, I first neutralize phonetic quality by studying variations across words and across dialects within the domain of a given nasal vowel. I then return to a comparison of the behaviors of the different nasal vowels in liaison.

I begin with [ɔ̃], as in *bon, mon, ton, son,* and *on,* since this nasal vowel is the one that exhibits the most variability across words and

---

17. See Rochet (1976) for arguments against the wave theory of vowel nasalization and in favor of the hypothesis that all vowels were nasalized at the same time. See also Ruhlen (1979) for further discussion of the issue.

across dialects in its liaison pronunciation. Table 2 illustrates the distribution of the oral and nasal pronunciations of this vowel across words in the five contemporary dialects of French discussed at the end of the preceding section.

Table 2

Words / Dialects	V	IV and I	II	III
1. *bon ami*	ṼnV	VnV	VnV	VnV
2. *mon ami*	ṼnV	ṼnV	VnV	VnV
3. *on a mis*	ṼnV	ṼnV	ṼnV	VnV

Table 2 shows that the distribution of oral and nasal pronunciations is not random, but that a law of solidarity operates. The staircase broken line that separates the oral pronunciations (above the line) from the nasal pronunciations (below the line) indicates that if *on* is denasalized, then so are *mon* and *bon,* and if *mon* is denasalized, then so is *bon*; conversely, if *bon* is nasal, then so are *mon* and *on,* and if *mon* is nasal, then so is *on*. In other words, in any row in a given column, an oral pronunciation implies an oral pronunciation in the rows above, and a nasal pronunciation implies a nasal pronunciation in the rows below. *Bon* and *on* are at the extremes of this chain, and *mon* occupies an intermediate position. This regularity is true not only of the five contemporary dialects considered here; it is also true of the past dialects for which the relevant information is available. For example, toward the end of the sixteenth century, *on* is attested with a nasal pronunciation, but *bon* is attested with both a nasal and an oral pronunciation; at the beginning of the eighteenth century Vaudelin reported the absence of vowel denasalization in *on,* but its application in *bon* and *mon, ton, son*; the same split was indicated by Littré at the end of the nineteenth century; and in the first half of the twentieth century the vowel of *bon* is always given as oral in liaison, the vowel of *on* is always given as nasal, and in most instances the vowels of *mon, ton,* and *son* are given as variable.

It is unlikely that this pervasive regularity is due to chance. Interestingly, the law of solidarity which regulates the respective behaviors of *bon, mon,* and *on* with regard to their pronunciation in liaison correlates with linguistic properties. At one end of the spectrum, *bon* belongs to the grammatical class of noun modifiers known as adjectives; it is variable, and it exhibits a regular masculine/feminine morphophonological alternation ([bɔ̃]/[bɔn]) which phonetically corresponds to the alternation created by vowel denasalization in liaison. At the other end of the spectrum, *on* belongs to the class of pronouns; it is invariable, that is, it does not exhibit grammatically governed alternations; in other words, vowel denasalization in liaison does not create an independently existing alternation. *Mon* occupies an intermediate position: as a possessive adjective, it is a noun modifier, like *bon*, and it exhibits a masculine/feminine morphophonological alternation, like *bon*; however, this alternation is of the suppletive type (*mon/ma*) and does not match the alternation created by vowel denasalization in liaison; in this regard, *mon* thus falls into the same category as *on*.

It would therefore seem that, whereas the pronunciation of nasal vowels in liaison is not affected by grammatical properties in Dialects V and III, in Dialects I and II, on the other hand, these factors are crucial. In Dialect I, the application of vowel denasalization appears to be reinforced by the existence of a morphophonological alternation phonetically identical with the one created by the sandhi rule itself, so that *bon*, but not *mon* or *on*, receives an oral pronunciation in liaison. In Dialect II, a different grammatical distinction seems to operate: vowel denasalization affects all types of noun modifiers, whether they offer an independent matching morphophonological alternation or not; in this dialect, vowel denasalization is thus closer to being phonetically governed, but it is not completely so, since the pronoun *on*, not a noun modifier, is not affected. It is only in Dialect III that vowel denasalization across words actually applies without regard to grammatical factors and is thus purely phonetically determined. The grammatical distinctions are also irrelevant in Dialect V, where the process does not operate at all.

The hypothesis just presented claims that two essential grammatical factors contribute to the selective application of vowel denasalization in liaison: (i) the existence of an independent alternation phonetically matching that created by the sandhi rule; (ii) the distinction between words that are noun modifiers and those that are not.

This hypothesis accounts for the distinctions that are made *within* dialects. The relations that exist *among* dialects remain to be explained, in particular the already mentioned trend toward a nasal pronunciation evidenced in Dialects II, I, and IV: Dialect II tends to merge into Dialect I, Dialect I into Dialect IV, and Dialect IV into Dialect V. I now consider the connection between Dialects II and I (the connections among Dialects I, IV, and V are examined later).

In Dialect II the oral pronunciation of the nasal vowel [ɔ̃] is restricted to noun modifiers (*bon, mon*). This means that, at the surface phonetic level, the adjective *bon* has two allomorphs: [bɔ̃] (the form used for the masculine before consonant-initial words and at the pause) and [bɔn] (the form used for the masculine before vowel-initial words and for the feminine). On the other hand, the possessive adjective *mon* has three allomorphs: [mɔ̃] (the form used for the masculine before consonant-initial words and at the pause), [mɔn] (the form used for the masculine and the feminine before vowel-initial words), and [ma] (the form used for the feminine before consonant-initial words and at the pause). In the case of the possessive adjectives (but not in the case of the adjective *bon*), vowel denasalization thus introduces paradigmatic variation that is more extensive than that which exists independently because of gender distinctions. Vennemann's (1972*a*) principle that conceptual analogy tends to restore the paradigmatic uniformity destroyed by phonological changes explains the tendency for Dialect II to merge into Dialect I: the surface allomorphy of possessive adjectives is reduced through the replacement by its nasal counterpart of the oral vowel found in the liaison forms of *mon, ton, son*.

I now examine the liaison behavior of the other nasal vowels in the light of the hypothesis proposed above for [ɔ̃]. For the nasal vowel [ã], there is only the invariable word *en* to be considered. No comparison along relevant grammatical parameters can be made in this case independently of vowel quality, but it is indicative to observe that, in both past and contemporary dialects, *en* always behaves together with *on*, rather than with *bon* or *mon*. This is expected within the grammatically based hypothesis proposed to account for the selective application of vowel denasalization in liaison.

For the nasal vowel [ɛ̃], I examine the cases where the oral counterpart is [ɛ] (the other cases are considered later). The words of this class belong to two different grammatical categories: adverbs (*bien, rien*) and adjectives (e.g., *ancien*). For such words all the logical combinations of oral and nasal liaison pronunciations are attested, except the one where *bien* and *rien* are denasalized and adjectives like *ancien* remain nasal. This distribution, which is exactly parallel to that concerning *on* and *bon,* is accounted for by the hypothesis, since *ancien,* but not *bien* or *rien,* is a noun modifier exhibiting a morphophonological alternation that is phonetically identical with the alternation created by vowel denasalization.

In general, *bien* and *rien,* which are invariable words exhibiting no independent alternation matching that which vowel denasalization can potentially create, expectedly behave like *on* and *en.* In three reports, however, *bien* is given an oral pronunciation in liaison, whereas *on* and *en* are not (see Littré 1881, Grammont 1914, and Bruneau 1931).[18] This subtle distinction between the behavior of *bien* and that of *on/en* could perhaps be attributed to the phonetic quality of the nasal vowels, if it could be shown independently that [ɛ̃] is more susceptible to vowel denasalization than [ɔ̃] and [ã]. A more plausible explanation lies in the observation that the split between *bien* and *on/en* correlates with the fact that *bien* is actually a modifier, like adjectives, whereas *on* and *en* are not. The grammatically based hypothesis can naturally accommodate this explanation, if it is refined to recognize, between variable modifiers like *bon/ancien/mon* and invariable nonmodifiers like *on/en,* the existence of an intermediate category of invariable modifiers like *bien.*

On the basis of several grammatical parameters, words commonly considered simply to belong to different categories can actually be ranked on what may almost be regarded as a continuum. This grammatically based classification accounts for important aspects of the selective application of vowel denasalization in liaison. These results are summarized in table 3.

Table 3

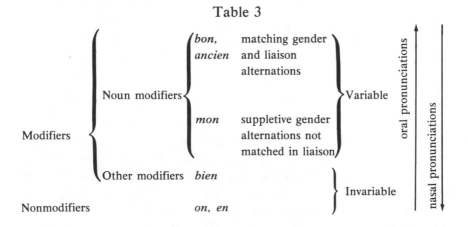

18. Littré and Grammont provide no information on the word *rien.* For Bruneau, an oral pronunciation is possible.

Another puzzle concerning the selective application of vowel denasalization in liaison has to do with the variations observed within the grammatical domain of noun modifiers, specifically adjectives and the determiners *un* and *aucun*. (I have already accounted for the difference between adjectives and possessive adjectives.) If noun modifiers are divided into categories based on the quality of the oral vowels that correspond to the nasal vowels, four classes emerge: 1. the *bon*-class ([ɔ̃]) ~ [ɔ]); 2. the *certain*-class ([ɛ̃] ~ [ɛ]); 3. the *un*-class (e.g., [œ̃] ~ [y]); and 4. the *fin*-class ([ɛ̃] ~ [i]). I will not consider category 4 any further, because adjectives in *-in* do not appear in prenominal position in the same productive fashion as the other words; the very few adjectives of this class which do appear in prenominal position are part of stock phrases such as *le divin enfant* [lədivinɑ̃fɑ̃] or *le malin esprit* [ləmalɛ̃nɛspri]. Category 3 is actually more complex than indicated by the alternation given; for the masculine indefinite article *un,* speakers have been reported to have the alternations [ɛ̃] ~ [ɛ] (Durand 1936:160–166) and [œ̃] ~ [œ] (Rousselot and Laclotte 1902; Martinon 1913; Dialect III); I have not been able to ascertain the existence of the alternation [ɛ̃] ~ [y].

Consideration of the liaison behavior of the first three categories of words in the five contemporary dialects previously established yields table 4.

Table 4

Words \ Dialects	V	IV	I and II	III
1. *bon ami*	ṼnV	VnV	VnV	VnV
2. *certain ami*	ṼnV	ṼnV	VnV	VnV
3. *un ami*	ṼnV	ṼnV	ṼnV	VnV

There are obvious regularities in the presentation of the facts given in table 4. The staircase broken line that separates the oral pronunciations (above the line) from the nasal pronunciations (below the line) reveals the same law of solidarity evidenced in table 2: in any row in a given column, a nasal pronunciation implies a nasal pronunciation in the rows below, and an oral pronunciation implies an oral pronunciation in the rows above. For the three categories of words considered, this pattern is not contradicted by past testimonies, but detailed relevant information did not become available until the beginning of the twentieth century; these past dialects follow the same general pattern as the contemporary ones. Thus, *bon* is always given an oral pronunciation in liaison; adjectives like *certain* are generally given an oral pronunciation too, with a few nasal pronunciations mentioned at the beginning of the century; and the vowel of *un* tends to be nasal.

As the testimonies of twentieth-century grammarians clearly establish, the first noun modifiers to succumb to a nasal pronunciation in liaison are those of category 3 in table 4, that is, *un, aucun, commun*. A number of factors seem to have contributed to this. Note that in the dialect where the denasalized vowel of these words is [y], the application of vowel denasalization creates the liaison alternation [œ̃] ~ [y]. The correspondence between the low-mid nasal vowel [œ̃] and the high oral vowel [y] is phonetically distant, compared with the relatively direct alternations [ɔ̃] ~ [ɔ] and [ɛ̃] ~ [ɛ] of categories 1 and 2. The import of this phonetic factor is underscored by the fact that the direct liaison alternation [œ̃] ~ [œ] apparently subsisted longer than the indirect liaison alternation [œ̃] ~ [y]. Thus, in the first thirty years of the twentieth century, all the grammarians' testimonies indicate that the alternation [œ̃] ~ [y] is dying or dead, but a few directly or indirectly mention the existence of the alternation [œ̃] ~ [œ] (Rousselot and Laclotte 1902; Martinon 1913; Bruneau 1931); this alternation is the one that I am aware of for Dialect III. The principle of minimum phonetic distance invoked here may be regarded as a case of conceptual analogy.

In areas where Dialects I and II are spoken, the disappearance of the [œ̃] ~ [œ] alternation may be related to the fact that it complicates the overall surface allomorphy of the indefinite article: [œ̃] and [œn] are used in the masculine, [yn] in the feminine. The disappearance of the nasal/oral liaison alternation with *un* may also be connected to the unrounding of [œ̃] into [ɛ̃]; a liaison alternation of the form [ɛ̃] ~ [y] would give rise to an even less direct phonetic correspondence than the liaison alternation [œ̃] ~ [y], and a liaison alternation of the form [ɛ̃] ~ [ɛ], although phonetically direct, also complicates the overall surface allomorphy of the indefinite article.

The elimination in liaison context of the denasalized [y]-versions of category 3 words may have another cause besides the minimum phonetic distance factor, at least if the adjective *commun* is excluded from consideration (perhaps with good reason since it does not productively appear in prenominal position). When adjectives like *bon* or *certain* occur before a masculine singular vowel-initial noun, they take on forms phonetically identical with those used for the feminine, but the gender of the noun is still unambiguously marked by the preceding indefinite article *un* or the definite article *le*. On the other hand, when *un* or *aucun* occurs before a masculine vowel-initial noun, it usually is the sole gender indicator, and the use of the denasalized form [yn] or [okyn] may create the impression of a gender error. The same goes for the word *chacun* in a phrase like *chacun un* 'one each' (masc.); *chacun* is the only gender marker and the use of the form [šakyn] may result in gender confusion (cf. *chacune un* [šakynœ] 'one each' (fem.)). This was noted in particular by Martinon (1913:389–390), who stated, in reference to Littré's pronunciation of *un homme* as [ynɔm]: "Cette prononciation a disparu à peu près complètement, à Paris du moins, chez les personnes instruites. Cela tient sans doute à ce que des confusions de genre se sont produites. Par exemple le peuple faisait *u-nomnibus* du féminin. Dès lors les personnes instruites ont craint peut-être qu'on ne les accusât de faire féminins des noms masculins, et l'usage s'est établi de faire la liaison sans décomposer: *un nhomme, un nami, un nun*." Nyrop's comment, cited above, that some speakers pronounce *un homme* [ynɔm], "tout comme si les hommes portaient des jupons" (1914:131), shows the possible validity of Martinon's theory. A personal experience further illustrates the plausibility of the gender confusion hypothesis. I remember my paternal grandmother, born toward the end of the nineteenth century, saying things like *un arbre* [ynarbr] or *un an* [ynã]. As a child I was puzzled by this use of [yn] instead of what I thought should have been [ɛn], and I considered then that my grandmother did not know the genders of nouns very well. It is interesting that I cannot remember any noun beginning in a consonant where she would make gender errors; nor can I remember a single instance when the confusion would involve a normally feminine noun that would have been masculine for her; in other words, her only "errors" occurred with vowel-initial masculine nouns. Obviously there was no error in gender, but simply vowel denasalization in liaison. At the time, however, my interpretation as a naive native speaker was to attribute this pronunciation to gender confusion. In sum, it is possible that, as suggested by Martinon, the denasalized pronunciation of *un* as [yn] disappeared because of the social pressure created by the wrong interpretation that it naturally suggested to many speakers. This functional and social factor should probably be viewed only as an element contributing to the demise of the denasalized [y]-versions of *un, aucun,* and *chacun,* rather than as the initiating cause of the change. This factor could have had an effect only when an alternative (nasal) pronunciation was already available, competing with the oral one, that is, when vowel denasalization in liaison was already regressing.[19]

The difference between categories 1 and 2 in table 4 remains to be accounted for. The last bastion where the oral pronunciation of nasal vowels in liaison subsists is the adjective *bon* (cf. Dialect IV). Note that *bon* is actually the only adjective in [ɔ̃] which occurs in prenominal position and which may therefore enter into liaison. It would thus not be unreasonable to presume that the masculine liaison form [bɔn] is not the result of the application of vowel denasalization, but rather is due to suppletion. This hypothesis provides a natural connection among Dialects I, IV, and V. The passage from Dialect I to Dialect IV can be explained by the principle of conceptual analogy invoked earlier: the elimination of the rule of vowel denasalization reduces surface allomorphy for masculine adjectives like *certain*; however, the elimination of the process does not affect *bon,* because the masculine liaison alternation [bɔ̃] ~ [bɔn] is suppletive. The passage from Dialect IV to Dialect V simply corresponds to the elimination of the suppletion itself.

In this section I have proposed explanations for the selective application of vowel denasalization in liaison. These explanations account for the distinctions that occur across words *within* dialects and for the relations that exist *among* dialects. Within dialects—that is, from a synchronic point of view—grammatical information, rather than purely phonological information, is of particular relevance. The distribution of oral and nasal pronunciations may thus depend on parameters such as whether or not a word is a modifier, whether or not it is a noun modifier, what type of gender variability is involved. Lexical constraints may in addition operate, limiting the range of occurrence of possible oral pronunciations within a given grammatical class. Across dialects—that is, from a diachronic perspective—the principles of conceptual analogy and minimum phonetic distance

19. As a partial explanation for the disappearance of the oral pronunciation of nasal vowels in liaison, the gender confusion hypothesis makes it more likely for vowel-initial adjectives like *ancien* than for consonant-initial adjectives like *certain* to occur with a nasal pronunciation when the definite article precedes, since *le* and *la* elide their (gender marking) vowels before vowel-initial words. I have no data bearing on this question.

contribute importantly to an explanation of both the instability of certain dialects and the directionality of the changes; the two principles tend to reduce differences between surface allomorphs.

This diachronic and dialectal study of nasal vowels in liaison indicates that liaison alternations between nasal and oral vowels were not purely phonological at least as early as Vaudelin's time, therefore that, for several centuries, nasal vowels have not been phonologically derivable from underlying /VN/ sequences, and thus that nasal vowels have long been lexical. In addition, the fact that vocalic nasal/oral alternations tend to be eliminated in liaison, but not in gender distinctions, confirms that these alternations are not of a uniform nature and that the phenomena of liaison and gender formation are to be treated differently if the account is to have psychological reality.

PART II
FINAL CONSONANTS

INTRODUCTION

The [V̄] ~ [VN] alternations examined in Part I are paralleled by [Ø] ~ [C] alternations, but the latter have an even wider range of occurrence when they are considered from a traditional classificatory perspective.

Like [V̄] ~ [VN] alternations, [Ø] ~ [C] alternations are found in gender distinctions among nouns and adjectives, in the conjugation of third-conjugation verbs, and in derivational morphology.

(i)   Gender distinctions:

(1)   (a) Adjectives:
   petit [pəti]/*petite* [pətit] 'little' (masc./fem.)
   bavard [bavar]/*bavarde* [bavard] 'talkative' (masc./fem.)
   gros [gro]/*grosse* [gros] 'big' (masc./fem.)
   long [lɔ̃]/*longue* [lɔ̃g] 'long' (masc./fem.)
   (b) Nouns:
   avocat [avɔka]/*avocate* [avɔkat] 'lawyer' (masc./fem.)
   chat [ša]/*chatte* [šat] 'cat' (masc./fem.)
   Danois [danwa]/*Danoise* [danwaz] 'Dane' (masc./fem.)
   lépreux [leprø]/*lépreuse* [leprøz] 'leper' (masc./fem.)

(ii)   Third-conjugation verbs:
(The examples are given in the third person)

(2)   Present indicative singular/plural:
   entend [ātā]/*entendent* [ātād] 'hear'
   sort [sɔr]/*sortent* [sɔrt] 'go out'
   dort [dɔr]/*dorment* [dɔrm] 'sleep'
   vit [vi]/*vivent* [viv] 'live'

(3) Present indicative/subjunctive:
entend [ātā]/*entende* [ātād] 'hear'
sort [sɔr]/*sorte* [sɔrt] 'go out'
dort [dɔr]/*dorme* [dɔrm] 'sleep'
vit [vi]/*vive*[viv] 'live'

(iii) Derivational morphology:

(4) Nouns/First-conjugation verbs:
drap [dra]/*draper* [drape] 'sheet'/'to drape'
chant [šã]/*chanter* [šãte] 'song'/'to sing'
filou [filu]/*filouter* [filute] 'swindler'/'to swindle'
sirop [siro]/*siroter* [sirɔte] 'syrup'/'to sip'
estomac [ɛstɔma]/*estomaquer* [ɛstɔmake] 'stomach'/
'to surprise'
escroc [ɛskro]/*escroquer* [ɛskrɔke] 'swindler'/'to swindle'
décès [desɛ]/*décéder* [desede] 'death'/'to die'
tracas [traka]/*tracasser* [trakase] 'worry'/'to worry'
tapis [tapi]/*tapisser* [tapise] 'carpet'/'to hang with tapestry'
accroc [akro]/*accrocher* [akrɔše] 'tear'/'to catch and tear'
nid [ni]/*nicher* [niše] 'nest'/'to nest'
impôt [ɛ̃po]/*imposer* [ɛ̃poze] 'tax'/'to tax'
bagou [bagu]/*bagouler* [bagule] 'gift of gab'/'to talk
constantly'
fusil [fyzi]/*fusiller* [fyzije] 'gun'/'to execute by shooting'
outil [uti]/*outiller* [utije] 'tool'/'to equip with tools'

(5) Word derivation by nonzero suffixation:
abricot [abriko]/*abricotier* [abrikɔtje] 'apricot'/'apricot tree'
bijou [bižu]/*bijoutier* [bižutje] 'jewel'/'jeweler'
chalut [šaly]/*chalutier* [šalytje] 'trawl'/'trawler'
lait [lɛ]/*laitier* [letje] 'milk'/'milkman'
tabac [taba]/*tabatière*[tabatjɛr] 'tobacco'/'tobacco pouch'
mari [mari]/*marital* [marital] 'husband'/'marital'
vie [vi]/*vital* [vital] 'life'/'vital'
soldat [sɔlda]/*soldatesque* [sɔldatɛsk] 'soldier'/'soldierlike'

The instances of liaison which exhibit a [Ø] ~ [C] alternation are more widespread than those with a [Ṽ] ~ [VN] or [Ṽ] ~ [ṼN] alternation. In both cases there are, for example, liaison with masculine singular adjectives and liaison with prepositions and adverbs, but [Ø] ~ [C] alternations are additionally found in plural liaison and verb liaison.

(iv) Liaison with masculine singular adjectives:

(6) *un petit écureuil* [ɛ̃ptitekyrœj] 'a little squirrel'
(cf. *un petit tamanoir* [ɛ̃ptitamanwar] 'a little anteater')
un gros ustensil [ɛ̃grozystãsil] 'a big utensil'
(cf. *un gros tonneau* [ɛ̃grotono] 'a big barrel')
un long été [ɛ̃lɔ̃gete] 'a long summer'
(cf. *un long printemps* [ɛ̃lɔ̃prɛ̃tã] 'a long spring')

(v) Liaison with prepositions and adverbs:

(7) *dans une heure* [dãzynœr] 'in an hour'
(cf. *dans deux heures* [dãdøzœr] 'in two hours')
après une heure [aprɛzynœr] 'after an hour'
(cf. *après deux heures* [aprɛdøzœr] 'after two hours')
trop important [tropɛ̃pɔrtã] 'too important'
(cf. *trop patient* [tropasjã] 'too patient')
assez important [asezɛ̃pɔrtã] 'important enough'
(cf. *assez patient* [asepasjã] 'patient enough')

(vi) Plural liaison:

(8) *les enfants* [lɛzãfã] 'the children'
(cf. *les parents* [lɛparã] 'the parents')
les petits animaux [lɛptizanimo] 'little animals'
(cf. *les petits crocodiles* [lɛptikrɔkɔdil] 'little crocodiles')
les athlètes américains [lɛzatlɛtzamerikɛ̃] 'American athletes'
(cf. *les athlètes français* [lɛzatlɛtfrãsɛ] 'French athletes')

(vii) Verb liaison:

(9) *il est anglais* [ilɛtãglɛ] 'he is English'
(cf. *il est danois* [ilɛdanwa] 'he is Danish')
il vit en France [ilvitãfrãs] 'he lives in France'
(cf. *il vit dans le Maine* [ilvidãlmɛn] 'he lives in Maine')
vous chantez agréablement [vušãtezagreabləmã] 'you sing pleasantly'
(cf. *vous chantez mal* [vušãtemal] 'you sing badly')
a-t-elle raison? [atɛlrezɔ̃] 'is she right?'
(cf. *as-tu raison?* [atyrezɔ̃] 'are you right?')

Other types of [Ø] ~ [C] alternations are governed by special conditions which do not affect [Ṽ] ~ [VN] alternations. For instance, the cardinal numbers *six* 'six', *huit* 'eight', and *dix* 'ten' exhibit no final consonant before a consonant-initial word, but they have one before vowel-initial words and at the pause:

(10) *huit familles* [ɥifamij] 'eight families'
  huit enfants [ɥitãfã] 'eight children'
  ils sont huit [ilsɔ̃ɥit] 'there are eight of them'

Nouns like *oeuf* 'egg', *boeuf* 'ox', and *os* 'bone' have a final consonant in the singular but not in the plural:

(11) *un oeuf* [ɛ̃nœf] 'an egg' *un os* [ɛ̃nɔs] 'a bone'
  des oeufs [dɛzø] 'eggs' *des os* [dɛzo] 'bones'

No [Ṽ] ~ [VN] alternation has distributions of the types illustrated in (10) and (11).

A basic issue concerning [Ø] ~ [C] alternations is whether they are to be accounted for uniformly or not. Since the alternations cut across many different morphological distinctions, and in some cases do not correspond to varying grammatical conditions, a uniform treatment must necessarily be phonological. Such a view has been advocated within the framework of generative grammar in numerous studies by Schane, Dell, and Selkirk. Basically, it is assumed that the consonants that alternate with zero are present underlyingly, and that a general phonologically conditioned process of final-consonant deletion eliminates them in the desired cases. This analysis is parallel to the abstract generative account of French nasal vowels, and I therefore similarly refer to it as the abstract, or standard, generative treatment of final consonants.

With the notable exception of Togeby (1951), where the same abstract approach is advocated, nongenerative accounts have generally assumed that [Ø] ~ [C] alternations do not constitute a uniform phonological phenomenon. Thus, in traditional treatises on French pronunciation (e.g., Grammont 1914; Fouché 1959), the phenomenon of liaison receives ample coverage, but the [Ø] ~ [C] alternations found in inflectional and derivational morphology are not even mentioned as a possibly related manifestation of the same process. American and Praguian structuralists considered that some of the [Ø] ~ [C] alternations are grammatically governed. For example, Bloomfield (1933:217) suggested that masculine adjectives be morphophonologically derived from the feminine forms; Gougenheim (1935:79) stated that "L'alternance consonne ∞ zero phonique joue un rôle dans la flexion des substantifs et des adjectifs et dans la conjugaison des verbes"; Hall (1948) recognized "the purely phonetic positions" (19) in which the alternations occur, but his classification otherwise reflects the crucial relevance of morphological factors.

Two divergent views of [Ø] ~ [C] alternations can thus be distinguished: one considers them as phonologically determined in their entirety, and the other regards them as in part morphologically governed. Despite this essential opposition, these analyses share some important characteristics: they include at their deepest levels of representation (underlying or morphophonemic) the consonants that alternate with zero, and consequently they assume the existence of some form of consonant-deletion process.

In the last five years or so, a third type of analysis has been developing, within the general framework of generative phonology but under the influence of the concrete views presented, for instance, by Kiparsky (1968a), Skousen (1975), and the proponents of natural generative phonology (e.g., Vennemann 1971; Hooper 1976). This approach, independently initiated by Klausenburger (1974) and Tranel (1974b, 1976b) and pursued in other studies (e.g., Kaye and Morin 1977; Klausenburger 1978a, b; Tranel 1978b), rejects the uniform phonological account of [Ø] ~ [C] alternations, like American and Praguian structuralism, but views consonant insertion, rather than consonant deletion, as an explanation for certain types of [Ø] ~ [C] alternations. The additional issue thus raised about the treatment of [Ø] ~ [C] alternations is not actually a novel opposition between consonant deletion and consonant insertion. For instance, concerning [Ø] ~ [C] gender alternations in nouns and adjectives, Bloomfield (1933:217) and Harris (1951:168–169) advocated taking the feminine forms as basic and deriving the masculine forms by deletion; Durand (1936), on the other hand, considered that "le féminin se forme en ajoutant des phonèmes au masculin pris pour base et ce phonème est une consonne" (32). Solutions mingling deletion and insertion have also been proposed. For example, Tranel (1974b, 1976b) suggested morphophonological consonant deletion for gender alternations and liaison with masculine singular adjectives, but consonant insertion for plural liaison, and Dumas (1978) even proposed a mixed analysis for plural liaison. For others (e.g., Schane 1978a), the deletion versus insertion issue may be nothing but a pseudocontroversy between notational variants.

In the last ten to fifteen years the standard generative analysis of final consonants has been the prevailing view, but attempts such as the recent ones mentioned above have provided the seeds of an interesting challenge.

The concrete analysis of [Ṽ] ~ [VN] alternations motivated in Part I and the close parallelism between the two types of alternation dictate and justify a similar treatment for [Ø] ~ [C] alternations. Here, however, I offer independent arguments substantiating the rejection of the abstract generative analysis of final consonants and the adoption of a concrete treatment.

The standard generative analysis of final consonants advocated by Schane, Dell, and Selkirk is comprehensive and explicit: it accounts for a wide range of static data, and the proposed formalizations make very precise claims. As mentioned above, it can also be considered as the established analysis. I therefore use it as a reference point. To this effect, I summarize it and point out its basic characteristics in chapter v. In chapter vi, I first criticize the abstract generative analysis by considering in detail the question of plural marking on nouns and adjectives in French and the related phenomenon of plural liaison. A central section presents arguments against the major phonological process of final-consonant deletion. Second, positive evidence is provided in favor of a treatment of plural liaison as /z/-insertion. In chapter vii, I extend the insertion analysis to other cases of liaison, and finally I account for the remaining [Ø] ~ [C] alternations that characterize inflectional and derivational morphology.

V

THE STANDARD GENERATIVE ANALYSIS

V.1. Basic claims

The abstract generative analysis of final consonants assumes that in all cases of [Ø] ~ [C] alternations, the long form is basic and the short form is derived. Mediating between the two is a phonological process of final-consonant deletion, which operates before a consonant-initial morpheme separated by a morpheme boundary (a) or a word boundary (b), and before two word boundaries (c):

(1) C → Ø / — +C   (a) e.g., *de petits écureuils*[1]
                         [dəptizekyrœj] 'small squirrels'
     — # C   (b) e.g., *un petit banc* [ɛ̃ptibɑ̄]
                         'a small bench'
     — # #   (c) e.g., *il est petit* [ilɛpti]
                         'he is small'

This analysis makes the important claim that all [Ø] ~ [C] alternations are to be uniformly accounted for and that the nature of the relation is purely phonological. It is also claimed that the consonant-deletion process is major.

To explain the numerous cases where a consonant opaquely appears at the surface phonetic level in the deletion environments specified in (1) (cf. the examples provided in (2)),

(2) (a)   *six* [sis] 'six'
          oeuf [œf] 'egg'
    (b)   *sept* [sɛt] 'seven'
          sept fois [sɛtfwa] 'seven times'

---

1. The plural morpheme /z/ is assumed to be attached with a morpheme boundary. For a different view see Tranel (1977*c*) and chapter vi, below.

      avec [avɛk] 'with'

      atlas [atlas] 'atlas'

(c) *honnête* [ɔnɛt] 'honest'

      honnêtement [ɔnɛtmã] 'honestly'

      honnête marchand [ɔnɛtmaršã] 'honest merchant'

      pilote [pilɔt] 'pilot'

(d) *petite* [ptit] 'small' (fem.)

      petite fenêtre [ptitfənɛtr] 'small window'

      petites étoiles [ptitzetwal] 'small stars'

(e) *il achète* [ilašɛt] 'he buys'

      qu'il sorte [kilsɔrt] 'that he leave'

it is assumed that the phonetic presence of these final consonants is either exceptional (e.g., (2a–b)) or due to the underlying existence of final schwas, which are deleted by late rules extrinsically ordered after final-consonant deletion in counterfeeding fashion (e.g., (2c–e)) (see sec. V.3.3.).

The basic claims of this analysis of final consonants are thus the same as those made in the abstract generative treatment of nasal vowels (cf. chap. i). A major phonological process is posited which uniformly accounts for a wide array of static data and crucially rests on the postulation of final schwas and on extrinsic rule ordering. The only difference between the two processes is that final-consonant deletion is not taken to apply morpheme-internally, whereas vowel nasalization was supposed to.

V.2. Basic motivation

The basic motivation for the abstract analysis of final consonants is closely connected to the evaluation measure of generative phonology (the simplicity metric). From a purely formal perspective, there is obviously no account preferable to one that handles all [Ø] ~ [C] alternations in a unified way. Schane (1968*b*) and Dell (1973*a, b*) particularly emphasize this aspect of the treatment in motivating the process of final-consonant deletion and the postulation of final schwas (see chap. viii for a discussion of the issue of final schwas). For example, Schane states: "Final schwas are structurally imperative if the consonant deletion rule is to operate in the *simplest* fashion" (156); "a mass of morphological facts can be *easily* accounted for if 'e muets' are postulated in the underlying representations. These underlying 'e muets' allow *generalizing* rules to cover forms which may at first appear as separate unrelated phenomena" (163) (emphases mine). Similarly, Dell comments that the analysis prevents the complications that obfuscate certain regularities in other solutions.

V.3. Formalizations

The standard generative analysis of final consonants has gone through various formal proposals and refinements. It is useful to consider them here, however briefly, not only because they reveal the approach itself but also because they reflect general preoccupations of a formal and substantive nature in linguistic theory, such as notational conventions, the role of syntactic structure in phonological operations, and the question of exceptions.

V.3.1. The formalization of the process of consonant deletion
V.3.1.1. Schane (1968a)

The first generative formulation of consonant deletion was proposed by Schane. In Schane (1968a:chap. 1), two separate rules account for [Ø] ~ [C] alternations:

(i) Truncation, which formally groups together the absence of liaison and the operation of elision (e.g., *petit camarade*/pǝtit#kamarad/ [pǝtikamarad] 'little friend'; *l'arbre*/lǝ#arbr/[larbr] 'the tree').

(ii) Final-consonant deletion, which applies in phrase-final position (e.g., *il est petit* [ilɛpǝti] 'he is small'), as well as under various grammatical and stylistic conditions (e.g., "optionally in a plural noun," hence *des camarades anglais* [dɛkamarad(z)ãglɛ] 'English friends').

These two rules apply cyclically, with truncation ordered before final-consonant deletion.

An additional rule of consonant deletion was postulated by Schane (1968a), namely, prefinal-consonant deletion (88):

(3) C → Ø / — C #

This rule serves to account for alternations such as those of (4):

(4) *respect* [rɛspɛ]/*respectable* [rɛspɛktabl] 'respect'/'respectable'
 sept [sɛt]/*septante* [sɛptãt] 'seven'/'seventy'

Prefinal-consonant deletion must precede final-consonant deletion to avoid being bled. It is assumed to follow truncation, presumably to ensure that it always affects the same consonant in a given word, whether it is singular or plural. The derivation of *respects* [rɛspɛ] 'respects' shows the operation of the three rules:

(5) *respects*   /rɛspɛkt+z/
    truncation   rɛspɛk +z
    prefinal-consonant deletion   rɛspɛ +z
    final-consonant deletion   rɛspɛ
                                            [rɛspɛ]

The main characteristics that distinguish this early generative formulation of consonant deletion from its descendants are that consonant truncation and final-consonant deletion are completely separate processes, and that the latter incorporates nonphonological (grammatical and stylistic) information. These aspects of the analysis were later argued against and abandoned by their own author (Schane 1974).

V.3.1.2. Schane (1974)

Schane (1974) argued that liaison and elision should not be collapsed into a truncation schema, but rather that consonant truncation and final-consonant deletion should be notationally combined.

In addition, following others (Milner 1967; Dell 1970), Schane assumed that "liaison is a consequence of the number of word boundaries" (96), and that prior to the application of the phonological rules, various conventions and readjustment rules combine to leave one word boundary in liaison cases, and two otherwise (see Selkirk 1972 for details and sec. V.3.2. for a summary).

The main results of these revisions are that the cycle can be dispensed with and that "final consonant deletion can be formulated uniquely in phonological terms" (97), as shown in (6):

(6) $C \rightarrow \emptyset$ / — [-seg] $\begin{cases} C \ (a) \\ \# \ (b) \end{cases}$

V.3.1.3. Dell (1970)

Owing to his rule of liaison (7),

(7) C # V
    1 2 3 $\Longrightarrow$ 2 1 3

Dell (1970) was able to collapse completely consonant truncation and final-consonant deletion and to eliminate the need for the rule of prefinal-consonant deletion:

(8) $C \rightarrow \emptyset$ / — C_o #

This proposal, which has been shown to be inadequate on multiple grounds (see Selkirk 1972; Tranel 1974*b*; sec. II.3.3.1. above), was not retained by Dell (1973*b*).

V.3.1.4. Dell (1973*b*)

Dell (1973*b*) postulated the following three rules of consonant deletion,

(9) $C \rightarrow \emptyset / - + C$

(10) $C \rightarrow \emptyset / - \# C$

(11) $C \rightarrow \emptyset / - \# \#$

which he collapsed into schema (12):

(12) $C \rightarrow \emptyset / - \left\{ \begin{matrix} \left\{ \begin{matrix} + \\ \# \end{matrix} \right\} C \\ \# \ \# \end{matrix} \right\}$ (a)

                                 (b)

(12) differs from Schane's schema (6) only with respect to the amount of collapsing performed. The two formulations are otherwise equivalent. As in Schane (1968*a*), consonant truncation (i.e., part (a) in both schemata) must be ordered before final-consonant deletion (i.e., part (b) in both schemata), since final-consonant deletion does not bleed truncation, as shown in (13):

(13) *petits* 'small' (masc., pl.)

    (a)   /pətit + z/

           consonant truncation   pəti + z

           final-consonant deletion   pəti

                                      [pəti]

    (b)   /pətit + z/

           final-consonant deletion   pətit

           consonant truncation   ———

                               *[pətit]

Also, both schemata make necessary the postulation of the rule of prefinal-consonant deletion proposed by Schane (1968*a*).

The need for this rule actually creates a problem for the collapsing of consonant truncation and final-consonant deletion, since prefinal-consonant deletion is best ordered between consonant truncation and final-consonant deletion (see sec. V.3.1.1.). This problem can be solved in a variety of ways. First, if it is assumed that the plural morpheme is attached by means of a word boundary rather than a morpheme boundary (as argued in Tranel 1977*c* and in chap. vi below), then prefinal-consonant deletion can be ordered before consonant truncation and final-consonant deletion while consistently deleting the same consonant in a given word, whether it is singular or plural. Alternatively, the need for the rule of prefinal-consonant deletion could be altogether avoided by allowing the schemata to apply iteratively from right to left, or, as in Selkirk (1972), by including C_0 in the environment immediately after the dash. The latter changes would also obviate the necessity to order extrinsically consonant truncation and final-consonant deletion.[2]

V.3.1.5. Selkirk (1972)

Selkirk (1972) similarly recognized the existence of the two processes of consonant truncation and final-consonant deletion, but she ultimately formulated them after Halle's (1971) suggestion concerning the role of word boundaries in rules,

(14) $C \rightarrow \emptyset$ / [# X — C_0 [-seg] C_1 V X #]

(15) $C \rightarrow \emptyset$ / [# X — C_0 #]

or, in collapsed form:

(16) $C \rightarrow \emptyset$ / [# X — C_0 ([-seg] C_1 V X) #]

The presence of C_0 and V in these rules is rendered necessary by the derivation of words like *petits*. If C_0 and V were not present in the environment of (16), truncation (the longest expansion of the schema) would apply first and delete the final /t/; but since truncation and final-consonant deletion are disjunctively ordered (by the parenthesis notation), final-consonant deletion could not operate to delete the plural marker /z/, hence the ungrammatical output *[pətiz]. The presence of V makes truncation inapplicable and final-consonant deletion eligible to apply; final-consonant deletion must now delete both the /t/ and the /z/; this is made possible by the presence of C_0. The presence of C_0 in the truncation rule is justified by the generation of phrases like *respects amicaux* /rɛspɛkt+z#amiko/ [rɛpɛzamiko] 'friendly respects'.

Selkirk's solution thus makes slightly different claims from those attached to Schane's (1974) and Dell's (1973*b*) schemata. According to the latter two, consonant truncation and final-consonant deletion are conjunctively and extrinsically ordered, whereas Selkirk's proposal is that they are disjunctively and intrinsically ordered. Also, in the derivation of words like *petits,* the elimination of the same consonant (/t/) is accomplished in Selkirk's system either by final-consonant deletion (as in *ils sont petits* [ilsɔ̃pəti] 'they are small') or by consonant truncation (as in *petits amis* [pətizami] 'little friends'); but in Schane's and Dell's systems, the deletion of this consonant is con-

---

2. This unordering might, however, create problems in the treatment of words like *oeuf* /œf/ [œf]/*oeufs* /œf+z/ [ø] 'egg'/'eggs', which are considered to be exceptions to final-consonant deletion but regular with respect to consonant truncation. In the derivation of the plural form, final-consonant deletion cannot be allowed to operate before consonant truncation; if it did, the /f/ could not be deleted; rather, consonant truncation must apply before final-consonant deletion (cf. sec. V.3.3.).

sistently performed by consonant truncation. Finally, Selkirk's schema (16) incorporates the effect of Schane's (1968a) rule of prefinal-consonant deletion, which is not true of Schane's schema (6) or Dell's schema (12).

V.3.2. The role of syntactic structure in liaison

The importance of the effect of syntactic structure on the phenomenon of liaison has long been recognized by traditional grammarians. In the framework of generative grammar, a number of authors (e.g., Milner 1967, 1973; Dell 1970; Schane 1974) have assumed that this type of information could be made available to the phonological component by the intermediary of the boundaries posited between words.

Selkirk (1972) provided detailed formal proposals to predict along these lines the syntactic contexts in which liaison could occur (see also Selkirk 1974). Her theory is that "the phonological phenomena characteristic of liaison operate when just one word boundary, #, separates one word from the next" (208–209), and that universal conventions on word boundaries and French-specific readjustment rules determine where there will be one or two word boundaries in the string.

Two conventions are assumed to govern the distribution of word boundaries universally:

(17) The boundary # is automatically inserted at the beginning and end of every string dominated by a major category, i.e., by one of the lexical categories "noun," "verb," "adjective," or by a category such as "sentence," "noun phrase," "verb phrase," which dominates a lexical category (Chomsky and Halle 1968:366).

(18) In a sequence W $\#]_X \#]_Y$ Z

or Z $_Y[\# \ _X[\# $ W, where Y $\neq$ S

delete the "inner" word boundary (Selkirk 1972:12; 1974: 578).

The first convention "defines where one will find word boundaries in surface structure. In particular, it predicts that nonlexical categories such as articles, complementizers, prepositions, modals, etc. are not flanked by word boundaries." The second convention "limits the number of word boundaries in a sequence; it eliminates long strings of word boundaries in surface structure." "The combined effect of conventions [(17)] and [(18)] is . . . that two words in surface structure may be separated by either zero, one, or, at most, two word boundaries" (Selkirk 1974:577–578).

These universal conventions account without further machinery for a number of liaison types which have been traditionally categorized as obligatory or assumed to be able to occur in any style of speech, including that of "conversation familière" (Selkirk's Style I). A few examples are given in (19):

(19) (a) Liaison with determiners:

un arbre [ɛ̃narbr] 'a tree'
ses amis [sɛzami] 'his friends'
les étranges fantômes [lɛzetrãžfãtom] 'the strange ghosts'
ces éminents savants [sɛzeminãsavã] 'these eminent scholars'

(b) Liaison involving clitic pronouns:

ils arrivent [ilzariv] 'they are coming'
chantait-il? [šãtɛtil] 'was he singing?'
allez-y [alezi] 'go there'
mettez-les-y [metelezi] 'place them there'

(c) Liaison with monosyllabic (nonlexical) prepositions and adverbs:

dans un fauteuil [dãzɛ̃fotœj] 'in an armchair'
sous une table [suzyntabl] 'under a table'
très intéressant [trɛzɛ̃teresã] 'very interesting'
plus important [plyzɛ̃pɔrtã] 'more important'

(d) Liaison with monosyllabic auxiliaries:

Paul est amoureux [pɔlɛtamurø] 'Paul is in love'
vous êtes arrivé [vuzɛtzarive] 'you have arrived'
je suis entré [žəsɥizãtre] 'I came in'
elles ont osé [ɛlzɔ̃toze] 'they dared'

An adequate description of Style I, however, requires the postulation of two French-specific readjustment rules to explain the obligatory liaison between an adjective and a noun and the absence of liaison after a polysyllabic nonlexical item. These two cases are illustrated in (20):

(20) (a) Liaison between adjective and noun:

un grand homme [ɛ̃grãtɔm] 'a great man'
de gros animaux [dəgrozanimo] 'big animals'

(b) Absence of liaison with polysyllabic nonlexical prepositions and adverbs:

pendant une heure [pãdã(t)ynœr] 'for an hour'
après une épidémie [aprɛ(z)ynepidemi] 'after an

epidemic'
assez intéressant [ase(z)ẽteresã] 'interesting enough'
(c) Absence of liaison with polysyllabic auxiliaries:
Paul était amoureux [pɔletɛ(t)amurø] 'Paul was in love'
vous étiez arrivé [vuzetje(z)arive] 'you had arrived'
j'étais entré [žetɛ(z)ãtre] 'I had come in'
elles avaient osé [ɛlzavɛ(t)oze] 'they had dared'

The effect of the first rule, the Adjective-Noun Rule, is to reduce to one the two word boundaries that the universal conventions would produce between the adjective and the noun. The second rule, the Polysyllabic Non-Lexical Category Rule, in fact provides between a polysyllabic nonlexical preposition, adverb, or auxiliary and the following word two word boundaries where the universal conventions would place only one.

Because it is generally claimed that the liaison types accounted for so far appear in any style of speech, Selkirk refers to them as "basic." The additional liaison types that occur in the language are dependent on stylistic factors; as speech becomes more elevated, a progressively richer repertoire of "stylistic" liaison types is allowed. These styles are characterized by different grammars from that of Style I. Thus, the grammar of Style II ("conversation soignée") does not contain the Polysyllabic Non-Lexical Category Rule, thereby permitting the occurrence of liaison in the examples of (20b–c), and it includes a "generalization" of the Adjective-Noun Rule, the Lexical Specifier Rule, which produces one word boundary instead of two between adjectives or adverbs and the words they modify, thus allowing the liaison types illustrated in (20a) and (21).

(21) Liaison with lexical adverbs:
extrêmement amusant [ɛkstrɛmmãtamyzã] 'extremely funny'
suffisamment attentif [syfizamãtatãtif] 'sufficiently attentive'

For Style III ("lecture et discours"), the grammar additionally contains the X-Comp Rule, whose effect is to reduce from two to one the number of word boundaries between inflected nouns, adjectives, or verbs and their complements, thus yielding liaison in the cases illustrated in (22):[3]

---

3. This brief summary contains the essence of Selkirk's proposals for handling the syntax of liaison. It does not do justice to many interesting and controversial aspects of the analysis (e.g., the role of traces; cf. Postal and Pullum 1978, Tranel 1978a). Also omitted from consideration here are the disagreements one might have regarding Selkirk's classification of permitted and nonpermitted liaison occurrences.

(22) (a) Noun + Complement:
  des gens obscurs [dežãzɔpskyr] 'obscure people'
  des robes en papier [dɛrɔbzãpapje] 'paper dresses'
(b) Adjective + Complement:
  doués en mathématiques [dwezãmatematik] 'gifted in mathematics'
  fidèles à leurs manies [fidɛlzalœrmani] 'faithful to their habits'
(c) Verb + Complement:
  il donnait un cours [ildɔnɛtẽkur] 'he was giving a course'
  vous écriviez à Paul [vuzekrivjezapɔl] 'you were writing to Paul'

The basic claim of this analysis is that universal and language-specific conventions on the distribution of word boundaries mediate between the syntax and the phonology. The formal consequence of this assumption is that consonant deletion can be formulated without directly referring to syntactic contexts and morphological markings. This is consistent with the claim maintained in the abstract generative analysis of final consonants that [Ø] ~ [C] alternations are, uniformly and exclusively, phonologically conditioned. In fact, the purely phonological treatment of final consonants crucially depends on the type of encoding performed by the word-boundary conventions proposed by Selkirk.

A perhaps less obvious and no doubt less central claim of Selkirk's proposals is that the grammar of Style II is less complex than those of Styles I and III. It is less complex than that of Style III since it contains one less rule, the X-Comp Rule. It is less complex than that of Style I, because it does not include the Polysyllabic Non-Lexical Category Rule, and its Lexical Specifier Rule is a more general version of Style I's Adjective-Noun Rule. The relative formal complexities of the grammars of Styles II and III naturally correlate with the observed general decline of liaison, but the same expected relation does not hold between the grammars of Styles I and II.

It should finally be observed that Selkirk's language-specific word-boundary readjustment rules generally result in comparatively stronger boundaries between words as speech becomes more casual and comparatively weaker boundaries as speech becomes more careful. This is paradoxical, because phonetic interactions between words commonly increase as speech becomes more casual and decrease as

speech becomes more careful, thus indicating that boundaries between words are comparatively weaker in casual speech and stronger
in careful speech.

V.3.3. Pronounced final consonants

As mentioned earlier, final consonants are pronounced in environments other than a single boundary followed by a vowel-initial morpheme. Such cases contradict, at least on the surface, the existence of
the major phonological process of consonant deletion given in (1).

When the pronounced consonants are followed by an *e* in the orthography, the proponents of the abstract generative treatment of
final consonants have invariably assumed that there is, correspondingly, an underlying final schwa present which protects the preceding
consonant from the effect of the consonant-deletion process. This
schwa may be a morphological marker (e.g., the feminine morpheme,
as in (2d); the thematic vowel of first conjugation verbs, or the subjunctive marker, as in (2e)), or it may be part of the lexical representation of words (e.g., (2c)).

When there is no *e* in the orthography, different authors have
adopted different solutions. Some continue to correlate underlying
representations with spelling and consider that these words are exceptions. The correlation, implicitly assumed by Schane, is explicitly
acknowledged by Selkirk (1972:328): "the spelling does reflect a division in the vocabulary . . . consonant-final words which are also
consonant-final in the spelling must be regarded as underlyingly
consonant-final and thus exceptions to either truncation or final consonant deletion." On the other hand, Dell (1970:60–62) assumed that
all words with a phonetic final consonant had underlying final schwas.
Dell (1973*b*:189 n. 20) modified this extreme position, recognizing the
necessary existence of certain exceptions.

Lexical items may be exceptions to consonant deletion in various
ways. First, there are words that are exceptions to final-consonant deletion, but not to truncation. As illustrated in the introduction to Part
II, the most notable examples are the numerals *six* /sis/ 'six', *huit*
/ɥit/ 'eight', and *dix* /dis/ 'ten', and the nouns *oeuf* /œf/ 'egg', *boeuf*
/bœf/ 'ox', and *os* /ɔs/ 'bone'. The former lose their final consonants
before a single word boundary followed by a consonant-initial morpheme (i.e., truncation applies), and they keep them not only before
a single word boundary followed by a vowel, but also before two word
boundaries; the latter lose their final consonants before the plural

marker /z/ (by truncation), but not in the singular (i.e., when they are followed by two word boundaries). This type of exception shows that a final schwa cannot be automatically postulated whenever a final consonant appears at the surface phonetic level.

Formally, words such as *six* and *oeuf* are thus lexically marked [–final consonant deletion]. Cases like *oeufs* [ø] (from /œf+z/) create a problem for Selkirk's (1972) formalization, as she pointed out herself (315). Recall that her truncation rule (14) is inapplicable in the derivation of this word, at least when no vowel follows the plural marker /z/ in a liaison context; her rule of final-consonant deletion (15) must therefore delete both the /z/ and the /f/; but it cannot delete the /f/, since the word has been marked as an exception to the rule (because of the singular *oeuf* [œf]). In the formulations proposed by Schane (1974) and by Dell (1973*b*), the problem is avoided owing to the conjunctive ordering of consonant truncation before final-consonant deletion.

There are also lexical items that are claimed to be exceptions to both truncation and final-consonant deletion (cf. (2b)). The question is whether these words are in fact exceptions or whether they have a final lexical schwa. Selkirk (1972:329–330) and Dell (1973*b*:189 n. 20) have argued that the behavior of such items before a so-called h-aspiré word is a reliable test to make a determination. For instance, they claim that before an h-aspiré word, *sept* [sɛt] 'seven' is pronounced without a schwa (e.g., *sept haies* 'seven hurdles'), whereas *cette* [sɛt] 'this' (fem.) is pronounced with a schwa (e.g., *cette haie* 'this hurdle'); *sept* is consequently assumed not to contain a final schwa, and it must therefore be an exception to both consonant truncation and final-consonant deletion (for further discussion see sec. VI.3.3.6. and Part III).

It is interesting, and rather perplexing, that no words are exceptions to truncation but are regular with respect to final-consonant deletion. Schane (1968*a*:9) captured this fact by a redundancy rule stating that "a morpheme which is an exception to the rule for truncation is also an exception to the rule for final consonant deletion."

Finally, there are exceptions that are dependent on the phonological ending of words. For example, it is generally considered that liquids and glides do not delete in word-final position; this is often incorporated directly in the rules themselves (cf. Schane 1968*a*; Dell 1970, 1973*b*; Selkirk 1974). It is also frequently pointed out that certain obstruents, for instance /k/ and /f/, are not normally subject to deletion (Dell 1970:62).

Schane (1973*b*) addressed himself to this particular issue in detail. He proposed that consonant deletion be very generally expressed by the following "natural" rule (826),

(23) $C \rightarrow \emptyset / - ([-\text{seg}]) \begin{Bmatrix} C \\ // \end{Bmatrix} \begin{matrix} \text{(a)} \\ \text{(b)} \end{matrix}$

(where $//$ = pause)

and that "phonologically predictable exceptions to this rule—the sub-regularities—be listed as a set of constraints" (828). Schane provided six partially ordered constraints (826–827): (i) nonnasal consonants are exempt from the deletion rule if they are immediately followed by a segment (e.g., *astre* [astr] 'star'); (ii) liquids and glides do not undergo the deletion rule either (e.g., *avril* [avril] 'April'; *soleil* [sɔlɛj] 'sun'), unless (iii) /e/ precedes /r/ and /i/ precedes /j/ (e.g., *parler* [parle] 'to speak'; *outil* [uti] 'tool'); but (iv) /r/ does not delete (even when preceded by /e/) if it occurs in a monosyllable (e.g., *mer* [mɛr] 'sea'); (v) the obstruents /k/, /b/, /g/, /f/, /v/, /z/ are exempt from the deletion rule (e.g., *avec* [avɛk] 'with'; *snob* [snɔb] 'snob'; *grog* [grɔg] 'hot wine'; *chef* [šɛf] 'chief'; *Kiev* [kjɛv] 'Kiev'; *fez* [fɛz] 'fez'),[4] unless (vi) in the case of /k/ and /g/ they are preceded by a nasal consonant (e.g., *banc* [bã] 'bench'; *long* [lɔ̃] 'long'). A constraint may thus not only exempt certain classes of consonants from the deletion rule; it may also undo the effect of a preceding more general constraint on a subclass of consonants. Complementing these interacting constraints, "minus features" are used to handle "lexical exceptions to either the rule or the constraints" (828). For example, the following exceptional markings appear in the lexicon: for *net* [nɛt] 'neat', [-rule (23)]; for *cul* [ky] 'ass', [-constraint (ii)]; for *enfer* [ãfɛr] 'hell', [-constraint (iii)]; for *escroc* [ɛskro] 'swindler', [-constraint (v)].

The intricate formalism suggested by Schane considerably adds to the power of the theory of exceptions without justification other than the assumption that the abstract generative analysis of French final consonants is basically correct. But the number and complexity of the restrictions on consonant deletion which are explicitly unveiled actually cast doubt on the psychological reality of the phonological deletion process postulated, as well as on the main motivation for the analysis, formal simplicity.

4. The inclusion of /z/ in the list forces one to assume that the plural marker, which regularly deletes, is /s/, and that it undergoes a voicing process in liaison (cf. Schane 1973*b*:833 n. 6). But there is no independent evidence that the plural morpheme is /s/, since it always shows up as [z] at the surface phonetic level.

V.4. Summary

The standard generative treatment of French phonology accounts for [Ø] ~ [C] alternations by assuming that the long forms are basic and that the short forms are uniformly derived by a major phonological process of consonant deletion. This process must apply after universal conventions on the distribution of word boundaries and French-specific readjustment rules have encoded morphological, syntactic, and stylistic information bearing on cohesion between words.

All proponents of the abstract generative analysis of final consonants have recognized the phonetic opacity of their phonological process of consonant deletion, and they have suggested in more or less detail ways to handle it formally, by resorting to the postulation of final protective schwas, in association with extrinsic rule ordering, and by assuming the existence of numerous exceptions.

VI

PLURAL MARKING AND LIAISON

VI.1. Introduction

In this chapter, I consider the question of plural marking on nouns and adjectives in Modern French. This particular aspect of French phonology and morphology is a very revealing window on the more general issue of liaison, and a detailed investigation of the phenomenon constitutes a convenient starting point for showing the inadequacy of the abstract generative analysis of final consonants and the necessity to assume the existence of consonant insertion in the treatment of [Ø] ~ [C] alternations.

Generative grammarians who have worked on the phonology and morphology of written languages such as English and French have often claimed that, contrary to the traditional complaints concerning the adequacy of spelling, orthography generally correlates very well with a psycholinguistically significant level of abstract representation.[1] For example, Chomsky and Halle (1968:69), in writing about English, note that "conventional orthography is remarkably close to the optimal phonological representation"; Schane (1968a:16-17) states that "French spelling, to a large extent, is highly morphophonemic" and, "by and large, quite satisfactory for the contemporary language"; writing about the question of word-final consonants in Modern French, Dell (1973b:193) comments that French orthography faithfully reflects linguistic reality.

1. The high degree of correlation observed between spelling and certain phonological analyses is no guarantee of the adequacy of spelling or of the well-foundedness of the linguistic accounts. It is simply caused by the fact that both orthography and abstract phonological solutions often reflect the past history of languages.

Since, for written French, the general rule of plural marking on nouns and adjectives is to add the letter *s* at the end of the singular forms of these words, it should come as no surprise that, in standard generative treatments of Modern French phonology and morphology, the plural marker on nouns and adjectives, the morpheme /z/, has been assumed, without much explicit motivation, to be systematically present at the underlying level of phonological representation, although it is sounded at the surface phonetic level only under very restricted conditions.[2] It is introduced at the underlying level by means of a spelling rule that automatically rewrites the feature [+Plural] as /z/ at the end of all nouns and adjectives thus marked (Dell 1973*b*: 183–184).

For ease of reference I call this analysis the systematic plural-suffix hypothesis. In this chapter I argue that this solution is incorrect. I first make explicit the main motivations for the analysis. Second, I show its lack of internal consistency with respect to the treatment of static data, and I also provide substantive evidence against it. Third, I substantiate and formalize a morphophonological treatment of plural liaison (/z/-insertion), which partially reflects the intuitions of traditional grammarians like Bauche (1951:78), Frei (1929:98), and Grevisse (1969:229), who felt that, as opposed to written French, plural marking in spoken French is a matter of prefixation rather than suffixation. From a more general perspective I demonstrate the inadequacy of the phonological process of final-consonant deletion which has been advocated in standard generative analyses of French phonology and morphology, and whose postulation necessarily accompanies the systematic plural-suffix hypothesis. The ground is thus prepared for an overall alternative treatment of [Ø] ~ [C] alternations based on substantive evidence, rather than on an apparent strict observance of the formal simplicity criterion (see chap. vii).

VI.2. Motivations for the systematic plural-suffix hypothesis

As opposed to English nouns or Spanish nouns and adjectives, the great majority of French nouns and adjectives are homophonous in the singular and in the plural when spoken in isolation:

---

2. Even closer to the orthography, the plural marker is posited as /s/ explicitly in Schane (1968*a*) and implicitly in Schane (1973*b*) (cf. chap. v, n. 4). Since this morpheme, however, shows up only as [z] phonetically, I assume here, as is elsewhere generally accepted, that the plural marker is /z/ rather than /s/.

(1) *chaise/chaises* [šɛz] 'chair'/'chairs'
   hublot/hublots [yblo] 'porthole'/'portholes'
   verte/vertes [vɛrt] 'green' (sg./pl.)
   bleu/bleus [blø] 'blue' (sg./pl.)

The absence of a straightforward phonetic manifestation of a plural meaning justifies a close inspection of the reasons that have led a number of linguists to postulate for Modern French nouns and adjectives a systematic plural suffix. Three main sets of static data may be taken to support the presumption of the existence of a systematic plural suffix.

VI.2.1. Liaison

One set of data has to do with liaison. As summarized in chapter v, in the abstract generative analysis of final consonants, [Ø] ~ [C] alternations such as those illustrated in (2)

(2) *petit* [pəti]/*petite* [pətit] 'small' (masc./fem.)
   petit chat [pətiša]/*petit écureuil* [pətitekyrœj]
   'small cat'   'small squirrel'

are handled by postulating lexical representations where final latent consonants are made part of the stems (e.g., /pətit/); a phonological process deletes morpheme-final consonants before consonant-initial morphemes (consonant truncation) and before two word boundaries (final-consonant deletion):[3]

(3) $C \rightarrow \emptyset / — \begin{cases} \text{[-seg] C} & \text{(a)} \\ \# \# & \text{(b)} \end{cases}$

Schema (3) thus deletes the final consonant of /pətit/ in the required instances, as shown in (4):

(4)

	petit	*petite*
	/pətit##/	/pətit + ə##/
Schema (3)	pəti	———
Other rules	———	pətit
	[pəti]	[pətit]
	petit chat	*petit écureuil*
	/pətit#ša/	/pətit#ekyrœj/
Schema (3)	pəti #ša	———
Other rules	———	———
	[pətiša]	[pətitekyrœj]

---

3. I use the type of formalization proposed by Schane (1974) and Dell (1973*b*) rather than that of Selkirk (1972) (see chap. v). Unless otherwise noted, this choice does not affect any of the arguments.

Parallel alternations with plural adjectives and nouns, exemplified in (5),[4]

(5) *jolis* [žɔli] 'pretty' (pl.)
    jolis chats [žɔliša] 'pretty cats'
    jolis écureuils [žɔlizekyrœj] 'pretty squirrels'
    penguins [pɛ̃gwɛ̃] 'penguins'
    penguins bavards [pɛ̃gwɛ̃bavar] 'talkative penguins'
    penguins adorables [pɛ̃gwɛ̃(z)adɔrabl] 'adorable penguins'

can be similarly accounted for if it is assumed that plural on nouns and adjectives is systematically marked, underlyingly, by means of the suffix /z/; this morpheme will simply be another example of a final consonant subject to deletion by schema (3).

VI.2.2. Singular/plural [al] ~ [o] alternations

For a few sets of nouns and adjectives the plural forms are phonetically different from the singular forms, even when the words are spoken in isolation. The most important of these groups is the one where the singular forms end in [al] and the plural forms end in [o]. This set of data, illustrated in (6), has been analyzed in a way that is dependent upon the systematic plural-suffix analysis.

(6) *journal* [žurnal]/*journaux* [žurno] 'newspaper'/'newspapers'
    cheval [šəval]/*chevaux* [šəvo] 'horse'/'horses'
    loyal [lwajal]/*loyaux* [lwajo] 'loyal' (sg./pl.)
    monumental [mɔnymãtal]/*monumentaux* [mɔnymãto]
    'monumental' (sg./pl.)

In order to account for the [al] ~ [o] alternations which also occur in the domain of verb conjugation (cf. (7a)), and across the learned/ nonlearned division in the area of derivational morphology (cf. (7b)),

(7) (a) *valons* [valɔ̃]/*vaut* [vo] '(we) are worth'/'(it) is worth'
       falloir [falwar]/*faut* [fo] 'to be necessary'/'(it) is
       necessary'
   (b) *altitude* [altityd]/*haut* [o], *haute* [ot] 'altitude'/'high'
       (masc./fem.)
       falsifier [falsifje]/*faux* [fo], *fausse* [fos] 'to falsify'/'false'
       (masc./fem.)

Schane (1968*a*:80–81), and later Selkirk (1972:307–308), posited the following two phonological rules:

---

4. As pointed out in chapter v, the optional liaison in *penguins adorables* is accounted for by means of a word-boundary readjustment rule whose application depends on style (Selkirk 1972).

(8) /l/-vocalization (/l/-VOC): l → u / — C
(9) /o/-conversion (/o/-CON): au → o

The application of these rules must be restricted so that the processes do not affect words such as *altitude* or *falsifier*, but the following sample derivations otherwise allow the generation of the correct outputs:

(10) (a)

	valons	vaut	haut
	/val + 5z/	/val +t/	/alt/
/l/-VOC	——	vau +t	aut
/o/-CON	——	vo +t	ot
schema (3)	val + 5	vo	o
	[val5]	[vo]	[o]

Provided the morpheme /z/ is systematically added to plural nouns and adjectives as a suffix attached with a morpheme boundary, /l/-vocalization and /o/-conversion will straightforwardly explain cases like those given in (6):

(10) (b)

	journaux	loyaux
	/žurnal +z/	/lwajal +z/
/l/-VOC	žurnau +z	lwajau +z
/o/-CON	žurno +z	lwajo +z
schema (3)	žurno	lwajo
	[žurno]	[lwajo]

VI.2.3. Singular/plural alternations of the type *oeuf* [œf]/*oeufs* [ø]

The third relevant set of data concerns words like *boeuf* 'ox', *oeuf* 'egg', and *os* 'bone', which are pronounced in standard normative French with their final written consonants *f* and *s* sounded in the singular but mute in the plural:

(11) (a) singular   (b) plural[5]
    boeuf [bœf]   *boeufs* [bø]
    oeuf [œf]   *oeufs* [ø]
    os [ɔs]   *os* [o]

As indicated in chapter v, the peculiar behavior of these words can be explained by the presence of the systematic plural suffix /z/ and the postulation of exception features. The lexical items *boeuf, oeuf,* and *os* are exceptions to the rule of final-consonant deletion (they are lexically marked [–rule (3b)]), but they normally undergo consonant truncation (rule (3a)). Since singular nouns are always followed by

5. The vowel quality adjustments found in the plural need not concern us here.

two word boundaries (Selkirk 1972), the final consonants in the singular words *boeuf, oeuf,* and *os* will never delete; on the other hand, since a single boundary separates noun stems from the plural morpheme /z/, the stem-final consonants of these words will delete in the plural:[6]

(12)

	oeuf	oeufs	os	os
	/œf##/	/œf+z##/	/ɔs##/	/ɔs+z##/
Rule (3a)	——	œ +z	——	ɔ +z
Rule (3b)	——	œ	——	ɔ
Other rules	——	ø	——	o
	[œf]	[ø]	[ɔs]	[o]

VI.2.4. Conclusion

The underlying presence of the plural morpheme /z/, in conjunction with the postulation of the major phonological consonant-deletion process (3), accounts for several distinct surface phenomena about plural marking in a unified fashion. This convergence of surface evidence lends plausibility to the systematic plural-suffix hypothesis. A central characteristic of the analyses just presented is that they are phonologically, rather than grammatically, governed. This particular feature is what makes the uniformity of treatment possible.

VI.3. Arguments against the systematic plural-suffix hypothesis

This section is devoted to the presentation of arguments against the systematic plural-suffix analysis, as they apply to each of the three groups of facts discussed above. The evidence provided is of two mutually reinforcing types: one type reveals inconsistencies in the analysis of static data within the framework that assumes the validity of the systematic plural-suffix hypothesis; the other demonstrates, by reference to external data, that many essential facets of the phonologically based analyses do not reflect appropriately what is actually characteristic of the native speakers' internalized knowledge of the language. The most important aspect of this section is the discussion of the evidence against the major phonological process of consonant deletion, since this process plays the essential role in accounting for liaison and other [Ø]∼[C] alternations in the standard generative treatment of French phonology and morphology.

---

6. The exceptionality of these words with respect to final-consonant deletion does not transfer to the plural morpheme /z/, which regularly undergoes rule (3b). This may contradict Chomsky and Halle's (1968) convention that "All non-phonological features of a given lexical item are distributed to every unit of this item" (374).

VI.3.1. The [al] ~ [o] alternation

The phonological treatment of the singular/plural [al] ~ [o] alternation crucially depends on the plural morpheme /z/ being attached at the end of noun and adjective stems by means of a morpheme boundary (+). Selkirk (1972:307–309) gives the following demonstration to show that this type of boundary is necessary in this particular instance: if a word boundary (#) were posited between a noun or an adjective and the plural suffix, the rule of /l/-vocalization would have to be stated as in (13):

(13) l → u / — (#) C

The problem with this solution is that /l/-vocalization would then incorrectly apply, for example, in the sequence *un loyal chevalier* /##ɛ̃#lwajal#šəvalje##/ 'a loyal knight', ultimately yielding *[ɛ̃lwajo-šəvalje] instead of [ɛ̃lwajalšəvalje].[7] Selkirk concludes that /l/-vocalization must be stated as in (8) and that "it must be a morpheme boundary which separates the plural marker from the stem" (308).

The postulation of a morpheme boundary between a noun or adjective stem and the plural suffix /z/, and the ensuing phonological analysis of the singular/plural [al] ~ [o] alternation, are, however, incompatible with a number of other facts. The inconsistencies arise in three domains: (i) universal grammar; (ii) the French-specific account of static data; and (iii) external evidence. Here I provide the essence of the arguments (see Tranel 1977c for details).

(i) From a general theoretical perspective, a word boundary, rather than a morpheme boundary, is the expected boundary for the attachment of the plural marker /z/ on French nouns and adjectives. Plural marking is a productive process, since all plural nouns and adjectives are automatically suffixed with the morpheme /z/; the meaning of a plural word is predictable from the meaning of the singular word and from that of the plural morpheme; and the grammar must clearly account for the phenomenon by rule rather than by listing in the lexicon the singular and plural forms of nouns and adjectives. These types of properties have been generally recognized in generative phonology as characteristic of the attachment of formatives by means of a word boundary (#) rather than a morpheme boundary (+) (see,

---

7. Given the universal word-boundary conventions postulated by Chomsky and Halle (1968) and by Selkirk (1972), there should be two word boundaries between *loyal* and *chevalier.* However, as indicated in chapter v, Selkirk also proposes that, to explain the basic liaison that occurs between an adjective and a following noun, an obligatory French-specific readjustment rule in effect reduces the two word boundaries to one.

for instance, Tranel (1976a) for a case study, and Aronoff (1976:chap. 6)). The formal universal conventions proposed in Chomsky and Halle (1968:85–86, 366–370) for the distribution of word boundaries will indeed place a word boundary, and not a morpheme boundary, at the border between a noun or adjective stem and the plural marker.

(ii) From a language-specific point of view, several essential rules postulated in the framework assuming the validity of the systematic plural-suffix hypothesis in fact require that a word boundary precede the plural marker, since the attachment of the plural morpheme /z/ has an effect upon the preceding word which is identical with that of a consonant-initial word separated from the preceding word by at least one word boundary.[8]

One such case involves the rule of Modern French given in (14), which raises /ɔ/ to /o/ at the end of a word:

(14) ɔ → o/ — #

Rule (14), already considered in chapter ii, has also been postulated by Selkirk (1972:324) and by Schane (1978b). The evidence that can be adduced to justify this process is illustrated again in (15):

(15) (a) *sotte* [sɔt]/*sot* [so] 'silly' (fem./masc.)
idiote [idjɔt]/*idiot* [idjo] 'stupid' (fem./masc.)

(b) *dormir* [dɔrmir]/*(faire) dodo* [dodo] 'to sleep'
communiste [kɔmynist]/*coco* [koko] 'communist'

(c) *héroïne* [erɔin]/*héros* [ero] 'heroine'/'hero'
noyauter [nwajɔte]/*noyau* [nwajo] 'to infiltrate'/'kernel'

(d) *métropolitain* [metrɔpɔlitɛ̃]/*métro* [metro] 'subway'
locomotive [lɔkɔmɔtiv]/*loco* [loko] 'locomotive'

(e) *jobard* [žɔbar]/*barjot* [baržo] (type of hoodlum)

(15a) illustrates feminine/masculine alternations in adjectives; (15b) shows the reduplication of word-initial consonant-vowel sequences (Morin 1972); (15c) draws from derivational morphology; (15d) exemplifies abbreviations by truncation of final syllables; and (15e) is taken from a secret language called *verlan* (= *l'envers* 'backward') (Monod 1968).

Consider now the data given in (16):

(16) (a) *(un bien) sot ami* [sɔtami] 'a really silly friend'
(b) *(de bien) sots amis* [sozami] 'really silly friends'

---

8. See the appendix in Tranel (1977c) for evidence that these rules cannot be justifiably formalized in a way compatible with the presence of a morpheme boundary before the plural marker.

(c) *(un bien) sot terrien* [sotɛrjẽ] 'a really silly earthman'

(d) *(un bien) sot zèbre* [sozɛbr] 'a really silly zebra'

The presence of the consonantal plural morpheme /z/ in (16b) coincides with the raising of the underlying /ɔ/ of *sots,* as does in (16c–d) the presence of a following consonant-initial word. If it is assumed that the plural morpheme /z/ is preceded by a word boundary, then rule (14) will straightforwardly account for the data provided in (16), as shown in (17):

(17)	*sot ami*	*sots amis*	*sot zèbre*
	/#sɔt#ami##/	/#sɔt#z#ami#z##/	/#sɔt#zɛbr##/
schema			
(3)	————	#sɔ #z#ami##	#sɔ #zɛbr##
/ɔ/-raising	————	#so #z#ami##	#so #zɛbr##
	[sɔtami]	[sozami]	[sozɛbr]

The process of /ɔ/-raising formulated as rule (14) is thus consistent with the presence of a word boundary between noun or adjective stems and the plural morpheme, but the occurrence of a morpheme boundary in that position is incompatible with rule (14); thus, Selkirk's and Schane's grammars will fail to derive the correct outputs for examples like (16b).

That the effect of the plural morpheme on a preceding word is similar to that of a consonant-initial word is also revealed by the domain of application of the three rules postulated by Dell (1970:70; 1973b:226, 236, 259) to account for the distribution of word-final schwas and liquids in the type of data exemplified in (18).

(18) (a) *la petite lampe* [lapətitlãp] 'the small lamp'

la grande chaise [lagrãdšɛz] 'the big chair'

(b) *la ferme typique* [lafɛrm(ə)tipik] 'the typical farm'

un contact pénible [ẽkõtakt(ə)penibl] 'a difficult contact'

il gouverne mal [ilguvɛrn(ə)mal] 'he governs badly'

(c) *un autre zéro* [ẽnot(rə)zero] 'another zero'

une table basse [yntab(lə)bas] 'a low table'

il tremble beaucoup [iltrãb(lə)boku] 'he is shaking a lot'

The three rules, which have also been considered in chapter ii, are the following:

(19) (a) Final-schwa deletion (obligatory):

$$ə \rightarrow \emptyset \;/\; VC_o \text{ —— } \#$$

(b) Schwa insertion (optional):

$$\emptyset \rightarrow ə \;/\; CC \text{ —— } \#_1 \; C$$

(c) Liquid deletion (obligatory):

$$L \rightarrow \emptyset \;/\; [-son] \text{ —— } \#_1 \; C$$

Their application is again illustrated in (20):

	(20)	*petite lampe*	*autre zéro*	*autre zéro*
		/pətit + ə#lãpə/	/otrə#zero/	/otrə#zero/
	(19a)	pətit #lãp	otr #zero	otr #zero
	(19b)	———	otrə#zero	———
	(19c)	———	———	ot #zero
		[pətitlãp]	[otrəzero]	[otzero]

These three processes, which operate across at least one word boundary, also apply before the plural morpheme /z/, as shown in (21):

(21) (a) *de petites étoiles* [dəpətitzetwal] 'small stars'
de grandes armoires [dəgrãdzarmwar] 'big wardrobes'

(b) *des fermes anglaises* [dɛfɛrm(ə)zãglɛz] 'English farms'
des contacts atroces [dɛkɔ̃takt(ə)zatrɔs] 'horrible contacts'

(c) *d'autres amis* [dot(rə)zami] 'other friends'
des tables adorables [dɛtab(lə)zadɔrabl] 'adorable tables'

The facts illustrated in (21) follow naturally from the rules given in (19) if a word boundary is assumed to precede the plural morpheme, but the attachment of the plural marker with a morpheme boundary is incompatible with the rules of (19).

Additionally, recall from chapter v that, at least in the grammar that contains the type of formalization of morpheme-final consonant deletion proposed by Schane (1974) and by Dell (1973*b*), a rule deleting prefinal consonants is needed which is best ordered between consonant truncation and final-consonant deletion (cf. (22a)). This ordering renders problematic the formal collapsing of consonant truncation and final-consonant deletion, but, as noted then, this difficulty can be eliminated if a word boundary is assumed to separate noun and adjective stems from the plural marker /z/, because prefinal-consonant deletion can consequently be considered to take place before consonant truncation and always affect the same consonant in a given word, whether it is singular or plural (cf. (22b)).

(22) *respects* [rɛspɛ] 'respects'

(a) /rɛspɛkt+z/

consonant truncation	rɛspɛk +z
prefinal-consonant deletion	rɛspɛ +z
final-consonant deletion	rɛspɛ
	[rɛspɛ]

(b)   /rɛspɛkt#z/
prefinal-consonant deletion   rɛspɛ t#z
consonant truncation   rɛspɛ #z
final-consonant deletion   rɛspɛ
                                               [rɛspɛ]

(iii) Formal universals and language-specific rules thus combine to support the attachment of the plural morpheme /z/ with a word boundary and therefore cast doubt on the validity of the phonological analysis of the singular/plural [al] ~ [o] alternation, which crucially depends on a morpheme boundary attachment of the plural marker.

Substantive evidence about the [al] ~ [o] alternations actually confirms the inadequacy of a uniform phonological analysis. A comparison of the singular/plural [al] ~ [o] alternations with those found in derivational morphology[9] reveals that the former type is unstable, whereas the latter is stable. For instance, speakers will in some cases hesitate between a plural in [al] and a plural in [o] (e.g., *final* 'final', *nasal* 'nasal'). In the area of derivational morphology, there is no such variability. In the phonological analysis of [al] ~ [o] alternations, there is no motivated ground to explain this difference in stability, since all the alternations are treated alike.

I have proposed (Tranel 1977c) a separate treatment for these two types of alternation. The singular/plural [al] ~ [o] alternation is accounted for by means of the minor rule given in (23):

(23) al → o / ——— #
$$\left. al \rightarrow o \middle/ \underline{\quad} \# \right] \quad \begin{array}{l} N \\ A \end{array} \begin{bmatrix} +\text{masc.} \\ +\text{plural} \end{bmatrix}$$

The main claims made by this rule are the following: (a) the change from /al/ to /o/ is a minor process; therefore, lexical items are not expected to undergo it; those that do are lexically marked; (b) rule (23) accounts only for the singular/plural [al] ~ [o] alternation; therefore the [al] ~ [o] alternations found in derivational morphology must be explained in a different way. It is suggested that this type of alternation be treated lexically; the alternants are entered in the lexicon in their classical phonemic forms (e.g., *altitude* /altityd/, *haut* /ot/), and they are related by means of a via rule (see Tranel 1977c for justifications).

---

9. I leave aside here the [al] ~ [o] alternation found in the conjugation of verbs, because only two verb stems actually exhibit it, namely /val/ and /fal/ (Tranel 1977c).

This dual treatment of [al] ~ [o] alternations explains why one type of alternation is stable, whereas the other is unstable. For the alternations found in derivational morphology, since each alternant is present in the lexicon in its classical phonemic form, there is no particular reason for variability to obtain. On the other hand, in the case of singular/plural alternations, only the singular forms are lexically entered (e.g., *cheval* /šəval/'horse'), and they are marked for taking a plural in /o/ ([+rule (23)]); this marking is an exception feature, a well-known unstable item in a grammar.

These exception features also predict a directionality in the instability of the singular/plural [al] ~ [o] alternation. One expects these markings to tend to be eliminated from lexical entries, and therefore one expects a neutralization of the alternation in favor of the pronunciation with [al]. This is borne out by the facts. Children often say, for instance, [šəval] instead of [šəvo] for the plural of *cheval* 'horse' (Cohen 1950:113), and it is not unusual for adults to use, for example, [kɔmɛrsjal] instead of [kɔmɛrsjo] for the plural of *commercial* 'commercial', as in *les centres* [kɔmɛrsjal] 'the shopping centers' (see also Sauvageot 1972:78–79, 81). From a diachronic perspective, there has been a general tendency since the seventeenth century to generalize the singular form of the words in *-al* (Nyrop 1968:221); this is naturally explained by the nonapplication of the minor process (23) to new words entering the language and by the removal of the exceptional lexical markings from the words that were marked.

The uniform phonological analysis of the [al] ~ [o] alternations cannot explain all these facts at the same time. If /l/-vocalization is assumed to be a major rule, it cannot correctly account for the types of "mistakes" mentioned above, the directionality of the diachronic trend, or the stability of the pronunciations of words with an [lC] sequence. If /l/-vocalization is considered to be a minor rule, it can explain correctly the instability of the singular/plural [al] ~ [o] alternation and the stability of the [lC] sequences, but it fails to account for the stability of words with [o], where this surface segment comes from underlying /al/ because of the existence of a derivationally related form with [al].

To come back to the main point of the discussion concerning the singular/plural [al] ~ [o] alternation, it is clear that this alternation is not phonologically, but morphophonologically, governed. The plural morpheme /z/ itself is not relevant to the treatment of the alternation; the grammatical feature [+Plural] is. The singular/plural

[al] ~ [o] alternation therefore cannot be used as an argument supporting the systematic plural-suffix hypothesis.

VI.3.2. Exceptions to final-consonant deletion

I will now show that, similarly, the singular/plural alternations noted about words such as *boeuf, oeuf,* and *os* cannot count as evidence for the existence of a systematic plural suffix.

It has been pointed out earlier that, within the framework of the systematic plural-suffix hypothesis and of schema (3), these words are marked [-rule (3b)] in standard normative French, that is, they are exceptions to final consonant deletion. If a change were to take place concerning these words, one would naturally expect the exceptional marking to be removed from the grammar; in other words, one would expect the singular forms to be pronounced like the plural forms, namely, with the final consonants [f] and [s] deleted. The fact is that the reverse is true; as noted by numerous grammarians (e.g., Frei 1929:207; Nyrop 1968:212), the plural forms tend to be pronounced like the singular forms, with the final consonants present.[10] The variability can be observed within the speech of a given speaker.

The phonological analysis that accounts for alternations such as *oeuf* [œf]/*oeufs* [ø] makes an incorrect prediction because it provides the wrong exceptional marking. What is actually irregular about the standard normative pronunciation of these words is the pronunciation of their plural forms; the phonological solution does not capture this at all, since it claims in effect that the singular forms are irregular and the plural forms are regular. A morphophonological analysis can capture the correct status of these forms by stating that the words under consideration behave exceptionally in that their stem-final consonants are deleted in the plural. The tendency to pronounce the plural forms like the singular forms is naturally explainable as the removal from the grammar of these exception features, a simplification of the lexicon.[11]

The important point here is that, again, the plural suffix /z/ itself

10. This pronunciation is especially common for *os,* less so for *oeuf* and *boeuf,* at least in my own speech.
11. Words other than *boeuf, oeuf,* and *os* have had parallel developments earlier in the history of French. For instance, according to Fouché (1966:676, 781–782) (see also Cohen 1966:163–164), words like *bec* [bɛk] 'beak', *coq* [kɔk] 'rooster', and *sac* [sak] 'bag' were once pronounced with their final /k/'s sounded in the singular but not in the plural. These alternations have also been resolved through the restoration of the final consonants in the plural, not through their elimination in the singular.

has nothing to do with the present-day absence of the stem-final consonants in the plural of the words *boeuf, oeuf,* and *os* in standard normative French. As indicated by a consideration of substantive evidence, the determining factor is the grammatical feature [+Plural]. The alternations undergone by these words therefore cannot be used as an argument in favor of the existence of a systematic plural suffix.

VI.3.3. Liaison

The only remaining supporting piece of evidence in favor of the systematic plural-suffix hypothesis rests with the phenomenon of liaison. Since liaison is essentially accounted for by schema (3), the systematic plural-suffix hypothesis ultimately depends on the well-foundedness of this process of consonant deletion.

At the outset, it is important to repeat very explicitly two of the main claims that go together with the postulation of schema (3) (cf. chap. v). Schema (3) is viewed as a major phonological process; therefore, (i) it is "abnormal" for a lexical item not to undergo the rule, and (ii) the process applies without regard to direct morphological or syntactic information (boundaries excepted).

I now consider several arguments against the view that Modern French is characterized by the existence of a major phonological process of consonant deletion. The first series of arguments (secs. VI.3.3.1. to VI.3.3.7.) deals in detail with the question of the descriptive adequacy of the process from the perspective of evidence usually omitted from consideration by the proponents of the abstract generative analysis of final consonants, or else treated in a rather mechanistic fashion. The second group of arguments (sec. VI.3.3.8.) is concerned with demonstrating in brief that what is usually considered as positive evidence in favor of schema (3), namely, the uniform treatment allowed for all types of [Ø] ~ [C] alternations, actually constitutes a spurious generalization.

VI.3.3.1. The restoration of final consonants

Since the seventeenth century, consonants that deleted in word-final position have reappeared in a large number of cases. Significantly, the restoration of final consonants is still occurring in contemporary French.

A. The cases of *cinq* and other cardinal numbers

It is generally assumed that *cinq* 'five' is pronounced [sɛ̃k] before vowel-initial words and at the pause, but [sɛ̃] before consonant-initial words (Léon 1966:132; Bras 1975:149; Valdman 1976:103):

(24) (a) *cinq enfants* [sɛ̃kãfã] 'five children'
   ils sont cinq [ilsɔ̃sɛ̃k] 'there are five of them'
   (b) *cinq femmes* [sɛ̃fam] 'five women'

This was actually true toward the beginning of the twentieth century, as the testimonies of linguists like Grammont (1914:94) and Martinon (1913:287) indicate. As I observed elsewhere (Tranel 1976*b*), however, a change has taken place since then, which Fouché (1959:479) noted in the fifties as characteristic of popular French, but which is quite widespread today: in contemporary French, *cinq* strongly tends to be pronounced with its final consonant restored before consonant-initial words:

(25) *cinq femmes* [sɛ̃kfam]

This particular change is not isolated. Thus, the numerals *sept* 'seven' and *neuf* 'nine' have already completed the same evolution. Grammont (1914:94–95), for example, indicated that these words were pronounced with their respective final consonants before vowel-initial morphemes and at the pause, but without them before consonant-initial morphemes:

(26) (a) *sept hommes* [sɛtɔm] 'seven men'
   neuf amis [nœfami] 'nine friends'
   ils sont sept [ilsɔ̃sɛt] 'there are seven of them'
   ils sont neuf [ilsɔ̃nœf] 'there are nine of them'
   (b) *sept femmes* [sɛfam] 'seven women'
   neuf tasses [nøtas] 'nine cups'

Almost half a century later, Fouché (1959:479) noted that the pronunciations [sɛ] and [nø] before consonant-initial words were disappearing. Such pronunciations have now completely vanished from the speech of Standard French speakers:

(27) *sept femmes* [sɛtfam]
   neuf tasses [nœftas]

This change in progress in the pronunciation of cardinal numbers cannot readily be explained in the context of the existence of schema (3). Within this framework, *cinq,* for example, must be marked as an exception to rule (3b) in order to account for the conservative pronunciation (cf. (24)). But since (3) is a major process, it is clear that, if any change is to affect *cinq,* its exceptional marking [−rule (3b)] should be lost from the grammar; in other words, the final /k/ of /sɛ̃k/ should delete at the pause as well as before consonant-initial morphemes. The fact that exactly the reverse takes place—that is, the final [k] is restored before consonant-initial morphemes—demonstrates that schema (3) captures certain facts about French phonology

backward. It is not the pronunciation of *cinq* as [sɛ̃k] at the pause
which is exceptional, but the pronunciation [sɛ̃] before consonant-initial morphemes.

The linguistic change observed, and its directionality, can be accounted for within a grammar that contains, instead of schema (3), a
minor phonological rule of consonant deletion such as (28) (Tranel
1976*b*):

(28) C → Ø / — # C

Rule (28) indicates that the final consonant of a word is deleted before
a consonant-initial morpheme separated by a word boundary. It is a
minor rule; that is, it applies to a given word if and only if that word is
marked in the lexicon as sensitive to the rule.

With a phonological component that includes rule (28) instead of
schema (3), the numeral *cinq* is marked [+rule (28)] in the grammars
of older or linguistically conservative speakers. This exception feature
on *cinq* can be considered to be on its way out in the grammars of
younger speakers, a very natural linguistic evolution. For the numerals *sept* and *neuf,* this lexical marking was presumably present in
the grammars of speakers at the turn of the century, but it has by now
been completely eliminated.

Under this analysis, the standard pronunciation of the numerals
six /sis/ 'six', *huit* /ɥit/ 'eight', and *dix* /dis/ 'ten' before consonant-
initial words and at the pause, which is illustrated again in (29),

(29) (a) *six cours* [sikur] 'six courses'
         huit cours [ɥikur] 'eight courses'
         dix cours [dikur] 'ten courses'
     (b) *ils sont six* [ilsɔ̃sis] 'there are six of them'
         ils sont huit [ilsɔ̃ɥit] 'there are eight of them'
         ils sont dix [ilsɔ̃dis] 'there are ten of them'

is accounted for by the lexical marking [+rule (28)]. Quite pre-
dictably, some French dialects have regularized the pronunciation of
these cardinal numbers. Thus, in Montreal French, as illustrated in
(30), *six, huit,* and *dix* are commonly pronounced with their respective final consonants sounded before consonant-initial words as well
as at the pause (and not without a final consonant in both environments, as predicted by their treatment within a framework where
schema (3) is posited):

(30) (a) *six cours* [sɪskur]
         huit cours [ɥɪtkur]
         dix cours [dɪskur]

(b) *ils sont six* [isɔ̃sɪs]
ils sont huit [isɔ̃ɥɪt]
ils sont dix [isɔ̃dɪs]

B. The cases of *boeufs, oeufs,* and *os*

As mentioned earlier, the plural forms of the nouns *boeuf, oeuf,* and *os* tend to be pronounced with the final consonants [f] and [s] restored. As with *cinq,* this is contrary to expectations, were schema (3) a major process: within the framework of schema (3), it has been seen that, in standard normative French, the nouns in question are marked with the exception feature [–rule (3b)]; it is therefore expected that any innovation in the pronunciation of these words should involve the removal of this exception feature from the grammar; in other words, the major phonological process of consonant deletion should generalize to the singular forms. That the reverse is actually occurring provides another clue to the basic inadequacy of schema (3).

As noted earlier, the proper characterization of these limited alternations is that the plural forms are exceptional in requiring deletion of the stem-final consonants.[12] This information is lexically encoded as exception features. Since exception features naturally tend to disappear from the grammar, this treatment provides an explanation for the observed trend to have the final consonants also pronounced in the plural.

C. The cases of optional final consonants

In a quantitative study of the speech of the "well-educated middle class of Paris," Malécot and Richman (1972) have pointed out that for a few words usually described as having an optional final consonant (e.g., *août* 'August', *but* 'goal', *fait* 'fact'), this consonant "is now generally pronounced in all contexts . . . in the sustained but relaxed conversation style" (84) ([ut], [byt], [fɛt]).

I would add that in these cases, as well as in others where there is an overall variability in the pronunciation of final consonants (e.g., *ananas* [anana] ~ [ananas] 'pineapple', *tandis que* [tɑ̃dikə] ~ [tɑ̃diskə]

12. If one wanted to maintain the role of the plural morpheme /z/ as a phonological conditioning factor, one would have to claim that schema (3) is a minor process and that *boeuf, oeuf,* and *os* are marked [+rule (3a)] in standard normative French. This solution is of course incompatible with the abstract generative analysis of final consonants. In addition, it would predict that, for example, the plural morpheme /z/, which would have to be marked [+schema (3)], should tend to appear on the surface before two word boundaries and before a single word boundary followed by a consonant-initial morpheme. Such predictions are not verified by any known data or intuitions.

'whereas', *exact* [ɛgza] ~ [ɛgzakt] 'exact'), the presence of the final consonants generally reflects a less conservative or more popular pronunciation than their absence.

The emerging domination of the pronunciations with the final consonants sounded contradicts the postulation of the major phonological process (3).

D. Consonantal regressions

The restoration of final consonants is not a new phenomenon. It has in fact been taking place for several centuries, since the second half of the seventeenth century, according to Fouché (1966:672): "Dans les mots qui existaient dans le lexique avant la seconde moitié du XVIIᵉ siècle, on peut considérer que la chute des consonnes finales a été générale. Cependant ces consonnes ont pu être rétablies par la suite. . . ." I repeat in (31) some of the examples provided by Fouché (1966:672-673, 679-680, 787-789):

(31) —final [p]: hanap, julep
     —final [t]: prétérit, zénith, bismuth, azimuth, occiput, mat, net, luth
     —final [k]: ammoniac, salamalech, basilic, alambic, manioc, estoc, caduc, aqueduc, turc, Marc
     —final [s]: hélas, jadis, maïs, aloès, iris, gratis, ibis, Raminagrobis, volubilis, rhinocéros, tétanos, blocus, lis, fils, os (sg.), tous (pronoun), ours, sens

Rosset (1911:240-243) also argues for final-consonant restoration in the case of [f]: "Dans le courant du XVIᵉ siècle, *f* final tendait à s'amuir; dans le peuple, l'amuissement fut rapide; il gagna même la prononciation correcte. . . . Aujourd'hui *f* se prononce toujours à la fin des mots; mais l'usage est tout récent pour certains." Some of the examples of restoration given by Rosset are reproduced in (32):

(32) couvrechef, boeuf, oeuf, chétif, juif, suif

Thus, as early as the second half of the seventeenth century the trend to restore deleted final consonants started. At least in the cases where these consonants never phonetically appeared in any environment, and where therefore they must not have been present underlyingly, orthography must have played a genuine role in influencing the pronunciation, as many grammarians have assumed. It is unlikely, however, that this type of final-consonant restoration would have been so successful in the long run if it had gone against the grain of a major phonological process. One can therefore justifiably say that orthography was allowed to have this effect only because the phonological process of final-consonant deletion was no longer productive.

Also characteristic of the inappropriateness of schema (3) are the instances of false regression mentioned by Fouché (1966:673–675), that is, cases where the etymologically incorrect consonants have been restored in word-final position. Some examples are provided in (33):

(33) orignal (for orignac), pluriel (for plurier), avril (for avri[j]), brancard (for brancal), caviar (for cavial), poignard (for poignal), brouillard (for brouillas), plumard (for plumas), Rue des Jeûneurs (for Rue des Jeux-Neufs), Honfleur (for Honfleu)

VI.3.3.2. New final consonants

When postconsonantal word-final schwas underwent deletion, a process that, according to Fouché (1969:524), was completed near the end of the seventeenth century or at the beginning of the eighteenth century, the consonants that thereby became word-final did not delete. This point also shows the long-standing opaque character and lack of productivity of schema (3) and underscores the contradiction inherent to the postulation of such a schema as a major phonological process of the language.

VI.3.3.3. New words

Since the seventeenth century new words have consistently entered the language with pronounced final consonants (Rosset 1911:230–232, 237–238, 241–242, 244, 246–247; Fouché 1966:670–671, 675–676, 680, 790–791). Examples are given in (34):

(34) —final [p]: croup, handicap
—final [t]: accessit, déficit, granit, transit, vermouth, mammouth, abrupt, cobalt, toast, verdict, volt, sprint
—final [k]: bivouac, ressac, loustic, hamac, mastoc, diagnostic, viaduc, mic mac, bric à brac, cric-crac, spoutnik
—final [f]: récif, tarif, golf, adjectives in -if
—final [s]: angelus, mordicus, prospectus, motus, atlas, albinos, albatros, kermès, vasistas, index, phénix, sphinx, biceps, forceps
—final [b]: baobab, nabab, club, snob, Jacob
—final [d]: David, Alfred, Madrid, Mohammed, week-end
—final [g]: grog, zigzag
—final [v]: Kiev, Tel-Aviv
—final [z]: Berlioz, fez, gaz

The relatively recent proliferation of acronyms has also added to the number of instances where final consonants appear phonetically:

(35) *CAPES* [kapɛs] (teacher's diploma)
    FNAC [fnak] (store chain)
    OPEP [opɛp] 'OPEC'
    SMIG [smig] (minimum wage)
    SNES [snɛs] (teachers' union)
    UNEF [ynɛf] (students' union)

Abbreviations whereby only the initial /C₀VC/ sequences of polysyllabic words are retained provide additional instances of final consonants created by language-internal processes:

(36) (a) *baccalauréat* [bakalɔrea] (high school diploma)
        → [bak]
      Boulevard Saint-Michel [bulvarsɛ̃mišɛl] (street name)
        → [bulmiš]
      capable [kapabl] 'capable' → [kap]
      faculté [fakylte] 'university' → [fak]
      maquereau [makro] 'pimp' → [mak]
      mathématiques [matematik] 'mathematics' → [mat]
      professeur [prɔfɛsœr] 'professor' → [prɔf]
      putain [pytɛ̃] 'whore' → [pyt]
      zéphyr [zefir] 'wind' → [zɛf]

A similar type of abbreviatory mechanism, which keeps the initial /C₀VC₀VC/ sequences of words, has led to the same results:

(36) (b) *agrégation* [agregasjɔ̃] (university-level exam)
        → [agrɛg]
      bénéfice [benefis] 'benefit' → [benɛf]
      certificat [sɛrtifika] 'certificate' → [sɛrtif]
      formidable [fɔrmidabl] 'terrific' → [fɔrmid]
      fortifications [fɔrtifikasjɔ̃] 'fortifications' → [fɔrtif]
      impeccable [ɛ̃pɛkabl] 'impeccable' → [ɛ̃pɛk]
      instituteur [ɛ̃stitytœr] 'schoolteacher' → [ɛ̃stit]
      manifestation [manifɛstasjɔ̃] 'demonstration'
        → [manif]
      occasion [ɔkazjɔ̃] 'deal' → [ɔkaz]
      à perpétuité [apɛrpetɥite] 'forever' → [apɛrpɛt]
      réactionnaire [reaksjɔnɛr] 'reactionary' → [reak]
      sensationnel [sãsasjɔnɛl] 'sensational' → [sãsas]
      sous-officier [suzɔfisje] 'noncommissioned officer'
        → [suzɔf]
      transatlantique [trãzatlãtik] 'transatlantic'
        → [trãzat]

The introduction into the language of words with final consonants, either through borrowing or by language-internal word-formation processes, constitutes another strong indication of the inadequacy of schema (3) as a major phonological process of French.

VI.3.3.4. Prefixes

Some prefixes, such as *dis-* and *trans-*, do not have their final consonants deleted before consonant-initial stems (cf. *disparaître* [disparɛtr] 'to disappear', *transporter* [trãspɔrte] 'to transport'); they must therefore be marked as exceptions to schema (3). But contrary to expectations, given that (3) is assumed to be a major process of the language, there is absolutely no tendency for these prefixes to conform to what is supposed to be the norm, that is, to get rid of their exception feature and to lose the final consonant before consonant-initial stems.

Instead of actually marking such prefixes as exceptions to consonant deletion, Selkirk (1972:384–389) assumes that they are attached to their stems by means of a special boundary =, which she labels the "prefix boundary." This particular boundary, as opposed to the morpheme boundary (+) and the word boundary (#), is considered not to allow the application of consonant truncation across it. But the postulation of the prefix boundary is arbitrary: it is specifically designed to prevent consonant deletion in prefixes like *dis-* and *trans-*. Selkirk attempted to motivate independently the existence of = by showing that its use with other prefixes can serve to make necessary distinctions among prefix attachments. For example, she argued that "the behavior of the prefixes *in-* and *con-* with respect to Nasalization supports the contention that there exists a special boundary '=' in French" (388). By positing a rule of "prefix nasal deletion" which "will delete prefix-final nasal consonants before '=' and either a liquid or a nasal consonant" (387), she accounts for data like the following:

(37) *immuable* [imɥabl] (from /in = mɥabl/) 'unchanging'
   illégal [ilegal] (from /in = legal/) 'illegal'
   irrévérent [ireverã] (from /in = reverã/) 'irreverent'
   commémoratif [kɔmemɔratif] (from /kɔn = memɔratif/) 'commemorative'
   collaborer [kɔlabɔre] (from /kɔn = labɔre/) 'to collaborate'
   corruption [kɔrypsjɔ̃] (from /kɔn = rypsjɔ̃/) 'corruption'
Selkirk did not, however, actually provide independent evidence

showing that the boundary = itself should serve to attach both prefixes like *dis-* and certain instances of the prefix *in-*. The connections
could conceivably be made by different boundaries. In fact, it is paradoxical that a boundary like =, which is specifically introduced to
bar one consonant-deletion process (consonant truncation), should
also have the exclusive property of allowing another one to apply
(nasal consonant deletion).

From a data-oriented perspective, Selkirk's prefix nasal-deletion
rule actually fails to derive the complete set of possible pronunciations
for *in-*prefixed words. Thus, note that her solution treats alike the two
prefixes *in-* and *con-*, but in reality they behave differently: in the type
of examples given, under nonemphatic conditions, the prefix *in-* may
show up on the surface with its underlying /n/ assimilated to the initial sonorant consonant of the stems ([immɥabl], [illegal], [irreverā]).
Such geminate consonants, on the other hand, are not possible with
the *con-*prefixed words, except in cases of emphatic stress. As noted
in section III.3.2., the historically *con-*prefixed words under consideration are best analyzed synchronically as *co-*prefixed words (*co-* is
an independently needed prefix); the *in-*prefixed words under consideration can be handled by a restricted assimilation rule and an optional degemination rule affecting prefixes (see Tranel 1976*a*).

Under an analysis where schema (3) is not postulated, no special
mechanism (exception features or arbitrary boundaries) is required to
explain the conservation of the final consonants in prefixes like *dis-*,
trans-, and *in-*.

There is another set of prefixes, *dés-*, *més-*, and *sous-*, whose members do exhibit a [Ø] ~ [C] alternation accountable for by schema (3)
(e.g., *désosser* [dezɔse] 'to bone' versus *défaire* [defɛr] 'to undo';
mésestimer [mezestime] 'to misjudge' versus *mécontenter* [mekɔ̃tāte]
'to displease'; *sous-entendre* [suzātādr] 'to imply' versus *soutenir* [sut-
nir] 'to support') (see sec. II.3.3.1.). In an analysis without schema
(3), other possibilities are open to explain these alternations. One
would be to posit a minor rule of consonant truncation similar to rule
(28), except that the process would take place across morpheme
boundaries. This solution cannot be retained, however, because it
leads to the incorrect expectation that the prefix-final consonants that
delete should tend to be restored. Another conceivable approach
would be to assume the existence of a process of intervocalic /z/-in-
sertion, which would apply to the prefixes /de/, /me/, and /su/ but
not to others like *anti-* and *pro-* (cf. *anti-atomique* [ātiatɔmik] *[āti-

zatɔmik] 'antiatomic'; *pro-avortement* [proavɔrtəmā] *[prozavɔrtə-mā] 'proabortion'). This process could be formalized as follows:

(38) $\begin{bmatrix} \text{de} \\ \text{me} \\ \text{su} \end{bmatrix}$ + V

$\qquad\qquad$ Prefix

$\qquad$ 1 $\quad$ 2 3 $\implies$ 1 2 z 2 3

The prefixes that need to be specified in rule (38) constitute a closed list with a very limited membership. Perhaps equivalently from a substantive perspective, it would also be possible to claim that the two allomorphs of each suffix exist independently of each other, and that rules of co-occurrence distribute them in the correct phonological environments.[13]

VI.3.3.5. The conditional

Recall from chapter ii that on occasion, in the speech of some speakers, there may be no thematic schwa between a verb stem of the first conjugation class and the conditional marker /r/. In such instances, schema (3) predicts that if the verb stem ends in a consonant (as in *demander* /dəmād+e/ [dəmāde] 'to ask'), this consonant should truncate. As shown in (39), this prediction is incorrect:

(39) *nous demanderions* [nudəmādrijɔ̃] *[nudəmār(i)jɔ̃] 'we would ask' (normally [nudəmāderjɔ̃])

Without schema (3) in the grammar, such data pose no problem.

VI.3.3.6. On the determination and treatment of exceptions

As all proponents of the major phonological process of consonant deletion have recognized, there are innumerable examples of word-final consonants appearing phonetically in the environments where schema (3) predicts they should not.

As noted in chapter v, Schane and Selkirk explain these occurrences by means of an underlying (morphological or lexical) final schwa (coupled with extrinsic rule ordering) when there is a final *e* in the orthography, and by means of an exception feature when there is no final *e* in the orthography. The number of cases thus considered as real exceptions to schema (3) is reduced, but nevertheless it remains

---

13. The prefix [de] irregularly shows up before a vowel-initial stem in the word *déodorant* [deɔdɔrā] 'deodorant'. This appears to be an isolated case, maybe a borrowing from English. (Cf. the regular *désodorisant* [dezɔdɔrizā].)

very high, and it is only natural to doubt the psychological reality of a major phonological process like (3) when it is exception-ridden.

Substantive evidence confirms the validity of these doubts. The words that are considered exceptional do not behave like exceptions: there is no tendency whatsoever for their final consonants to conform to the pattern described by schema (3), that is, to delete. In addition, as indicated earlier, in instances where there is variability concerning the pronunciation of final consonants, the overriding trend is for these consonants to be sounded, a fact that also contradicts the predictions made by the setting up of the exception markings required by the postulation of schema (3).

The actual determination of which words are exceptional and which words are regular in the abstract generative analysis of final consonants leads, in the first place, to learnability problems. It is obvious that the distinction between words that do not have an underlying final schwa (i.e., those that are lexically marked as exceptions to schema (3)) and words that do contain one (i.e., those that are regular) cannot be based on orthography, since the construction of a grammar would then be impossible for children who have not yet learned how to read and write and for illiterate people in general. Selkirk (1972:329–330) claims, however, that the behavior of a word before a so-called h-aspiré morpheme indicates whether its phonetic final consonant is followed, underlyingly, by a final schwa or not: if it is, this schwa will appear before h-aspiré words. The practical question of how the distinction can actually be learned nevertheless remains. Even if Selkirk's claim concerning the telltale role of h-aspiré words were correct (see Part III for a discussion of the reliability of the information provided by h-aspiré words), it must still be true that each relevant word must have been heard before an h-aspiré word in order for a determination based solely on pronunciation (and not spelling) to be made. But this clearly does not happen in the lifetime of an individual for each word involved, if only because of collocation restrictions between words. For the proponents of schema (3), a crucial question thus arises concerning the learnability of the grammar they propose.

In an analysis where no major phonological process of consonant deletion is postulated, this learnability problem does not exist, since word-final consonants are not considered as anything contrary to any essential aspect of the grammar of the language. In addition, the incorrect substantive claims made by the postulation of exceptions to schema (3) are avoided.

VI.3.3.7. Summary

The arguments provided so far against the postulation for Modern French of a major phonological process of consonant deletion have dealt with a wide array of substantive evidence. It has been shown that the grammar that contains such a process makes incorrect claims about the directionality of language change, and that it fails to explain the introduction into French, through borrowing or language-internal processes, of an abundance of words with final consonants. It has also been pointed out that the number of exceptions actually recognized as such by the advocates of the analysis in itself makes the existence of the process rather doubtful, especially in light of the fact that these exceptions do not tend to conform to the pattern described by the process. Finally, it has been indicated that the distinction between regular consonant-final words and irregular ones is in fact not learnable. The elimination of schema (3) as a major phonological process of the language results in a corresponding solution to these problems. Certain adjustments that consequently need to be made in the grammar (e.g., the postulation of minor rules such as (23) and (28)) have been demonstrated to be well motivated to handle both static and external data.

The type of evidence presented above has been generally ignored by the proponents of the abstract generative treatment of French final consonants, who have instead emphasized what they consider to be positive evidence in favor of their analysis, namely, the generalizations allowed by schema (3) concerning the handling of [Ø] ~ [C] alternations. I now turn briefly to these data so as to point out some reasons why they should not in fact be treated uniformly. Detailed arguments and proposals follow in section VI.4. and in chapter vii.

VI.3.3.8. On the generalizations allowed by consonant deletion

The proponents of the major phonological process of consonant deletion have argued (see in particular Schane 1968b and Dell 1973a, b) that their analysis captures a linguistically significant characteristic of Modern French because, in addition to accounting for liaison, it allows for a unified treatment of [Ø] ~ [C] alternations affecting areas of the language traditionally considered separately (e.g., inflectional and derivational morphology; see introduction to Part II and chap. v).

This formal argument is essentially correct in the sense that schema (3) (together with other assumptions; see chap. v) provides a uniform mechanistic analysis of almost all [Ø] ~ [C] alternations. As is pointed out in this section, however, from a substantive point of view these various alternations are in fact different in nature, and it is therefore misleading and inadequate to collapse them into one phenomenon. That the standard theory of generative phonology as presently formulated may allow us, and even force us, to do so is not an indication that they should be collapsed, but rather that the theory is incorrect. Clearly, the weight of substantive evidence must be more important than the weight of a simplicity metric that has been independently shown to be deficient (see sec. II.2.2.1. for illustrations and references). It is also shown in this section that schema (3) is in fact insufficient to account for all the data where a [Ø] ~ (C) alternation occurs.

A. Inflectional morphology

The standard and Montreal dialects of French are different in a number of respects, but to switch from one to the other, either in production or in perception, requires no particular adjustments concerning the [Ø] ~ [C] alternations that operate in the conjugation of third-class verbs (e.g., *battre* 'to beat': *(il) bat* [ba]/*(ils) battent* [bat]) or in gender distinctions among nouns and adjectives (e.g., *français* [frãsɛ] /*française* [frãsɛz] 'French' (masc./fem.)). One can therefore reasonably assume that these alternations are to be treated in the same fashion in the two dialects.

One difference between the two dialects is that there exists in Montreal French a productive phonetic process of final-consonant deletion which does not operate in Standard French (Pupier and Drapeau 1973). The effect of this process is similar to a phonological rule found in Sanskrit (Whitney 1971:150–151): word-final consonants are iteratively deleted from right to left, until only one final consonant remains; a final consonant does not delete if it is preceded by a liquid. This is illustrated in (40):

(40) (a) *contact* [kɔ̃tak] 'contact'
      correct/correcte [kɔrɛk] 'correct' (masc./fem.)
      journaliste, journalisme [žurnalis] 'journalist',
      'journalism'
      ministre [minis] 'minister'
   (b) *calme* [kalm] *[kal] 'calm'
      courte [kurt] *[kur] 'short' (fem.)
      monarque [mɔnark] *[mɔnar] 'monarch'
      tarte [tart] *[tar] (type of pie)

Within the framework of the abstract generative treatment of final consonants, Montreal French would thus have two different major phonological processes of consonant deletion, schema (3) and the iterative rule just described. That these rules are indeed different is made clear by the fact that schema (3) must be ordered before final-schwa deletion, whereas the iterative rule must be ordered after it. Also, schema (3) is not constrained by the liquid restriction that affects the iterative rule. Yet the two processes are similar in that they are both major phonological processes eliminating word-final consonants. This type of coexistence in a grammar is unexpected and suspicious. The phonological component of Montreal French actually becomes much more plausible if it is recognized, as is done in traditional accounts, that alternations like *bat* [ba]/*battent* [bat] and *français* [frãsɛ]/*française* [frãsɛz] are morphologically conditioned, a fact that schema (3) hides by treating them phonologically. If these alternations are to be accounted for in Montreal French by means of morphophonological rules, as seems to be the case, it follows from what is pointed out at the beginning of this section that the same alternations in Standard French also ought to be treated by direct reference to grammatical information (see chap. vii).

Another way of looking at the evidence just presented is to say that one would not expect a language with schema (3) to add another major phonological process of final-consonant deletion similar to the one that operates in Sanskrit, for example. Yet a dialect of French, Montreal French, is such a language. One could of course decide to revise one's expectations about the types of rules which may coexist in a grammar, but a more reasonable path is to doubt the validity of schema (3) as an explanation for the [Ø] ~ [C] alternations found in inflectional morphology and to assume that these are grammatically governed instead.

This argument is perhaps strengthened by Yves Morin's observation (personal communication) that the type of pronunciation illustrated in (40) is also regularly found in the speech of some Parisian speakers (e.g., [minis] for *ministre* [ministr] 'minister', [artis] for *artiste* [artist] 'artist', [katešis] for cathéchisme [katešism] 'catechism', [rymatis] for *rhumatisme* [rymatism] 'rheumatism').

Another argument in support of the grammatical conditioning of the [Ø] ~ [C] alternations found in gender distinctions and verb conjugation concerns the remarkable overall pattern followed by the restoration of final consonants in French since its inception. Final consonants have been restored precisely in cases where they can be said to play no grammatical role. Thus we find, for example, that [t] and [s] have reappeared in grammatically invariable words like *août* [ut] 'August' and *ananas* [ananas] 'pineapple', but not in grammatically variable adjectives and verbs like *petit* [pəti] 'small' (masc.), *gros* [gro] 'big' (masc.), and *bat* [ba] '(he) beats'.[14] This distribution of restored final consonants can be explained straightforwardly if it is assumed that the process of final-consonant deletion has ceased to exist as a major phonological rule of French, and that it is a different type of rules, namely morphologically conditioned ones, which accounts for alternations like *petit* [pəti]/*petite* [pətit] 'small' (masc./fem.), *gros* [gro]/*grosse* [gros] 'big' (masc./fem.), and *bat* [ba]/*batte* [bat] 'beat' (ind./subj.).

The psychological reality of the assumption that gender alternations are morphologically anchored in the minds of native speakers, rather than phonologically motivated, is further evidenced by the creation, mostly (but not exclusively) in popular speech, of alternating adjectives from normally invariable ones (e.g., *pécuniaire* [pekynjɛr] 'monetary': [pekynje]/[pekunjɛr]; *bizarre* [bizar] 'strange': [bizar]/[bizard]; see chaps. iii and vii).

B. Derivational morphology

The hypotheses that the [Ø] ~ [C] alternations found in gender distinctions and verb conjugation are grammatically governed, and that schema (3) must be eliminated from the grammar, leave [Ø] ~ [C] alternations found in derivational morphology (e.g., *vie* [vi]/*vital* [vital] 'life'/'vital') unaccounted for. But as I have briefly pointed out (Tranel 1976*b*), schema (3) cannot in fact explain all such alternations. To take a simple and clear example, consider the data given in (41):

(41) *petit* [pəti]/*petite* [pətit]/*petitesse* [pətitɛs]
　　　'small' (masc.) 'small' (fem.) 'smallness'
　　　hardi [ardi]/*hardie* [ardi]/*hardiesse* [ardjɛs]
　　　'bold' (masc.) 'bold' (fem.) 'boldness'
　　　poli [pɔli]/*polie* [pɔli]/*politesse* [pɔlitɛs]
　　　'polite' (masc.) 'polite' (fem.) 'politeness'
Poli behaves like *hardi* as far as gender alternations are concerned,

---

14. Two possible exceptions to the pattern have come to my attention: for the adjectives *mat* [mat] 'mat' and *net* [nɛt] 'neat', pronunciations without the final consonants ([ma], [nɛ]) are attested (Fouché 1966:679). This implies consonant restoration in formerly alternating adjectives (if [ma], [nɛ] were used only in the masculine and [mat], [nɛt] in the feminine). These two cases, however, appear to be isolated, especially when compared with the number of grammatically invariable words that have undergone final-consonant restoration.

but like *petit* as far as derivational morphology is concerned. The first point of this example is that schema (3) cannot uniformly account for [Ø] ~ [C] alternations in inflectional and derivational morphology. Since the [t] of *politesse* cannot be part of the lexical representation of the adjective (one would then expect the feminine to be *[pɔlit]), it must be accounted for by some other means than schema (3). Several solutions may be contemplated: a rule of /t/-insertion (which *poli* must be marked to undergo), the postulation of an extended suffix *-tesse* (for *poli*), or a via rule (relating *poli* and *politesse*). These treatments all have in common that they are lexical in nature, rather than phonological. The second point of the example then is that, even if schema (3) is postulated, lexical mechanisms must be additionally resorted to in order to account for at least some [Ø] ~ [C] alternations found in derivational morphology.

Additional cases involving [Ø] ~ [C] alternations in derivational morphology cannot be explained by schema (3). Consider morphemes that apparently exhibit an alternation between zero (when used without a suffix) and not just one but several consonants or one consonant and zero (when used before suffixes):

(42) (a) *tabac* [taba] 'tobacco'
tabatière [tabatjɛr] 'tobacco pouch'
(cf. *sel* [sɛl]/*salière* [saljɛr] 'salt'/'saltshaker')
tabagique [tabažik] 'tobacco-related'
(cf. *atome* [atom]/*atomique* [atɔmik] 'atom'/'atomic')

(b) *sirop* [siro] 'syrup'
sirupeux [sirypø] 'syrupy'
(cf. *peur* [pœr]/*peureux* [pørø] 'fear'/'fearful')
siroter [sirɔte] 'to sip'
(cf. *goutte* [gut]/*goutter* [gute] 'drop'/'to drip')

(c) *clou* [klu] 'nail'
clouer [klue] 'to nail'
clouter [klute] 'to stud with nails'

(d) *café* [kafe] 'coffee'
caféine [kafein] 'caffeine'
cafetière [kaftjɛr] 'coffeepot'
(cf. *thé* [te]/*théière* [tejɛr] 'tea'/'teapot')

These morphemes must clearly be interpreted as not containing a final consonant (/taba/, /siro/, /klu/, /kafe/), and again some form of lexical treatment is necessary to account for the presence of the consonants between the stems and suffixes.

In many instances the consonant in [Ø] ~ [C] alternations found in derivational morphology has appeared intrusively in the process of the creation of the new words. Nyrop (1936:55–62) and others have provided abundant illustrations of the existence of these "consonnes intercalaires."

    (43) *bazar* [bazar] 'bazaar'/*bazarder* [bazarder] 'to get rid of'
        cauchemar [košmar] 'nightmare'/*cauchemarder*
        [košmarde] 'to have a nightmare'
        Marivaux [marivo] (French writer)/*marivaudage*
        [marivodaž] (witty and affected conversation in the style of
        Marivaux)
        fer blanc [fɛrblā 'tin'/*ferblantier* [fɛrblātje] 'tinker'
        tréma [trema] 'diaeresis'/*trémater* [tremate] 'to put a
        diaeresis on'
        biseau [bizo] 'bevel'/*biseauter* [bizɔte] 'to bevel'
        chapeau [šapo] 'hat'/*chapeauter* [šapɔte] 'to hat'
        queue [kø] 'line'/*queuter* [køte] 'to wait in line'
        abri [abri] 'shelter'/*abriter* [abrite] 'to shelter'
        piano [pjano] 'piano'/*pianoter* [pjanɔte] 'to strum on the
        piano'
        bijou [bižu] 'jewel'/*bijoutier* [bižutje] 'jeweler'
        cailloux [kaju] 'pebble'/*caillouteux* [kajutø] 'pebbly'
        morue [mɔry] 'cod'/*morutier* [mɔrytje] 'cod-fishing boat'
        banlieue [bāljø] 'suburb'/*banlieusard* [bāljøzar] 'suburban'

It could perhaps be claimed that, synchronically, the inserted consonants have been reinterpreted as being part of the stems and that the alternations can now be accounted for by schema (3). However, examples parallel to those of (43), but involving vowel-final acronyms, cannot be reinterpreted in such a way, since the stem-final consonant would have no word corresponding to it.

    (44) *les troupes onusiennes* [lɛtrup(z)ɔnyzjɛn] 'the UN troops'
        (cf. *ONU* [ɔny] (United Nations))

Such cases provide strong evidence against a consonant-deletion account.

    In a framework that includes schema (3), other mechanisms are thus required to relate derivationally connected words exhibiting [Ø] ~ [C] alternations. The fact that this process cannot account for all cases of [Ø] ~ [C] alternations found in derivational morphology shows that it does not have the generality claimed by the proponents of the abstract generative treatment of final consonants. In addition, the necessary lexical nature of the mechanisms needed independently of schema (3) reveals both the nonuniform character of [Ø] ~ [C] alternations and aspects of their nonphonological characteristics.

From a more constructive perspective, the elimination of schema (3) from the grammar simply means, for derivational morphology, the extension of lexical mechanisms (e.g., via rules) to a larger number of cases where a [Ø] ~ [C] alternation is involved (see chap. vii).

C. Liaison

The third main type of [Ø] ~ [C] alternations, liaison, is treated by schema (3) on a par with the [Ø] ~ [C] alternations found in inflectional and derivational morphology. But it is clearly a different kind of phenomenon. For example, whereas there is no tendency to level the alternations in variable adjectives [15] by eliminating the consonant-final alternants (or the other alternants for that matter), the use of linking consonants in general has been regressing, even in cases of so-called obligatory or basic liaison. This is illustrated in (45) with monosyllabic (nonlexical) prepositions after which universal conventions predict the presence of a single word boundary.

(45) *dans un mois* [dãɛ̃mwa] 'in a month'

     sous un toit [suɛ̃twa] 'under a roof'

Liaison consonants also tend to have a different effect on a preceding word than gender consonants do, as illustrated in (46) with the [e] ~ [ɛ] alternation:

(46) *premier ami* [prəmjerami] 'first friend' (masc.)

     première amie [prəmjɛrami] 'first friend' (fem.)

These kinds of arguments, developed in more detail in chapter vii, indicate that liaison is a type of [Ø] ~ [C] alternation which is distinct, for instance, from gender alternations; they thus argue against the uniformity of treatment of [Ø] ~ [C] alternations captured by the postulation of schema (3).

VI.3.3.9. Conclusion on consonant deletion

Schema (3) improperly collapses into one phonologically conditioned process what are in fact separate phenomena in Modern French. These phenomena have in common only the fact that they

---

15. There are common instances of lack of agreement (e.g., *la lettre qu'il a écrit* instead of *la lettre qu'il a écrite* 'the letter that he wrote') or of incorrect agreement (e.g., *elle a l'air idiote* instead of *elle a l'air idiot* 'she looks stupid'), but such examples reflect the particular operation of syntactic agreement rules, not inflectional leveling.

arose historically in a similar fashion, owing to the advent of a phonetic process of consonant deletion which started as consonant truncation and then generalized to include final-consonant deletion. But
this process, which operated until the seventeenth century at the latest
in popular French (Rosset 1911), has ceased to be productive; it is
now extinct, except under the form of minor rules. Schema (3) is thus
a reflection of the past, not an accurate characterization of the language today. No wonder, then, that it is insufficient to account for the
static data it is supposed to explain and that its postulation makes
predictions about external data which are exactly the reverse of what
is actually occurring.

VI.3.4. Conclusion on the systematic plural-suffix hypothesis

Schema (3) thus cannot be a major process of Modern French.
With it, there disappears the last and in fact the essential basis for the
systematic plural-suffix hypothesis: if schema (3) does not exist, then
the systematic plural morpheme /z/ cannot be deleted to account for
its absence before consonant-initial morphemes and before two word
boundaries. Consequently, /z/ cannot be systematically present, underlyingly, owing to a spelling rule rewriting the feature [+Plural].
Instead, it must be inserted only when it is actually present on the surface, that is, when the plural noun or adjective is followed by a vowel-
initial word and the syntactic and stylistic conditions for liaison are
met. A provisional formulation of this principle follows:

$$(47) \quad \begin{bmatrix} X \\ \begin{matrix} N \\ A \end{matrix} [+\text{plural}] \end{bmatrix} \quad \# \quad [+\text{syll}]$$

$$1 \qquad\qquad 2 \quad 3 \implies 1 \ 2 \ z \ 2 \ 3$$

For ease of reference I call this analysis the plural /z/-insertion analysis. In the next section I provide positive supporting arguments for
this treatment and refine the formulation of the rule.

VI.4. The plural /z/-insertion analysis
VI.4.1. Positive evidence

The plural /z/-insertion analysis is made necessary by the inadequacy of the systematic plural-suffix hypothesis and schema (3). I
would like, however, to provide in this section substantive evidence
demonstrating that it is not simply a solution that must be adopted by
default, but also one that actually provides new insights into French

phonology and morphology and captures correct generalizations about the native speaker's knowledge of the language.

VI.4.1.1. Direct mapping

The insertion analysis directly reflects the surface phonetic facts: the plural marker [z] shows up phonetically only when the word following the plural noun or adjective begins in a vowel; this is exactly where rule (47) inserts the plural morpheme.

Concerning language acquisition, the learning of this process is correspondingly straightforward; everything else being equal, the more directly a rule reflects the surface facts, the less the grammar faces learnability problems.

VI.4.1.2. Plural /z/ as a connective morpheme

The insertion analysis claims that the plural morpheme /z/ is not a suffix tacked onto plural words but rather a connecting element. The transformational format adopted to formalize the insertion process reflects this by having, in the structural change, a word boundary on both sides of the inserted /z/. It is thus assumed that /z/ does not belong to the (preceding) plural word any more than it belongs to the (following) vowel-initial word.

Historically, then, I suggest that the plural morpheme, which used to be a suffix, has now become a connecting morpheme. It is interesting to note that, especially in the speech of children and in popular French, there are data suggesting that the plural morpheme /z/ might actually be considered as a prefix on plural nouns and adjectives.[16]

Cohen (1963:111–112) notes that children often make the "mistake" of saying [trozørø] for *trop heureux* [tro(p)ørø] 'too happy'. This pronunciation is also found in popular speech and as an occasional slip by speakers of Standard French. The crucial fact here is that, according to Cohen, such an "error" is especially frequent when *heureux* is plural; since the adverb *trop* cannot presumably be marked for number, [z] is best interpreted as a plural prefix on the adjective.[17]

16. Data of a similar indicative nature might be found in French Creoles, but I have not investigated this domain.

17. *Trop* also links with [z] when the following word is singular. The explanation given in the text accounts for the frequency of liaison with /z/ when the following word is plural. The fact that *trop* "incorrectly" links in the first place is discussed in chapter vii.

Cohen (1963:107; 1972:90) also observes that, in Standard French, phrases like *Vous êtes Algérien(s)/Auvergnat(s)* 'You are Algerian/Auvergnat' (sg./pl.) are pronounced with a linking [z] between *êtes* and *Algérien(s)* or *Auvergnat(s)* more frequently when *vous* (and therefore *Algériens/Auvergnats*) is semantically plural than when it is the semantically singular polite form of address.

These observations of a quantitative nature are suggestive of a trend where plural marking, from suffixation through connection, would be moving in the direction of prefixation.

Bauche (1951:78) gives data drawn from popular French which can perhaps be considered to confirm this trend: [bokudzjø] for *beaucoup d'yeux (dans le bouillon)* 'many fat globules (in the broth)', [yndizɛndəzuvrijɛr] for *(j'ai chez moi) une dizaine d'ouvrières* '(I have at home) about ten employees'. In these cases, however, rule (47) will straightforwardly account for the facts if one makes the reasonable assumption that *beaucoup de* and *une dizaine de* are interpreted by some speakers as unitary plural nominal modifiers which trigger the insertion of plural /z/.

Some of Frei's examples (1929:98) may be more indicative, as they exemplify the occurrence of a plural [z] between a word that is presumably not marked for the feature [Plural] and a following plural noun: [maldəzjø] for *mal d'yeux* 'eye irritation', [kɔmzɔm] for *(les Français ne sont pas plus beaux,) comme hommes* '(the French are not more handsome,) as men.'

Although rule (47) has not been formulated to account directly for the interpretation of the plural marker [z] as a prefix, it does constitute a plausible intermediate stage between the suffixation stage of the past and a prefixation stage perhaps already announced.

VI.4.1.3. On the pronunciation of *oeufs*

Extremely revealing data gathered by Orr (1951) provide additional substantive evidence for the insertion analysis and, at the same time, against the systematic plural-suffix hypothesis. The crucial data observed by Orr in the speech of a Parisian grocer are given in (48) (see also Fouché (1959:421) and Cohen (1963:100) for reports of similar facts):

(48) (a) *un oeuf* [ɛ̃nœf]

      (b) *quatre oeufs* [katrœf], *cinq oeufs* [sɛ̃kœf]
           sept oeufs [sɛtœf], *huit oeufs* [ɥitœf]

      (c) *deux oeufs* [døzø], *trois oeufs* [trwazø]
           six oeufs [sizø], *dix oeufs* [dizø]

In this type of speech, as in the standard dialect, the word *oeufs* is obviously marked [+Plural] in the examples (48b–c). Therefore, according to the systematic plural-suffix hypothesis, the spelling rule that rewrites [+Plural] as /z/ must apply. The problem is that, in this framework, consonant truncation (rule (3a)) apparently applies in (48c), where /f/ deletes, but not in (48b), where /f/ does not delete. Clearly, the deletion of /f/ in (48c) cannot be due to the postulated presence of the systematic plural suffix /z/ and to the ensuing application of rule (3a). This reinforces the arguments given earlier against the treatment of these words within the framework of schema (3) and against the systematic plural-suffix hypothesis. Nor can it be said, however, that in this type of speech the stem-final consonant is lost in the plural (cf. (48b)), as is the case in standard normative French.

Interestingly, the dichotomy between (48b) and (48c) is in correspondence with the segment type that precedes the word *oeufs*: the absence/presence of the final consonant /f/ correlates exactly with the presence/absence of a preceding /z/. A question that arises is whether *any* preceding /z/ entails the pronunciation [ø] for *oeufs*. For example, in the dialect investigated by Orr, what is the pronunciation of *quinze oeufs* or *seize oeufs*? Unfortunately, Orr did not elicit data beyond *dix oeufs*. However, even with speakers who claim to use the "correct" singular and plural forms of the French word for *egg*, it is possible to obtain judgments of relative grammaticality which correspond to the facts of (48); such speakers reported, for instance, that [sɛ̃kœf] (for *cinq oeufs*) is not too shocking, whereas [døzœf] (for *deux oeufs*) is to be totally rejected. When asked about sequences such as *quinze oeufs*, the same speakers judged [kɛ̃zœf] on the same level of grammaticality as [sɛ̃kœf], that is, more acceptable than the impossible *[døzœf]. Similarly, in my judgment, [sɛzœf] could refer to *seize oeufs*, but not to *ses oeufs* or *ces oeufs*, which must be pronounced [sɛzø]. One can capture these distinctions by claiming that, whereas in the pronunciation of *quinze oeufs* and *seize oeufs* [z] is simply and obviously the last consonant of *quinze* and *seize*, in the pronunciation of *deux oeufs* and *ses oeufs*, *ces oeufs*, [z] is interpreted as a plural marker rather than as the last underlying segment of *deux* and *ses*, *ces*. Note that the [z] in *six oeufs* and *dix oeufs* must consequently be considered to be the plural marker also (the final /s/ of *six* and *dix* being eliminated by consonant deletion; see rule (28)), rather than the result of a voicing of the final /s/ (cf. Schane 1973*b*:833 n. 6).

In the dialect probed by Orr, it is apparent that it is not just the grammatical feature [+Plural] which triggers the deletion of the final /f/ in *oeufs*; the presence of a preceding [z], presumably when it is the plural marker, is also required. This is further supported by the data reported by Orr concerning *nine eggs*. Orr first found it impossible to surreptitiously elicit *neuf* directly followed by *oeufs*; the grocer would consistently say *neuf beaux oeufs* [nœfbozø] 'nine beautiful eggs'. When Orr finally asked the grocer directly why he would not say *neuf* immediately followed by *oeufs,* the grocer's answer was extremely revealing: "Mon bon Monsieur, avec *neuf,* je dis toujours: [nœfbozø]. [nœfœf], voyez-vous, ça jure; [nœfzø], au fond, ça serait peut-être bien plus correct" (Orr 1951:12).

Orr's data reflect both the inadequacy of the systematic plural-suffix hypothesis and the strong plausibility of the proposed plural /z/-insertion treatment. The judgments of relative grammaticality made by native speakers of Standard French are equally revealing because they demonstrate the speakers' readiness to interpret the data in the same fashion as Orr's grocer. This would probably not be possible if plural marking could not also be the result of an insertion process in their grammar.

VI.4.1.4. Plural marking and cardinal numbers

The data from Orr (1951) naturally call for a more detailed investigation of the evidence that the liaison behavior of cardinal numbers brings to bear on the issue of the treatment of plural marking.

It has been seen that, in the dialect of Orr's grocer, as well as in Standard French, the linking [z] that appears, for example, between *deux* or *trois* and *oeufs* is in all likelihood the plural marker. This interpretation of the data is in fact necessary if, as has been argued earlier, schema (3) is to be discarded. In the framework that includes schema (3), *deux* and *trois* have, in accord with etymology, lexical representations with final consonants, namely /døz/ and /trwaz/; these final consonants show up phonetically before vowel-initial words, but they are deleted before consonant-initial words and before two word boundaries. If schema (3) is rejected, it follows that the consonant that shows up phonetically between *deux* or *trois* and a following vowel-initial word like *oeufs* must be inserted rather than underlying; in this case the rule of plural /z/-insertion accounts for the surface phonetic facts.

The insertion analysis thus claims that, historically, the lexical representations of *deux* and *trois* have been restructured from /døz/

and /trwaz/ to /dø/ and /trwa/, and that the [z] that appears in liaison is due to insertion rather than the absence of deletion.

As noted elsewhere (Tranel 1976b), further evidence for this view comes from the pronunciation of these numerals in conjunction with names of months. In such cases the cardinal numbers do not express plurality; rather, they have the semantic value of ordinal numbers. As the plural /z/-insertion analysis predicts, the following pronunciations occur, with no linking /z/ present:

(49) *le deux octobre* [lədøɔktɔbr] 'October 2d'

le trois avril [lətrwaavril] 'April 3d'

The advocates of schema (3), who claim that /døz/ and /trwaz/ are the underlying representations for *deux* and *trois,* must explain the possible absence of liaison in such instances. There does not seem to be any well-motivated way of doing this. One possibility would be to postulate two word boundaries between the cardinal number and the name of the month, a move that could perhaps be justified syntactically and semantically if one wished to argue that such phrases are the result of a syntactic reduction rule operating on underlying strings of the type *le deuxième jour d'octobre* 'the second day of October', *le troisième jour d'avril* 'the third day of April'. The problem is that, since in the abstract framework that includes schema (3), the numerals *six* /sis/, *huit* /ɥit/, and *dix* /dis/ are exceptions to the process of final-consonant deletion before two word boundaries, one would expect the following to occur:

(50) *le six janvier* [ləsisžãvje] 'January 6th'

le huit mars [ləɥitmars] 'March 8th'

le dix novembre [lədisnɔvãbr] 'November 10th'

Although data such as (50) are found in the speech of some speakers, they are typical of conservative dialects (Grammont 1914:94–95; Fouché 1959:479).[18] In nonconservative dialects the following seems to be the norm:

(51) *le six janvier* [ləsižãvje]

le huit mars [ləɥimars]

le dix novembre [lədinɔvãbr]

The pronunciations exemplified in the sets (49) and (51) thus constitute homogeneous data,[19] and in the framework that includes sche-

18. For an account of the data of (50) in conservative speech, see Tranel (1976b). Pronunciations like those of (50) are also found in dialects such as Montreal French, but for different reasons: Montreal speakers do not as a rule delete the final consonants of *six, huit,* and *dix* before consonant-initial words (cf. the examples in (30a)).

19. For example, they are characteristic of my speech.

ma (3), the two-word boundary solution cannot explain both sets at the same time.

In conservative and/or elevated speech, liaison may take place between *deux* or *trois* and the following vowel-initial name of a month:

(52) *le deux octobre* [lədøzɔktɔbr]

le trois avril [lətrwazavril]

In the framework of the insertion analysis, such pronunciations (which are probably reinforced by the orthography, a not unusual phenomenon in this type of speech) are handled by means of a minor rule of /z/-insertion, which is distinct from the major process of plural /z/-insertion. Thus, *deux* and *trois,* whose lexical representations are assumed to be /dø/ and /trwa/, respectively, are marked to undergo this minor rule in certain dialects and/or styles (see chap. vii).

It may seem like a severe generalization loss to require two processes of /z/-insertion to account for liaison phenomena with *deux* and *trois*. As I have indicated, however, this division of labor between a minor /z/-insertion rule and the major plural /z/-insertion rule reflects substantive differences. In particular, the minor process accounts for cases of nonplural liaison which tend to disappear from the language; the major process accounts for cases of plural liaison which seem to be relatively solidly established in the language at the present time. In addition, as is shown in chapter vii, the minor insertion rule postulated here will account for other vanishing cases of nonplural liaison with /z/; other such minor rules are also posited and justified.

It has been assumed that numerals like *deux* and *trois,* when they have a semantically plural value, trigger the rule of plural /z/-insertion. In standard speech, numerals like *quatre* or *neuf* do not. Such items are therefore exceptionally marked [–rule (47)]. In keeping with what is known about exception features—that is, they tend to be removed from grammars—it is not surprising to observe that such numerals do become regular in the speech of many and that they trigger the insertion of plural /z/; the type of liaison illustrated in (53) is thus relatively common:

(53) *quatre enfants* [katzãfã] 'four children'

huit épreuves [ɥizeprœv] 'eight events'

neuf oeufs [nœfzø] 'nine eggs'

vingt-cinq années [vɛ̃tsɛ̃kzane] 'twenty-five years'

trois mille évêques [trwamilzevɛk] 'three thousand bishops'

VI.4.2. On the formulation and application of the plural /z/-insertion process

As I have already implied, the context for the application of the rule should include plural cardinal numbers in addition to plural nouns and adjectives. Other plural lexical items that trigger this process are determiners (*les, des, aux, ces, mes, tes, ses, nos, vos, leurs*), quantifiers (e.g., *certains, plusieurs*), and personal pronouns (*nous, vous, les, ils, elles*). The plural /z/-insertion rule can thus be generalized to apply after words marked [+Plural]:

(54) $\left.\begin{array}{c} X \\ \\ [+\text{plural}] \end{array}\right]$ # [+syll]

   1   2   3 $\implies$ 1 2 z 2 3

Conjugated verbs are meant to be excluded from the domain of application of this rule; first and second person plural verbs do link with [z], but the third person links with [t] (cf. sec. VII.2.1.). In the framework of the systematic plural-suffix hypothesis, the spelling rule that rewrites [+Plural] as /z/ has to be similarly constrained.

The pronoun *leur* must be exempt from rule (54) (cf. *il leur a dit* [illœradi] *[illœrzadi] 'he told them'). The analysis would therefore predict "mistakes" here, that is, the pronoun *leur* linking with [z]. To my knowedge such "errors" do not occur.[20] This problem with the pronoun *leur* is not specific to the insertion analysis. Except for Milner (1973:161, 163), the usual practice in the abstract generative framework seems to be to represent underlyingly certain determiners and personal pronouns (e.g., *les, ses, nous*) with a final /z/ which is part of the lexical representations (/lɛz/, /sɛz/, /nuz/), rather than the plural morpheme (/lɛ+z/, /sɛ+z/, /nu+z/). Presumably, the reason for doing so is that there are no corresponding singular forms (*/lɛ/, */sɛ/, */nu/) to which the plural morpheme can be added.

---

20. It is interesting to note, however, that in school, emphasis is often placed on the absence of an *s* in the orthography at the end of the pronoun *leur*, as opposed to the possibility of one at the end of the possessive adjective *leur(s)*. This reflects the tendency of children to spell the pronoun *leur* with an *s*, and maybe to make it link with [z] in the pronunciation. Martinon (1913:357) does report [illœrzadi] for *il leur a dit* [illœradi] 'he told them', but as a pronunciation "autrefois" admitted "par les personnes les plus distinguées"; he similarly mentions [ɔza] for *on a* [ɔna] 'one has'. Vaugelas (1647:436–437) condemned the use of the linking [z] with *on* (see chap. iv). In the French dialect of St. Thomas, the pronoun *leur* does link with [z]: [palœrdilistwa] 'Don't tell them the story', [ʒəlœrzedɔneœntitbeke] 'I gave them a little bit' (Highfield 1979:74).

However, the underlying representations of the plural possessive adjective *leurs* and of the plural personal pronouns *ils* and *elles* are in all likelihood assumed to be /lœr+z/, /il+z/, and /ɛlə+z/, respectively, since there are corresponding singular forms (*leur* /lœr/, *il* /il/, *elle* /ɛlə/). This means that the spelling rule that automatically rewrites [+Plural] as /z/ applies in the cases of *leurs, ils,* and *elles* but must be restricted so as not to affect the pronoun *leur* and items like *les, ses,* and *nous.* (If it did apply to items like *les, ses,* and *nous,* there would be no reason to assume that they have a final lexical /z/.) If the lexical representations of items like *les, ses,* and *nous* are assumed to be /lɛ/, /sɛ/, and /nu/, then the application of the spelling rule need not be constrained, except for the still necessary restriction that the pronoun *leur* must not be affected. The absence of plural liaison with the pronoun *leur* thus needs to be marked in any analysis.

As is well known, plural liaison is not equally possible in all syntactic contexts where a plural word is followed by a vowel-initial word. It has been traditionally recognized that plural liaison may be obligatory (e.g., between an article and a noun, as in *les enfants* [lɛzãfã] 'the children', or between a clitic pronoun and a verb, as in *ils arrivent* [ilzariv] 'they are coming'), optional (e.g., between a noun and an adjective, as in *des tableaux affreux* [dɛtablo(z)afrø] 'horrible paintings'), or practically prohibited (e.g., between a noun and a verb, as in *les soldats arrivent* [lɛsɔldaariv] 'the soldiers are coming'). In standard generative treatments this question has been handled by assuming that liaison takes place across one word boundary but is blocked across two word boundaries, and that a set of universal and language-specific conventions specifies the distribution of word boundaries; certain occurrences of # and ## are categorically determined, giving rise to obligatory and prohibited liaison, respectively; others are variably determined, depending on style; these give rise to the optional cases (see chap. v and Selkirk 1972). This general hypothesis has also been assumed for the plural /z/-insertion analysis, as rule (54) has been written to apply only when a single word boundary separates the plural word from the following vowel-initial word.

Another conceivable approach to the question would be to consider that the application of the insertion process is directly sensitive to the degree of syntactic cohesion between words: everything else being equal, the less tight the cohesion, the less likely the insertion. Style would of course be an additional variable affecting the application of the rule: the more elevated the style, the more likely the insertion. This approach has the advantage over the word-boundary solution of capturing directly the genuine relation that exists between the syntax/style and the phonology. The elimination of at least some word-boundary readjustment rules is also an advantage because it is not always obvious that their existence corresponds to any substantive point about the language. As to the Adjective-Noun Rule, which reduces from two to one the number of word boundaries between an adjective and a noun, it is clear that the point is to capture the fact that there is tighter cohesion between an adjective and a noun than between a noun and an adjective. The substance of the X-Comp Rule, which reduces from two to one the number of word boundaries between an inflected noun, adjective, or verb and its complement, is, however, more difficult to determine; this readjustment rule cannot reasonably mean that in elevated speech the cohesion between these words is stronger than when the nouns, adjectives, or verbs are uninflected, stronger than in less elevated styles, and the same as the cohesion between an adjective and a noun; but then what is the meaning of the readjustment beyond its purely mechanistic function of allowing the formal operation of liaison to apply correctly? The direct approach to the relation between the syntax/style and the phonology, in combination with the insertion treatment of plural liaison, avoids the lack of substance attached to such word-boundary readjustment rules. Another advantage of the direct approach is that it allows for a more differentiated scale of potential liaison contexts. In the word-boundary solution, only three types of separation between words are recognized: zero, one, and two word boundaries. A number of different degrees of syntactic cohesion are thereby merged, apparently incorrectly. For instance, the Adjective-Noun Rule merges the cohesion between an adjective and a noun with that between an article and a noun. Yet, although plural liaison is to my knowledge categorically present after an article, I have heard cases where it did not occur between an adjective and a noun:

(55) *deux longs arrêts* [dølɔ̃arɛ] 'two long stops'
les autres avions [lɛzotravjɔ̃] 'the other planes'
deux autres enfants [døzotrɑ̃fɑ̃] 'two other children'

As another example, note that in elevated speech plural liaison may actually occur between a noun phrase and a verb (e.g., *les soldats avancèrent* [lɛsɔldazavɑ̃sɛr] 'the soldiers moved forward'; cf. Fouché 1959:443), but that everything else being equal, it is less expected in this context than between a noun and an adjective; yet in both cases two word boundaries are assumed. The difference here also is directly captured by the syntax, as is actually recognized by Selkirk (1972), who bases her readjustment from two word boundaries to one between a noun and an adjective on syntactic structure, thereby avoiding a similar reduction in the case of the noun phrase plus verb sequence. It might thus be more accurate to consider plural liaison as a variable process directly affected by the factors of syntactic cohesion and style, rather than as a categorical rule whose application is mediated by word-boundary readjustment rules.[21]

Variability in plural liaison is also introduced along the phonological axis. Consider the syntactic context Adjective + Noun. As observed above, plural liaison may fail to apply in this environment. In the great majority of cases I have noticed, however, the nonapplication of the insertion process correlates with the presence of a final consonant in the preceding word.

(56) *les autres engagés* [lɛzotrãgaže] 'the other participants'
les autres otages [lɛzotrotaž] 'the other hostages'
d'autres associations [dotrasɔsjasjɔ̃] 'other associations'
les autres agences de presse [lɛzotražãsdəprɛs] 'the other press agencies'
d'autres exigences [dotrɛgzižãs] 'other demands'
dix-huit autres appareils [dizɥitotraparɛj] 'eighteen other planes'
cinq autres essais [sɛ̃kotrɛsɛ] 'five other attempts'
les autres années [lɛzotrane] 'the other years'
vingt-cinq autres écrivains [vɛ̃tsɛ̃kotrekrivɛ̃] 'twenty-five other writers'
les intouchables Américains [lɛzɛ̃tušablamerikɛ̃] 'the invincible Americans'
de véritables exploits [dəveritablɛksplwa] 'real feats'
dix-sept mille petites entrées [dissɛtmilpətitãtre] 'seventeen thousand small tickets'
dix-sept nouvelles exécutions [dissɛtnuvɛlɛgzekysjɔ̃] 'seventeen new executions'
des éventuels acquéreurs [dɛzevãtɥelakerœr] 'potential buyers'
les petites et moyennes entreprises [lɛptitemwajɛnãtrəpriz] 'small and average businesses'

21. The direct approach also avoids the paradoxes inherent to the word-boundary readjustment solution which were mentioned at the end of section V.3.2.

les quatre dernières années [lɛkatdɛrnjɛrane] 'the last four years'

les seize premières années [lesɛzprəmjɛrane] 'the first sixteen years'

une ou plusieurs entrées gratuites [ynuplyzjœrãtregratɥit] 'one or several free tickets'

plusieurs écologistes [plyzjœrekɔlɔžist] 'several ecologists'

The operating constraint is phonetically explainable: the presence of the plural marker creates a more complex syllable structure when there is already in the string, at the insertion site, a word-final consonant which can provide an "enchaînement" with the following vowel-initial word. The constraint, however, is not categorical, since plural /z/ only tends not to be inserted if the preceding word ends in a consonant. The phonetic character of the restriction can be naturally incorporated into the framework of the insertion analysis, since the insertion rule, as already noted, has the property of reflecting surface facts directly: it is sufficient to place a variable constraint on rule (54) indicating that the insertion is not favored if X is a consonant. In contrast, the systematic plural-suffix spelling rule and schema (3), which are deeply embedded in the phonological component and opaque with respect to the surface phonetic level (in particular, they are ordered before final-schwa deletion), allow no revealing account of the phenomenon.

VII

A TREATMENT OF [Ø] ~ [C] ALTERNATIONS

VII.1. Introduction

Chapter VI was devoted in part to demonstrating the inadequacy of the abstract generative analysis of French final consonants. The absence of a major phonological process of consonant deletion has drastic implications for the treatment of [Ø] ~ [C] alternations. The main general consequence is that these alternations cannot be handled in a uniform fashion. Arguments provided in section VI.3.3.8. indicate that the various types of [Ø] ~ [C] alternations traditionally recognized are in fact different in nature and thus should not be considered as the reflections of a single phenomenon. Additional evidence is presented in this chapter.

The preceding chapter also offered a motivated analysis of plural liaison based on a direct morphophonological insertion of the plural morpheme /z/ where it appears phonetically. Although plural liaison constitutes an essential aspect of French phonology and morphology (both because of its pervasiveness and crucial functional role in the language, and because of its importance as a testing ground for competing analyses), it represents only part of the linking phenomenon that characterizes Modern French, and an even smaller portion of the [Ø] ~ [C] alternations that pervade the language. This chapter provides a motivated treatment of these phenomena.

The goals of this chapter are thus threefold: (i) to account for the types of liaison encountered in French apart from plural liaison, (ii) to explain the remaining [Ø] ~ [C] alternations found in inflectional and derivational morphology, and (iii) to attempt in every case to anchor the proposed treatment in substantive evidence, and in particular to develop further the type of argumentation already sketched in chapter vi concerning the nonuniform essence of [Ø] ~ [C] alternations.

VII.2. Liaison

In addition to plural liaison, three main areas can be delimited where [Ø] ~ [C] alternations are due to what has been traditionally considered as linking:

(i) Liaison with verbs:

This type of liaison can be divided into three categories:

(a) Optional liaison with person endings:

(1) *nous vivons à Paris* [nuvivɔ̃(z)apari] 'we live in Paris'
ils chantent en choeur [ilšãt(t)ãkœr] 'they sing in chorus'

(b) Obligatory liaison with person endings:

(2) *allons-y* [alɔ̃zi] 'let's go'
chante-t-il? [šãttil] 'does he sing?'

(c) Infinitive liaison:

(3) *chanter en choeur* [šãte(r)ãkœr] 'to sing in chorus'
donner un espoir [dɔne(r)ɛ̃nɛspwar] 'to give hope'

(ii) Liaison with masculine singular adjectives:

A few illustrative examples are:

(4) *un petit écureuil* [ɛ̃ptitekyrœj] 'a small squirrel'
un gros amiral [ɛ̃grozamiral] 'a fat admiral'
un long été [ɛ̃lɔ̃gete] 'a long summer'
le premier invité [ləprəmjerɛ̃vite] 'the first guest'

(iii) Liaison with invariable words:

This type of liaison refers essentially to linking with prepositions and adverbs:

(5) *dans un mois* [dãzɛ̃mwa] 'in a month'
pendant un mois [pãdãtɛ̃mwa] 'for a month'
trop intelligent [tropɛ̃tɛližã] 'too intelligent'
assez intelligent [asezɛ̃tɛližã] 'intelligent enough'

These three cases of liaison, though handled by different systems of rules, all share the feature of resulting from consonant insertion.

VII.2.1. Verb liaison
VII.2.1.1. Optional verb liaison with person endings

The type of verb liaison considered in this section occurs with conjugated forms, provided certain syntactic, morphological, and stylistic conditions are met. For ease of exposition it is assumed that universal and language-specific conventions on the distribution of word boundaries provide a single word boundary between the verb and the next word when these factors are present, and two word boundaries when they are not (see chap. v and Selkirk 1972). I am thus concerned here with predicting the consonant that is inserted when a single word boundary occurs. The analysis does not crucially rest, however, on a necessary mediation by word boundaries.

With conjugated verb forms there are actually only two possible linking consonants, /z/ and /t/. /z/ correlates with the first and second persons, /t/ with the third person. Morphophonological rules comparable to the rule of plural /z/-insertion can thus be written inserting /z/ and /t/ between verbs and vowel-initial words separated by a single word boundary.

With plural verb forms, the insertions are straightforward, as there are no particular restrictions on the processes. The examples given in (6) are wholly representative:

(6) (a) *nous arriverons ensemble* [nuzarivrɔ̃(z)āsābl]
      'we will arrive together'
      vous chantiez encore [vušātje(z)ākɔr]
      'you were still singing'
   (b) *ils arrivent ensemble* [ilzariv(t)āsābl]
      'they are arriving together'
      elles chantèrent encore [ɛlšātɛr(t)ākɔr]
      'they sang again'

Plural verb liaison can thus be formally captured by the following rules:

$$(7) \quad (a) \quad \left. X \right]_V \left[\begin{array}{l} -\text{third person} \\ +\text{plural} \end{array} \right] \quad \# \; [+\text{syll}]$$

$$1 \qquad\qquad\qquad 2 \quad 3 \implies 1 \; 2 \; z \; 2 \; 3$$

$$(b) \quad \left. X \right]_V \left[\begin{array}{l} +\text{third person} \\ +\text{plural} \end{array} \right] \quad \# \; [+\text{syll}]$$

$$1 \qquad\qquad\qquad 2 \quad 3 \implies 1 \; 2 \; t \; 2 \; 3$$

In the singular, verb liaison is more complex, as the type of information provided in rules (7a–b) is insufficient to account for the data. Singular verb liaison is parallel to plural verb liaison in that, if liaison is possible at all, it will be with /z/ in the first and second persons and with /t/ in the third person, as shown in (8) with the imperfect:

(8) (a) *je chantais encore* [žəšātɛ(z)ākɔr]
　　　'I was still singing'
　　　tu chantais encore [tyšātɛ(z)ākɔr]
　　　'you were still singing'
　　(b) *il chantait encore* [ilšātɛ(t)ākɔr]
　　　'he was still singing'

Additional grammatical information is necesssary, however, because in the singular the possibility of verb linking varies, depending on the conjugation classes, moods, and tenses. This is illustrated in (9), with verbs from the first and third groups conjugated in the third person present, passé simple, future, and imperfect of the indicative, and in the third person present of the conditional. (Second-group verbs, e.g., *finir* 'to finish', behave like third-group verbs with respect to liaison.)

(9)

	First-group verbs (e.g., *chanter* 'to sing')	Third-group verbs (e.g., *entendre* 'to hear')
Indicative present	*il chante encore* [ilšāt(*t)ākɔr]	*il entend encore* [ilātā(t)ākɔr]
Passé simple	*il chanta encore* [ilšāta(*t)ākɔr]	*il entendit encore* [ilātādi(t)ākɔr]
Future	*il chantera encore* [ilšātra(*t)ākɔr]	*il entendra encore* [ilātādra(*t)ākɔr]
Imperfect	*il chantait encore* [ilšātɛ(t)ākɔr]	*il entendait encore* [ilātādɛ(t)ākɔr]
Conditional present	*il chanterait encore* [ilšātrɛ(t)ākɔr]	*il entendrait encore* [ilātādrɛ(t)ākɔr]

The grammatical restrictions on singular verb liaison are well known: they affect first-group verbs in the indicative present and passé simple, and in the imperative, and all verb groups in the future and subjunctive.

The rules of consonant insertion for singular verb liaison can be written in a general form similar to that of rules (7a–b), but with an additional set of conditions specifying when they must not apply:

(10) (a) $\left.\begin{matrix} X \\ \\ 1 \end{matrix}\right]_V \begin{bmatrix} -\text{third person} \\ +\text{singular} \end{bmatrix}$ # [+syll]

　　　1　　　　　　　　　　　　2　　3　$\Longrightarrow$　1　2　z　2　3

Conditions: not applicable if
V = first-group indicative present
passé simple
imperative
V = future
subjunctive

(b) X $\Big]$
V [+third person
+singular]
[+syll]

1   2   3   ⟹   1   2   t   2   3

Conditions: not applicable if
V = first-group indicative present
passé simple
V = future
subjunctive present

The conditions on these two rules differ slightly. The imperative restriction is not mentioned in (10b) because there is no third person imperative. In (10b), subjunctive present is specified, as opposed to simply subjunctive for (10a), because liaison may occur in the third person singular of the past subjunctive (e.g., *il eût fallu qu'il chantât encore* [ilyfalykilšāta(t)ākɔr] 'it would have been necessary that he sing again').

There are a few instances the restrictions on (10a–b) do not handle. *Ai* [ɛ], *as* [a], *a* [a] (singular present indicative of *avoir* 'to have'), and *vas* [va], *va* [va] (second and third person singular present indicative of *aller* 'to go') do not link, although the verbs do not belong to the first-conjugation class. This behavior is not surprising, however, since these verbs are irregular in many other respects. In some speakers, liaison is sometimes found after *as* and *vas*, and also after the second person singular of the indicative present and passé simple of first-conjugation verbs (e.g., *tu chantes, tu chantas*), and in the second person singular of the future and subjunctive in all conjugation groups (e.g., *tu chanteras, tu chantes; tu finiras, tu finisses; tu entendras, tu entendes*); the occurrence of liaison with these forms is probably due to the presence of a final *s* in the orthography.

Instead of restricting the process of consonant insertion in singular verb liaison, the framework in which the linking consonants are systematically present underlyingly must enforce deletion; Schane (1968*a*:72) and Selkirk (1972:367) thus postulate a rule of "singular person deletion''; this rule is stated as eliminating the person ending consonants /z/ and /t/ at a word boundary, when they are preceded by the vowels /ə/ or /a/ followed by a morpheme boundary. (The presence of this juncture in the structural description of the rule avoids the deletion of /t/ in the third person plural ending posited to be /ət/.) Because of its phonological conditioning, "singular person deletion" accounts for the absence of liaison with *as, a, vas,* and *va*; it does not, however, cover the absence of liaison with *ai* and, more important, it does not cover the absence of liaison with the first person singular of the passé simple of first-group verbs (e.g., *je chantai* [žəšātɛ]), or with the first person singular of the future of any verb (e.g., *je chanterai* [žəšātrɛ], *je finirai* [žəfinirɛ], *j'entendrai* [žātādrɛ]). That the absence of singular verb liaison in certain cases is directly linked to grammatical factors rather than being governed by the quality of the preceding vowel is further demonstrated by the fact that homophonous verb forms allow or disallow liaison depending on the mood and tense in which they are conjugated; this is illustrated in (11):

(11) (a) *je chantais une chanson* [žəšātɛ(z)ynšãsɔ̄]
'I was singing a song' (imperfect)
je chantai une chanson [žəšātɛ(*z)ynšãsɔ̄]
'I sang a song' (passé simple)
(b) *je chanterais une chanson* [žəšātrɛ(z)ynšãsɔ̄]
'I would sing a song' (conditional present)
je chanterai une chanson [žəšātrɛ(*z)ynšãsɔ̄]
'I will sing a song' (future)

In addition to the grammatical conditions that limit singular verb liaison, there is a phonological restriction also in effect, although perhaps not for all speakers. As attested in a number of pronunciation treatises (e.g., Fouché 1959:462; Léon 1966:120), singular verb liaison is blocked if the verb ends in /r/. In practice, this restriction affects only the indicative present and the imperative of third-conjugation verbs like *dormir* 'to sleep', *courir* 'to run', and *mordre* 'to bite'. Other tenses and moods of third-group verbs have additional segments between the /r/ of the stem and the potential linking consonants; first-conjugation verbs do not link in the cases where the restriction would be operative (cf. the conditions on rules (10a-b)); and conjugated forms of second-group verbs never end in /r/ because of the presence of the thematic vowel /i/ (e.g., *tu guéris* [tygeri] 'you are getting better'). Illustrations of the application of the constraint are given in (12):

(12) *je dors encore* [žədɔr(*z)ākɔr] 'I am still sleeping'
    tu cours encore [tykur(*z)ākɔr] 'you still run'
    il mord encore [ilmɔr(*t)ākɔr] 'he still bites'
    cours encore [kur(*z)ākɔr] 'run again'

For speakers with this phonological restriction, an additional specification must be included in rules (10a-b), namely, X ≠ /r/. This condition does not affect plural verb liaison (e.g., *ils courent encore* [ilkur(t)ākɔr] 'they still run').

The sets of rules (7) and (10) make the claim that the linking consonants are separated from the verb forms by a word boundary. This is consistent with their conditioning of the processes of optional schwa insertion after a consonant cluster and liquid deletion after an obstruent, since these rules apply at word boundaries (see chaps. ii, vi; Tranel 1977*c*; Dell 1970:21-23; 1973*b*:226, 236-238; 1976; 1978*b*):

(13) (a) *elles marchent encore* [ɛlmarš(ə)tākɔr]
        'they are still working'
        (cf. *elles marchent toujours* [ɛlmarš(ə)tužur]
        'they always work')
        ils mordent encore [ilmɔrd(ə)tākɔr]
        'they are still biting'
        (cf. *ils mordent toujours* [ilmɔrd(ə)tužur]
        'they always bite')
    (b) *elles tremblent encore* [ɛltrāb(lə)tākɔr]
        'they are still shaking'
        (cf. *elles tremblent toujours* [ɛltrāb(lə)tužur]
        'they always shake')
        ils rentrent en classe [ilrāt(rə)tāklas]
        'they are going to class'
        (cf. *ils rentrent dans un mur* [ilrāt(rə)dāzɛ̃myr]
        'they are running into a wall')

With respect to the sets of rules (7) and (10), two main types of deviations may occur. First, it is not uncommon to generalize (10) by removing the restrictions on it; thus, one may find "mistakes" like those of (14a) (Sauvageot 1972:135 and personal observations):

(14) (a) *ce règlement devra être révisé*
        [sərɛgləmādəvratɛtrərevize]
        'this regulation will have to be revised'
        en dépit d'une circulation que chacun continue à
        trouver fluide
        [ādepidynsirkylasjɔ̃kəšakɛ̃kɔ̃tinytatruveflɥid]
        'despite a traffic that everybody continues to find fluid'

le nouveau commence à remonter
[lənuvokɔmãstarəmɔ̃te]
'the new one is beginning to come back'
The second type of deviation concerns both sets of rules: an "error" is
made on the linking consonant; the "mistakes" appear to be in the
direction of using /z/ for /t/ rather than the reverse. The examples
given in (14b) are from Sauvageot (1972:135), Jacques Capelovici (see
his column "télé-langage" in the French television guide *Télé 7 Jours*),
and personal observations.

(14) (b) *souhaitons que le ministre soit entendu*
[swɛtɔ̃kələministrəswazãtãdy]
'let us hope that the minister will be heard'
d'on ne sait où [dɔ̃nsɛzu]
'from nowhere'
une qui était encore . . . [ynkietɛzãkɔr]
'one that was still . . .'
ceux qui ne pourront en prendre [søkinəpurɔ̃zãprãdr]
'those that won't be able to take some'
être prêts dès que les Bretons nous feront appel
[ɛtrəpredekələbrətɔ̃nufərɔ̃zapɛl]
'to be ready as soon as the Bretons will call us'
The latter type of deviation is particularly informative with respect
to the debate on consonant deletion versus consonant insertion. In the
framework of the abstract generative analysis of final consonants, it is
assumed that the linking consonants under consideration are part of
the lexical representations of person endings (Schane 1968a:92): /z/,
/z/, /t/ for the singular, /ɔ̃z/, /ez/, /ət/ (/ɔ̃t/ in the future) for the
plural; the linking consonants are thus systematically present underlyingly, and they are deleted in the appropriate cases. This representation of the linking consonants means that, for instance, the /z/ of
/ɔ̃z/ and /ez/ and the /t/ of /ɔ̃t/ have the same lexical status as the
/ɔ̃/ and /e/ of these endings. However, "errors" are not made where
one would use, for example, /ɔ̃z/ instead of /ez/, or vice versa. The
question therefore is why the vocalic part of these endings is stable
whereas speakers make "mistakes" with the linking consonants. The
most probable answer is that these consonants have a different status
from the rest of the endings. The deletion analysis does not capture
this distinction. On the other hand, the analysis proposed here does
by claiming that the person endings are /Ø/ in the singular, /ɔ̃/, /e/,
/Ø/ (/ɔ̃/ for the future) in the plural, and that they are systematically
introduced by spelling rules, whereas the consonants that appear in

liaison are directly inserted by morphophonological rules where they appear phonetically.

The explanatory value of the insertion analysis is also revealed by the consideration of the often noted observation that verb liaison has been declining. In order to explain this fact in the abstract framework, one would have to contend that the readjustment process which, in elevated speech, reduces to one the two word boundaries that would otherwise occur between a verb and its complement (see chap. v) is disappearing from use. Although this might be legitimately considered as a factor, it is not a sufficient explanation. There are cases where the theory predicts a single word boundary after a conjugated verb form (e.g., after the monosyllabic auxiliary *est* 'is'), and yet, although liaison is common after it, it is not obligatory (Malécot 1975*a*):

(15) *il est arrivé* [ilɛ(t)arive] 'he has arrived'

　　elle est amoureuse [ɛlɛ(t)amurøz] 'she is in love'

The regression of liaison in cases like these cannot be accommodated straightforwardly in the context of a consonant-deletion solution.[1] On the other hand, it can easily be explained as the reduced use and progressive loss of the consonant-insertion processes proposed here for optional verb liaison.

The formulation of the verb liaison insertion rules (7a–b) and (10a–b) took for granted the type of word-boundary readjustment rules proposed in Selkirk (1972), in particular the X-Comp Rule. Alternatively, as for plural /z/-insertion, it could be assumed that these consonant-insertion processes are directly sensitive to syntactic structure and style. The same explanation as that given above would account for the general decline of optional verb liaison.

VII.2.1.2. Obligatory verb liaison with person endings

In some instances verb liaison obligatorily occurs, namely, when the verb is followed by a cliticized pronoun.[2] The relevant clitic pro-

---

1. One would have to posit the existence of an additional readjustment rule comparable to Selkirk's (1972) Polysyllabic Non-Lexical Category Rule (see chap. v). This would result in a paradoxical complication of the grammar (cf. sec. VII.2.3.2.). Note also that two word boundaries rather than just one would actually need to be inserted when two auxiliaries are contiguous and are not linked (e.g., *ils ont été appelés à Rome* [ilzɔ̃eteaplearɔm] 'they were called to Rome').

2. When clitic pronouns are cliticized to the following rather than to the preceding verb, verb liaison between the first verb and the following clitic pronoun is of course not obligatory (e.g., *Courez en attraper un* [kure(z)ɑ̃natrapeɛ̃] 'Run and catch one').

nouns (relevant because they are vowel-initial) are the following: *il(s),* *elle(s), on, en,* and *y.* As the examples given in (16) show, the pertinent grammatical environments are interrogative and imperative constructions.

(16) (a) *va-t-il partir?* [vatilpartir] 'is he going to leave?'
  marche-t-elle? [maršətɛl] 'does she walk?'
  traversera-t-on? [travɛrsəratɔ̃] 'will we cross?'
  iront-ils? [irɔ̃til] 'will they go?'
  (b) *manges-en* [mãžžã] 'eat some'
  écrivez-en une [ekrivezãyn] 'write one'
  passes-y [paszy] 'go by there'
  allons-y [alɔ̃zy] 'let's go'

As in optional verb liaison, the linking consonants used in these obligatory cases are [z] for the first and second persons and [t] for the third person. One might therefore think that the same rules as those proposed in the preceding section could be used, the only distinction being one of obligatoriness versus optionality. If it were only a question of obligatoriness which distinguished verb liaison in verb + clitic combinations from verb liaison elsewhere, the close syntactic link between verbs and clitics (see Kayne 1975:chap. 2) would probably be sufficient to explain the difference. In verb + clitic combinations, however, verb liaison, besides being obligatory, is also allowed with verb forms that do not otherwise link (cf. the conditions on rules (10a–b)). Compare (17), for instance, with some of the examples of (16) (the examples given in parentheses in (17) show that these structures allow liaison):

(17) *il va arriver* [ilva(*t)arive] 'he is going to arrive'
  (cf. *je vais arriver* [žəvɛ(z)arive] 'I am going to arrive')
  elle marche encore [ɛlmarš(*t)ãkɔr] 'she is still walking'
  (cf. *elle marchait encore* [ɛlmaršɛ(t)ãkɔr] 'she was still walking')
  on traversera encore [ɔ̃travɛrsəra(*t)ãkɔr] 'we will cross again'
  (cf. *on traverserait encore* [ɔ̃travɛrsərɛ(t)ãkɔr] 'we would cross again')
  mange une poire [mãž(*z)ynpwar] 'eat a pear' (sg.)
  (cf. *mangez une poire* [mãže(z)ynpwar] 'eat a pear' (pl.))
  passe un fruit [pas(*z)ɛ̃frɥi] 'pass a piece of fruit' (sg.)
  (cf. *passez un fruit* [pase(z)ɛ̃frɥi] 'pass a piece of fruit' (pl.))

In addition, as noted earlier, optional verb liaison is declining; in contrast, in verb + clitic combinations, there is absolutely no tendency for liaison not to occur. Finally, the phonological restriction on optional singular verb liaison exemplified in (12) does not operate in obligatory verb liaison, as illustrated in (18):

(18) (a) *il dort encore* [ildɔrãkɔr] *[ildɔrtãkɔr] 'he is still sleeping'
dort-il? *[dɔril] [dɔrtil] 'is he sleeping?'
(b) *cours encore* [kurãkɔr] *[kurzãkɔr] 'run again'
cours-y *[kuri] [kurzi] 'run there'

In verb + clitic combinations, the obligatory insertion of the linking consonants is therefore taken to constitute a process distinct from optional verb liaison, and it is accounted for by a separate system of rules.[3] The rules needed are given in (19):

$$(19)\ (a)\quad \begin{bmatrix} X \\ V \end{bmatrix} \text{Verb [−third person]}\quad \# \quad \text{Clitic} \begin{bmatrix} [+\text{syll}] \end{bmatrix}$$

$$1 \qquad\qquad\qquad 2 \qquad\quad 3 \implies 1\ 2\ z\ 2\ 3$$

$$(b)\quad \begin{bmatrix} X \\ V \end{bmatrix} \text{Verb [+third person]}\quad \# \quad \text{Clitic} \begin{bmatrix} [+\text{syll}] \end{bmatrix}$$

$$1 \qquad\qquad\qquad 2 \qquad\quad 3 \implies 1\ 2\ t\ 2\ 3$$

3. In her framework, Selkirk (1972:358–367) avoids the application of "singular person deletion" in verb + clitic combinations by postulating a readjustment rule that eliminates the word boundary between the verb and the cliticized pronoun. Selkirk finds independent justification for this readjustment rule in the particular domain of application of a process of vowel harmony which switches /ɛ/ to [e] when the next syllable contains a high or high mid vowel: according to Selkirk, this process does not operate between words (e.g., with *très* [trɛ] 'very' and *après* [aprɛ] 'after'), except between verbs and clitics. The readjustment rule she proposes explains this exception, since it eliminates the word boundary between verbs and clitics.

Dialects may vary with respect to vowel harmony (see Dell 1973*b*:215 n. 41). Nevertheless, the following observations appear relevant and may throw some doubt on Selkirk's analysis (see also n. 4, below). Although the pronunciations [ety] for *es-tu* 'are you' and [etil] for *est-il* 'is he' sound natural to me, the pronunciations [avetil] for *avait-il* 'had he', [alety] for *allais-tu* 'were you going', and [ekrivetil] for *écrivait-il* 'was he writing', which Selkirk also provides as illustrations, sound rather unnatural. It is interesting that the grammarians on whom Selkirk relied for her analysis of vowel harmony (Grammont 1914 and Fouché 1959; cf. Selkirk 1972:361, 406 n. 37) gave examples of vowel harmony between verbs and clitics only with the forms *es* and *est* of the auxiliary *être* 'to be', not with other verb forms. (Their actual examples had the pronoun *y* 'there' incorporated: *tu y es* and *il y est* with [ɛ] versus *y es-tu?* and *y est-il?* with [e] (Grammont 1914:41–42; Fouché 1959:71); in these particular instances, the

Like sets (7) and (10), rules (19a–b) claim that a word boundary separates the verb from the linking consonant. Again, optional schwa insertion and liquid deletion operate on such strings in a way consistent with this type of attachment, as shown in (20).[4]

(20) (a) *marche-t-elle?* [marš(ə)tɛl] 'is she walking?'
  traverses-en [travers(ə)zã] 'go across some'
  (b) *tremble-t-il beaucoup?* [trãb(lə)tilboku]
  'is he shaking much?'
  offres-en un [ɔf(rə)zãɛ̃] 'offer one'

---

process of vowel harmony is further motivated phonetically by the presence of a high vowel both before and after the /ɛ/ of the auxiliary.) In addition, vowel harmony may take place in *es* and *est* when, for example, the following word is the pronoun *où* [u] 'where': *tu es où?* [tyeu], *il est où?* [ileu], *elle est où?* [ɛleu]. Since liaison is not obligatory in these examples, it cannot be the case that *où* is cliticized to the verbs and that there is no word boundary between the auxiliaries and the pronoun. It would thus appear that the verb forms *es* and *est* are generally sensitive to vowel harmony, independently of cliticization. The phenomenon actually extends beyond *es* and *est,* as I find this sensitivity to vowel harmony also true of the articles *les* and *des,* the object pronoun *les,* and the possessive adjectives *mes, tes, ses,* although not of *très* 'very' or *après* 'after'. This dichotomy may be explained by the fact that the words in the first group contain a front mid unrounded vowel which can actually vary between [e] and [ɛ] independently of vowel harmony (cf. *il est arrivé* [iletarive] ∼ [ilɛtarive] 'he arrived'; *mes enfants* [mezãfã] ∼ [mɛzãfã] 'my children'), whereas *très* and *après* definitely contain /ɛ/ (cf. *très enfantin* *[trezãfãtɛ̃] [trɛzãfãtɛ̃] 'very childish'; *après avoir vu* *[aprezavwarvy] [aprɛzavwarvy] 'after having seen').

Dell (1973*b*:252) proposes apparently supportive evidence for Selkirk's readjustment rule, but his interpretation of the scope of the rule is actually too narrow to explain all instances of obligatory verb liaison. In Dell's framework, final schwas are obligatorily lost in polysyllabic words. The fact that the clitics *ce* and *je* always lose the schwa in questions with subject inversion (cf. *qui est-ce?* [kies] 'who is it?', *où suis-je?* [usɥiž] 'where am I?') is automatically accounted for if there is no word boundary between the verbs and the clitics. Dell, however, assumes that Selkirk's readjustment rule operates only between verbs and subject clitics, because in verb + object clitic combinations, the schwa of clitics is never lost (cf. *prends-le* [prãlə] 'take it'), except under elision (cf. *donne-m'en* [dɔnmã] 'give me some', *force-l'y* [fɔrsli] 'force him to'). If Selkirk's rule is limited to verb + subject clitic combinations, then "singular person deletion" will apply in verb + object clitic combinations, and obligatory verb liaison in cases like *donnes-en* [dɔnzã] 'give some' will fail to occur (*[dɔnã]). If her rule is applied to all verb + clitic combinations, as she intends, then Dell's rule of final-schwa deletion will incorrectly yield phrases like *[prãl] for *prends-le.*

4. The application of optional schwa insertion and liquid deletion in verb + clitic combinations also argues against the absence of an intervening word boundary advocated by Selkirk (1972) (see n. 3 above). In the environment CC — + C, the presence of a schwa is obligatory (e.g., *gendarme* [žãdarm] 'police officer'/*gendarmerie* [žãdarməri] *[žãdarmri] 'police station'), and in the environment C — + C, liquid deletion is impossible (e.g., *souffle* [sufl] 'puff' (of wind)/*soufflerie* *[sufri] [sufləri] 'wind tunnel') (see Tranel 1977*c*).

VII.2.1.3. Generalizing the rules

The three sets of rules given in (7), (10), and (19) to account for liaison with conjugated verb forms share the characteristics that the only linking consonants are [z] and [t] and that [z] is used in the first and second persons, [t] in the third person. This generalization can be captured by formulating rules inserting a consonantal segment /C/ in the required contexts and by having a separate statement specifying which consonant is to be used, depending on the person of the verb.

$$(7') \quad \left. \begin{matrix} \overline{X} \\ \text{Verb } [+\text{plural}] \end{matrix} \right] \qquad \# \ [+\text{syll}]$$
$$ \quad 1 \qquad\qquad\qquad 2 \quad 3 \ \Longrightarrow \ 1 \ 2 \ C \ 2 \ 3$$

$$(10') \quad \left. \begin{matrix} \overline{X} \\ \text{Verb } [+\text{singular}] \end{matrix} \right] \qquad \# \ [+\text{syll}]$$
$$ \quad 1 \qquad\qquad\qquad 2 \quad 3 \ \Longrightarrow \ 1 \ 2 \ C \ 2 \ 3$$
$$ \quad \text{Conditions: (see (10a–b))}$$

$$(19') \quad \begin{bmatrix} \left. \begin{matrix} \overline{X} \\ \text{Verb} \end{matrix} \right] \\ V \end{bmatrix} \quad \# \quad \text{Clitic} \quad \begin{bmatrix} [+\text{syll}] \end{bmatrix}$$
$$ \quad\quad 1 \qquad 2 \qquad\quad 3 \ \Longrightarrow \ 1 \ 2 \ C \ 2 \ 3$$

Specification of inserted consonant:
     If Verb = [−third person], then C = /z/
     If Verb = [+third person], then C = /t/

VII.2.1.4. Infinitive liaison

/z/ and /t/ are the only linking consonants for conjugated verbs. But /r/ is also a possible linking consonant in verb liaison, namely, when an infinitive of the first-conjugation group is followed by a vowel-initial word:

    (21) *adopter un enfant* [adɔpte(r)ɛ̃nãfã] 'to adopt a child'
         mener un combat [məne(r)ɛ̃kɔ̃ba] 'to lead a fight'
         traverser une crise [travɛrse(r)ynkriz] 'to go through a crisis'

Another rule must therefore be added to the grammar, of the form given in (22):

$$(22) \quad \left. \begin{matrix} e \\ \text{Verb} \begin{bmatrix} +\text{infinitive} \\ +\text{first conjugation} \end{bmatrix} \end{matrix} \right] \qquad\qquad \# \ [+\text{syll}]$$
$$ \quad 1 \qquad\qquad\qquad\qquad\qquad\qquad 2 \quad 3 \ \Longrightarrow 1 \ 2 \ r \ 2 \ 3$$

Since the type of liaison illustrated in (21) is nowadays extremely rare and limited to certain oratory styles, it is assumed that rule (22) belongs only to the grammar of linguistically very conservative speakers, and perhaps only in elevated styles.[5]

The minor character of rule (22) is underscored by data that reveal imperfect knowledge of this process in certain speakers. The "mistakes" that occur can often be interpreted as hypercorrections toward an elevated type of norm; for instance, I heard *tous décidés à* 'all determined to' pronounced [tusdesidera] instead of [tusdesidea]; here the /e/ ending of the past participle misled the speaker into inserting the infinitive linking consonant /r/. Conversely, when there is an infinitive, a consonant other than /r/ may sometimes be inserted, as in *pour remédier aux manifestations* 'to remedy demonstrations', pronounced [purrəmedjezomanifɛstasjɔ̃] instead of [purrəmedje(r)omanifɛstasjɔ̃] (Sauvageot 1972:135). (The intrusive [z] may be a prefixal plural marker; see sec. VI.4.1.2.)

VII.2.2. Adjective liaison

Liaison between a masculine singular adjective and a following noun is also accounted for by morphophonological consonant insertion. In chapter iii (sec. III.5.3.3.) and in chapter vi (sec. VI.3.) several arguments are developed against a treatment based on consonant deletion, whether morphophonological or phonological. The insertion approach itself, however, faces two important problems, which have to do with consonant prediction and the existing correlation between the liaison consonants and the gender consonants. This section is devoted to a resolution of these questions. The presentation of most of the positive evidence in favor of the insertion analysis in adjective liaison is delayed until [Ø] ~ [C] gender alternations are taken up (see sec. VII.3.2.).

There is more than one way in which masculine singular adjectives are connected with a following noun: there may be no linking consonant present at all, or one of five consonants may occur (/t/, /z/, /g/ (/k/ for some speakers), and /r/; /n/ must also be added to this list (cf. Part I)). This is illustrated in (23):

(23) *un joli étang* [ɛ̃ʒɔlietɑ̃] 'a pretty lake'
un grand écrivain [ɛ̃grɑ̃tekrivɛ̃] 'a great writer'

5. For some speakers, infinitive liaison is reported to be accompanied by an opening of /e/ to [ɛ] (e.g., *mener un combat* [mənɛrɛ̃kɔ̃ba]). See section VII.3.2.2. for a brief discussion of this phenomenon.

un gros intérêt [ẽgrozẽterɛ] 'a big interest'
un long après-midi [ẽlɔ̃gaprɛmidi] 'a long afternoon'
un léger incident [ẽležerẽsidã] 'a slight incident'
un certain auteur [ẽsɛrtɛnotœr] 'a certain author'

As often observed, it is not possible to predict absolutely, on the basis of the form of the masculine singular adjective, whether liaison will take place, and if it does, which linking consonant will appear. This is shown briefly by the following pairs of contrasting examples:

(24) (a) *joli* [žɔli] 'pretty' (masc.)/*petit* [pəti] 'small' (masc.)
    un joli étang [ẽžɔlietã] 'a pretty lake'
    un petit étang [ẽpətitetã] 'a small lake'
(b) *gros* [gro] 'big' (masc.)/*haut* [o] 'high' (masc.)
    un gros intérêt [ẽgrozẽterɛ] 'a big interest'
    un haut intérêt [ẽotẽterɛ] 'a high interest'

There is, however, a definite correlation between the type of linking which a masculine singular adjective allows and the form of its feminine counterpart. Thus, when the feminine adjective has no final consonant distinguishing it from the masculine form, no liaison is possible; when there is a distinguishing final consonant in the feminine, there is in general a linking consonant with the masculine singular form, and this consonant is either the same as the feminine consonant or a phonetically closely related one. (Specifically, if the feminine consonant is /d/, the liaison consonant is /t/; if the feminine consonant is /s/, the liaison consonant is /z/; and for some speakers, if the feminine consonant if /g/, the liaison consonant is /k/.) To illustrate this, the feminine forms of the adjectives used in (23) are given in (25):

(25) *jolie* [žɔli]
    grande [grãd]
    grosse [gros]
    longue [lɔ̃g]
    légère [ležɛr]
    certaine [sɛrtɛn]

The advantage provided within the frameworks assuming consonant deletion (e.g., Schane 1968*a,* Tranel 1974*b*) was that the consonants that appear in the feminine forms were posited lexically (as part of the phonological representations of the adjectives). The question of predicting the consonants was thereby eliminated, and the correlation between the existence and nature of a final consonant in the feminine and the existence and nature of a linking consonant in the masculine singular was captured immediately.

Although certain predictions based on the form of the masculine adjectives can be made about the existence and nature of these consonants (see sec. VII.3.2.1.), it is clearly correct to consider that the knowledge of whether or not a consonant may be present, and which it is if there is one, is sufficiently idiosyncratic to be regarded as lexical in nature. This does not mean, however, that one must abandon the idea of an insertion approach and adopt a deletion solution, for in this instance one may have the best of both worlds.

Under an insertion analysis of linking consonants with masculine singular adjectives, the grammar would seem to require as many rules of consonant insertion as there are possible liaison consonants, and lexical markings on adjectives determining which insertion rule (if any) they are supposed to undergo. The postulation of several different insertion rules offers the disadvantage of not capturing the unity of the process involved. In addition, this solution would be equivalent to having adjective classes, the /t/ class, the /z/ class, and so on. The notion of adjective class is not without merit, but as will be seen in section VII.3.2.1., it should in general be based on the phonological and/or morphological properties of masculine adjectives rather than on the liaison or gender consonants they take; for example, one can legitimately define the class of adjectives ending in the suffix -eux /ø/ (they take /z/); on the other hand, there are no grounds for considering all the adjectives taking /z/ as a homogeneous class.

Following a suggestion made by Schane (1978a), I assume that there is a single rule generally inserting an unspecified consonantal segment /C/ between a masculine singular adjective and a following noun. A provisional formulation of this rule is given in (26):

$$(26) \quad \begin{bmatrix} +\text{syll} \end{bmatrix} \Big]_A \begin{bmatrix} +\text{masc} \\ +\text{sg} \end{bmatrix} \quad \# \quad N\begin{bmatrix} +\text{syll} \end{bmatrix}$$

$$1 \qquad\qquad 2 \qquad 3 \implies 1\ 2\ C\ 2\ 3$$

Adjectives are lexically specified as to which linking consonant, if any, they require; by convention, the features of this consonant fill in the unspecified features of the inserted /C/; if an adjective has no such lexical consonant, then /C/ automatically receives a null phonetic realization. Provisional partial lexical entries are illustrated in (27):

(27) *joli*   /žɔli/
    petit   /pəti/   (/t/)
    grand   /grã/   (/t/)
    gros   /gro/   (/z/)
    long   /lɔ̃/   (/g/)
    léger   /leže/   (/r/)
    certain /sɛrtɛ̃/   (/n/)

This approach is intuitively appealing; in essence, it states directly that the language provides for a consonantal liaison process between masculine singular adjectives and nouns, but that only certain adjectives may link with certain consonants; which adjectives link and which linking consonants are associated with which adjectives is lexically determined. With respect to this lexical determination, it is important to emphasize that the consonants given in parentheses in (27) are not part of the phonological representations of the adjectives; rather, they are idiosyncratic phonological markings which are simply part of the lexical entries. This is a crucial difference between the insertion and the deletion analyses (see sec. VII.3.2.).

It is immediately apparent that this type of treatment allows for an explanation of the existing correlation between linking consonants and feminine consonants. Assume that instead of indicating in the lexicon which linking consonant is associated with which adjective, the gender consonants are thus specified (see sec. VII.3.2. for details on the treatment of masculine/feminine [Ø] ~ [C] alternations):

(28) *joli*   /žɔli/
    petit   /pəti/   (/t/)
    grand   /grã/   (/d/)
    gros   /gro/   (/s/)
    long   /lɔ̃/   (/g/)
    léger   /leže/   (/r/)
    certain /sɛrtɛ̃/   (/n/)

It can be redundantly assumed that this lexically specified consonant is chosen for linking as well as for gender marking. In linking, additional rules will automatically change /d/ to /t/, /s/ to /z/, and in some dialects /g/ to /k/. That the gender consonants rather than the linking consonants should be lexically specified is only natural, since the latter have a much more restricted role than the former; in particular, nouns that exhibit a masculine/feminine [Ø] ~ [C] alternation do not normally enter into liaison in the masculine singular, and many adjectives that also exhibit this type of gender alternation cannot occur in prenominal position and therefore do not link in the masculine singular either.

For adjective liaison, rule (26) is assumed to replace rule (51) of chapter iii, which specifically inserted /n/. (The minor rule of vowel denasalization given there as (52) continues to operate as before.) The explicit inclusion in the scope of (26) of adjective liaison with /n/ requires a few modifications in the formulation of the rule. Liaison with the possessive adjectives *mon, ton, son,* is supposed to be handled by rule (26). But in some instances words like *mon* must in fact be marked [+feminine], namely, when they are used with a following vowel-initial feminine word (e.g., *mon amie* [mɔ̃nami] 'my friend' (fem.)); the presence of the feature [+masculine] in rule (26) incorrectly prevents such outputs. The specification [+masculine] is actually not necessary in the formulation of the process; as argued in chapter iii, when an adjective is feminine and part of a string that meets the structural description of adjective liaison (because of the absence of the feature [+masculine] in the rule), feminine formation automatically takes precedence. The removal of the specification [+masculine] from the rule of adjective liaison is thus a legitimate simplification, and it allows for liaison with words like *mon* in feminine strings.

In addition to occurring before nouns, words like *mon* and the article *un* also appear before adjectives and enter into liaison with them (e.g., *son admirable courage* [sɔ̃nadmirabləkuraž] 'his admirable courage'); rule (26) fails to account for such linking because item 3 of the rule is specified as a noun. It must also be specified as an adjective. Rule (26) might also be considered to fail to apply with items like *mon* and *un* because these words, strictly speaking, are not adjectives. They do, however, fall into a class with adjectives, namely, that of noun modifiers.

The rule of adjective liaison will therefore be written as follows, with the understanding that the symbol A covers noun modifiers:

$$(29) \quad [+\text{syll}]\Big]_A \;[+\text{sg}] \quad \# \quad N\begin{bmatrix}[+\text{syll}] \\ A\end{bmatrix}$$

$$1 \qquad\qquad 2 \qquad 3 \;\Longrightarrow\; 1\;2\;C\;2\;3$$

VII.2.3. Liaison with invariable words

The type of morphological information which plays a crucial part in the treatment of the liaison phenomena considered so far (plural liaison, verb liaison, and adjective liaison) is not relevant to invariable words like prepositions and adverbs. A consonant-insertion treatment of liaison with prepositions and adverbs thus slightly distinct in character from the other cases just mentioned will now be proposed and justified.

VII.2.3.1. Formal proposal

As in the cases of liaison dependent on morphological information, the analysis of liaison with prepositions and adverbs assumes that short forms, or citation forms, are basic. To account for the occurrences of the long forms, I postulate minor rules of consonant insertion which prepositions and adverbs, as well as a few other words, are lexically marked to undergo. The rules given in (30) insert /z/, /t/, /p/, and /n/; I provide in each case examples of words subject to the rule.

(30) (a) X # [+syll]

    1 2   3 $\Longrightarrow$ 1 2 z 2 3

    — prepositions: *dans* /dā/ 'in'; *chez* /še/ 'at';
            sans /sā/ 'without'; *sous* /su/ 'under';
            après /aprɛ/ 'after'; *depuis* /dəpųi/ 'since'
    — adverbs: *très* /trɛ/ 'very'; *moins* /mwɛ̃/ 'less';
            assez /ase/ 'enough'
    — also *deux* /dø/ 'second'; *trois* /trwa/ 'third'
            (i.e., when not plural; see sec. VI.4.)

(b) X # [+syll]

    1 2   3 $\Longrightarrow$ 1 2 t 2 3

    — prepositions: *devant* /dəvā/ 'in front of';
            durant /dyrā/ 'during'; *pendant* /pādā/ 'during'
    — adverbs: *tant* /tā/ 'so'; *fort* /fɔr/ 'very'; *-ment* /-mā/
            '-ly' adverbs (e.g., *absolument* [apsɔlymā]
            'absolutely')
    — also *vingt* /vɛ̃/ 'twenty'; *cent* /sā/ 'one hundred';
            dont /dɔ̃/ (relative pronoun)

(c) X # [+syll]

    1 2   3 $\Longrightarrow$ 1 2 p 2 3

    — only two words: *trop* /tro/ 'too much'; *beaucoup*
            /boku/ 'much'

(d) $\begin{bmatrix} V \\ +\text{nasal} \end{bmatrix}$ # [+syll]

            1   2   3 $\Longrightarrow$ 1 2 n 2 3

— the preposition *en* /ã/ 'in'
— adverbs: *bien* /bjẽ/ 'well'; *rien* /rjẽ/ 'nothing'
— pronouns: *en* /ã/ (de NP); *on* /õ/ 'one'

For rule (30b) it is probable that every *-ment* adverb is not marked individually, but that there exists a redundancy rule stating that these words are automatically marked [+rule (30b)]. This redundancy rule is actually necessary if all such adverbs are not lexically entered, as is likely. Rule (30d) supersedes rule (51) of chapter iii for words that are not noun modifiers (for noun modifiers, see sec. VII.2.2.).

For prepositions and adverbs, it is well known that the length of the word plays a role in liaison: everything else being equal, liaison with monosyllabic prepositions and adverbs is more basic than liaison with polysyllabic ones. It is also well known that liaison becomes more widespread with polysyllabic items as style becomes more elevated. These facts can be accounted for by means of word-boundary readjustment rules which are sensitive to word length and style (cf. Selkirk's 1972 Polysyllabic Non-Lexical Category Rule and Lexical Specifier Rule) and which leave one word boundary in cases of liaison, two otherwise. This hypothesis has been assumed in the formalizations provided in (30), as indicated by the single word boundary written in the structural descriptions of the rules. Alternatively, the insertion processes could be made directly sensitive to the length of the prepositions and adverbs and to style. Such alternatives were already briefly discussed and compared in the contexts of the studies on plural liaison (sec. VI.4.) and verb liaison (sec. VII.2.1.). I return to this topic toward the end of the following section. Otherwise I concentrate on providing positive evidence for the consonant-insertion approach by means of minor rules, as opposed to the deletion treatment via a major phonological process.

VII.2.3.2. Justification of the analysis

Besides the difference in liaison behavior between monosyllabic and polysyllabic prepositions and adverbs, and besides the role played by style, other important distinctions and tendencies must be recognized and explained in the area of linking with invariable words. The insertion analysis proposed here is of particular explanatory value in these respects.

There are clearly different liaison patterns for the monosyllabic adverbs *très* and *trop*. According to Cohen (1963:111–112), "L'adverbe le plus usuel, *très*, paraît comporter normalement la liaison:

'très-z-agréable, très-z-agréablement'. . . . Pour *trop,* il y a plus de flottement. J'ai noté récemment sur moi-même 'sans trop-p-attendre' et à la radio 'une idée tro(p) incomplète'." Also in need of an explanation is the fact that some native speakers occasionally make a "mistake" and link *trop* with [z], whereas, to my knowledge, *très* never links with [p] (or any other "incorrect" consonant).

The analysis proposed here explains these matters in a straightforward fashion. A relatively large number of lexical items are marked to undergo the /z/-insertion rule (30a); on the other hand, only two words may actually undergo the /p/-insertion rule (30c). Thus, although both minor, rules (30a) and (30c) differ in the sense that (30c) is "more minor" than (30a). In addition, the process of /z/-insertion by rule (30a) may be reinforced by the existence of other /z/-insertion rules (e.g., plural liaison); no such reinforcement applies for rule (30c). These differences between rules (30a) and (30c) explain the comparatively low application rate of /p/-insertion with *trop* and "mistakes" of the type [trozelegā] instead of [tro(p)elegā] for *trop élégant* 'too elegant'; native speakers tend not to apply a very minor rule such as (30c), or they know that *trop* can trigger a consonant-insertion process, but they use the "incorrect" consonant, one that is otherwise inserted with relative frequency.

In a deletion analysis the linking consonants are assumed to be part of the phonological representations (*très* /trɛz/, *trop* /trop/); they thus have the same status as the other segments in the words and the same status as one another. Therefore no ground exists to explain why the final consonant of *trop* may "mistakenly" appear as [z], whereas the other segments (/t/, /r/, /o/) never fail to appear correctly, and why it is the /p/ of *trop*, rather than the /z/ of *très*, which creates "difficulties" for native speakers.

Another important trend leading to problems in a deletion treatment, but easily explained within the insertion framework developed here, concerns the general regression of liaison with prepositions and adverbs. It has traditionally been assumed (Delattre 1951:27, 30, 33; Selkirk 1972:211–218) that monosyllabic prepositions and adverbs obligatorily link with a following vowel-initial word, whereas polysyllabic prepositions and adverbs exhibit the variability usually associated with style. Although it remains true, as mentioned earlier, that everything else being equal, liaison with monosyllabic prepositions and adverbs is more basic than liaison with polysyllabic prepositions and adverbs, it is actually false to claim that liaison with monosyllabic prepositions and adverbs is obligatory in contemporary French. Independent observations by several linguists point to the tendency to suppress liaison with monosyllabic prepositions and adverbs. For example, Cohen (1963:111–112) says: "Je dis 'dans-z-une heure', 'sous-z-un arbre'; 'dan(s) une heure', 'sou(s) un arbre' me paraît un peu plaisant, ou *langage de jeune*. . . . Devant infinitif, je dis 'sans-z-essayer', comme 'sans-z-aucun doute', mais j'ai recueilli, *d'intellectuels pas tout jeunes,* 'san(s) essayer', 'san(s) appliquer ça', 'san(s) y répondre' " (emphases mine). Concerning adverbs, as noted above, Cohen finds that if *très* normally links, the same is certainly not true for *trop*; however, Cohen also adds about *très*: "L'absence de [z] est *ou est encore* insolite" (emphasis mine), thus suggesting a sporadic absence of liaison with *très* as the beginning of a possible trend (see Malécot 1975*a*, cited below, for confirmation of Cohen's foresight). For *plus,* Cohen indicates that "la liaison est habituelle; mais j'ai une fiche 'plu(s) assidument'." On the basis of data gathered in systematic fashion a few years later, Malécot (1975*a*:176) states in the same vein: "Monosyllabic adverbs and prepositions were formally said always to make the liaison with a following word. Our analysis has proven what many of us have observed for quite some time, namely that the liaison for a number of these is optional rather than obligatory. Cultivated people now often say *très intéressant* and the like without making the liaison."

Parallel to this regression of liaison with monosyllabic prepositions and adverbs, the tendency seems to be for liaison with polysyllabic prepositions and adverbs to be restricted to more elevated styles than it formerly was. According to Cohen (1963:111–112), ". . . en conversation, il me semble bien que c'est 'aprè(s) enquête', 'aprè(s) une visite aussi prolongée' qui me sont naturels. . . . En ce qui concerne *assez,* je pense qu'il échappe plus souvent à la liaison [que *plus*], pour avoir recueilli récemment dans un commentaire diplomatique de Radio-Luxembourg: 'les opinions demeurent asse(z) éloignées' et 'la vie économique semble avoir été asse(z) active' de la bouche d'un très savant paléographe." Similarly, Malécot (1975*a*) indicates that, in "natural conversations by members of the educated middle class of Paris" (161), "polysyllabic adverbs almost never make the liaison to the following word" and "polysyllabic prepositions never make the liaison to the following word" (165).

For short-term diachronic perspective, Cohen's and Malécot's observations, based on material collected in the sixties, may be contrasted with those of Martinon (1913:374): "La liaison est encore nécessaire avec les prépositions monosyllabiques, *dans, dès, sans, chez, sous,* devant leurs régimes . . . elle est un peu moins indis-pensable avec *après* ou *depuis*. . . . La liaison doit se faire aussi cor-rectement avec les mots négatifs *pas, plus, jamais,* si peu qu'ils soient liés au mot suivant . . . de même avec les adverbes de quantité *plus, moins, très, assez,* portant sur le mot qui suit."

This trend toward a general decline of liaison with prepositions and adverbs (whether they are monosyllabic or polysyllabic) is ac-counted for very naturally in the analysis proposed here. The insertion rules are minor rules; in other words, the lexical items marked to undergo them have lexical entries that are complicated by the exis-tence of a special feature. The elimination of this marking, an ex-pected change in the grammar, leads to the increasing absence of liai-son noted by observers.

In an analysis of liaison based on consonant deletion rather than on consonant insertion, certain paradoxes arise when one attempts to account for this decline. For instance, in Selkirk's (1972) analysis, universal conventions concerning the placement of word boundaries stipulate that prepositions and adverbs like *dans, sous, très, trop,* are separated from the next word by at most a single word boundary. (Since these words are not considered to belong to lexical categories, they do not carry word boundaries at their sides.) They are therefore always in the correct syntactic environment for liaison, and it be-comes rather difficult to explain why linking with such words is disappearing.

In the spirit of Selkirk's framework, one would perhaps argue that this elimination of liaison can be accounted for by means of a word-boundary readjustment rule inserting the necessary word boundaries in the relevant contexts, thus forcing the application of the process of final consonant deletion. A similar rule is actually posited by Selkirk to account for the fact that basic liaison does not take place, for in-stance, between a polysyllabic adverb like *assez* and a following word (cf. her Polysyllabic Non-Lexical Category Rule). The generalization of this boundary-reinforcing rule to monosyllabic nonlexical preposi-tions and adverbs (and also auxiliaries; see sec. VII.2.1.1. and n. 1 above) in a certain type of familiar speech would, however, be para-doxical, because boundaries between words actually ought to be as-sumed to be less strong in relatively casual speech than in relatively careful speech, since sandhi processes normally take place in the lan-guages of the world more often and in more places in casual, rapid speech than in careful, slow speech. (As noted in chapter v, this paradox is inherent in Selkirk's language-specific word boundary readjustment rules.) In the insertion treatment, on the other hand, there is no paradox, because we are in the presence of minor rules of consonant insertion which can accommodate an account where liaison is made directly sensitive to syntactic structure and style rather than being dependent on word-boundary readjustments (cf. secs. VI.4. and VII.2.1.), and which will naturally tend not to apply under the stylistic and tempo conditions ordinarily favoring the application of major phonetically motivated sandhi rules.

The insertion treatment proposed for liaison with invariable words receives additional support when one compares liaison after monosyllabic prepositions and adverbs with adjective liaison and prenominal plural liaison. All three types of liaison occur in syntactic structures of comparable cohesion, and they have been traditionally considered as prime examples of obligatory or basic liaison. However, whereas linking has remained practically obligatory in adjective and prenominal plural liaison,[6] a different trend has been operating in monosyllabic preposition and adverb liaison, as noted above. This distinction shows that native speakers conceive of liaison in these two groups as different in character. The explanation for the difference is straightforward within the framework developed here. One group exhibits [Ø] ~ [C] liaison alternations which are governed by grammatical factors (plural marking in plural liaison), or which are paralleled by morphological distinctions (gender in adjective liaison). On the other hand, in the case of prepositions and adverbs, there is an obvious absence of independent motivation for latent consonants, a fact that may be the key to a real explanation of the tendency for prepositions and adverbs to eliminate linking with following words. Whereas the approach to liaison advocated here captures this explanation directly, in a treatment where liaison is accounted for uniformly by assuming that latent consonants are part of the underlying representations and that their surface distribution is the result of a phonological process of final consonant deletion, one simply cannot straightforwardly account for the split that has taken place in the contemporary realization of the phenomenon of liaison in syntactic structures of comparable cohesion.

Concerning numerals, *deux* and *trois* are marked to undergo rule (30a) when they have an ordinal value ('second', 'third'). As seen

6. For some violations of this obligatoriness, see secs. VI.4.2. and VII.3.2.2.

earlier (sec. VI.4.1.4.), this type of linking is in regression, a phenomenon in keeping with the minor character of this rule of /z/-insertion. The numerals *vingt* 'twenty' and *cent* 'a hundred' are supposed to undergo rule (30b), that is, to link with /t/ (e.g., *vingt hommes* [vɛ̃tɔm] 'twenty men'; *cent hommes* [sãtɔm] 'a hundred men'), but they frequently fail to do so, as predicted by the analysis. When used with a plural value, they tend to link with /z/, that is, to undergo the rule of plural /z/-insertion. This tendency may be more common with *cent* than with *vingt*. Cohen (1972:16) reports an experiment in which 47 children between the ages of six and fourteen were asked to say 'a hundred eggs'; to the difficulty of the linking was of course added the problem of the pronunciation of the word *oeuf* in the plural (cf. sec. VI.4.1.3.); the "right" answer is supposed to be [sãtø]. None of the children actually provided a completely "correct" answer: a large majority (37) expectedly used [z] as the linking consonant (32 said [sãzø] and 5 said [sãzœf]); 8 did not use a linking consonant at all (2 said [sãø] and 6 said [sãœf]); and only 2 used the linking consonant [t] (but they said [sãtœf]). When *vingt* has an ordinal value (with names of months), the linking with [t], by rule (30a), tends not to occur, as predicted, and the linking with [z], by plural /z/-insertion, is expectedly impossible (e.g., *le vingt octobre* [ləvɛ̃(t)ɔktɔbr] *[ləvɛ̃zɔktɔbr] 'October 20th').

VII.2.3.3. Apparent exceptions

There are a few apparent exceptions to the trend of declining liaison with invariable words. The first concerns the preposition *chez* when it is followed by the vowel-initial pronouns *eux* and *elle(s)*: *chez eux* [šezø] *[šeø] 'at their place' (masc.), *chez elle(s)* [šezɛl] *[šeɛl] 'at her (their) place' (fem.). Although liaison with *chez* is optional when a full noun phrase follows (*chez Irène* [še(z)irɛn] 'at Irene's', *chez un ami* [še(z)ɛ̃nami] 'at a friend's'), it is not just the distinction pronoun/full noun phrase which is relevant, because with other prepositions, liaison is optional with pronouns as well as with full noun phrases (e.g., *sans elle* [sã(z)ɛl] 'without her', *sans Irène* [sã(z)irɛn] 'without Irene', *sans un ami* [sã(z)ɛ̃nami] 'without a friend'). The semantics of the expressions *chez eux* and *chez elle(s)* have apparently contributed to a lexicalization of these word combinations with liaison which is comparable to the lexicalization with obligatory liaison after a noun in phrases like *accent aigu* [aksãtegy] *[aksãegy] 'acute accent', *Etats-Unis* [etazyni] *[etayni] 'United States', and *pot au feu* [potofø] *[poofø] 'stew'.

Another apparent exception is the preposition *en* (cf. *en elle* [ānɛl] *[āɛl] 'in her'; *en Irlande* [ānirlād] *[āirlād] 'in Ireland'; *en un mois* [ānɛ̃mwa] ?*[āɛ̃mwa] 'in a month'). Here, since the use of linking with the preposition *en* is unlimited, one cannot claim that phrase lexicalization has taken place. The explanation for the absence of a nonlinking alternative appears to reside in the nature of rule (30d), which accounts for the presence of the /n/ in liaison with invariable words. This rule has a less arbitrary status than the other rules of liaison given in (30). As pointed out in chapter iii, /n/ is inserted only when a nasal vowel precedes.[7] In a sense, then, this process is phonologically motivated, at least to a point that is not reached by the other rules (cf. Beauzée 1765:1–2, cited in chap. iv). This partial phonological motivation may reinforce the use of the process and explain its obligatoriness with *en*. This obligatoriness also affects the clitic pronouns *en* and *on* (*il en apporte* [ilānapɔrt] *[ilāapɔrt] 'he is bringing some'; *on arrive* [ɔ̃nariv] *[ɔ̃ariv] 'we are coming'), although in the case of *on* the [n] may fail to be inserted before the clitic pronoun *y* /i/ when it is realized as [j] before a vowel-initial verb (*on y arrivera* [ɔ̃njarivra] ~ [ɔ̃jarivra] 'we'll get there'). Concerning the preposition *en* and its use in Parisian French, Yves Morin (personal communication) has actually observed the absence of liaison when *en* is followed by the indefinite article (e.g., *en un mois* [āɛ̃mwa] 'in a month', *en une heure* [āynœr] 'in an hour'), but never when there is no article (e.g., *en argent* *[āaržā] 'in silver'). My own intuition runs parallel to these data in that I find the former type of examples relatively acceptable compared with the latter (?*[āɛ̃mwa], ?*[āynœr] versus *[āaržā]). Yves Morin's observations and my judgments of relative grammaticality may be explained by direct reference to surface syntactic configurations, the cohesion between *en* and what follows being structurally less tight in the first instance than in the second ($_{PP}[_P[en]_{NP}[_{ART}[un]_N[mois]]]$ versus $_{PP}[_P[en]_N[argent]]$).

With the adverbs *bien* and *rien*, liaison is not obligatory (e.g., *il est bien arrivé* [ilɛbjɛ̃(n)arive] 'he arrived safely'; *il (n') est rien arrivé* [ilɛrjɛ̃(n)arive] 'nothing happened'). The difference with *en* and *on* might be attributable to a relatively stronger degree of syntactic cohesion between the preposition *en* and its object and between the pronouns *en* or *on* and their verbs than between the adverbs *bien* and

---

7. It does not follow that all words ending in a nasal vowel take /n/ as a linking consonant. Cf. *dans, sans,* which link with /z/; *tant, dont,* which link with /t/; and *selon,* which does not normally link (but I have heard the phrase *selon eux* 'according to them' pronounced [səlɔ̃tø] instead of [səlɔ̃ø]).

rien and the words they modify. A prepositional phrase or a clitic + verb combination do seem to form a tighter unit than an adverb + adjective combination; in particular, whereas the preposition and pronoun *en* may not be emphatically stressed or intonationally detached, the adverbs *bien* and *rien* may, which attests to their greater independence. The word *on* may marginally be stressed and intonationally detached when the emphasis is placed on the anonymity of those hiding behind *on* 'they' (*on a dit que . . . 'they* said that . . .'); but precisely in this case there is no linking ([ɔ́adikə]) (cf. Martinon 1913:391), as *on* functions in the NP slot rather than as a clitic.

VII.3. Remaining [Ø] ~ [C] alternations

There remain three types of [Ø] ~ [C] alternations to consider:

(i) The verb-stem alternations found in the conjugation of third-group verbs:

(31) (*il*) *sort* [sɔr]   /(*ils*) *sortent* [sɔrt]
      '(he) goes out' '(they) go out' (indicative)
                      /(*il*) *sorte* [sɔrt]
                      '(he) go out' (subjunctive)
    (*il*) *dort* [dɔr] /(*il*) *dorment* [dɔrm]
    '(he) sleeps'   '(they) sleep' (indicative)
                      /(*il*) *dorme* [dɔrm]
                      '(he) sleep' (subjunctive)

(ii) The masculine/feminine alternations in nouns and adjectives:

(32) *avocat* [avɔka]/*avocate* [avɔkat] 'lawyer'
      teinturier [tɛ̃tyrje]/*teinturière* [tɛ̃tyrjɛr] 'dry cleaner'
      heureux [ørø]/*heureuse* [ørøz] 'happy'
      chaud [šo]/*chaude* [šod] 'hot'

(iii) The alternations found in derivational morphology:

(33) *galop* [galo]/*galoper* [galɔpe] 'gallop'/'to gallop'
      poli [pɔli]/*politesse* [pɔlitɛs] 'polite'/'politeness'
      ami [ami]/*amical* [amikal] 'friend'/'friendly'

VII.3.1. Verb-stem alternations

These alternations are characteristic of third-conjugation verbs. The presence/absence of the consonant depends on the grammatical features of number, tense, and mood. Thus, the consonant is absent in the present singular indicative and imperative, and present elsewhere.

These grammatically governed alternations can be formalized in various ways. For instance, the consonant could be considered as a type of thematic consonant present under certain grammatical conditions. Verbs belonging to the third-conjugation class would thus be divided into various groups, depending on which thematic consonant they take, as illustrated in (34):

(34) (i) /d/ e.g., *entendre* 'to hear', *attendre* 'to wait'
  (ii) /t/ e.g., *sortir* 'to go out', *sentir* 'to feel'
  (iii) /m/ e.g., *dormir* 'to sleep'
  (iv) /v/ e.g., *vivre* 'to live'
  (v) /k/ e.g., *vaincre* 'to defeat'

This treatment would be comparable to the one commonly assumed for second-conjugation verbs (e.g., *finir* 'to finish', *alunir* 'to land on the moon'). These verbs take a thematic vowel /i/ and a thematic consonant /s/. The /s/, however, is absent not only in the present singular indicative and imperative, but also in the infinitive, future, and conditional.

This type of analysis of third-group verbs essentially assumes that the short forms are basic. Instead, one could postulate, as I suggested elsewhere (Tranel 1974*b*:196–197; 1978*b*:48–49), that the base forms include the consonants and that a morphophonological rule of final-consonant deletion such as (35) eliminates the stem-final consonants in the required grammatical contexts.

$$(35) \quad C \quad \#\left.\begin{array}{l} \\ \\ \\ \end{array}\right] \left[\begin{array}{l} -\text{subjunctive} \\ +\text{present} \\ +\text{singular} \\ +\text{third conj.} \end{array}\right]$$
$$1 \quad 2 \qquad\qquad\qquad \Longrightarrow \quad \varnothing \quad 2$$

A third alternative would be to posit in the lexicon both the short form and the long form of these verbs, and to have rules distributing the allomorphs in the correct environments.

The first two solutions share the claim that there is a basic form and a derived form for each stem; the third suggestion is neutral in this respect. The latter alternative appears preferable, because there does not seem to be any convincing substantive evidence justifying the decision to make one form of the stems primary rather than the other. In particular, the occurrence of the short forms in the present singular indicative and imperative and of the long forms elsewhere exhibits great stability, with no encroachment of one form over the domain of the other. In fact, this strict dichotomy tends to spread to verbs that normally do not have short and long forms and therefore do not normally show such a division of labor. For instance, Frei (1929:76) says that for the verbs *croire* 'to believe' and *voir* 'to see', which are in standard speech pronounced [krwa] and [vwa] in the indicative and subjunctive present singular and third person plural, a final yod is produced in popular French in the indicative present third person plural and in the subjunctive ([krwaj], [vwaj]) (see also Bauche 1951: 114–115). One might decide to view these data as evidence that a final consonant is indeed a marker for the indicative plural and for the subjunctive, and therefore that short forms are basic; but it could equally well be assumed that, since a yod does appear in these verbs in the first and second person plural of the indicative and subjunctive in both standard and popular speech (cf. *nous croyons* [nukrwajɔ̃] 'we believe', *vous voyez* [vuvwaje] 'you see'), the yod has been reinterpreted in popular speech as being part of the stem, and that it is deleted in the indicative present singular. Other examples found in popular French also show the general tendency to use long forms in grammatical contexts other than the indicative and imperative present singular: *elle pouvra* [ɛlpuvra] instead of *elle pourra* [ɛlpura] 'she will be able to'; *j'écriverai* [žekrivrɛ] instead of *j'écrirai* [žekrirɛ] 'I will write' (cf. Frei 1929:168–171). Data from popular French additionally reveal the trend to regularize the consonants that appear in long forms (e.g., *que je save* [kəžəsav] instead of *que je sache* [kəžəsaš] 'that I know' (subj.); *qu'on veule* [kɔ̃vœl] instead of *qu'on veuille* [kɔ̃vœj] 'that one want' (subj.); cf. Frei 1929:168–171); this shows that among the long stems a verb may have, one is primary, but it does not establish the primariness of this particular form over the short stem.

As with the corresponding [Ṽ] ~ [VN] alternations (see sec. III.5.3.2.), I therefore prefer to retain a treatment in which both the short and long forms of third-group verbs exhibiting [Ø] ~ [C] alternations are lexically entered and distributed in the correct grammatical contexts by traditional rules of allomorphy. At any rate, it should remain clear that [Ø] ~ [C] alternations in third-group verbs are directly governed by grammatical information rather than being phonologically determined. In this respect it is of interest to point out that a grammatically based analysis straightforwardly accounts for the fact that the long forms of third-group verbs are generally used before the consonantal morpheme /r/ (i.e., in the infinitive, future, and conditional; e.g., *suivre* [sɥivr] 'to follow', *nous suivrons* [nusɥivrɔ̃] 'we'll follow', *nous suivrions* [nusɥivrijɔ̃] 'we would follow'). On the other hand, a purely phonological analysis based on consonant deletion requires either the presence of an underlying thematic vowel which never appears phonetically, as proposed in Schane (1968*a*:101–103), or else, as proposed in Dell (1973*b*:244 n. 51), numerous exception markings which make incorrect predictions, since, as evidenced above by the data from popular French, the true exceptions are not the many verbs that behave like *suivre,* but rather the few verbs that, like *écrire,* make use of the short form of the stem before /r/ in Standard French (e.g., *nous écrirons* [nuzekrirɔ̃] 'we'll write').

VII.3.2. Masculine/feminine alternations

This type of [Ø] ~ [C] alternations affects nouns and adjectives. Its formal treatment has been partially outlined in section VII.2.2. The masculine forms are considered to be basic; the feminine forms are derived by a general morphophonological rule inserting an unspecified consonant in word-final position:

$$(36) \quad \left. \begin{array}{l} X \quad \# \\ \\ \qquad \left. \begin{array}{l} N \\ A \end{array} \right] [+\text{fem}] \end{array} \right.$$

$$1 \quad 2 \qquad \qquad \Longrightarrow \ 1 \ C \ 2$$

The actual consonant that needs to be inserted is lexically specified for each adjective and noun, and its features automatically fill in the unspecified features of /C/. If no consonant is specified in the lexicon for a given adjective or noun, the inserted /C/ receives a phonetically null representation.

This approach is now explored in detail along two axes. First, I consider more closely the question of the relation between the basic masculine forms of nouns and adjectives and the lexically specified gender consonants; in particular, I attempt to determine the degree to which the existence and nature of gender consonants are idiosyncratic or predictable. Second, I justify the insertion analysis by showing the need to recognize distinct derivational paths (i.e., rules (29) and (36)) to account for adjective liaison and gender marking.

VII.3.2.1. On the predictability of gender consonants

This section is based in part on Durand's (1936) study of gender in French, in particular on her list of 5,630 nouns and adjectives representing the "vocabulaire commun des Français cultivés" (104), her statistics on these data, and her comments on the various classes of gender formation she established. The main goal of this section is to show that gender consonants have properties that justify their status as lexical pieces of phonological information which are not strictly part of the phonological representations of nouns and adjectives.

The consonants that may yield feminine adjectives and nouns by being added to masculine forms are /t/, /d/, /k/, /g/, /n/, /ñ/, /v/, /s/, /z/, /š/, /r/, /l/, and /j/; the use of these thirteen consonants is illustrated in (37):

(37) *petit* [pəti]/*petite* [pətit] 'small'
　　grand [grã]/*grande* [grãd] 'tall'
　　franc [frã]/*franque* [frãk] 'Frank'
　　long [lɔ̃]/*longue* [lɔ̃g] 'long'
　　plein [plɛ̃]/*pleine* [plɛn] 'full'
　　bénin [benɛ̃]/*bénigne* [beniñ] 'not serious'
　　loup [lu]/*louve* [luv] 'wolf'
　　gros [gro]/*grosse* [gros] 'big'
　　heureux [ørø]/*heureuse* [ørøz] 'happy'
　　blanc [blã]/*blanche* [blãš] 'white'
　　entier [ãtje]/*entière* [ãtjɛr] 'entire'
　　soûl [su]/*soûle* [sul] 'drunk'
　　gentil [žãti]/*gentille* [žãtij] 'nice'

Out of the twenty consonants that exist in Modern French (excluding /ŋ/), eighteen can occur in word-final position (the exceptions are the glides /ɥ/ and /w/). Of these eighteen, thirteen can thus mark the feminine of adjectives and nouns (the five consonants ruled out are /p/, /b/, /m/, /f/, and /ž/). Given this proportion, it might appear surprising, within the framework of the insertion analysis, that so relatively few "errors" of feminine formation are made by native speakers, since these consonants have been assumed so far to be idiosyncratic markings on adjectives and nouns. The reason for the absence of innumerable deviations from the norm is that the lexically specified gender consonants can in fact be predicted in a significant proportion on the basis of the short forms posited as phonological representations.

As a first step, observe that only adjectives and nouns that end in a vowel or in /r/ in phonological representations can exhibit a masculine/feminine [Ø] ~ [C] alternation. Adjectives and nouns ending in /p/, /b/, /t/, /d/, /k/, /g/, /m/, /n/, /ñ/, /f/, /v/, /s/, /z/, /š/, /ž/, /l/, and /j/ cannot. Although this particular distribution historically arose as the result of phonological constraints on possible word-final consonant clusters, this is not the synchronic explanation. Some of the sequences formed by one of the consonants just listed plus a gender consonant are still barred from occurring in word-final position, but many are now actually possible, as illustrated in (38):

(38) *apte* [apt] 'apt'
acte [akt] 'act'
sprint [sprint] 'sprint'
aphte [aft] 'canker'
est [ɛst] 'east'
il cach'te [ilkašt] 'he seals'
halte [alt] 'stop'

The gaps that exist in the insertion of gender consonants after the final segments of phonological representations thus cannot be generally accounted for by sequential morpheme structure constraints. This observation is important, because if these gaps had all been phonologically explainable, the analysis that assumes that the gender consonants are present in phonological representations would have been able to account for them in revealing fashion; this would have constituted a serious argument in favor of a deletion analysis. As it is, however, the generalization is simply that only vowel-final or /r/-final adjectives and nouns can exhibit a masculine/feminine [Ø]~[C] alternation. This kind of arbitrary phonological distinction is typical of morphological processes and thus reinforces the idea that [Ø]~[C] gender alternations are to be treated morphophonologically rather than phonologically.

In the preceding paragraph, I have determined in part the restricted phonological domain where masculine/feminine [Ø]~[C] alternations may be found. But this does not mean that all adjectives and nouns ending in a vowel or /r/ exhibit such an alternation. In fact, it remains to be ascertained what properties (if any) of an adjective or noun ending in a vowel or /r/ correlate with its gender invariability or variability, and if it is variable, what properties (if any) govern the addition of a particular consonant.

The following two additional considerations further restrict the field of investigation. First, only words ending in certain vowels + /r/ may actually take a consonant in the feminine. Other words ending in /r/—in particular, words ending in an obstruent followed by /r/ (e.g., *pauvre* [povr] 'poor')—are invariable. Second, not all gender consonants have the same generality of use. Some occur so seldom that as a rule they need not be of much concern, as the alternations in these instances can be considered truly idiosyncratic. Five consonants occur in only one word, the one given in (37): /k/, /g/, /v/, /l/, and /j/. /š/ occurs in just three adjectives (*blanc* [blā]/*blanche* [blāš] 'white'; *franc* [frā]/*franche* [frāš] 'frank, sincere'; *frais* [frɛ]/*fraîche* [frɛš] 'fresh'). /ñ/ occurs in only two adjectives (*malin* [malɛ̃]/*maligne* [maliñ] 'sly'; *bénin* [benɛ̃]/*bénigne* [beniñ] 'not serious'); these two words are less idiosyncratic than the preceding ones, in the sense that a nasal consonant is added to a form ending in a nasal vowel; however, the idiosyncrasy lies in the fact that the palatal nasal consonant, rather than the usual dental nasal consonant, is inserted; in this light, it is not surprising that one of the two adjectives, *malin*, has formed a new feminine, *maline* [malin], which conforms to the regular pattern (see chap. iii and below).

With the elimination of these isolated and idiosyncratic gender consonants, six consonants remain which are used with any generality at all as gender consonants: /t/, /d/, /n/, /s/, /z/, and /r/. I will now show that a large proportion of the [∅] ~ [C] gender alternations involving these consonants can actually be predicted on the basis of morphological and phonological information characterizing the lexical representations postulated. The majority of invariable cases will also be similarly predicted. There will, nevertheless, remain numerous instances that appear idiosyncratic. The established generalizations are assumed to take the form of redundancy rules. In this way the consonant-insertion rules of adjective liaison and gender formation can still be regarded as uniformly picking the needed consonant (if any) from the lexical entries, but in some cases the consonant (if any) will be truly idiosyncratic, whereas in others the burden of memory on the native speaker will not be so heavy, because of the general patterns involved. It will also be seen that the "mistakes" in gender formation which are actually attested are not random, but rather conform to these generalizations.

(i) Words ending in /i/:

Apart from the isolated case of *gentil* [žāti]/*gentille* [žātij], cited above, words ending in /i/ are invariable, or they take /t/ or /z/ in the feminine.

All past participles of second-group verbs are invariable (e.g., *finir* 'to finish': *fini/finie* [fini]). All past participles of third-group verbs in *-ire* take /t/ (e.g., *dire* 'to say': *dit* [di]/*dite* [dit]). The rest of the third-group verbs which have a past participle in /i/ take /z/ (e.g., *acquérir* 'to acquire': *acquis* [aki]/*acquise* [akiz]; *mettre* 'to put': *mis* [mi]/*mise* [miz]; *prendre* 'to take': *pris* [pri]/*prise* [priz]).

These generalizations leave a few words whose feminines are unexplained and must therefore be considered idiosyncratic. Examples of invariable words are *ami* [ami] 'friend'; *apprenti* [aprãti] 'apprentice'; *ennemi* [ɛnmi] 'enemy'; *hardi* [ardi] 'bold'; *joli* [žɔli] 'pretty'; *poli* [pɔli] 'polite'. Examples of words taking /t/ are *favori* [favɔri] 'favorite'; *gratuit* [gratyi] 'free'; *inédit* [inedi] 'unpublished'; *manuscrit* [manyskri] 'manuscript'; *petit* [pəti] 'small'. Examples of words taking /z/ are *concis* [kõsi] 'concise'; *Denis* [dəni] (first name); *exquis* [ɛkski] 'exquisite'; *gris* [gri] 'gray'; *indécis* [ẽdesi] 'indecisive'; *Louis* [lwi] (first name); *précis* [presi] 'precise'.

(ii) Words ending in /e/:

These words are either invariable or they have a feminine in /ɛr/.

All past participles of first-group verbs are invariable (e.g., *chanter* 'to sing': *chanté/chantée* [šãte]). Almost all other words in /e/ have feminines in /ɛr/. A few exceptions are *carré* [kare] 'square', *pygmé* [pigme] 'pygmy', *René* [rəne] (first name), *zélé* [zele] 'zealous', which are invariable.

Another generalization is that all words containing the suffix *-ier* (*-er* after /š/ and /ž/)[8] take /ɛr/ (e.g., *côte* 'coast': *côtier* [kotje]/*côtière* [kotjɛr] 'coastal'; *gauche* [goš] 'left': *gaucher* [goše]/*gauchère* [gošɛr] 'left-handed'; *mensonge* [mãsõž] 'lie': *mensonger* [mãsõže]/*mensongère* [mãsõžɛr] 'untrue'). The four words *dernier* [dɛrnje] 'last', *entier* [ãtje] 'entire', *léger* [leže] 'light', and *premier* [prəmje] 'first' cannot strictly be said to contain the suffix *-(i)er,* but they also have a feminine in /ɛr/. The force of the [je]/[jɛr] alternation has drawn into its fold the invariable word *pécuniaire* [pekynjɛr] 'monetary': [pekynje]/[pekynjɛr], even in educated speakers of Standard French (Durand 1936:136). Despite the fact that no genuine stems seem to be recoverable by removing *-(i)er* from *dernier, entier, léger, premier,* and *"pécunier",* it may be that speakers nevertheless

---

8. Historically, the [j] of the suffix *-ier* did not occur after the alveopalatal fricatives [š] and [ž]. As pointed out by Pichon (1942:38–39), this constraint has ceased to operate in the language, as indicated by the following examples:

pistache [pistaš]/*pistachier* [pistašje] 'pistachio' (seed/tree)
fiche [fiš]/*fichier* [fišje] 'card'/'card catalogue'
éponge [epõž]/*épongier* [epõžje] 'sponge'/'sponger'

Pichon also cites the interesting story of a child who, at three years and four months of age, said [ɔrãžje] instead of [ɔrãže] for *oranger* 'orange tree', before learning the "correct" word a few weeks later.

feel the presence of a boundary (/dɛrn+je/, /āt+je/, /lež+e/, /prəm+je/, /pekyn+je/). The same phenomenon is perhaps more clearly seen in instances like *menuisier* [mənɥizje] 'carpenter' and *boucher* [buše] 'butcher'; the stems /mənɥiz/ and /buš/ are synchronically meaningless, but the endings [je] and [e] are nevertheless undoubtedly felt as separate morphemes (/mənɥiz+je/, /buš+e/); in these examples, however, this intuition may be reinforced by the existence of the words *menuiserie* [mənɥizri] 'carpentry' and *boucherie* [bušri] 'butcher shop', interpreted synchronically as /mənɥiz+ri/ and /buš+ri/.

The vowel quality change from /e/ to [ɛ] which occurs when /r/ is added could be considered to be part of a separate process of feminine formation by /r/-insertion, since the feminine consonant /r/ is added only to words ending in /e/ and it automatically triggers the vowel-quality change. Alternatively, the switch from /e/ to [ɛ] may preferably be regarded as an adjustment of a more general nature, since at the end of a word the only front mid unrounded vowel that may occur in a closed syllable is [ɛ], no matter what the final consonant is. The examples given in (39) illustrate the operation of this word-internal vowel-quality change in areas other than feminine formation (for (39a), see sec. VI.3.3.3.):

(39) (a) *agrégation* [agregasjɔ̃] → [agrɛg] (university-level examination)
bénéfice [benefis] → [benɛf] 'benefit'
(b) *céder* [sede]/*(il) cède* [sɛd] 'to yield'/'(he) yields'
gérer [žere]/*(il) gère* [žɛr] 'to manage'/'(he) manages'

The switch from /e/ to [ɛ] which occurs in feminine formation by /r/-insertion can therefore be accounted for by the independently motivated rule given in (40):

(40) e → ɛ/ — C #

(iii) Words ending in /ɛ/:

A few of these words are isolated and must be considered as idiosyncratic in their feminine formation. Three are invariable (*bai/baie* [bɛ] 'bay'; *gai/gaie* [gɛ] 'happy'; *vrai/vraie* [vrɛ] 'true'); one takes /d/ (*laid* [lɛ]/*laide* [lɛd] 'ugly'); and one takes /s/ (*épais* [epɛ]/*épaisse* [epɛs] 'thick'). Durand gives three words taking /kt/ (*abject* [abžɛ]/*abjecte* [abžɛkt] 'abject'; *circonspect* [sirkɔ̃spɛ]/*circonspecte* [sirkɔ̃spɛkt] 'circumspect'; *suspect* [syspɛ]/*suspecte* [syspɛkt] 'suspect'); [abžɛ], rather than [abžɛkt], for *abject* (masc.) actually sounds impossible to me, and *suspect* strongly tends to be pronounced with [kt] in the masculine as well as in the feminine.

The quantitatively important groups are those whose members take /t/ and /z/ in the feminine. Among the words taking /t/ is the class of diminutives with the suffix *-et* (e.g., *grassouillet* [grasujɛ]/ *grassouillette* [grasujɛt] 'plump'). Also included in this group are the past participles of third-group verbs in *-aire* (e.g., *faire* 'to do': *fait* [fɛ]/*faite* [fɛt]). Examples of words taking /t/, but apparently not falling into any general pattern, are *complet* [kɔ̃plɛ] 'complete', *concret* [kɔ̃krɛ] 'concrete', *discret* [diskrɛ] 'discrete', *muet* [mɥɛ] 'mute', *préfet* [prefɛ] 'prefect', *inquiet* [ɛ̃kjɛ] 'worried', *sujet* [syžɛ] 'subject'.

Practically all the words that take /z/ contain the suffix *-ais,* whose function is to indicate origin (e.g., *Ecosse* 'Scotland': *écossais* [ekɔsɛ]/*écossaise* [ekɔsɛz]). Not falling into this category, but nevertheless taking /z/, are only the two adjectives *mauvais* [mɔvɛ] 'bad' and *niais* [njɛ] 'stupid', which must be regarded as idiosyncratic.

(iv) Words ending in /a/:

A few isolated cases must be considered idiosyncratic: two words are invariable (*angora* [ãgɔra] 'Angora', *extra* [ɛkstra] 'extra') and three take /s/ (*bas* [ba]/*basse* [bas] 'low'; *gras* [gra]/*grasse* [gras] 'fat'; *las* [la]/*lasse* [las] 'tired'). For some speakers, *exact* 'exact' exhibits a [Ø]~[kt] alternation (*exact* [ɛgza]/*exacte* [ɛgzakt]), but the tendency is for [kt] to be pronounced in both genders.

The two groups that include respectable numbers of items are those where /t/ and /z/ are added in the feminine. The words taking /t/ do not seem to exhibit any pattern (cf. *auvergnat* [overña]/ *auvergnate* [overñat] 'from Auvergne'; *chat* [ša]/*chatte* [šăt] 'cat'; *droit* [drwa]/*droite* [drwat] 'straight'; *étroit* [etrwa]/*étroite* [etrwat] 'narrow'; *plat* [pla]/*plate* [plat] 'flat'; *scélérat* [selera]/*scélérate* [selerat] 'scoundrel'). They are regarded as idiosyncratic.

On the other hand, the words taking /z/ present an interesting generalization: most of them end in the suffix *-ois*, which indicates origin (e.g., *Prague*: *pragois* [pragwa]/*pragoise* [pragwaz]). A few words ending in /wa/ and taking /z/ cannot be said to contain this suffix of origin; they are *François* [frãswa] (first name), *grivois* [grivwa] 'lewd', *narquois* [narkwa] 'cunning', *pantois* [pãtwa] 'stunned', and *sournois* [surnwa] 'sly'; they must be regarded as idiosyncratic (cf. *droit/droite; étroit/étroite*). One additional word taking /z/ is the isolated adjective *ras* 'flat' (*ras* [ra]/*rase* [raz]).

(v) Words ending in /y/:

Most words ending in /y/ are invariable. They fall into two main categories: first, past participles of third-group verbs (e.g., *entendre* 'to hear': *entendu/entendue* [ãtãdy]; *lire* 'to read': *lu/lue* [ly]; *recevoir* 'to receive': *reçu/reçue* [rəsy]; *vaincre* 'to defeat': *vaincu/vaincue* [vɛ̃ky]); second, denominal adjectives with the suffix -*u* (e.g., *barbe* 'beard': *barbu/barbue* [barby]; *moustache* 'moustache': *moustachu/moustachue* [mustašy]; *ventre* 'abdomen': *ventru/ventrue* [vãtry]). A few other invariable words in /y/ remain outside the scope of these two generalizations (e.g., *absolu/absolue* [apsɔly] 'absolute'; *aigu/aiguë* [egy] 'acute'; *crépu/crépue* [krepy] 'frizzy'; *exigu/exiguë* [egzigy] 'cramped').

According to Durand, only eleven words in /y/ are supposed to take /z/. Some of them are rare (*contus* [kɔ̃ty] 'bruised'; *profus* [prɔfy] 'profuse'); others are used practically exclusively in association with a single noun (*camus: un nez camus* [ɛ̃nekamy] 'a snub nose'; *infus: la science infuse* [lasjãsɛ̃fyz] 'spontaneous knowledge'); a third group seems to me to be used invariably (*inclus* [ɛ̃kly] 'included'; *intrus* [ɛ̃try] 'intruder'; *obtus* [ɔpty] 'obtuse'; *perclus* [pɛrkly] 'stiff-jointed'). Only three words in /y/ genuinely appear to take /z/ in the feminine (*confus* [kɔ̃fy]/*confuse* [kɔ̃fyz] 'confused'; *diffus* [dify]/*diffuse* [difyz] 'diffuse'; *reclus* [rəkly]/*recluse* [rəklyz] 'recluse').

The overall tendency thus seems to be that adjectives and nouns ending in /y/ are or become invariable.

(vi) Words ending in /ø/:

Except for *bleu* [blø] 'blue', which is invariable, and *hébreu* [ebrø] 'Hebrew', whose feminine is *hébraïque* [ebraik], all these words take /z/ in the feminine. In the large majority of them the suffix -*eux* is recognizable (e.g., *scandale* 'scandal': *scandaleux* [skãdalø]/*scandaleuse* [skãdaløz]).

The feminine *bleuse* [bløz] for *bleue* [blø] was independently attested by Bauche (1951:94) and Durand (1936:127). Even though this form may be rare, it is interesting that the consonant [z] rather than another consonant is always chosen to mark the feminine. "Que ce féminin insolite soit ou non une plaisanterie, il indique peut-être une tendance bien timide de ce mot à subir l'analogie du grand groupe concurrent" (Durand 1936:127). For *hébreu*, one of the readers of Jacques Capelovici's column "télé-langage" in *Télé 7 Jours* wrote: "Quel est, au juste, le féminin de l'adjectif *hébreu*? La forme *hé-*

breuse est-elle tolérée ou constitue-t-elle une faute?" This query also indicates the power of attraction of the [ø]~[øz] alternation.

(vii) Words ending in /u/:

According to Durand, only a dozen nouns and adjectives in /u/ are of direct relevance here. They all appear to be isolated idiosyncratic cases. Three words are invariable (*flou/floue* [flu] 'vague'; *hindou/hindoue* [ẽdu] 'Indian'; *mandchou/mandchoue* [mãtšu] 'Manchurian'); three take /z/ (*andalou* [ãdalu]/*andalouse* [ãdaluz] 'Andalusian'; *époux* [epu]/*épouse* [epuz] 'spouse'; *jaloux* [žalu]/*jalouse* [žaluz] 'jealous'); three take /t/ (*absout* [apsu]/*absoute* [apsut] 'absolved'; *dissout* [disu]/*dissoute* [disut] 'dissolved'; *tout* [tu]/*toute* [tut] 'all'); two take /s/ (*doux* [du]/*douce* [dus] 'sweet'; *roux* [ru]/*rousse* [rus] 'red-haired'); and one takes /l/ (the already mentioned *soûl* 'drunk').

Also idiosyncratic are the following two instances of masculine/feminine alternations which fall outside the proper domain of [Ø]~[C] alternations: *fou* [fu]/*folle* [fɔl] 'mad'; *mou* [mu]/*molle* [mɔl] 'soft'. In each instance, both alternants are assumed to be entered in the lexicon in their entirety (/fu/, /fɔl/; /mu/, /mɔl/).

(viii) Words ending in /o/:

Some isolated cases must be treated idiosyncratically. Two adjectives are invariable (*dingo* [dẽgo] 'crazy'; *rococo* [rokoko] 'rococo'), one takes /t/ without a change in vowel quality (*haut* [o]/*haute* [ot] 'high'), two take /s/ (*faux* [fo]/*fausse* [fos] 'false'; *gros* [gro]/*grosse* [gros] 'big'), and two take /z/ (*clos* [klo]/*close* [kloz] 'shut'; *dispos* [dispo]/*dispose* [dispoz] 'fit').

The interesting groups are those whose members take /t/ (with an opening of the vowel to [ɔ]) and /d/. The words that take /d/ include those with the suffix *-aud* (e.g., *lourd* 'heavy': *lourdaud* [lurdo]/*lourdaude* [lurdod]; *noir* 'black': *noiraud* [nwaro]/*noiraud* [nwarod]). A few words remain idiosyncratic (e.g., *chaud* [sǒ]/*chaude* [šod] 'hot').

The second of the two groups includes words built with the diminutive suffix *-ot* (e.g., *Charles* (first name): *Charlot* [šarlo]/*Charlotte* [šarlɔt]; *petit* 'small': *petiot* [pətjo]/*petiote* [pətjɔt]). This particular type of gender formation appears to be productive, as new words in /o/ (excluding those formed with the suffix *-aud*) tend to have this masculine/feminine pattern, even if the suffix *-ot* is not involved (e.g., *rigolo* [rigolo]/*rigolote* [rigɔlɔt] 'funny'). Words like *sot* 'silly' (*sot* [so]/*sotte* [sɔt]) and *idiot* 'stupid' (*idiot* [idjo]/*idiote* [idjɔt]) may therefore be part of a general pattern rather than be idiosyncratic.

Durand cites eleven cases of masculine/feminine [o] ~ [ɛl] alternation (e.g., *beau* [bo]/*belle* [bɛl] 'beautiful'; *nouveau* [nuvo] /*nouvelle* [nuvɛl] 'new'). The members of this closed list are assumed to be entered in the lexicon in full (/bo/, /bɛl/; /nuvo/, /nuvɛl/).

(ix) Words ending in a nasal vowel:

— Words ending in /ã/:

Most of these words form their feminine in /t/. An important generalization is that deverbal adjectives in -*ant* (present participles) always take /t/ (e.g., *mériter* 'to deserve': *méritant* [meritã]/ *méritante* [meritãt]). Other words in /ã/ taking /t/ may have to be treated idiosyncratically (e.g., *lent* [lã]/*lente* [lãt] 'slow'; *opulent* [ɔpylã]/*opulente* [ɔpylãt] 'opulent'; *urgent* [yrʒã]/*urgente* [yrʒãt] 'urgent'). But the power of attraction of this alternation, illustrated by the fact that the invariable adjective *gnangnan* [ñãñã] 'not energetic' takes /t/ in the feminine when made variable, may indicate that these items follow a regular pattern for words ending in /ã/.

Some words in /ã/, however, systematically form their feminines in /n/ (with denasalization of /ã/) rather than in /t/. Here the emerging regularity is that most of these words contain the suffix -*an* (e.g., *Castille*: *castillan* [kastijã]/*castillane* [kastijan]; *Perse*: *persan* [pɛrsã]/*persane* [pɛrsan]). Examples of words not falling under this or other generalizations are *artisan* [artizã]/*artisane* [artizan] 'craftsman'; *faisan* [fəzã]/*faisane* [fəzan] 'pheasant'; *paon* [pã]/*paonne* [pan] 'peacock'; *plan* [plã]/*plane* [plan] 'flat'.

A few other words in /ã/ do not take /t/ or /n/ in the feminine and are assumed to be idiosyncratic. A dozen words take /d/ (e.g., *allemand* [almã]/*allemande* [almãd] 'German'; *grand* [grã]/*grande* [grãd] 'tall'), and there are the isolated cases mentioned earlier, with /š/ and /k/ (*blanc* [blã]/*blanche* [blãš] 'white', *franc* [frã]/*franche* [frãš] 'frank, sincere'; *franc* [frã]/*franque* [frãk] 'Frank').

— Words ending in /õ/:

There is one word that takes /t/ in the feminine (*prompt* [prõ]/*prompte* [prõt] 'prompt'), one that takes /g/ (*long* [lõ]/*longue* [lõg] 'long'), and a dozen that take /d/ (e.g., *blond* [blõ]/*blonde* [blõd] 'blond'; *profond* [prɔfõ]/*profonde* [prɔfõd] 'deep'; *rond* [rõ]/ *ronde* [rõd] 'round'). Since no special pattern emerges in these few instances, they are assumed to be idiosyncratic.

The great majority of words ending in /õ/ have feminines in /n/, with denasalization of the nasal vowel. An important proportion of them contain the morpheme -on, either in diminutives (e.g., *maigre* 'skinny': *maigrichon* [megriš5]/*maigrichonne* [megrišɔn]) or as a suffix denoting origin (e.g., *Bretagne*: *breton* [brət5]/*bretonne* [brətɔn]). Other words with a masculine/feminine [5] ~ [ɔn] alternation fall into neither of these two categories (e.g., *baron* [bar5]/*baronne* [barɔn] 'baron'; *bon* [b5]/*bonne* [bɔn] 'good'; *lion* [lj5]/*lionne* [ljɔn] 'lion'; *mignon* [miñ5]/*mignonne* [miñɔn] 'cute'; *patron* [patr5]/*patronne* [patrɔn] 'owner'). The power of attraction of this particular alternation, indicated by the fact that invariable adjectives in /5/ tend to pattern after it (*marron* [mar5]/*marronne* [marɔn] 'brown'; *ronchon* [r5š5]/*ronchonne* [r5šɔn] 'grumpy'), may show, however, that the unmarked pattern is for words in /5/ to form their feminines in /n/, whether they contain a suffix -*on* or not.

— Words ending in /ɛ̃/[9]

Past participles of third-group verbs automatically take /t/ in the feminine (e.g., *éteindre* 'to extinguish': *éteint* [etɛ̃]/*éteinte* [etɛ̃t]). A few idiosyncratic words taking /t/ are *défunt* [defɛ̃] 'deceased', *maint* [mɛ̃] 'many', *saint* [sɛ̃] 'saint', *succinct* [syksɛ̃] 'succinct'.

Also idiosyncratic is the word *distinct* 'distinct', which exhibits a [Ø] ~ [kt] alternation (*distinct* [distɛ̃]/*distincte* [distɛ̃kt]). According to Durand, the word *succinct* may also undergo this alternation.

The remaining words in this group take a nasal consonant in the feminine, with denasalization of the vowel. The nasal consonant is generally /n/; as mentioned earlier, the nasal consonant is /ñ/ in just two instances (*malin, bénin*), and at least in the case of *malin*, the tendency is for /n/ to replace /ñ/. As noted in Part I, the main question is to determine the quality of the oral vowel in the feminine; there are three candidates: /y/, /ɛ/, and /i/. In chapter iii it was assumed that one had to resort to lexical markings entirely. In fact, although lexical markings are apparently necessary in a number of cases, a certain number of predictions can also be made which importantly reduce the burden of memory on speakers.

Durand gives seven words for which the feminine forms have /y/: *un* [ɛ̃]/*une* [yn] 'a', *aucun* [okɛ̃]/*aucune* [okyn] 'no', *chacun* [šakɛ̃]/*chacune* [šakyn] 'each', *commun* [kɔmɛ̃]/*commune* [kɔmyn] 'common', *brun* [brɛ̃]/*brune* [bryn] 'brown', *importun* [ɛ̃pɔrtɛ̃]/*importune* [ɛ̃pɔrtyn] 'disturbing', *opportun* [ɔpɔrtɛ̃]/*opportune* [ɔpɔrtyn] 'oppor-

---

9. Unlike Durand, I assume a dialect where [œ̃] has merged into [ɛ̃].

tune.' For speakers who have preserved the [œ̃]/[ɛ̃] distinction, the oral vowel in these feminine forms is easily predictable, since the nasal vowel in the masculine forms is [œ̃], and [œ̃] uniquely corresponds to [y]. For speakers who have merged the distinction between [œ̃] and [ɛ̃], it appears that the feminine vowel must be idiosyncratically learned and lexically marked. One conceivable generalization concerning the first three words given is that they might be regarded as a special class of grammatical items or as a class of items all containing the morpheme -un.

The large majority of the words under consideration actually have /ɛ/ or /i/ in the feminine. An important generalization is that when the nasal vowel /ɛ̃/ is preceded by /j/ or /e/, the oral vowel is always /ɛ/. This occurs in particular with the suffixes -ien and -éen (e.g., *Canada*: *canadien* [kanadjɛ̃]/*canadienne* [kanadjɛn]; *Panama*: *panaméen* [panameɛ̃]/*panaméenne* [panameɛn]), but also with monomorphemic words (e.g., *chien* [šjɛ̃]/*chienne* [šjɛn] 'dog'; *doyen* [dwajɛ̃]/*doyenne* [dwajɛn] 'dean'; *mien* [mjɛ̃]/*mienne* [mjɛn] 'mine').

The suffix written -ain also yields a feminine with /ɛ/ (e.g., *Afrique* 'Africa': *africain* [afrikɛ̃]/*africaine* [afrikɛn]; *Amérique* 'America': *américain* [amerikɛ̃]/*américaine* [amerikɛn]), but it is not clear whether it can be distinguished on independent grounds from the suffix written -in, which yields feminines with /i/ (e.g., *Alpes* 'Alps': *alpin* [alpɛ̃]/*alpine* [alpin]; *Gironde* (French department): *girondin* [žirɔ̃dɛ̃]/*girondine* [žirɔ̃din]). Words ending in the suffixes -ain and -in may therefore have to be regarded as idiosyncratic, together with monomorphemic words such as *certain* [sɛrtɛ̃]/*certaine* [sɛrtɛn] 'certain', *plein* [plɛ̃]/*pleine* [plɛn] 'full', *fin* [fɛ̃]/*fine* [fin] 'thin', and *taquin* [takɛ̃]/*taquine* [takin] 'teasing'.

As observed in chapter iii, however, and excluding words with endings commanding a feminine with /ɛ/, the productive feminine formation with words ending in /ɛ̃/ is clearly with /i/ rather than /ɛ/. Durand (1936:121) also emphasized this point, noting that the [ɛ̃] ~[in] alternation seems to exercise "une action analogique aux dépens de [ɛ̃] ~ [ɛn]" (e.g., *sacristain* [sakristɛ̃]/*sacristine* [sakristin] 'sexton'), and that "les mots d'argot ou simplement familiers font tous partie de la subdivision [ɛ̃] ~ [in]" (e.g., *copain* [kɔpɛ̃]/*copine* [kɔpin] 'pal'; *crétin* [kretɛ̃]/*crétine* [kretin] 'imbecile'; *frangin* [frãžɛ̃] /*frangine* [frãžin] 'brother'/'sister'; *gamin* [gamɛ̃]/*gamine* [gamin] 'child').

The process of feminine formation by /n/-insertion may have a different status from that of the other widely used processes of gender consonant insertion. As noted in this section and also in chapter iii, /n/ appears to be exclusively inserted after phonological representations ending in a nasal vowel. This means not only that one can legitimately define a class of adjectives and nouns by reference to the consonantal ending /n/ which they take in the feminine (a type of characteristic shared only with the phonologically homogeneous class of adjectives and nouns ending in /e/ and taking /r/ in the feminine); it means also that there exists in the process of feminine /n/-insertion a phonological motivation (nasality) which is absent in all other cases.

The morphophonological processes of /n/-insertion and vowel denasalization proposed in chapter iii as rule (50) can be considered as a special case of the general schema given in (36) at the beginning of this section. What is special is that the insertion of the consonant is accompanied by a vowel change. In the case of feminine formation by /r/-insertion, the vowel change from /e/ to [ɛ] was explained by a separate phonological process (rule (40)). Vowel denasalization in feminine formation by /n/-insertion is not accounted for by a rule distinct from /n/-insertion because it is not a purely phonological independent process: the nasal vowel /ɛ̃/ may yield [y], [ɛ], or [i], and nasal vowels phonetically occur before word-final nasal consonants (cf. *nous tînmes* [nutɛ̃m] 'we held', *nous vînmes* [nuvɛ̃m] 'we came'). Vowel denasalization is thus an integral part of feminine formation by /n/-insertion, and it must therefore remain combined with the process of /n/-insertion.

(x) Words ending in /Vr/:

A large group of these words is invariable; otherwise, /d/, /t/, and /s/ are used to form feminines.

No particular pattern emerges for the few items that take /s/ (e.g., *divers* [divɛr]/*diverse* [divɛrs] 'varied'; *épars* [epar]/*éparse* [epars] 'scattered'; *pervers* [pɛrvɛr]/*perverse* [pɛrvɛrs] 'perverse').

Among the words taking /t/, past participles of third-group verbs form a small but coherent group (e.g., *couvrir* 'to cover': *couvert* [kuvɛr]/*couverte* [kuvɛrt]; *mourir* 'to die': *mort* [mɔr]/*morte* [mɔrt]; *offrir* 'to offer': *offert* [ɔfɛr]/*offerte* [ɔfɛrt]). Only a few words remain idiosyncratic (e.g., *court* [kur]/*courte* [kurt] 'short'; *fort* [fɔr]/*forte* [fɔrt] 'strong'; *vert* [vɛr]/*verte* [vɛrt] 'green').

The words that take /d/ typically contain what is felt to be the suffix *-ard* (e.g., *banlieue* 'suburb': *banlieusard* [bāljøzar]/*banlieusarde* [bāljøzard]; *clochard* [klɔšar]/*clocharde* [klɔšard] 'tramp'). This

[ar] ~ [ard] alternation appears to be productive, as it tends to be extended to invariable adjectives in /ar/ (e.g., *avare* 'stingy': [avar]/ [avard]; Durand (1936:118) attested the existence of the feminine *avarde* in the 404 points of her dialectal study, which encompassed a 50-kilometer-wide area 25 kilometers outside and around Paris). *Lourd* [lur]/*lourde* [lurd] 'heavy' and *sourd* [sur]/*sourde* [surd] 'deaf' are idiosyncratic (cf. *court/courte*).

Invariable words in /Vr/ fall into several predictable categories, but not all instances are part of a general pattern. The suffix *-aire* correlates with invariability (e.g., *supplément* 'supplement': *supplémentaire* [syplemãtɛr]); so does the suffix *-oire* (e.g., *contradiction* 'contradiction': *contradictoire* [kɔ̃tradiktwar]); also invariable are the words ending in /yr/ (e.g., *dur/dure* [dyr] 'hard') and /ir/ (e.g., *pire* [pir] 'worse'). Among invariable words, examples falling into no particular pattern are *cher/chère* [šɛr] 'expensive', *sévère* [sevɛr] 'severe' (cf. *vert/verte*); *avare* [avar] 'stingy', *bizarre* [bizar] 'strange' (cf. *blafard* [blafar]/*blafarde* [blafard] 'pale'); *multicolore* [myltikɔlɔr] 'multicolored', *sonore* [sɔnɔr] 'voiced' (cf. *fort/forte*).

Words ending in /œr/ are particularly interesting. They are invariable (e.g., *antérieur/antérieure* [ãterjœr] 'anterior'; *majeur/majeure* [mažœr] 'adult') unless they end in the noun-forming suffix *-eur*. When this suffix is present, two main possibilities are open for feminine formation, which fall outside the proper domain of [Ø] ~ [C] gender alternations: the feminine may be in *-euse* [øz] or in *-rice* [ris]. Practically all the feminines in *-rice* appear after /t/. This distribution between feminines in *-euse* and feminines in *-rice* is predictable. When the noun in *-eur* is directly derived from a verb stem, the feminine is in *-euse* (e.g., *acheter* 'to buy': *acheteur* [aštœr]/*acheteuse* [aštøz] 'buyer'; *jouer* 'to play': *joueur* [žwœr]/*joueuse* [žwøz] 'player'). Otherwise, *-rice* is the ending in the feminine (e.g., *adapter* 'to adapt': *adaptateur* [adaptatœr]/*adaptatrice* [adaptatris] 'adapter'; *corriger* 'to correct': *correcteur* [kɔrɛktœr]/*correctrice* [kɔrɛktris] 'corrector'; *orateur* [ɔratœr]/*oratrice* [ɔratris] 'orator'; *rédiger* 'to write': *rédacteur* [redaktœr]/*rédactrice* [redaktris] 'editor'). *Ambassadeur* [ãbasadœr]/*ambassadrice* [ãbasadris] 'ambassador', which may be the only example of *-rice* not preceded by /t/, follows the general principle given, since *ambassadeur* is directly derived from a noun (*ambassade* 'embassy') rather than from a verb.

(xi) Other gender alternations

In the course of the examination of the predictability of gender consonants, I have mentioned a few cases of masculine/feminine alternations which fell outside the proper scope of [Ø] ~ [C] alternations, specifically [u] ~ [ol] (e.g., *fou/folle*), [o] ~ [ɛl] (e.g., *beau/belle*), *-eur/-euse* (e.g., *acheteur/acheteuse*), and *-teur/-trice* (e.g., *adaptateur/adaptatrice*). Three other kinds of masculine/feminine alternations are not strictly of the [Ø] ~ [C] type either; I here consider them briefly for the sake of completeness.

First, in the isolated case of *sec* [sɛk]/*sèche* [sɛš] 'dry', these two words are assumed to be listed in full in the lexicon.

Second, Durand cites about forty words that may use the feminine suffix *-esse* /ɛs/ (e.g., *âne* [an]/*ânesse* [anɛs] 'donkey', *maître* [mɛtr]/*maîtresse* [mɛtrɛs] 'schoolteacher', *ogre* [ɔgr]/*ogresse* [ɔgrɛs] 'ogre', *tigre* [tigr]/*tigresse* [tigrɛs] 'tiger', *pécheur* [pešœr]/*pécheresse* [pešrɛs] 'sinner'). I assume that the masculine forms of these words are marked in the lexicon as being able to take *-esse*. The list of words thus marked may vary from speaker to speaker.

Finally, as to the [f] ~ [v] masculine/feminine alternation, practically all nouns and adjectives ending in /f/ take /v/ in the feminine. The productive group is formed by the adjectives in *-if* (e.g., *actif* [aktif]/*active* [aktiv] 'active', *vif* [vif]/*vive* [viv] 'quick'). The only other words in /f/ which take /v/ in the feminine are: *neuf* [nœf]/*neuve* [nœv] 'new', *veuf* [vœf]/*veuve* [vœv] 'widower'/'widow'; *bref* [brɛf]/*brève* [brɛv] 'brief'; *sauf* [sof]/*sauve* [sov] 'safe'. The only exceptions to this regularity are words ending in the suffix *-graphe* /graf/ (e.g., *géographe* [žeɔgraf] 'geographer') and in the sequence *-ophe* /ɔf/ (e.g., *limitrophe* [limitrɔf] 'bordering', *philosophe* [filɔsɔf] 'philosopher'), which are invariable.

Summary.

Whether a noun or an adjective is invariable or not, and what type of feminine it takes if it is variable, can to a large extent be predicted on the basis of morphological and arbitrary phonological information provided by the masculine forms entered in the lexicon. As an example of arbitrary, but determining, phonological information, it has been seen that only words ending in a vowel or certain vowels followed by /r/ can be variable. As an example of relevant morphological information, it has been seen that all present participle adjectives form their feminines in /t/. As an example of the role played by both types of information combined, it has been seen that the feminines of past participles are predictable on the basis of their final segment and the conjugation class to which the verbs belong.

The fact that a large number of restrictions on gender consonants cannot be made to follow from independently valid morpheme structure conditions, and the fact that their existence and nature can be predicted on the basis of morphological and generally arbitrary phonological information indicate that gender consonants are distinct from other word-final segments. On the other hand, the fact that gender consonants cannot be predicted in all cases points to their basic lexical character. It therefore makes sense not to include gender consonants directly in phonological representations, but to set them apart as special lexical markings. This formalism allows an encoding of both the existing regularities (by means of redundancy rules) and the idiosyncrasies.

The hypothesis that masculine forms are basic can also be maintained, in agreement with the commonly held assumption that the masculine is the unmarked gender and the feminine the marked one. When masculine/feminine alternations do not appear to offer any particular motivation for deriving the masculine from the feminine or vice versa (as seems to be the case in the -if/-ive alternation), a choice can be made which is based on universal principles. When the suffix -esse is used to form feminines, there is no doubt that the masculine forms must be regarded as basic in any analysis; the treatment advocated here inherently allows a uniform characterization of gender relations by positing in general that the masculine is basic.

VII.3.2.2. Justification of the insertion analysis

The correspondence that exists in Standard French between adjective liaison and gender marking (see sec. VII.2.2.) has in general been a central motivation for assuming that the two phenomena ought to be accounted for uniformly. On this basis, it has frequently been posited that liaison/gender consonants are part of the phonological representations of nouns and adjectives (as stem-final consonants), and that a single consonant-deletion operation is responsible when they do not appear at the surface phonetic level. (A phonological rule of final-consonant deletion was postulated in the framework of the standard generative analysis of final consonants (see chap. v); a morphophonological rule of final-consonant deletion was proposed in less abstract treatments (e.g., Bloomfield 1933; Tranel 1974b)).

Arguments developed in both chapters iii and vi have already shown the inadequacy of such deletion solutions. In addition, as pointed out in section VII.2.2., the correspondence between liaison consonants and gender consonants can also be captured in an insertion approach by having the consonants as phonological markings in the lexical entries of the words, rather than as part of the phonological representations themselves. The preceding section partially justifies this approach by showing that these consonants have a different status from that of other segments in words, namely, the constraints on their possible occurrence go beyond morpheme structure conditions. The consonants used in adjective liaison and gender marking are thus lexically entered in both the deletion and insertion approaches, but in crucially distinct ways.

The insertion analysis also differs from any deletion treatment by claiming that liaison consonants and gender consonants are derived by the application of different rules, namely, rules of liaison and rules of gender formation. In this section, I point out major differences between liaison and gender marking which justify the postulation of distinct generating paths for consonant insertion in adjective liaison and for consonant insertion in the formation of feminine adjectives.

In the insertion analysis, liaison consonants are assumed to be separated from the preceding adjective by a word boundary, whereas gender consonants are placed directly after the last segment of the basic masculine forms. This difference captures the fact that liaison consonants are in essence, as indicated by their name, connective elements between words, whereas gender consonants are markers on words which contribute to the formation of other words having an existence of their own. Thus, the phonetic sequence [pətit] in itself is felt to be the feminine of the adjective meaning 'small'; it is not felt to be a potential masculine form.

This distinction also explains that certain lexically specified consonants undergo phonological changes in liaison which they do not undergo as gender consonants. Thus, as already noted, /d/ becomes /t/ and /s/ becomes /z/ in liaison, but not as feminine markers:

(41) *grand* [grã]/*grande* [grãd] 'great' (masc./fem.)
un grand homme [ɛ̃grãtɔm] 'a great man'
une grande armée [yngrãdarme] 'a great army'
gros [gro]/*grosse* [gros] 'big' (masc./fem.)
un gros orage [ɛ̃grozɔraž] 'a big storm'
une grosse orange [yngrosɔrãž] 'a big orange'

If [Ø[~ [C] alternations in adjective liaison and in gender distinctions really constituted a uniform phenomenon, as is claimed in the deletion analyses, one should expect the same facts in both cases.[10]

As observed earlier, masculine adjectives like *court* [kur] 'short' and *lourd* [lur] 'heavy' do not link with [t], although the feminine counterparts are *courte* [kurt] and *lourde* [lurd] in all contexts:

(42) *court* [kur]/*courte* [kurt] 'short' (masc./fem.)

un court instant [ɛ̃kurɛ̃stã] *[ɛ̃kurtɛ̃stã] 'a short time'
une courte interruption [ynkurtɛ̃terypsjɔ̃] ' a short interruption'
lourd [lur]/*lourde* [lurd] 'heavy' (masc./fem.)
un lourd objet [ɛ̃lurɔbʒɛ] *[ɛ̃lurtɔbʒɛ] 'a heavy object'
une lourde objection [ynlurdɔbʒɛksjɔ̃] 'a heavy objection'

Such cases similarly argue for a separate treatment of adjective liaison and feminine formation, and therefore against any uniform deletion treatment of the phenomena and in favor of the dual-insertion approach. In the analysis proposed here, the consonant-insertion rule of liaison, rule (29), states that the adjective must end in a vowel in order for liaison to take place; it thus straightforwardly accounts for the facts, since *court* and *lourd* both end in /r/ in their phonological representations. In a deletion analysis, the absence of the [t] in liaison has to be treated as an exception, since the phonological representations of these words include a final /t/ and a final /d/, respectively, which must be deleted before a vowel-initial word; any such account must be incorrect, however, because there is no tendency to eliminate the presumed exceptions and say *[ɛ̃kurtɛ̃stã] or *[ɛ̃lurtɔbʒɛ] (see part B of sec. III.5.3.3.).

In addition to the cases where liaison consonants and gender consonants actually behave in different ways with respect to their own ultimate phonetic shapes, there are also instances where they have different phonological effects on the preceding vowel. For example, in Montreal French, a high vowel becomes lax in closed syllables, as illustrated in (43):

(43) *petit* [pti]/*petite* [ptɪt] 'small' (masc./fem.)

lu [ly]/*lutte* [lYt] 'read'/'wrestling'
doux [du]/*douce* [dɔs] 'soft' (masc./fem.)

---

10. This does not mean that one cannot formally crank out the correct outputs in a deletion framework. For example, Schane (1968*b*:157–158) assumes the existence of a devoicing rule taking /d/ to /t/ at a word boundary (thus accounting for [grãtami] 'great friend' (masc.) from /grãd#ami/) and ordered before final-schwa deletion (thus accounting for [grãdami] 'great friend' (fem.) from /grãd + ə#ami + ə/).

Interestingly, whereas *petit ami* 'boyfriend' can only be pronounced [ptitami], *petite amie* 'girl friend' may be pronounced either [ptitami] or [ptɪtami], showing that whereas the linking consonant [t] in *petit ami* automatically belongs to the next syllable, the gender consonant [t] in *petite amie* may close the preceding syllable. Native speakers thus seem to consider that the two [t]'s have different statuses and that the [t] of the feminine is more closely attached to the adjective than the [t] of liaison. These facts are directly reflected in the insertion analysis, since it is assumed that liaison consonants are connective elements whereas gender consonants are truly part of the feminine words. Thus, after insertion, *petit ami* has the structure /pti#t#ami/, whereas *petite amie* has the structure /ptit#ami/. In Montreal French, there is no reason for the high vowel laxing rule to apply in the first case. In the second case, on a purely phonetic basis, there is also no reason for the rule to operate; this yields an output identical with that of the masculine phrase. On the basis of word structure, however, the final /t/ of /ptit/ does close a syllable with a high vowel, hence the possible application of the laxing rule.

Data of a parallel nature occur in Standard French. Consider the following examples:

(44) (a) *premier* [prəmje] 'first' (masc.)
   le premier étage [ləprəmjeretaž] 'the first floor'
   son premier amour [sɔ̃prəmjeramur] 'his first love'
  (b) *première* [prəmjɛr] 'first' (fem.)
   la première étagère [laprəmjɛretažɛr] 'the first shelf'
   sa première amourette [saprəmjɛramurɛt] 'his first flirt'

Whereas the feminine consonant [r] opens the preceding /e/ to [ɛ], the linking consonant [r] does not. These facts are consistent with the analysis proposed here. After insertion, *premier étage* and *première étagère* have the following respective structures: /prəmje#r#etaž/, /prəmjer#etažɛr/. The rule that changes /e/ to [ɛ] operates only in word-final closed syllables (cf. rule (40)); it will therefore apply only in the feminine.

In some conservative dialects, the final vowel of *premier* also appears as [ɛ] in liaison cases (e.g., *le premier étage* [ləprəmjɛretaž]). It is possible that, in the grammar of these speakers, the liaison consonants are inserted to the left of the word boundary, as the gender consonants are for all speakers. Such grammars would constitute a plausible intermediate stage between the times when all [Ø] ~ [C] alternations probably formed a uniform phenomenon to be accounted for by deletion, and the present stage. Linguistically conservative speakers seem to operate in a like manner when linking with infinitives of the first-conjugation class: the ending /e/ is opened to [ɛ] in liaison; thus, they say [alɛralamɛs] rather than [aleralamɛs] for *aller à la messe* 'to go to Mass'.

The adjective *sot* 'silly' (*sot* [so]/*sotte* [sɔt]) exhibits a comparable interesting behavior in the somewhat marginal construction where it is used in prenominal position. It has usually been considered, in various generative works on French phonology (e.g., Schane 1978*b*; Selkirk 1972; Tranel 1974*b*, 1977*c*), that the liaison pronunciation of the masculine singular adjective *sot* is always [sɔt], as in *un bien sot ami* [ɛ̃bjɛ̃sɔtami] 'a really silly friend'. When I asked native speakers to produce such phrases, however, some came up with sequences like [soami] or [sotami] or both; they did not themselves volunteer [sɔtami], and they usually seemed to feel quite uneasy with it, generally considering it the least acceptable of the three strings when it was suggested to them. For these speakers at least, these facts constitute another example of a linking consonant and a gender consonant acting differently on a preceding vowel, the linking consonant correlating with a closed [o] and the gender consonant correlating with an open [ɔ]; the presence of the closed [o] with the linking consonant is expected since a word boundary is assumed to separate the vowel from the connective consonant, and, as is well known, [o], rather than [ɔ], must occur in word-final position. The elicitation of [soami] also demonstrates the possibility for the linking consonant not to be inserted at all; the gender consonant, on the other hand, never fails to appear (*sotte* [sɔt]) (see below for a discussion of this difference between liaison and gender consonants). For speakers who do say [sɔtami], it may be that they insert the linking consonant to the left rather than to the right of the word boundary; this hypothesis would be likely if they also produced an open [ɛ] in liaison with words like *premier* and first-group verb infinitives. However, when this pronunciation ([sɔtami]) is isolated, as I know it is for some, then it probably ought to be regarded as due to suppletion, as suggested earlier for the adjective *bon* (cf. *bon ami* [bɔnami] *[bonami] 'good friend') (see part E of sec. III.5.3.3. and n. 13).

Another distinction between adjective liaison and gender formation has to do with the differing stability of the two processes. As noted in particular by Cohen (1963:106) and as verified by myself in many personal observations, liaison between an adjective and a noun may not always take place:

(45) *un violent incendie* [ɛ̃vjɔlãɛ̃sãdi] 'a violent blaze'
un important effort [ɛ̃nɛ̃pɔrtãefɔr] 'an important effort'
un étonnant engouement [ɛ̃netɔnããgumã] 'a surprising craze'
l'éclatant arc-en-ciel [leklatãarkãsjɛl] 'the bright rainbow'
le blond Italien [ləblɔ̃italjɛ̃] 'the blond Italian'
un audacieux à-propos [ɛ̃nodasjøapropo] 'a bold opportuneness'
un chaleureux accueil [ɛ̃šalørøakœj] 'a warm welcome'
l'odieux assassinat [lodjøasasina] 'the horrible murder'
un gros avantage [ɛ̃groavãtaž] 'a big advantage'
un gros oignon [ɛ̃groɔñɔ̃] 'a big onion'
un long entretien [ɛ̃lɔ̃ãtrətjɛ̃] 'a long talk'
ce long effort [səlɔ̃efɔr] 'this long effort'
un léger inconvénient [ɛ̃leže ɛ̃kɔ̃venjã] 'a slight drawback'
au premier étage [oprəmjeetaž] 'on the first floor'
le premier anneau [ləprəmjeano] 'the first loop'
un dernier entretien [ɛ̃dɛrnjeãtrətjɛ̃] 'a last talk'

These examples illustrate the sporadic nonapplication of rule (29) and demonstrate the relatively unstable status of adjective liaison. In contrast, the consonants found in feminine marking exhibit great stability. This difference indicates that the two operations of adjective liaison and gender marking are indeed distinct. The insertion approach not only captures the fact that speakers make a distinction; it provides in addition an explanation for the fact that the liaison phenomenon is less stable than feminine formation: in adjective liaison, linking consonants are regarded as mere connective segments that fulfill no particular functional role; in particular, it cannot be argued that they serve to eliminate hiatus, since the language tolerates them very well. On the other hand, gender consonants are considered to be a more integral part of the words and to fulfill a grammatical function that in many cases is directly connected to semantics (cf. Kiparsky 1972 and the notion of conservation of functional distinctions).

This pattern is confirmed by the existence of dialects from which adjective liaison has apparently completely disappeared, but where gender distinctions based on [Ø]~[C] alternations have remained. The illustrative data provided in (46) are from a Belgian dialect of French (Adriaens 1975).

(46) *petit* [pti]/*petite* [ptit] 'small' (masc./fem.)
petit homme [ptiɔm] 'small man'
grand [grã]/*grande* [grãd] 'great' (masc./fem.)

grand ami [grãami] 'great friend'
grand homme [grãɔm] 'great man'
gros [gro]/*grosse* [gros] 'big' (masc./fem.)
gros avion [groavjɔ̃] 'big plane'

To my knowledge, there are no dialects of French where adjective liaison has been maintained, but not [Ø] ~ [C] gender distinctions.

VII.3.2.3. Summary

The insertion analysis draws a three-way distinction among stem-final consonants, gender consonants, and liaison consonants, whereas deletion analyses conflate the three notions. The evidence shows that the distinction is warranted, as it corresponds to genuine differences in the behavior of these three types of consonants.

VII.3.3. Derivational morphology alternations

The [Ø] ~ [C] alternations found in derivationally related words are accounted for lexically. Consider again the type of examples given in part B of section VI.3.3.8.

(47) *petit* [pəti]/*petite* [pətit]/*petitesse* [pətitɛs]
    'small' (masc.) 'small' (fem.) 'smallness'
    joli [žɔli]/*jolie* [žɔli]/*joliesse* [žɔliɛs]
    'pretty' (masc.) 'pretty' (fem.) 'prettiness'
    poli [pɔli]/*polie* [pɔli]/*politesse* [pɔlitɛs]
    'polite' (masc.) 'polite' (fem.) 'politeness'

The adjectives and the derived nouns are entered in the lexicon as follows:

(48) (a) *petit* /pəti/ (/t/)
        petitesse /pətit+ɛs/
    (b) *joli* /žɔli/
        joliesse /žɔli+ɛs/
    (c) *poli* /pɔli/
        politesse /pɔli+t+ɛs/ or /pɔli+tɛs/

A general word-formation rule of Modern French states that nouns can be created by adding the suffix *-esse* to the feminine forms of adjectives (cf. *mou* [mu]/*molle* [mɔl] 'soft' (masc./fem.)/*mollesse* [mɔlɛs] 'softness'). The existence of this rule and of the rule of feminine formation accounts directly for cases (48a–b). For *politesse,* however, there is an intrusive /t/ present. Native speakers may either interpret this /t/ as just that, that is, "une consonne intercalaire"

(/pɔli+t+ɛs/), or they may assume that *poli* does not take *-esse,* but rather an extended suffix *-tesse* (/pɔli+tɛs/). The analysis may vary from speaker to speaker. But no matter how the presence of this /t/ is analyzed, it is completely idiosyncratic, from a synchronic perspective (cf. the case of *joli*), and speakers have to learn that one says [pɔlitɛs] rather than *[pɔliɛs]; they must therefore enter the existence of this /t/ in their lexicon, and the [ø]~[C] alternation that is exhibited in the pair *poli/politesse* has to be lexical in nature.

Consider now the verb *enjoliver* [ãžɔlive] 'to make pretty'. This verb, based on the adjective *joli,* is entered in the lexicon as /ã+žɔli+v/. This representation symbolizes the recognition by native speakers of the fact that this word is formed by the concatenation of the prefix /ã/ followed by the adjective *joli* and the (idiosyncratic) verb-forming consonant /v/. The [ø]~[C] alternation between the adjective *joli* and the verb *enjoliver* is a purely lexical matter, as was the [ø]~[C] alternation between *poli* and *politesse.*

The relation between nouns and first-conjugation verbs exhibiting a [ø]~[C] alternation is treated in a fashion parallel to the corresponding [Ṽ]~[VN] alternation examined in section III.5.3.1. The same type of productive process of denominal verb formation which was postulated to operate on nouns ending in a nasal vowel is assumed to operate on nouns ending in an oral vowel; the only difference is that in this case, the verb stems have a final [t] rather than a final [n] (Nyrop 1936:204–205; Morin 1972):

    (49) *biseau* [bizo]/*biseauter* [bizɔte] 'bevel'/'to bevel'
        caoutchouc [kautšu]/*caoutchouter* [kautšute] 'rubber'/'to rubberize'
        chouchou [šušu]/*chouchouter* [šušute] 'teacher's pet'/'to favor'
        filou [filu]/*filouter* [filute] 'swindler'/'to swindle'
        queue [kø]/*queuter* [køte] 'line'/'to stand in line'
        yeux [jø]/*zyeuter* [zjøte] 'eyes'/'to ogle'

This word-formation process can be formalized as follows:

$$(50) \quad \left[X \begin{bmatrix} V \\ -\text{nasal} \end{bmatrix} \right]_{\text{Noun}} \Rightarrow \left[X \begin{bmatrix} V \\ -\text{nasal} \end{bmatrix} t \right]_{\text{Verb}}$$

Like its nasal counterpart of chapter iii, rule (50) is considered to have a dual function: that of a once-only process creating new denominal verbs and that of a lexical rule relating noun/verb pairs. Not all noun/verb pairs exhibiting a [ø]~[C] alternation can, however, be the object of a relation through rule (50); a more encompassing lexicon-restricted rule of correspondence (i.e., the via rule [Ø] ⟺ [C]) is required to account for phonologically nonproductive cases such as *décès* [desɛ]/*décéder* [desede] 'death'/'to die', *estomac* [ɛstɔma]/*estomaquer* [ɛstɔmake] 'stomach'/'to surprise', *galop* [galo]/*galoper* [galɔpe] 'gallop'/'to gallop', *hiver* [ivɛr]/*hiberner* [ibɛrne] 'winter'/'to hibernate', *nid* [ni]/*nicher* [niše] 'nest'/'to nest', *outil* [uti]/*outiller* [utije] 'tool'/'to equip with tools.'

In general, [Ø] ~ [C] alternations in derivationally related words are directly accounted for by the analyzing function of word-formation rules and via rules (cf. Aronoff 1976; Vennemann 1972c; sec. III.5.3.1.). Sometimes it is necessary for native speakers to recognize in addition the existence of "consonnes intercalaires" or of extended suffixes. This is automatically provided by the splitting up of complex words into recognizable morphemes, at least for the speakers who do make the semantic and phonological connections.

This approach predicts that speakers may relate words in different degrees and ways, as is borne out by common experience and by folk etymology. For example, I have synchronically related the verb *tabasser* [tabase] 'to beat up' to *tabac* [taba] in *passer à tabac* [paseataba] 'to beat up' and to *tabac* [taba] 'tobacco' (Tranel 1976b); Pichon (1942:29) and Yves Morin (personal communication) do not think, however, that this connection is diachronically justified; nevertheless, the relation is real in the grammars of many speakers (see, e.g., Dauzat 1919:77).

[Ø] ~ [C] alternations found in derivational morphology are not grammatically determined, as opposed to those found in plural liaison, verb liaison, and adjective liaison. Thus, if one wanted to relate them to the linking phenomenon, as is done in the framework of the abstract generative treatment of final consonants, they would have to be classified together with the type of liaison found with invariable words like prepositions and adverbs. But, as noted in section VII.2.3., the [Ø] ~ [C] alternations typical of liaison with prepositions and adverbs are unstable, and they are in fact being neutralized in favor of the forms with no final consonants. On the other hand, the [Ø] ~ [C] alternations found in derivational morphology are a model of stability and therefore are clearly of a different nature. The analysis proposed here expresses this distinction straightforwardly: it has been seen that liaison with prepositions and adverbs is the result of the application of minor rules; the linking consonants are inserted because of a particular lexical marking on the words, which naturally tends to be removed from the grammar. In derived words, the consonants are lexically present; since they are an integral part of the words, there is no reason for them to be eliminated.

The [∅]~[C] alternations found in derivationally related noun/ verb pairs also differ from a superficially similar type of [∅]~[C] alternations treated separately in the present framework, namely, [∅]~[C] gender alternations. In the latter case, it makes sense to have a unique underlying representation for a given adjective or noun, and to derive generatively one gender from the other, because the syntactic and semantic properties of the masculine and feminine forms are identical, and remain so.[11] On the other hand, in noun/verb pairs, the syntactic properties of the alternants are different, and the semantic connections between them can become quite idiosyncratic (cf. *drap* [dra]/*draper* [drape] 'sheet'/'to drape'; *tapis* [tapi]/*tapisser* [tapise] 'carpet'/'to hang with tapestry'); as already noted in section III.5.3.1., this also indicates that derivationally related words are best accounted for lexically rather than generatively.

VII.4. Conclusion

The final section of chapter vi and this chapter offer a treatment of [∅]~[C] alternations in Modern French within a framework rejecting the major phonological process of consonant deletion assumed in standard generative analyses of French phonology and morphology. The well-motivated abandonment of this process makes it necessary to forego a uniform account of [∅]~[C] alternations, but it has been shown that the different properties that characterize the various types of [∅]~[C] alternations actually warrant a nonuniform solution.

For the [∅]~[C] alternations found in verb stems of the third-conjugation group, it has been suggested that the alternants are both entered in the lexicon, and that rules of distribution account for their occurrence in the correct grammatical contexts. For the [∅]~[C] alternations found in derivational morphology, it has been proposed that the words have separate lexical entries and that they are related within the lexicon rather than generatively.

11. In chapter iii, one case of semantic drift is noted between the masculine and the feminine of an adjective (*malin* [malɛ̃]/*maligne* [maliɲ]). But in this instance the occurrence of the drift was observed to correlate with an unexpected process of feminine formation (the addition of /ɲ/ instead of /n/) which was hypothesized to have led to separate lexical entries.

Liaison phenomena (plural liaison, verb liaison, adjective liaison, liaison with invariable words) and feminine formation are on the other hand treated generatively by postulating one form as basic and deriving the other by rule. The following general observations can be drawn from this generative treatment:

(i) The distinction "basic" versus "derived" coincides with the traditional dichotomy between "unmarked" and "marked." Thus, basic forms turn out to be citation forms, and when grammatical information is relevant, forms that are singular or masculine. Derived forms, on the other hand, turn out to be forms that may not be used in isolation, or forms that are plural or feminine. This type of correlation is intuitively appealing, and it has actually been proposed as a theoretical postulate in the framework of natural generative phonology (Vennemann 1971).

(ii) The relations between basic and derived forms are established by rules of consonant insertion which are governed by phonological, grammatical, and lexical information. This attests to widespread and drastic historical changes in the grammar of French, starting with the stage where $[\emptyset] \sim [C]$ alternations were presumably the outcome of a uniform phonological process of consonant deletion. The consonant-insertion approach thus reveals a complex body of data wherein the phenomenon of rule inversion (Vennemann 1972c) has operated.

(iii) It has been suggested (Schane 1978a) that the debate on consonant deletion versus consonant insertion is a pseudocontroversy and that the two approaches to $[\emptyset] \sim [C]$ alternations are notational variants. A close look at the data and a detailed consideration of substantive evidence have shown that consonant deletion and consonant insertion make in many respects widely different claims about French phonology and morphology, and that the consonant-insertion treatment presents a much more plausible psychological picture of the linguistic knowledge internalized by native speakers.

(iv) The treatment of $[\emptyset] \sim [C]$ alternations advocated here reflects surface phonetic facts rather directly. In this sense it is more concrete than the standard generative analysis of final consonants. In particular, it does not require the postulation of final schwas which do not appear on the surface, and it does not require recourse to extrinsic rule ordering.

PART III
PROTECTIVE SCHWAS AND H-ASPIRÉ WORDS

INTRODUCTION

1. A note on terminology

The term "schwa" and the corresponding symbol "ə" are commonly used to refer to the segment phonetically realized as [œ] but subject to alternations such as those of (1):

(1) *le bel arbre* [ləbɛlarbr] ([lœbɛlarbr])/*l'arbre* [larbr]
    'the beautiful tree'   'the tree'
    cinq chemises [sɛ̃kšəmiz] ([sɛ̃kšœmiz]) 'five shirts'
    /*deux chemises* [døšmiz] 'two shirts'
    un énorme camion [ɛ̃nɔrm(ə)kamjɔ̃] ([ɛ̃nɔrm(œ)kamjɔ̃])
    'a huge truck'

This notation offers the typographical convenience of allowing us to distinguish between two kinds of front rounded low-mid vowels, the one that alternates with zero and the one that does not:

(2) (a) *genêt*   /žənɛ/   [žənɛ] ~ [žnɛ] 'furze'
       neveu   /nəvø/   [nəvø] ~ [nvø] 'nephew'
   (b) *jeunet*   /žœnɛ/   [žœnɛ] *[žnɛ] 'young'
       neuvaine   /nœvɛn/   [nœvɛn] *[nvɛn] 'novena'

This practice, which has been generally adopted implicitly, should not detract from the fact that there are actually two /œ/'s in Modern French, one unstable, the other stable (for an explicit recognition of this state of affairs, see, for example, Dell 1973*b*:196–197, Tranel 1977*b*:694, and especially Morin 1978).

"H-aspiré words" is the standard phrase used to refer to lexical items like *héros* 'hero' and *hache* 'axe', which phonetically begin in a vowel but do not, for example, govern elision or liaison:

(3) (a) *héros* [ero]
     hache [aš]
  (b) *le héros* [ləero] *[lero] 'the hero'
     la hache [laaš] *[laš] 'the axe'
  (c) *les héros* [lɛero] *[lɛzero] 'the heroes'
     les haches [lɛaš] *[lɛzaš] 'the axes'

The terminology is doubly inaccurate: there is no [h] present in the pronunciation, and the occurrence or absence of the letter *h* in the orthography does not constitute a reliable indication of a word's behavior with respect to elision and liaison, as shown in (4):

(4) (a) *homme* [ɔm] 'man'
     onze [ɔ̃z] 'eleven'
  (b) *l'homme*   [lɔm]   *[ləɔm] 'the man'
     le onze (tricolore) *[lɔ̃z]   [ləɔ̃z]
     (the French national soccer team)
  (c) *les hommes*   [lɛzɔm]*[lɛɔm] 'the men'
     les onze (joueurs) *[lɛzɔ̃z] [lɛɔ̃z] 'the eleven players'

Nevertheless, throughout chapters viii and ix, I retain the use of the terms "schwa" and "h-aspiré words" because, as part of the traditional terminology, they readily identify the types of phenomena investigated.

2. Purpose

Schwas and h-aspiré words have played an important role in the standard generative analysis of French nasal vowels and final consonants. As already mentioned (see chaps. i and v), in this abstract framework schwas are posited underlyingly in certain positions with the specific purpose of protecting /VN/ sequences from the effects of vowel nasalization (e.g., *samedi* /samədi/ [samdi] 'Saturday'; *homme* /ɔmə/ [ɔm] 'man'; *bonne* /bɔn+ə/ [bɔn] 'good' (fem.)) and final consonants from the effects of consonant deletion (e.g., *honnête* /ɔnɛtə/ [ɔnɛt] 'honest'; *petite* /pətit+ə/ [pətit] 'small' (fem.)). These protective schwas, which are deleted by obligatory rules extrinsically ordered after vowel nasalization and consonant deletion, are structurally indispensable to a uniform phonological treatment of [Ṽ] ~ [VN] and [Ø] ~ [C] alternations (Schane 1968*b*; Dell 1973*a*).

H-aspiré words have also figured prominently in this analysis. As mentioned in sections V.3.3. and VI.3.3.6., they are considered to trigger the surface realization of underlying word-final protective schwas and thus to provide a phonetic basis for the postulation of these segments (Schane 1968*b*; Selkirk 1972; Dell 1973*a, b*). On a wider scale, h-aspiré words have played a part in the debate on abstractness initiated by Kiparsky (1968*a*) and opposing the use of imaginary underlying segments to that of rule features. Within the framework of the standard generative analysis of nasal vowels and final consonants, a rule-feature treatment of h-aspiré words has been shown to be impossible, whereas the lexical postulation of an initial consonantal segment (systematically deleted by a late phonetic rule) has been claimed to explain the behavior of these words (Selkirk and Vergnaud 1973).

My goal in chapter viii is to show that there is no basis for the postulation of protective schwas; converging evidence for this view comes from a phonological perspective and from a structural perspective, as well as from the viewpoint of language acquisition. My goal in chapter ix is to provide a critical review of the abstract segment analysis of h-aspiré words and to motivate a treatment based on the use of rule features and integrated into the concrete analysis of nasal vowels and final consonants presented in Parts I and II. By providing arguments against the postulation of two rather well-established abstract segments, Part III supports the view that a universal theoretical principle bars the use of abstract segments in the grammars constructed by native speakers.

VIII

PROTECTIVE SCHWAS

VIII.1. Introduction

As pointed out in chapters i and v, two types of protective schwas have been postulated in the framework of the abstract generative analysis of nasal vowels and final consonants: morphological and lexical schwas. Morphological schwas represent grammatical morphemes inserted in underlying representations by spelling rules. Three protective morphological schwas have been assumed. One is the feminine marker; it is rewritten at the end of feminine nouns and adjectives, as exemplified in (1):

(1) (a) *paysanne*　/peizan+ə/　[peizan]　'peasant'
　　　bonne　　/bɔn+ə/　　[bɔn]　　'good'
　　(b) *avocate*　/avɔkat+ə/　[avɔkat]　'lawyer'
　　　petite　　/pətit+ə/　　[pətit]　'small'

Another protective morphological schwa is the thematic vowel posited for first-conjugation verbs. The examples given in (2) include the person markings assumed to be systematically present at the underlying level in the standard generative analysis (see sec. VII.2.1.).

(2) (a) *je donne*　/žə#dɔn+ə+z/　[žədɔn]　'I give'
　　(b) *il arrive*　/il#ariv+ə+t/　[ilariv]　'he is coming'

The third protective morphological schwa is the subjunctive marker postulated to occur with all verbs, whatever their conjugation class. This is illustrated in (3) with verbs of the third group:

(3) (a) *je vienne*　/žə#vjɛn+ə+z/　[žəvjɛn]　'I come'
　　(b) *il morde*　/il#mɔrd+ə+t/　[ilmɔrd]　'he bite'

Lexical schwas are part of the phonological representations of words.

Protective lexical schwas have been posited morpheme-internally (at least to prevent the application of vowel nasalization) and word-finally, as exemplified in (4):

(4) (a) *samedi*   /samədi/   [samdi]   'Saturday'
     jaune   /žonə/   [žon]   'yellow' (masc.)
   (b) *pilote*   /pilɔt/   [pilɔt]   'pilot'
     honnête   /ɔnɛtə/   [ɔnɛt]   'honest' (masc.)

In this chapter, I argue against the postulation of protective schwas from three perspectives: (i) I show that they exhibit no phonetic reflexes, and therefore that they are entirely abstract segments; drawing from Parts I and II, I then briefly reemphasize (ii) that protective schwas are not structurally necessary to a correct account of [Ṽ] ~ [VN] and [Ø] ~ [C] alternations, and (iii) that the existence of protective schwas is not naturally learnable.

The status of protective schwas is to be clearly separated from that of the following four types of schwas:

(i) Elision schwas:

Grammatical morphemes like the definite article *le*, the subject pronouns *je* and *ce*, the object pronouns *me*, *te*, *se*, *le*, the preposition *de*, the conjunction *que*, and the negative particle *ne* enter into alternations like those given in (5):

(5) *le nouvel étudiant* [lənuvɛletydjã]/*l'étudiant* [letydjã]
     'the new student'   'the student'
   ce sera fait [səsərafɛ]/*c'était fait* [setɛfɛ]
     'it will be done'   'it was done'
   Luc le voit [lykləvwa]/*Luc l'entend* [lyklãtã]
     'Luke sees it'   'Luke hears it'
   il ne viendra pas [ilnəvjẽdrapa] 'he won't come'/
   il n'arrivera pas [ilnarivrapa] 'he won't arrive'

I take these words to contain an underlying schwa which is subject to obligatory elision before vowel-initial words (Dell 1973*b*:203–204, 251–252).[1]

(ii) Optional schwas:

The schwas of the monosyllabic morphemes given above are also subject to an optional process of schwa deletion under certain conditions, in particular when they are not preceded by more than one consonant:

1. Elision in addition affects the /a/ of the definite article and pronoun *la*. Under certain conditions, optional elision affects other vowels in other grammatical morphemes (*tu* [ty] 'you' (sg.); *si* [si] 'if'; *qui* [ki] 'that'; see Tranel 1978*a*).

(6) *Luc le voit* [lyklǝvwa]/*Henri le voit* [ãril(ǝ)vwa]
    'Luke sees it'   'Henry sees it'
    la bouteille de vin [labutɛjdǝvɛ̃] 'the bottle of wine'/
    beaucoup de vin [bokud(ǝ)vɛ̃] 'much wine'
    ce gâteau est bon [sǝgatoɛbɔ̃] ~ [sgatoɛbɔ̃]
    'this cake is good'

The same alternations are found in the initial syllable of polysyllabic words:

(7) *il part demain* [ilpardǝmɛ̃] 'he leaves tomorrow'/
    il partira demain [ilpartirad(ǝ)mɛ̃] 'he will leave tomorrow'
    sept chemins [sɛtšǝmɛ̃]/*un chemin* [ɛ̃š(ǝ)mɛ̃]
    'seven paths'   'one path'
    venons-en aux faits [vǝnɔ̃zãofɛ] ~ [vnɔ̃zãofɛ]
    'let's get to the facts'

I take these alternations to require that the schwas be present underlyingly and deleted by rule (see Dell (1973*b*:187, 238–242) and Morin (1974:73) for convincing arguments against an insertion treatment).[2]

(iii) Schwas alternating with [ɛ]:

At the surface phonetic level schwas may also enter into alternations with zero and [ɛ], as illustrated in (8):

(8) (a) *hôtelier* [otǝlje]/*hôtel* [otɛl] 'innkeeper'/'hotel'
    (b) *mener* [m(ǝ)ne]/*il mène* [ilmɛn] 'to lead'/'he leads'
    (c) *acheter* [ašte]/*il achète* [ilašɛt] 'to buy'/'he buys'

The treatment of these alternations is controversial. Selkirk (1972: 345–348) assumes the presence of an underlying /ɛ/; Dell (1973*b*: chap. v) presupposes that of an underlying /ǝ/; and Morin (1978: 124–135), basing his analysis on a wide array of data from various dialects, argues for different underlying segments, depending on the cases: he suggests /ɛ/ in nominal alternations like (8a), /ǝ/ in verbal alternations like (8b), and zero in verbal alternations like (8c). Whatever the analysis, the schwas that do show up at the surface phonetic level (cf. (8a–b)) appear to require the presence of an underlying segment (/ɛ/ or /ǝ/).

(iv) Future and conditional schwas:

In the future of first-conjugation verbs a schwa may appear pho-

---

2. This particular schwa ~ zero alternation has been the object of many studies. From a general theoretical point of view it has frequently been considered in relation to the debate on rule application (simultaneous versus iterative) (see Dell 1970:23–38, 1973*b*:244–250; Howard 1972:138–140; Johnson 1970:77; Morin and Friedman 1971:48–52; Morin 1974; Tranel 1974*a*).

netically between the stem and the future marker /r/ if the stem ends
in a consonant cluster; the presence of the schwa is obligatory if the
stem ends in an obstruent + liquid cluster. This is illustrated in (9):

(9) (a) *nous prétexterons* [nupretɛkst(ə)rɔ̃] 'we will pretend'
    vous parlerez [vuparl(ə)re] 'you will speak'
  (b) *nous tremblerons* [nutrãblərɔ̃] 'we will tremble'
    vous vinaigrerez [vuvinɛgrəre] 'you will use vinegar'

It has usually been assumed that this schwa is the phonetic reflex of
an underlying thematic vowel which may undergo deletion after any
consonant cluster, except an obstruent + liquid sequence (Dell
1973*b*:231–232; see also Dell 1976). The same process is also assumed
to take place in the conditional, except in the first and second person
plural:

(10) (a) *je prétexterais* [žəpretɛkst(ə)rɛ] 'I would pretend'
    tu parlerais [typarl(ə)rɛ] 'you would speak'
    il tremblerait [iltrãblərɛ] 'he would tremble'
  (b) *nous prétexterions* [nupretɛkstərjɔ̃] 'we would pretend'
    vous parleriez [vuparlərje] 'you would speak'

The impossible deletion of the schwa in the examples in (10b) is attributable to the constraint preventing the occurrence of sequences of
consonant + liquid + yod + vowel in the same syllable (Morin
1971; Tranel 1972; part C of sec. II.4.3.2.).

The distribution of future and conditional schwas has thus been
commonly considered to result from the variable application to an
underlying thematic schwa of a deletion rule subject to various blocking conditions (cf. Morin (1978:115–121) for alternative hypotheses
presented in the light of additional data).

The first three categories of schwas just mentioned do not perform
a protective function, but it might be argued that future and conditional schwas do, because their underlying presence apparently prevents the application of vowel nasalization and consonant deletion, as
shown in (11):

(11) (a) *j'aimerai* 'I will like'
    /zə#ɛm+ə+r+ɛ/   [žemrɛ] *[žẽrɛ]
  (b) *je demanderai* 'I will ask'
    /žə#dəmãd+ə+r+ɛ/   [žədəmãdrɛ] *[žədəmãrɛ]

As observed in part C of section II.4.3.2. and in section VI.3.3.5.,
however, pronunciations like those of (12),

(12) *nous aimerions* [nuzɛmrijɔ̃] 'we would like'
   nous demanderions [nudəmãdrijɔ̃] 'we would ask'

which are sporadically found in speakers of Standard French and which can be explained only by the absence of the underlying thematic schwa, demonstrate that future and conditional schwas cannot be responsible for the blocking of vowel nasalization and consonant deletion.

I am not concerned any further in this chapter with these four categories of schwas. Instead, I will concentrate on what I have defined as protective schwas.

VIII.2. On the phonetic evidence for protective schwas

In the standard generative analysis of French phonology, final protective schwas are systematically eliminated by late rules extrinsically ordered after vowel nasalization and consonant deletion (Dell 1970; 1973*a, b*). This across-the-board deletion makes the case for final protective schwas weak, because it claims in effect that, since these schwas have no phonetic reflexes, they are completely abstract constructs. These constructs are posited as schwa, an existing segment in the phonological inventory of Modern French, but one might as well have picked a nonexisting vowel in the system, for example, /i/ or /ɯ/. In one particular case, however, it has been argued that final protective schwas do show up phonetically, namely, before h-aspiré words. In this section, I consider the evidence provided by h-aspiré words concerning final protective schwas, as well as other phonetic realizations of schwa which could conceivably be interpreted as surface reflexes of underlying protective schwas. I show that there is actually no basis for recognizing a correspondence between protective schwas and surface manifestations of schwa, and that protective schwas thus remain abstract segments.

VIII.2.1. Schwa and h-aspiré words

The argument that final protective schwas actually show up phonetically before h-aspiré words is found in Schane (1968*b*:162), Selkirk (1972:329–330), and Dell (1973*a*:35; 1973*b*:186). Dell, for instance, states that *quelle housse* 'what a covering' may be pronounced [kɛləus], but that *quel hêtre* 'what a beech tree' cannot be pronounced *[kɛləɛtr]. This surface distribution of schwa before h-aspiré words seems to correspond exactly to the underlying distribution of final protective morphological schwas: *quelle* has a final schwa underlyingly because it is feminine (/kɛl + ə/), but *quel* does not because it is masculine (/kɛl/). On the basis of similar observations, Selkirk argues that final protective lexical schwas are present in "such words as *mince, étrange, onze, fantastique, chouette, vide,* etc, which are identical in the masculine and the feminine," whereas they are absent in words like *"sept, cinq, avec, net, chic, bref, répulsif,* etc" because the words of the first group, but not those of the second, are pronounced with a final schwa before h-aspiré words. Selkirk specifically mentions the contrast between *sept haies* 'seven hurdles', pronounced without a schwa between the two words, and *cette haie* 'this hurdle', pronounced [sɛtəɛ].

The facts, however, are not so clear-cut as these observations based on normative French might lead one to think. I have observed, in spontaneous speech, the phrase *quel hasard* 'what a coincidence' pronounced [kɛləazar]; this pronunciation has also been attested by Yves Morin (personal communication). Since *hasard* is masculine, it cannot be argued that the schwa is the feminine marker. In direct elicitation of the pronunciations of *sept haies* 'seven hurdles' and *cette haie* 'this hurdle', I have obtained [sɛtəɛ] for *sept haies,* when this phrase was requested first; however, as soon as the contrast with *cette haie* was introduced, [sɛt/ɛ] was used for *sept haies* and [sɛtəɛ] for *cette haie* (the slanted bar indicates the absence of "enchaînement" between the preceding consonant and the following vowel; that is, the [t] is not syllabified with the following [ɛ]). Phrases like [avwarəɔ̃t] for *avoir honte* 'to be ashamed', where no lexical protective schwa has been postulated which would correspond to the surface one, are actually attested in spontaneous speech (Martinon 1913:249).

Such data indicate that h-aspiré words, rather than revealing the underlying existence of final protective schwas, generally govern an optional rule of schwa insertion when the preceding word ends in a consonant. This process is optional, as the following examples show:

(13) *un jeune héros* [ɛ̃ʒœnəero] ~ [ɛ̃ʒœn/ero] 'a young hero'
  une bonne hache [ynbɔnəaš] ~ [ynbɔn/aš] 'a good axe'
  en légère hausse [ãležɛrəos] ~ [ãležɛr/os] 'slightly gaining'

In addition, the insertion is constrained by the orthography: the presence/absence of a final *e* at the end of the preceding word tends to reinforce the occurrence/nonoccurrence of the schwa. The rule can be provisionally written as follows (see chap. ix for refinements):

(14) Ø → ə/ C — # h-aspiré words
  Variable condition: Application of the rule is reinforced/ inhibited by the presence/absence of an orthographic *e* after C

This analysis explains why, in spontaneous speech, schwa insertion may take place regardless of the orthography, whereas in normative French or in an artificial elicitation situation, schwa insertion occurs only in accordance with the orthography; spelling expectedly has a stronger influence under the latter two conditions. Rule (14) is a doubly marginal process of the language: first, it is triggered by a very small class of words; second, these words are in many ways anomalous (see chap. ix). It should therefore not be considered fanciful to assume that speakers, at least on certain occasions, rely on the spelling to constrain the process of schwa insertion before h-aspiré words.

The historical scenario of the emergence of rule (14) can be hypothesized to have been approximately as follows: when final schwas were deleted before vowel-initial words, h-aspiré words had to be considered as exceptions, because they could cause the retention of an immediately preceding schwa. With the later deletion of final schwas before consonant-initial words, the schwas that appeared before h-aspiré words were reinterpreted as inserted segments, since there was otherwise no motivation for their underlying presence; in other words, rule inversion took place. As noted, there is accordingly a tendency to generalize the insertion of schwas in cases where they are not etymological, but this trend is curbed by orthography, most notably and expectedly in normative French.

VIII.2.2. Schwa and consonant clusters

When a word ends in a consonant cluster and is followed by a consonant-initial word, a schwa may appear between the two words, as illustrated in (15):

(15) *un énorme camion* [ɛ̃nenɔrm(ə)kamjɔ̃] 'a huge truck'
une veste déchirée [ynvɛst(ə)dešire] 'a torn jacket'
il s'offusque toujours [ilsɔfysk(ə)tužur] 'he is always hurt'
ils perdent beaucoup [ilpɛrd(ə)boku] 'they lose a lot'

Dell (1970:21–23; 1973b:236–238) has shown that these cases are best handled by a grammar including an optional process of schwa insertion like (16), because rule (16) is needed independently.

(16) $\emptyset \rightarrow$ ə $/ CC - \#_1 C$

A schwa may appear "à la fin de certaines formes des verbes *ouvrir, couvrir, offrir, souffrir* lorsque le mot suivant commence par une consonne. Ces verbes appartiennent à la troisième conjugaison, comme *peindre, servir,* etc. Leur représentation phonologique ne contient pas de voyelle thématique, et parallèlement à *il peint* /pɛñ+t/, *il sert* /sɛrv+t/, on doit attribuer à *il ouvre, il offre* les représentations phonologiques /uvr+t/, /ɔfr+t/, où n'apparaît aucune voyelle dont on puisse dériver le schwa qui apparaît facultativement dans *il ouv(re) la porte, il m'off(re) du feu"* (Dell 1973*b*:237). A similar argument may be adduced from words like *contact* [kɔ̃takt] 'contact', which, at least according to the view shared by Schane and Selkirk (see chap. v), do not contain a final lexical schwa and thus require the existence of rule (16) (cf. *des contacts pénibles* [dɛkɔ̃takt(ə)penibl] 'painful contacts'). The schwas that may appear phonetically at the border between words to break up consonant clusters are thus not the phonetic reflexes of final protective schwas (see Dell 1976, 1977, 1978*b* for additional observations concerning these epenthetic schwas).

Final protective schwas might also be taken to occur phonetically in derived words, when a consonant-initial suffix is added to a form ending in a consonant cluster. The obligatory presence of a schwa in such environments is illustrated in (17):

(17) *correctement* [kɔrɛktəmã] 'correctly'
 (cf. the adjective *correct* [kɔrɛkt] 'correct')
 gouvernement [guvɛrnəmã] 'government'
 (cf. the verb *gouverner* [guvɛrne] 'to govern')
 brusquerie [bryskəri] 'brusqueness'
 (cf. the adjective *brusque* [brysk] 'brusque')
 gendarmerie [žãdarməri] 'police station'
 (cf. the noun *gendarme* [žãdarm] 'police officer')

Dell (1978*a*) has shown, however, that these schwas cannot be the phonetic reflexes of protective schwas such as the feminine marker or the first-conjugation thematic vowel, because they also occur in words where no such schwas can be postulated (e.g., *recouvrement* [rəkuvrəmã] 'recovery'; cf. the third-conjugation verb *recouvrir* [rəkuvrir] 'to recover'). He therefore proposes that these schwas are the result of an obligatory rule inserting a schwa before any derivational suffix. I also consider (Tranel 1977*c*) the schwas found in words like those of (17) to be the result of an obligatory insertion process, but since they occur only when a stem ends in a consonant cluster and the suffix begins in a consonant, the insertion rule is limited to operate in this context. At any rate, the schwas that appear phonetically before derivational suffixes are not the phonetic reflexes of protective schwas.

VIII.2.3. Schwa and *rien*

Another potential piece of phonetic evidence for final protective schwas concerns the possible pronunciations of first-conjugation verbs in the indicative and subjunctive present singular before the word *rien* [rjẽ] 'nothing'. These forms may exhibit, at the surface phonetic level, what could be interpreted as the thematic vowel postulated in first-conjugation verbs:

(18) *il ne mange rien* [ilnəmãž(ə)rjẽ] 'he eats nothing'

   il ne capture rien [ilnəkaptyr(ə)rjẽ] 'he captures nothing'

The presence of a phonetic schwa before *rien* is also possible, however, after words that cannot be claimed to have a final protective schwa. For instance, a schwa may occur before *rien* when it is preceded by third-conjugation verbs that do not have thematic vowels:

(19) *il ne perd rien pour attendre* [ilnəpɛr(ə)rjẽpuratãdr]

   'his turn will come' (threat)

   il ne mord rien [ilnəmɔr(ə)rjẽ]

   'he bites nothing'

   si je sors rien [sižsɔr(ə)rjẽ]

   'if I roll nothing' (dice)

The same phenomenon may also take place when *rien* is combined with words like *avec* 'with', *pour* 'for', and *toujours* 'still, always':

(20) *avec rien* [avɛk(ə)rjẽ] 'with nothing'

   pour rien [pur(ə)rjẽ] 'for nothing'

   toujours rien [tužur(ə)rjẽ] 'still nothing'

The words *avec* and *pour* are usually assumed not to contain a final lexical schwa, and the word *toujours* presumably cannot, since the fact that it may link with /z/ (e.g., *toujours ensemble* [tužurzãsãbl] 'always together') necessitates in the standard generative analysis of final consonants the underlying representation /tužurz/.[3]

The phonetic presence of schwa in cases like (18) is thus not to be taken as evidence for the underlying existence of final protective schwas. It can be straightforwardly accounted for by the following independently necessary optional rule:

(21) $\emptyset \rightarrow$ ə / C — # rjẽ

The existence of rule (21) may be related to the general constraint that prohibits sequences of consonant + liquid + yod + vowel in the same syllable (see Morin 1971; Tranel 1972; part C of sec. II.4.3.2.).

---

3. /tužurəz/ would actually have to be proposed, but this form would phonetically yield *[tužurɛ], at least in Dell's framework (1973*b*:198–212) (see sec. II.2.2.4.).

Because *rien* is a separate word, a slight pause can be maintained before it (e.g., *avec rien* [avɛk/rjɛ̃]) and therefore make unnecessary the application of the schwa-insertion process.

VIII.2.4. Schwa and other dialects

Schane (1972) has suggested that the actual phonetic realizations of schwa in other dialects of French (e.g., Southern French) support the position that protective schwas exist underlyingly in the standard dialect.

Concerning Southern French, there is to my knowledge no particular evidence that the schwas that do show up phonetically between words are present underlyingly. In fact, I have observed that the alleged "underlying final schwas" curiously surface in cases where the abstract generative analysis does not postulate them, as, for example, after infinitives in *-ir* (*finir* [finir] 'to finish', *dormir* [dɔrmir] 'to sleep'); I have also observed the pronunciation [œnavwarəfamiljal] for *un avoir familial* 'a family possession' by a speaker from the Southwest of France. A detailed investigation of these dialects is certainly warranted, but I would hypothesize that a rather general rule of interconsonantal schwa insertion at word boundaries would correctly account for the presence of schwas between words in *spontaneous* speech in Southern French.

Even if it were conclusively proven that final protective schwas must be posited to account for southern speech, it would not automatically follow that they ought to be posited in the dialect of Standard French. A simple example will demonstrate the fallacy of the view that all dialects of the same language must have the same underlying representations and, further, that in French the common underlying representations must be the ones of the dialect that has schwas on the surface. Consider abstract internal schwas in Modern French, for which Schane (1972) suggested the same type of dialectal evidence to justify their postulation in Standard French. According to Schane, "concrete" evidence for an underlying schwa in *samedi* 'Saturday' comes from the fact that southern speakers pronounce the word [samədi]; for northern speakers, then, the underlying representation for this word is /samədi/, although they always say [samdi]; the difference between the underlying representation and the surface form is accounted for by the obligatory application of a rule of internal-schwa deletion. But note that speakers of some dialects of French say [ɛksəprɛ] for *exprès* 'on purpose'; although northern speakers always pronounce [ɛksprɛ], one must conclude from Schane's argument that the underlying representation for this word is /ɛksəprɛ/; the problem is that there is no independently motivated rule of schwa deletion to account for the surface form [ɛksprɛ], since schwa cannot normally delete if it is preceded by more than one consonant (cf. *avec ce prêt* [avɛksəprɛ] *[avɛksprɛ] 'with this loan'; *fixement* [fiksəmã] *[fiksmã] 'fixedly').

The evidence for protective schwas which is based on the assumption that they occur phonetically in southern dialects is at best clearly irrelevant.

VIII.2.5. Schwa in songs and poetry

Schane (1972) also argued that protective schwas appear phonetically in songs and in poetry. The pronunciation of schwas in these circumstances, however, is strictly based on orthography, and it cannot be taken as evidence for a corresponding underlying presence.

Dell (1970:61) noted, for example, that in songs one can expect *asile* [azil] 'shelter' to be pronounced with a final schwa ([azilə]), but not *avril* [avril] *[avrilə] 'April', simply because of the different spellings. The role of orthography is also crucial in poetry. Classical Alexandrine lines, for instance, require the pronunciation (as schwas) of interconsonantal *e*'s in order to have the correct number of feet. That spelling is indeed the relevant factor is reflected in the poetic license that authorized writers to spell *avec* 'with' either *avec* or *avecque,* and *encore* 'again' either *encore* or *encor,* to fit their rhythmic needs. Note that nowadays it is so unnatural for northern speakers to produce these schwas that French teachers must relentlessly, and most of the time quite in vain, drill their students to put them in; even the trained actors of the Comédie Française occasionally deliver a few "limping" lines (Gilbert Puech, personal communication).

The pronunciation of schwas in songs and poetry is thus to be attributed to a special competence that includes some specific rules based on orthography.

VIII.2.6. Schwa and slow speech

Morpheme-internal schwas not normally pronounced may show up phonetically in slow speech. They may in particular occur in correspondence with postulated lexical protective schwas (e.g., *samedi* [samdi] 'Saturday' may be pronounced [samədi] in slow speech). Dell (1970:56) considered this pronunciation to be evidence for an underlying presence (/samədi/).

As observed in sections II.2.2.3. and II.4.3.1., however, not all speakers produce a phonetic schwa under these circumstances (some consistently give [samdi] for *samedi* in slow speech), and not all words allow the occurrence of such phonetic schwas (e.g., *amnistie* 'amnesty' never yields *[amənisti] in slow speech, only [amnisti]).

The pronunciation of morpheme-internal schwas in slow speech appears to be generally governed by the spelling. In a significantly asymmetric fashion, speakers who do not resort to their orthographic competence do not pronounce morpheme-internal schwas anywhere in slow speech (unless of course they are required in normal speech), rather than putting them in even when they are not "present" in the spelling.

The facts concerning the pronunciation of schwas in slow speech are thus closely related to what occurs in poetry and do not in the least provide any evidence for protective schwas.

VIII.2.7. Conclusion

I have explored a number of potential cases where the occurrence of surface schwas might be taken as evidence for the existence of underlying protective schwas. In all instances the phonetic basis for protective schwas must be dismissed.

VIII.3. On the structural evidence for protective schwas

Schane (1968*b*) and Dell (1973*a*) have argued that protective schwas are structurally necessary because they allow a uniform and economical phonological treatment of [Ṽ] ~ [VN] and [Ø] ~ [C] alternations (see chap. v). In Parts I and II, however, I have shown, quite independently of the question of protective schwas, that the phonological rules of vowel nasalization and consonant deletion were inadequate to characterize the phonology of nasal vowels and final consonants in Modern French, and that in fact these alternations did not warrant a uniform treatment. Structural necessity is thus an invalid argument for maintaining the underlying existence of protective schwas in spite of the absence of phonetic evidence.

VIII.4. Protective schwas and learnability

Ultimately, the only solid correlation that protective schwas enter into is with the presence of an *e* in the orthography, as is implicitly admitted by Schane and explicitly recognized by Selkirk (1972) (see chap. v). This means that a pivotal aspect of the standard generative analysis of Modern French phonology depends on a skill which children do not usually master until after they have acquired language and which illiterates do not possess. Such a grammar is obviously not naturally learnable (see also sec. VI.3.3.6.).

VIII.5. Conclusion

Protective schwas are not justified underlying segments in Modern French. They have no phonetic reflexes, they have no structural raison d'être, and they are not naturally learnable.

Most instances of protective schwas were in word-final position (they were postulated morpheme-internally only to bar the application of vowel nasalization). The rejection of their existence does not mean, however, that there are no word-final schwas in phonological representations. In general, lexical final schwas are needed when they appear phonetically in the citation form of words. They are thus postulated in monosyllabic words such as those mentioned in section VIII.1. under the heading "Elision schwa." The underlying schwas of these words are pronounced, unless they undergo obligatory elision or optional schwa deletion (see sec. VIII.1.). Word-final schwas are also lexically required in stock expressions like *et ce* [esə] 'and this' and *sur ce* [syrsə] 'whereupon', where they are actually always pronounced since these phrases occur only before a pause. Finally, lexical word-final schwas are posited in conjunctions like *lorsque* [lɔrskə] 'when', *parce que* [parskə] 'because', *puisque* [pɥiskə] 'since', *tandis que* [tãdi(s)kə] 'as'. The final schwas of these words behave like the schwas of the monosyllabic words mentioned above, that is, they undergo elision, and optional schwa deletion when they are preceded by only one consonant; this behavior may indicate that these words are to be interpreted as containing the conjunction *que*.

The grammar thus does not require any process of final-schwa deletion systematically eliminating underlying schwas in all contexts in polysyllabic words.[4] The processes that do erase word-final schwas (elision and optional schwa deletion) do so in restricted environments, and the lexical schwas subject to these rules are easily recoverable from the surface phonetic level; in particular, they occur when the words are given in citation form.

4. The absence of a rule of schwa deletion at the end of words poses the problem of accounting for the pronunciation of *ce* and *je* in questions like *qui est-ce?* [kiɛs] 'who is it?' and *où suis-je?* [usɥiž] 'where am I?' (cf. Dell 1973*b*:252; sec. VII.2.1.2. n. 3). Following Morin's suggestion for *je* (1978:128), I assume that the subject clitics *ce* and *je* have been reanalyzed as the suffixes /s/ and /ž/ in questions with subject inversion.

IX

H-ASPIRÉ WORDS

IX.1. Introduction

In this chapter, I recognize the existence of several categories of h-aspiré words and present an inventory of their main characteristics. The abstract segment analysis of h-aspiré words is evaluated and rejected. I also show that exclusive recourse to syllable boundaries to explain the behavior of these words is inadequate. An account of h-aspiré words based on rule features is motivated and integrated into the general concrete framework of French phonology advocated in Parts I and II.

IX.2. H-aspiré words and elision, liaison, and suppletion

The essential descriptive claim traditionally made about h-aspiré words is that, although phonetically vowel-initial, they behave like consonant-initial words. Generative phonologists have generally focused their attention on this particular characteristic (Schane 1968a:7; Selkirk and Vergnaud 1973:251), and the phonological representations of these lexical items have been accordingly assumed to contain an initial consonantal segment. The exact nature of this consonant is uncertain; for example, Schane (1968a:7-8; 128-129 n. 15) and Dell (1970:90, 102) have suggested /h/ or /x/, and in an effort to give the abstract consonant a better phonetic basis, Dell (1973b:256 n. 72) and Freeman (1975) have proposed /ʔ/, because [ʔ] does occur phonetically in the language, in particular in conjunction with h-aspiré words. Following the noncommittal notation adopted by Selkirk and Vergnaud (1973:251), I will simply call this segment /H/.

The presence of an initial lexical /H/ in h-aspiré words accounts for their patterning with consonant-initial words rather than with vowel-initial words in the following cases:

(i) Elision:

Elision occurs before vowel-initial words but not before consonant-initial words and h-aspiré words, as illustrated in (1):

(1) (a) *l'étau* [leto] 'the vise' (cf. *le petit étau*)
   l'anse [lãs] 'the handle' (cf. *la petite anse*)
   (b) *le terreau* [lətero] 'the soil'
   la tache [lataš] 'the stain'
   (c) *le héros* [ləero] 'the hero'
   la hache [laaš] 'the axe'

(ii) Liaison:

Liaison takes place before vowel-initial words but not before consonant-initial words and h-aspiré words. In terms of the standard generative analysis of nasal vowels and final consonants (see chaps. i and v), the rules of vowel nasalization and consonant deletion fail to apply before vowel-initial words, but they do operate before consonant-initial words and h-aspiré words. This is exemplified in (2):

(2) (a) *un certain étau* [ɛ̃sɛrtɛneto] 'a certain vise'
   un mauvais étau [ɛ̃mɔvɛzeto] 'a bad vise'
   (b) *un certain terreau* [ɛ̃sɛrtɛ̃tero] 'a certain soil'
   un mauvais terreau [ɛ̃mɔvɛtero] 'a bad soil'
   (c) *un certain héros* [ɛ̃sɛrtɛ̃ero] 'a certain hero'
   un mauvais héros [ɛ̃mɔvɛero] 'a bad hero'

(iii) Suppletion:

In the use of suppletive forms, h-aspiré words pattern after consonant-initial words, not after vowel-initial words, as shown in (3):

(3) (a) *cet étau* [sɛteto] 'this vise'
   un nouvel étau [ɛ̃nuvɛleto] 'a new vise'
   son anse [sɔ̃nãs] 'his handle'
   (b) *ce terreau* [sətero] 'this soil'
   un nouveau terreau [ɛ̃nuvotero] 'a new soil'
   sa tache [sataš] 'his stain'
   (c) *ce héros* [səero] 'this hero'
   un nouveau héros [ɛ̃nuvoero] 'a new hero'
   sa hache [saaš] 'his axe'

Also, as a direct result of the absence of elision before consonant-initial words and h-aspiré words, the forms *du* (from *de* + *le*) and *au* (from *à* + *le*) are used with these words but not with vowel-initial words, as illustrated in (4):

(4) (a) *de l'étau* [dəleto]
   à l'étau [aleto]
   (b) *du terreau* [dytero]
   au terreau [otero]
   (c) *du héros* [dyero]
   au héros [oero]

The postulation of an initial lexical consonant in h-aspiré words straightforwardly and uniformly explains the facts described in (i)–(iii).

Selkirk and Vergnaud (1973) argue for the necessity of this analysis as opposed to one that would consist in assuming that h-aspiré words are lexically vowel-initial and marked by rule features: "In the case of Consonant Truncation and Nasalization, a treatment of the h aspiré exceptions in terms of rule features is impossible. The sequences 'consonant # "h aspiré" X' and 'vowel nasal consonant # "h aspiré" X' do not satisfy the structural descriptions of Consonant Truncation and Nasalization, respectively (if one were to assume that h aspiré words are vowel-initial). Yet, the rules apply to these sequences" (252). But in a treatment of nasal vowels and final consonants such as the one proposed in Parts I and II, a rule-feature analysis would of course be possible, since h-aspiré words could be marked as [–context Consonant Insertion] in addition to [–context Elision] and [–context Suppletion].[1]

The possibility of considering h-aspiré words as vowel-initial in their lexical representations is particularly attractive, because of a number of problems caused by the postulation of an abstract initial consonant in these words. First, as shown below, h-aspiré words do not actually behave like consonant-initial words "in every respect," contrary to what is claimed by Selkirk and Vergnaud (1973:251). Second, the postulation of /H/ leads to problems in the area of phoneme distribution (Dell 1970:91–92; Cornulier 1974). /H/ has a very restricted domain of occurrence: it does not occur before or after consonants or in word-final position; it occurs only before vowels. This defective distribution requires the postulation of otherwise unnecessary /H/-specific morpheme structure conditions. In addition, unlike other consonants, /H/ never occurs before schwa; this additional restriction obscures an otherwise general characteristic of the language, namely, that schwa never occurs in word-initial position.

1. As shown in Coats (1970), Kenstowicz and Kisseberth (1977), and Kisseberth (1970*b*), the theory must allow exceptional rule environment features.

Selkirk and Vergnaud (1973), however, see an important advantage offered by the abstract segment analysis of h-aspiré words over a rule-feature solution. The latter would require "a separate rule feature for each process involved. It would thus fail to express an important generalization, i.e., that the h aspiré words behave in every respect as if they begin with a consonant. The rule feature analysis does not immediately explain, for example, why there are not words which entail Nasalization, but not Consonant Truncation, or why there are not words which do entail Vowel Elision and don't entail Suppletion. In order to explain these dependencies the rule feature analysis would have to include redundancy rules which have no natural foundations, e.g.,

[–context Vowel Elision] → [–context Suppletion]
and so on" (251).

Schane (1978*a*, *b*) has suggested a treatment of h-aspiré words which potentially eliminates both the postulation of /H/ and the lack of generalization of a rule-feature analysis. He proposes that h-aspiré words be entered in the lexicon preceded by a syllable boundary, which presumably cannot be removed from this position by the standard rules of syllabification (see Tranel 1979). The application of consonant truncation before h-aspiré words is accounted for by rewriting the phonological process of consonant deletion so that it operates before grammatical boundaries when they coincide with a syllable boundary. The application of vowel nasalization before h-aspiré words would be obtained in similar fashion (see Schane 1978*c*). In order to account for the absence of elision before h-aspiré words, Schane assumes that the process does not apply across a grammatical boundary that coincides with a syllable boundary. This, however, incorrectly prevents elision from occurring when it should, since, for example, in the underlying representation for *l'arbre* [larbr] 'the tree', /lə#arbr/, the standard rules of syllabification will presumably place a syllable boundary between the article and the noun (between two vowels). Concerning elision, Schane's proposal must therefore receive the following interpretation (see Tranel 1979): if elision occurred before an h-aspiré word, the standard rules of syllabification would automatically attach the consonant of the elided word to the initial vowel of the h-aspiré word; it would follow that this vowel is no longer syllable-initial, and thus that the string is ungrammatical; elision therefore cannot apply. It is important to emphasize that, in this type of analysis, it must be explicitly specified that the initial vowel of h-aspiré words must remain syllable-initial. Entering h-aspiré words in the lexicon with an initial syllable boundary is therefore not sufficient; it may not even be relevant, since, as mentioned above, regular vowel-initial words can receive an initial syllable boundary, and nothing distinguishes a syllable boundary before an h-aspiré word from a syllable boundary before a regular vowel-initial word. Thus what is really needed is some sort of derivational constraint (Kisseberth 1970a, c) ensuring that the initial vowel of h-aspiré words remains syllable-initial. In sum, Schane's proposal turns out to be a rule-feature analysis, since h-aspiré words must be marked for the constraint, but it avoids the postulation of the abstract segment /H/ and it preserves the idea that a single factor is responsible for the behavior of h-aspiré words with respect to elision and liaison.[2]

It is generally taken for granted (even in /H/-less analyses such as Cornulier 1974, Klausenburger 1977, Gaatone 1978) that h-aspiré words behave uniformly with respect to elision, liaison, and suppletion, and that therefore the absence of elision, liaison, and suppletion before h-aspiré words must be due to one and the same reason. But there are data indicating that h-aspiré words do not actually behave uniformly with respect to elision, liaison, and suppletion. For instance, Cohen (1963:138) noticed the following about the word hameçon [amsɔ̃] 'hook': "Tout le monde dit 'mordre à l'hameçon', au propre et au figuré. Il y a partage pour d'autres combinaisons; il faudrait un référendum pour savoir quelle est la majorité: 'un-n-hameçon', 'mon-n-hameçon', ou absence de liaison, comme s'il y avait un h aspiré (je dis ainsi)?" Only an analysis based on separate rule features can explain Cohen's observation about the behavior of the word hameçon in his dialect:[3] hameçon is lexically marked [- context Consonant Insertion], but it is regular with regard to elision.

With respect to the phenomena of elision, liaison, and suppletion, there is another reason that makes a rule-feature analysis of h-aspiré words preferable to an abstract segment solution. Speakers show wide variability in the categorization into h-aspiré words and regular vowel-

2. As shown below, the rule feature needed in Schane's proposal cannot in fact be maintained because of other characteristics of h-aspiré words which are not shared by consonant-initial words. Also it is not clear how this analysis would prevent suppletion before h-aspiré words and avoid the derivation of incorrect outputs such as *[sɔ̃aš] for sa hache [saaš] 'his axe'.

3. Cohen's l'hameçon [lamsɔ̃], un hameçon [ɛ̃amsɔ̃], mon hameçon [mɔ̃amsɔ̃], sound natural to me, although I do not know whether they actually reflect my spontaneous speech.

initial words. The following examples, taken from Jacques Capelovici's column "télé-langage" in *Télé 7 Jours,* Cohen (1963:chap. 28), Sauvageot (1972:138), and personal observations, illustrate the tendency to use h-aspiré words as regular vowel-initial words:

(5) (a) Elision:

aux environs d'onze heures [ozãvirɔ̃dɔ̃zœr]
'around eleven o'clock'
nous étions des sortes d'héros [nuzetjɔ̃desɔrtdero]
'we were heroes in a way'
cette escrimeuse est trop nerveuse, ce qui l'handicappe
[setɛskrimøzɛtronɛrvøzskilãdikap]
'this fencer is too nervous, which handicaps her'
plusieurs bombardements d'harcèlement
[plyzjœrbɔ̃bardəmãdarsɛlmã]
'several harrying bombings'
l'haricot [lariko]
(term used to refer to a small child or person)

(b) Liaison:

des haricots [dɛzariko] 'beans'
un haut-parleur [ɛ̃noparlœr] 'a loudspeaker'
un hasard [ɛ̃nazar] 'a coincidence'
à tout hasard [atutazar] 'on the off chance'
le petit Hollandais [ləpətitɔllãdɛ] 'the little Dutchman'
moins hardi [mwɛ̃zardi] 'less bold'
des victimes hongroises [dɛviktimzɔ̃grwaz] 'Hungarian victims'
une moto était hors course [ynmotoetɛtɔrkurs]
'a motorcycle was out of the race'
ils sont hors jeu [ilsɔ̃tɔržø] 'they are offside'
les femmes sont harnachées de bijoux somptueux
[lɛfamsɔ̃tarnašedəbižusɔ̃ptɥø]
'the women are covered with sumptuous jewelry'
les handicappés [lɛzãdikape] 'the handicapped'
aux handicappés [ozãdikape] 'to the handicapped'
un handicap [ɛ̃nadikap] 'a handicap'
un gros handicap [ɛ̃grozãdikap] 'a big handicap'
de jeunes handicappés [dəžœnzãdikape]
'young handicapped people'
une fusée qui les handicappe [ynfyzekilɛzãdikap]
'a rocket that handicaps them'

(c) Suppletion:

cet handicap [sɛtãdikap] 'this handicap'
un bel harnachement [ɛ̃bɛlarnašmã] 'beautiful trappings'
le nouvel héros [lənuvɛlero] 'the new hero'
nouvel Hitler [nuvɛlitlɛr] 'new Hitler'

If h-aspiré words, like regular consonant-initial words, contained an initial lexical consonant, it would be surprising that they would thus tend to lose it, since word-initial consonants are stable in French. On the other hand, if h-aspiré words are marked as exceptions, as they are under a rule-feature analysis, it is expected that these lexical markings should tend to be removed from the grammar.

H-aspiré words are therefore taken to be marked [−context Elision], [−context Consonant Insertion], and [−context Suppletion]. For speakers for whom these exception features always go together, redundancy rules can be assumed to specify the dependencies.[4]

The lexical markings just postulated for vowel-initial h-aspiré words are also valid for the class of h-aspiré words that begin in a glide and are thus distinguished from the glide-initial words that do undergo elision, liaison, and suppletion.[5] Contrastive examples are provided in (6):

(6) (i) Elision:

    (a) *la hiérarchie* [lajerarši] 'the hierarchy'
        le huitième [ləɥitjɛm] 'the eighth'
        le whisky [ləwiski] 'the whisky'
    (b) *l'ion* [ljɔ̃] 'the ion'
        l'huître [lɥitr] 'the oyster'
        l'oiseau [lwazo] 'the bird'

(ii) Liaison:

    (a) *les hiérarchies* [lɛjerarši] 'the hierarchies'

---

4. It is possible that h-aspiré words behave differently with respect to different processes of consonant insertion. For example, whereas I accept *ils sont hors jeu* [ilsɔ̃tɔržø], I would reject *les hors jeux* *[lɛzɔržø] 'the offsides'; whereas I find *le petit Hollandais* ?[ləptitɔllãdɛ] marginally acceptable, I would rate *les petits Hollandais* ?*[lɛptizɔllãdɛ] as worse and reject completely *des Hollandais* *[dezɔllãdɛ] 'Dutchmen'. The syntactic environments in which liaison occurs may partly determine such degrees of grammaticality; I feel that the tighter the syntactic cohesion between a word and an h-aspiré word, the least likely the constraint on the absence of liaison is to be waived.

5. The glide-initial words that are considered regular (see examples (b) in (6)) are taken to be glide-initial underlyingly. Therefore, elision, consonant insertion, and suppletion are assumed to operate before words beginning in a [−consonantal] segment (vowels and glides), rather than a [+syllabic] segment (vowels).

        les huitièmes [lɛɥitjɛm] 'the eighths'
        les whiskys [lɛwiski] 'the whiskies'
    (b) *les ions* [lɛzjɔ̃] 'the ions'
        les huîtres [lɛzɥitr] 'the oysters'
        les oiseaux [lɛzwazo] 'the birds'
  (iii) Suppletion:
    (a) *sa hiérarchie* [sajerarši] 'his hierarchy'
        un beau huitième [ɛ̃boɥitjɛm] 'a beautiful eighth'
        ce whisky [səwiski] 'this whisky'
    (b) *son huître* [sɔ̃nɥitr] 'his oyster'
        un bel oiseau [ɛ̃bɛlwazo] 'a beautiful bird'
        cet ion [sɛtjɔ̃] 'this ion'

The behavior of the glide-initial morpheme *huit* [ɥit] 'eight' may also argue against an abstract segment analysis of h-aspiré words and in favor of a rule-feature treatment. The numeral *huit* is an h-aspiré word, as shown in (7a):

  (7) (a) (i) Elision:
        le huit [ləɥit] 'the eight'
     (ii) Liaison:
        les huit livres [lɛɥilivr] 'the eight books'
        un gros huit [ɛ̃groɥit] 'a big eight'
     (iii) Suppletion:
        un beau huit [ɛ̃boɥit] 'a beautiful eight'
        ce huit [səɥit] 'this eight'

The morpheme *huit* also behaves like an h-aspiré morpheme when it enters in combination with *cent* 'a hundred' to form the word *cent huit* 'a hundred and eight': liaison does not occur.

  (7) (b) *cent huit* [sɑ̃ɥit] *[sɑ̃tɥit]

It behaves like a regular glide-initial morpheme, however, when combined with *dix* 'ten' and *vingt* 'twenty' to form the words *dix-huit* 'eighteen' and *vingt-huit* 'twenty-eight': liaison occurs.

  (7) (c) *dix-huit* [dizɥit] *[diɥit] *[disɥit]
        vingt-huit [vɛ̃tɥit] *[vɛ̃ɥit]

In the abstract segment analysis, the morpheme *huit* may thus require one phonological representation in *huit* and *cent huit* (namely /Hɥit/), and another in *dix-huit* and *vingt-huit* (namely /ɥit/).[6] The

---

6. In the case of *vingt-huit*, the proponents of the abstract segment analysis might argue that the presence of an initial /H/ is not impossible, since in the series going from twenty-one to twenty-nine, the *t* of *vingt* is always pronounced, even before consonant-initial numerals (e.g., *vingt-quatre* [vɛ̃tkatr] 'twenty-four'). In the case of

existence of these two distinct representations presents problems for capturing the fact that the same morpheme is actually involved, since phonological representations are presumably the seat of such generalizations. On the other hand, in the rule-feature analysis, there is no difference in the segmental makeup of the morpheme *huit* in the various words where it appears; it is always /ɥit/. There is therefore no problem in capturing the intuition of native speakers that it is the same morpheme in all cases. The fact that it behaves as an h-aspiré morpheme in some of the lexical combinations in which it enters is a particular idiosyncrasy of the whole words; thus, in the cases of the numerals *huit* and *cent huit,* but not in the cases of *dix-huit* and *vingt-huit,* /ɥit/ is marked with the rule features typical of h-aspiré words.

IX.3. H-aspiré words and optional schwa deletion

As mentioned earlier, contrary to the traditional descriptive claim made about h-aspiré words, these items do not behave like consonant-initial words in all respects. For example, consonant-initial words allow the application of the optional rule of schwa deletion in a preceding monosyllabic word (see sec. VIII.1.), but vowel-initial h-aspiré words do not. This difference is illustrated in (8):

(8) (a) *il faut le visser* [ilfol(ə)vise] 'it is necessary to screw it'
      dans le bas [dāl(ə)ba] 'at the bottom'
      ce terreau-là [s(ə)terola] 'this soil'
  (b) *il faut le hisser* [ilfoləise] *[ilfolise]
      'it is necessary to hoist it'
      dans le haut [dāləo] *[dālo] 'at the top'
      ce héros-là [səerola] *[serola] 'this hero'

Within the framework of the abstract segment analysis, in order to account for this behavior and also for the fact that h-aspiré words exhibit no inherent initial consonant phonetically, a rule that systematically deletes /H/ must be postulated and extrinsically ordered after elision, liaison, and suppletion are handled and before optional schwa deletion takes place. In addition, optional schwa deletion must be rewritten so as to include in its environment the presence of a following consonant; it is thus changed from (9a) to (9b) (Dell 1970:88; 1973*b*:252–253):

---

dix-huit, the presence of the final consonant in *dix* might be similarly explained (cf. *dix-sept* [dissɛt] 'seventeen'), but its voicing from /s/ to [z] would presumably require the previous application of the /H/-deletion rule.

(9) (a) $\vartheta \rightarrow \emptyset$ / $\left\{ {//\atop V\ \#_1} \right\}$ C —

(b) $\vartheta \rightarrow \emptyset$ / $\left\{ {//\atop V\ \#_1} \right\}$ C — (#) C

where // indicates a pause

The added optional boundary is independently motivated because, as pointed out by Dell (1973b:252), "la séquence #Cə sujette à la règle est soit la première syllabe d'un polysyllabe, soit un monosyllabe #Cə# qui est séparé du mot suivant par une seule frontière #. Bref, elle est très étroitement liée à ce qui suit." Thus, the process does not apply, for instance, in cases like *fais-le attendre* /fɛ#lə##atãdr/ [fɛləatãdr] *[fɛlatãdr] 'make him wait' and *fais-le manger* /fɛ#lə##mãže/ [fɛlə-mãže] *[fɛlmãže] 'make him eat' (contrast *fais le manger* /fɛ##lə#-mãže/ [fɛl(ə)mãže] 'make the dinner'). The consonant added to the environment is specifically incorporated by Dell to avoid the optional deletion of schwa when it is followed by h-aspiré morphemes that have been made vowel-initial by the rule of /H/-deletion.

In an analysis where h-aspiré words are lexically vowel-initial, the rewriting of optional schwa deletion as (9b) is sufficient to account for the nonapplication of the process before vowel-initial h-aspiré words, and there is no need to resort to rule ordering.

In the preceding section it has been seen that the class of h-aspiré words that begin in a glide behave like vowel-initial h-aspiré words with respect to elision, liaison, and suppletion. With respect to optional schwa deletion, however, the two categories of h-aspiré words do not behave alike: glide-initial h-aspiré words do allow the application of optional schwa deletion (Dell 1970:95), as illustrated in (10):

(10) *dans le yaourt* [dãl(ə)jaurt] 'in the yogurt'
   prends le huitième [prãl(ə)ɥitjem] 'take the eighth'
   ce whisky-là [s(ə)wiskila] 'this whisky'

This behavior can be accounted for by assuming that optional schwa deletion should be rewritten as (11) rather than (9b):

(11) $\vartheta \rightarrow \emptyset$ / $\left\{ {//\atop V\ \#_1} \right\}$ C — (#) [−syll]

An analysis that explains the facts of elision, liaison, and suppletion with h-aspiré words by assuming that these words must be syllabically separated from the preceding consonant (Schane 1978a, b; see sec. IX.2.) cannot account for the behavior of glide-initial h-aspiré words with respect to optional schwa deletion, since the constraint would not allow sequences like *ce whisky-là* [swiskila] to surface.[7]

Assuming that (11) is the correct formulation of the process of optional schwa deletion, h-aspiré words are thus regular with regard to it: vowel-initial h-aspiré words do not trigger the deletion simply because they do not provide the correct environment for it; glide-initial h-aspiré words do trigger the deletion by virtue of providing the correct context for it. It might be tempting to try to relate the behavior of vowel-initial h-aspiré words with respect to elision to their behavior with respect to optional schwa deletion, but the fact that glide-initial h-aspiré words behave differently with respect to the two processes seems to constitute a serious obstacle.[8]

IX.4. H-aspiré words and enchaînement

As pointed out by Cornulier (1974), vowel-initial h-aspiré words can be divided into two categories with respect to "enchaînement." Some h-aspiré words (e.g., *héros* [ero] 'hero', *hache* [aš] 'axe') do not generally allow a preceding consonant to be syllabified with their initial vowel:

(12) (a) *cinq héros* [sẽk/ero] *[sẽkero] 'five heroes'
       une hache [yn/aš] *[ynaš] 'an axe'
       where the slanted bar indicates absence of
       enchaînement

Others (e.g., *Hollandais* [ɔllãdɛ] 'Dutchman', *hauteur* [otœr] 'height') do tolerate enchaînement:

(12) (b) *cinq Hollandais* [sẽk/ɔllãdɛ] ~ [sẽkɔllãdɛ]
       'five Dutchmen'
       une hauteur [yn/otœr] ~ [ynotœr] 'a height'

The data illustrated in (12b) show clearly that an analysis that argues that h-aspiré words must always have a syllable boundary before the initial vowel is inadequate (cf. Schane 1978*a, b*; sec. IX.2.). It should also be clear that an abstract segment analysis of h-aspiré words cannot attribute the facts concerning enchaînement to the presence of /H/, unless two kinds of abstract /H/'s are postulated, as is in effect proposed by Freeman (1975).

7. These data also appear to contradict Cornulier's (1974) principle that h-aspiré words cannot be preceded by a consonantal clitic.

8. This obstacle might be lifted if one assumed that glide-initial h-aspiré words do not undergo elision because elision applies only before vowel-initial words. This would imply, however, that regular glide-initial words, which do undergo elision, must be considered vowel-initial underlyingly (cf. n. 5).

In the framework of the rule-feature analysis being constructed here, it is sufficient to assume that words like *héros* and *hache* are lexically marked as being unable to undergo the normal processes of syllabification, whereas words like *Hollandais* and *hauteur* are marked as optional exceptions to these rules.

Wide variability can be observed in this domain. Not all speakers have the same words marked in the same way. For example, the h-aspiré word *hausse* [os] 'increase' appears to tolerate enchaînement in Montreal French (cf. *une maudite hausse* [ynmoditos] 'a goddamn increase'), but not in Parisian French (cf. *une maudite hausse* [ynmodit/os]). This is expected in the framework of a rule-feature account.

IX.5. H-aspiré words and final schwas

H-aspiré words have a characteristic shared by neither consonant-initial words nor vowel-initial words. They may trigger the phonetic presence of a schwa at the end of a preceding consonant-final word, as illustrated in (13):

(13) (a) *une anse* [ynās] *[ynəās] 'a handle'
    (b) *une tache* [yntaš] *[ynətaš] 'a stain'
    (c) *une hache* [yn/aš] [ynəaš] 'an axe'

In the framework of the standard generative analysis of French phonology, these schwas are considered to be the phonetic reflexes of underlying schwas (see sec. VIII.2.1.). In order to account for this property of h-aspiré words to govern the retention of a preceding final schwa, three solutions have to my knowledge been proposed. Dell (1970:86–88) resorts to crucially ordered rules of word-boundary readjustment in front of /H/. For instance, in the case of *une hache* /yn+ə#Haš/ [ynəaš], a rule ordered before final schwa deletion removes the word boundary that separates the schwa from /H/, yielding /yn+əHaš/, a representation to which the rule of word-final schwa deletion is inapplicable. The rule of obligatory internal-schwa deletion postulated by Dell (1970:14; 1973b:229) (cf. *samedi* /samədi/ [samdi]) does not apply either, because it is ordered after /H/-deletion, and it requires the presence of a following consonant (Dell 1970:88; 1973b:253). The elision process assumed by Dell (1970:6; 1973b:203–204, 252) to apply morpheme-internally as well as across a single boundary also fails to take place, because it is ordered before /H/-deletion. Selkirk (1972:374–375) assumes that schwa is a lax vowel, and that there exists a rule tensing pre-/H/ schwas and thereby preventing them from deleting. These two treatments are evidently ad hoc. Dell's solution in effect claims that the lexical units in *une hache* lose their individuality as words, at least when the phrase is pronounced [ynəaš]; if anything, the presence of the schwa actually serves to enhance the fact that there are two words. Selkirk's proposal makes the assumption that schwa is a lax vowel, but there is no evidence for this claim (Tranel 1977*b*:694). These unjustified operations, although written as conditioned by the presence of /H/, are ill-disguised rule features stating that a schwa may appear phonetically before an h-aspiré word; the presence of /H/ certainly does not provide any phonological motivation to the phenomenon of schwa retention in the sense that was argued for in the cases of elision, liaison, and suppletion. The third solution to schwa retention before h-aspiré words was proposed by Freeman (1975). He suggests that final-schwa deletion is blocked by virtue of a presumably universal constraint disjunctively ordering elision and final-schwa deletion. The problem with this solution is that, since elision does not apply before h-aspiré words, final-schwa deletion should always occur.

As shown in section VIII.2.1., the schwas that may appear before h-aspiré words are in fact not the reflexes of underlying word-final protective schwas. Rather, they are the result of an optional insertion rule triggered by h-aspiré words when they are preceded by a consonant-final word. Orthography was seen to constrain the process. Three other factors are also known to influence the occurrence of the schwas (cf. Dell 1970:86–88; 1973*b*:257):

(i) Length of h-aspiré words:

Everything else being equal, schwa tends to appear more readily before monosyllabic h-aspiré words than before polysyllabic ones. Thus, in the pairs of examples given in (14), the schwa is more likely to occur in the first member than in the second.

    (14) (a) *cette hausse* [sɛtəos] 'this increase'
            cette hauteur [sɛtəotœr] 'this height'
      (b) *il parle haut* [ilparləo] 'he speaks loudly'
           il parle hautement [ilparləotmā] 'he speaks haughtily'

As suggested by Dell (1970:86–88), stress may be the relevant factor.

(ii) Syntactic cohesion:

The degree of syntactic cohesion between a consonant-final word and a following h-aspiré word also plays a role.[9] Everything else being

---

9. This is probably to be related to the observation made in n. 4.

equal, the tighter the syntactic cohesion, the more readily a schwa will occur. Thus, in (15), the schwa is more expected between an adjective and a noun than between a noun phrase and a verb.

(15) (a) *une énorme hache* [ynenɔrməaš] 'a huge axe'
    un clown énorme hurle [ɛ̃klunenɔrməyrl]
    'a huge clown is yelling'
  (b) *une énorme hachure* [ynenɔrməašyr] 'a huge striation'
    un clown énorme hurlait [ɛ̃klunenɔrməyrlɛ]
    'a huge clown was yelling'

(iii) The number of preceding consonants:

Everything else being equal, the more complex the coda of the final syllable in the word preceding the h-aspiré word, the more expected the presence of a schwa. Thus, a schwa is more likely to occur in the first member of each pair given in (16) than in the second member.

(16) (a) *une énorme hache* [ynenɔrməaš] 'a huge axe'
    une grande hache [yngrɑ̃dəaš] 'a big axe'
  (b) *un artiste honteux* [ɛ̃nartistəɔ̃tø] 'an ashamed artist'
    un homme honteux ?*[ɛ̃nɔməɔ̃tø] 'an ashamed man'

The second example in (16b) lacks three of the reinforcing factors for schwa insertion, which accounts for its doubtful grammaticality. If one uses the monosyllabic h-aspiré adjective *hâve* [av] 'emaciated' instead of *honteux,* the insertion of schwa yields a slightly better output: *un homme hâve* ??[ɛ̃nɔməav].

To account for the possible presence of a schwa between a consonant-final word and an h-aspiré word, I therefore propose the analysis summarized in (17):

(17) H-aspiré words are marked to allow the possibility of schwa insertion after a preceding consonant-final word. This process is a variable rule whose application is favored (i) by the presence of an *e* in the orthography at the end of the consonant-final word, (ii) by monosyllabic h-aspiré words, (iii) by a strong syntactic cohesion between the consonant-final word and the h-aspiré word, and (iv) by a complex syllable coda in the final syllable of the word preceding the h-aspiré word.

IX.6. H-aspiré words and liquid deletion

Liquid deletion is a process that may eliminate the liquid of word-final obstruent + liquid clusters when a consonant-initial word follows; if the rule does not apply, a schwa generally appears after the liquid (see Dell 1970:21–23; 1973*b*:236–238; 1976).

(18) *un arbre pourri* [ɛ̃narbpuri] ~ [ɛ̃narbrəpuri] 'a rotten tree'
une table pourrie [yntabpuri] ~ [yntabləpuri] 'a rotten table'
Liquid deletion may also occur before a vowel-initial word or at the pause; this phenomenon characterizes more familiar speech.

(19) (a) *votre ami* [vɔtami] ~ [vɔtrami] 'your friend'
une table en bois [yntabābwa] ~ [yntablābwa]
'a wooden table'

(b) *à la vôtre!* [alavot] ~ [alavotr]
'cheers!' (when making a toast)
à table! [atab] ~ [atabl] (= 'dinner is ready')

With vowel-initial h-aspiré words, one finds the following pronunciations, using as an example the phrase *l'autre hameau* 'the other village' picked by Dell (1970:89):

(20) (a) [lotramo]
(b) [lotrəamo]
(c) [lotamo]

In the analysis that claims h-aspiré words to be vowel-initial, these data are accounted for straightforwardly: (20a) corresponds to the application of none of the relevant rules to the underlying representation /lə#otr#amo/; (20b) corresponds to the application of the optional rule of schwa insertion proposed in the preceding section; and (20c) corresponds to the application of liquid deletion in any context (in particular before vowel-initial words) in familiar speech.

With glide-initial h-aspiré words and regular glide-initial words, my judgments on the data are as follows (cf. Dell 1970:96, 101–103):

(21) (a) *l'autre hiérarchie* ?*[lotrjerarši] 'the other hierarchy'
l'autre huitième ?*[lotrɥitjɛm] 'the other eighth'
l'autre whisky ?*[lotrwiski] 'the other whisky'

(b) [lotrəjerarši]
[lotrəɥitjɛm]
[lotrəwiski]

(c) [lotjerarši]
[lotɥitjɛm]
[lotwiski]

(22) (a) *l'autre ion* ?*[lotrjɔ̃] 'the other ion'
l'autre huître ?*[lotrɥitr] 'the other oyster'
l'autre oiseau ?*[lotrwazo] 'the other bird'

(b) *[lotrəjɔ̃]
*[lotrəɥitr]
*[lotrəwazo]

(c) [lotjɔ̃]

[lotɥitr]

[lotwazo]

(21c) and (22c) are explained like (20c). (21b) is explained like (20b); (22b) is ungrammatical because regular glide-initial words are not marked for triggering the rule of schwa insertion (17). (21a) and (22a) are practically unacceptable because the concatenation of the words yields sequences (obstruent + liquid + glide + vowel) whose creation the language generally avoids and for which alternative pronunciations are provided (cf. *sablier* /sabl+je/ [sablije] *[sablje] 'hourglass'; *engluer* /ãgly+e/ [ãglye] *[ãglɥe] 'to ensnare'; *trouer* /tru+e/ [true] *[trwe] 'to make a hole'). The validity of this explanation is confirmed by the following data, where the outputs created by liquid deletion are also practically unacceptable:

(23) *l'autre rien* ?*[lotrjɛ̃] 'the other nothing'

l'autre ruisseau ?*[lotrɥiso] 'the other river'

l'autre roi ?*[lotrwa] 'the other king'

(21a), (22a), and (23) become more acceptable when a slight pause is provided at the border between the words.

In summary of the interaction between h-aspiré words and liquid deletion, it can be said that h-aspiré words behave regularly, apart from the fact that they allow the triggering of schwa insertion when the liquid does not delete. Actually, they may trigger the insertion even if the liquid has been eliminated; thus, I have heard in spontaneous speech the phrase *une autre housse* 'another covering' pronounced [ynotəus]; such outputs are predicted by (17).

IX.7. H-aspiré words and glottal stops

A glottal stop may occur before an h-aspiré word, in particular when it is preceded by a consonant-final word (Dell 1973*b*:256 n. 72; Freeman 1975).

(24) *il hache la viande* [ilʔašlavjãd] 'he is grinding the meat'

sept héros [sɛtʔero] 'seven heroes'

une Hollandaise [ynʔɔllãdɛz] 'a Dutchwoman'

As pointed out by Cornulier (1978:50), the appearance of a glottal stop is not an exclusive property of h-aspiré words. For example, regular vowel-initial words may also exhibit it (Malécot 1975*b*).

(25) *cet émoussement* [sɛtʔemusmã] 'this dulling'

le verbe acheter [ləvɛrbʔašte] 'the verb to buy'

The function of the glottal stop may be different when it occurs before h-aspiré words from when it occurs before regular vowel-initial words. In the latter case, its function is generally "contrastive, emphatic, or citational" (Freeman 1975), whereas in the former case, it is not necessarily so. From a phonological perspective, however, the source of these glottal stops can be considered to be the same, namely, the possible consequence of the nonapplication of the standard syllabification rules. For regular vowel-initial words, "contrastive, emphatic, or citational" situations often suspend the normal application of syllabification rules; for h-aspiré words, this occurs as a direct result of these items being either optional or obligatory exceptions to the standard syllabification processes (sec. IX.4.).

A general optional rule of glottal-stop insertion can thus be written as follows:

$$(26) \quad \emptyset \rightarrow ? \ / \ C \ {}^{\$}_{\#_1} \ - V$$

(26) states that a glottal stop may be inserted between a consonant-final word and a vowel-initial word when the standard syllabification rules have failed to apply (for one reason or another) and have thus left a syllable boundary at the border between the two words.[10]

To recapitulate what has been proposed in the sections on enchaînement, schwa insertion, and glottal-stop insertion, consider the phrase *une hausse* 'an increase'. The word *hausse* is, at least in my speech, an obligatory exception to the standard rules of syllabification. This accounts for the ungrammaticality of *[ynos] and the grammaticality of [yn/os]. This phonetic output, however, is not the only possible pronunciation. Schwa insertion may apply, yielding [ynəos], or glottal-stop insertion may apply, yielding [yn?os]. All the possible outputs are obtained very directly, without recourse to abstract segments or extrinsic rule ordering.

IX.8. H-aspiré words and deletable final consonants

Before h-aspiré words, the morphemes *six* [sis] 'six', *huit* [ɥit] 'eight', and *dix* [dis] 'ten' lose their final consonants, as they do before consonant-initial words in Standard French:

(27) (a) *six héros* [siero] 'six heroes'
    huit haches [ɥiaš] 'eight axes'
    dix yaourts [dijaurt] 'ten yogurts'

---

10. Glottal stops may of course also appear in environments other than between a consonant-final word and a vowel-initial word (see Malécot 1975*b*). Rule (26) is thus only a very partial account of the phonetic occurrences of glottal stops in Modern French.

(b) *six bureaux* [sibyro] 'six desks'
huit taches [ɥitaš] 'eight stains'
dix valises [divaliz] 'ten suitcases'

In part A of section VI.3.3.1. it is shown that such words have a final underlying consonant (/sis/, /ɥit/, /dis/), and that they are marked to undergo the following minor rule:

(28) $C \rightarrow \emptyset \, / \, - \, \# \, C$

Rule (28) accounts for the facts illustrated in (27b), but it leaves the data given in (27a) unexplained. A rule feature is not even possible, since h-aspiré words, being vowel-initial, do not meet the structural description of rule (28).

Words like *six* have created difficulties for all the analyses of h-aspiré words. Schane's (1978*a*, *b*) proposal incorrectly provides for the deletion of the underlying final consonants of *six, huit,* and *dix* at the pause, since his new rule of consonant deletion applies when a word-final consonant is syllable-final (see sec. IX.2.). Kiparsky (1973: 88–92) treated h-aspiré words as phonological islands, that is, words always preceded by two word boundaries; but, as pointed out by Schane (1978*b*:140), before two word boundaries, *six, huit,* and *dix* keep their final consonants (e.g., *six arrivent* /sis##ariv/ [sisariv] 'six are coming'). Cornulier's (1974) framework does not seem to accommodate the facts either. In essence, Cornulier proposed that h-aspiré words require to their left the presence of the disjunctive variant of a word (i.e., its unmarked form or citation form); but the unmarked or citation forms of *six, huit,* and *dix* contain a final consonant. The abstract segment analysis of h-aspiré words itself does not fare well. Consider the word *cinq* [sɛ̃k] 'five' in the dialect where it behaves like *huit,* that is, keeps its final underlying consonant before vowel-initial words and at the pause (e.g., *cinq étaux* [sɛ̃keto] 'five vises'; *ils sont cinq* [ilsɔ̃sɛ̃k] 'there of five of them') and loses it before consonant-initial words (e.g., *cinq taches* [sɛ̃taš] 'five stains'). According to Cornulier (1974), in this dialect *cinq* may lose its final consonant before glide-initial h-aspiré words (e.g., *cinq yaourts* [sɛ̃jaurt]), but it must keep it before vowel-initial h-aspiré words (e.g., *cinq héros* [sɛ̃k/ero] *[sɛ̃ero]); although presumably there was a stage when vowel-initial h-aspiré words also triggered the loss of the final consonant of *cinq,* this is no longer the case, hence the problem for the abstract segment analysis. It should not be surprising that words like *six* and *cinq* are the source of difficulties in the treatment of exceptional words like h-aspiré words, because they themselves behave irregularly.[11]

Let us consider the solution to which the rule-feature framework proposed here leads. Since rule (28) cannot be used to explain the deletion of the final consonants in words like *six* before h-aspiré words, a special rule must be postulated, which can be informally written as (29):

(29) C → Ø / — # h-aspiré words

(29) is a minor rule that requires both the words to which it applies and the environments in which it applies to be marked; thus, words like *six* are marked to undergo the process and h-aspiré words are marked to trigger it. This formally ensures the generation of the data illustrated in (27a).

The grammar now has two separate rules of consonant truncation for words like *six*. One would expect these rules, which are both minor rules, to tend not to apply, but in independent ways, since they are distinct processes. The case of *cinq* in the dialect described by Cornulier (1974) provides some evidence for this prediction: rule (28) continues to operate (e.g., *cinq francs* [sɛ̃frã] 'five francs'), but rule (29) may apply only in the context of one class of h-aspiré words, those that are glide-initial. According to the data provided by Freeman (1975), there also appears to be a dialect where rule (28) applies (e.g., *huit garçons* [ɥigarsɔ̃] 'eight boys'), and where rule (29) does not apply (or optionally applies) before vowel-initial h-aspiré words that tolerate enchaînement (e.g., *huit Hongrois* [ɥitɔ̃grwa] 'eight Hungarians'), but still obligatorily applies before vowel-initial h-aspiré words that do not tolerate it (e.g., *huit héros* [ɥiero] 'eight heroes') and before glide-initial h-aspiré words (e.g., *huit yachts* [ɥijɔt] 'eight yachts'). For a more complete test of the independent existence of rules (28) and (29), it would be desirable to find a dialect from which rule (28) has disappeared but where rule (29) still operates. Such a dialect might be difficult to find, because rule (29), by virtue of being minor from the perspectives of both its focus and its environment, is likely to disappear before rule (28), which is minor only from the perspective of its focus.

---

11. As noted in part A of section VI.3.3.1., *cinq* has regularized in the speech of many speakers.

IX.9. Conclusion

This chapter provides evidence (i) motivating the treatment of h-aspiré words by means of rule features, and (ii) showing the weaknesses of solutions based on the postulation of an abstract lexical initial consonant or on exclusive reliance on syllable boundaries.

H-aspiré words are taken to behave regularly with respect to optional schwa deletion, liquid deletion, and glottal-stop insertion. The question of enchaînement is clearly established as proof of the necessary existence of a rule feature obligatorily or optionally barring the application of the standard syllabification processes. Schwa insertion is shown to be a variable rule for which h-aspiré words are also lexically marked. Finally, although the facts surrounding elision, consonant insertion, consonant deletion, and suppletion might initially appear to be of a unified nature, it is indicated that the absence of uniformity which actually exists across these phenomena for a given word in the speech of a given speaker, across categories of h-aspiré words, and across speakers, legitimizes the concept of separate rule features, without eliminating the possibility of a network of redundancy rules expressing the dependencies between the rule features in the grammar of certain speakers.

REFERENCES

Adriaens, J.-L. 1975. Problèmes de phonologie flexionnelle et dérivationnelle à propos des adjectifs du dialecte wallon de Roux. In *Contributions à la question phonologique,* ed. R. Rongen, 197–223. Université Catholique de Louvain.

Anderson, S. 1969. West Scandinavian vowel systems and the ordering of phonological rules. Ph.D. dissertation, MIT.

———. 1970. On Grassmann's Law in Sanskrit. *Linguistic Inquiry* 1:387–396.

———. 1974. *The organization of phonology.* New York: Academic Press.

Anonyme. 1624. *Ecloge praecipuarum legum gallicae pronunciationis.* See Thurot I:xlix.

Antonini. 1753. *Principes de la grammaire françoise pratique et raisonnée.* See Thurot I:lxxxi.

Aronoff, M. 1976. *Word formation in generative grammar.* Cambridge, MA: MIT Press.

Basbøll, H. 1978. Boundaries and ranking of rules in French phonology. In *Etudes de phonologie française,* ed. B. de Cornulier and F. Dell, 3–18. Paris: Editions du CNRS.

Bauche, H. 1951. *Le langage populaire.* Nouvelle édition revue et corrigée. Paris: Payot.

Beauzée, N. 1765. N. In *Encyclopédie ou dictionnaire raisonné des sciences, des arts et des métiers,* Vol. XI, ed. Diderot and d'Alembert, 1–2. Neuchâtel.

Bescherelle. 1959. *Le nouveau Bescherelle. L'art de conjuguer. Dictionnaire des huit mille verbes usuels.* Edition renouvelée et mise à jour (36ᵉ). Paris: Hatier.

Bèze, T. de. 1584. *De Francicae linguae recta pronuntiatione.* Geneva. See Thurot I: xxxix–xl.

Bibeau, G. 1975. *Introduction à la phonologie générative du français.* Montreal: Didier.

Bloomfield, L. 1933. *Language.* New York: Holt, Rinehart and Winston.

Boulliette. 1760. *Traité des sons de la langue françoise et des caracteres qui les representent.* See Thurot I:lxxxii–lxxxiii.

Bourciez, E. and J. 1967. *Phonétique française: étude historique.* Paris: Klincksieck.

Bras, M. 1975. *Your guide to French pronunciation.* Paris: Larousse.

Bruneau, C. 1931. *Manuel de phonétique pratique*. Deuxième édition revue et complétée. Paris: Berger-Levrault.

Chen, M. 1973. On the formal expression of natural rules in phonology. *Journal of Linguistics* 9:223–249.

Chen, M., and W. Wang. 1975. Sound change: actuation and implementation. *Language* 51:255–281.

Cherrier, S. 1766. *Equivoques et bizarreries de l'orthographe françoise, avec les moiiens d'y remedier*. See Thurot I:lxxxiv.

Chifflet, L. 1659. *Essay d'une parfaite grammaire de la langue françoise*. Anvers. See Thurot I:lx–lxi.

Chomsky, N. 1957. *Syntactic structures*. The Hague: Mouton.

———. 1965. *Aspects of the theory of syntax*. Cambridge, MA: MIT Press.

———. 1972*a*. Remarks on nominalizations. In *Studies on semantics in generative grammar*, by N. Chomsky, 11–61. The Hague: Mouton.

———. 1972*b*. *Studies on semantics in generative grammar*. The Hague: Mouton.

———. 1975. *Reflections on language*. New York: Pantheon.

Chomsky, N., and M. Halle. 1968. *The sound pattern of English*. New York: Harper and Row.

Churma, D. 1977. On choosing between linguistic analyses: a reply to Klausenburger. *Lingua* 42:131–152.

Clayton, M. 1976. The redundance of underlying morpheme-structure conditions. *Language* 52:295–313.

Coats, H. 1970. Rule environment features in phonology. *Papers in Linguistics* 2:110–140.

Cohen, M. 1946. *Le français en 1700 d'après le témoignage de Gile Vaudelin*. Paris: Champion.

———. 1950. *Regards sur la langue française*. Paris: SEDES.

———. 1962. Quelques éclaircissements préalables à propos de l'acquisition du langage. In *Etudes sur le langage de l'enfant*, ed. M. Cohen, 7–32. Paris: Scarabée.

———. 1963. *Nouveaux regards sur la langue française*. Paris: Editions Sociales.

———. 1966. *Encore des regards sur la langue française*. Paris: Editions Sociales.

———. 1972. *Une fois de plus des regards sur la langue française*. Paris: Editions Sociales.

Corneille, T. 1687. Notes sur *Remarques sur la langue françoise de Monsieur de Vaugelas*. See Thurot I:lxvii.

Cornulier, B. de. 1974. Expressions disjonctives: h et la syllabicité. MS, UER de Luminy.

———. 1977. Le remplacement d'e muet par "è" et la morphologie des enclitiques. In *Actes du colloque franco-allemand de linguistique théorique*, ed. C. Rohrer, 155–180. Tübingen: Max Niemeyer Verlag.

———. 1978. Syllabe et suite de phonèmes en phonologie du français. In *Etudes de phonologie française*, ed. B. de Cornulier and F. Dell, 31–69. Paris: Editions du CNRS.

Dangeau, L. de. 1694. *Lettres d'un académicien à un autre*. See Thurot I:lxxi.

Dauzat, A. 1919. *L'argot de la guerre*. Paris: Colin.

De la Touche, P. 1696. *L'art de bien parler françois*. Amsterdam. See Thurot I: lxxii.

Delattre, P. 1951. *Principes de phonétique française à l'usage des étudiants anglo-américains*. 2d ed. Middlebury College: The College Store.

———. 1965. La nasalité vocalique en français et en anglais. *French Review* 39:92–109.

———. 1966. Le mot est-il une entité phonétique en français? In *Studies in French and comparative phonetics*, by P. Delattre, 141–149. The Hague: Mouton.

Dell, F. 1970. Les règles phonologiques tardives et la morphologie dérivationnelle du français. Ph.D. dissertation, MIT.

———. 1973a. "e muet," fiction graphique ou réalité linguistique? In *A Festschrift for Morris Halle*, ed. S. Anderson and P. Kiparsky, 26–50. New York: Holt, Rinehart and Winston.

———. 1973b. *Les règles et les sons*. Paris: Hermann.

———. 1973c. Two cases of exceptional rule ordering. In *Generative grammar in Europe*, ed. F. Kiefer and N. Ruwet, 141–153. Dordrecht: Reidel.

———. 1976. Schwa précédé d'un groupe obstruante-liquide. *Recherches Linguistiques* 4, Université de Paris VIII, Vincennes.

———. 1977. Paramètres syntaxiques et phonologiques qui favorisent l'épenthèse de schwa en français moderne. In *Actes du colloque franco-allemand de linguistique théorique*, ed. C. Rohrer, 141–153. Tübingen: Max Niemeyer Verlag.

———. 1978a. Certains corrélats de la distinction entre morphologie dérivationnelle et morphologie flexionnelle dans la phonologie du français. *Recherches Linguistiques à Montréal* 10:1–10.

———. 1978b. Epenthèse et effacement de schwa dans des syllabes contiguës en français. In *Etudes de phonologie française*, ed. B. de Cornulier and F. Dell, 75–81. Paris: Editions du CNRS.

Dell, F., and E. Selkirk. 1978. On a morphologically governed vowel alternation in French. In *Recent transformational studies in European languages*, ed. S. Keyser, 1–51. Cambridge, MA: MIT Press.

De Longue, P. 1725. *Principes de l'orthographe françoise*. See Thurot I:lxxvii–lxxviii.

Demandre, A. 1769. *Dictionnaire de l'élocution françoise*. Paris. See Thurot I:lxxxv.

De Soule, B. 1698. *Traité de l'orthographe françoise ou l'orthographe en sa pureté*. Reveu, corrigé et augmenté par l'auteur, 2d ed. See Thurot I:lxxiii.

De Wailly, N. F. 1770. *Principes généraux et particuliers de la langue françoise*. 6th ed. Paris. 1st ed., 1754.

Domergue, U. 1805. *Manuel des étrangers amateurs de la langue françoise*. See Thurot I:lxxxvi.

Dubois, J. 1962. *Etude sur la dérivation suffixale en français moderne et contemporain*. Paris: Larousse.

Dubroca, L. 1824. *Traité de la prononciation des consonnes et des voyelles finales des mots français*. Paris.

Dumarsais, C. 1751. Baillement. In *Encyclopédie ou dictionnaire raisonné des sciences, des arts et des métiers*, Vol. II, ed. Diderot and d'Alembert, 17–18. Paris.

Dumas, D. 1978. La querelle des abstraits et des concrets, ses a priori idéologiques et la liaison de pluriel en français contemporain. In *Etudes de phonologie française*, ed. B. de Cornulier and F. Dell, 83–106. Paris: Editions du CNRS.

Dumas, L. 1733. *La bibliotheque des enfans*. See Thurot I:lxxviii–lxxix.

Duperré de Lisle, F. 1883. *Etude sur la prononciation française.* Paris: Delagrave.

Durand, M. 1936. *Le genre grammatical en français parlé.* Paris: d'Artrey.

Ewert, A. 1933. *The French language.* London: Faber.

Féline, A. 1851. *Dictionnaire de la prononciation de la langue française.* Paris: Firmin Didot.

Ferguson, C. 1977. New directions in phonological theory: language acquisition and universals research. In *Current issues in linguistic theory,* ed. R. Cole, 247–299. Bloomington: Indiana University Press.

Fouché, P. 1959. *Traité de prononciation française.* 2d ed. Paris: Klincksieck. 1st ed., 1956.

———. 1966. *Phonétique historique du français.* Vol. III. *Les consonnes.* 2ᵉ édition revue et corrigée. Paris: Klincksieck.

———. 1969. *Phonétique historique du français.* Vol. II. *Les voyelles.* 2ᵉ édition revue et corrigée. Paris: Klincksieck.

Freeman, M. 1975. Is French phonology abstract or just elsewhere: boundary phenomena and 'h aspiré' = [?], not #?! Unpublished MS, Harvard University.

Frei, H. 1929. *La grammaire des fautes.* Paris: Geuthner.

Fromkin, V. 1971. Simplicity is a complicated question. *Working Papers in Linguistics,* 17:76–84, University of California, Los Angeles.

Gaatone, D. 1978. Phonologie abstraite et phonologie concrète. A propos de h aspiré en français. *Linguisticae Investigationes* 2:3–22.

Galmace, A. 1767. *Llave nueva y universal para aprender con brevedad y perfeccion la lengua francesa.* See Thurot I:lxxxiv–lxxxv.

Girault-Duvivier, Ch.-P. 1843. *Grammaire des grammaires.* Nouvelle édition. Bruxelles: Société Belge de Librairie, Hauman et Cᵉ. 1st ed., 1811.

Gougenheim, G. 1935. *Eléments de phonologie française.* Paris: Les Belles Lettres.

Grammont, M. 1914. *Traité pratique de prononciation française.* Paris: Delagrave.

Grevisse, M. 1969. *Le bon usage.* Neuvième édition revue. Paris: Hatier.

Guillaume, P. 1927. Le développement des éléments formels dans le langage de l'enfant. *Journal de Psychologie* 24:203–229.

Guillet, A. 1971. Morphologie des dérivations. Les nominalisations adjectivales en -té. *Langue Française* 11:46–60.

Hall, R. 1948. *French.* Language Monograph no. 24, Structural Sketches 1. Baltimore: Waverly Press.

Halle, M. 1961. On the role of simplicity in linguistic description. In *Structure of language and its mathematical aspects,* ed. R. Jakobson, 89–94. Providence: American Mathematical Society.

———. 1971. Word boundaries as environments in rules. *Linguistic Inquiry* 2:540–541.

Harris, J. 1973. On the order of certain phonological rules in Spanish. In *A Festschrift for Morris Halle,* ed. S. Anderson and P. Kiparsky, 59–76. New York: Holt, Rinehart and Winston.

Harris, Z. 1951. *Structural linguistics.* Chicago: University of Chicago Press.

Highfield, A. 1979. *The French dialect of St. Thomas, U.S. Virgin Islands.* Ann Arbor: Karoma.

Hindret, J. 1696. *L'art de prononcer parfaitement la langue françoise.* Seconde édition, revue, corrigée et augmentée par l'auteur. See Thurot I:lxviii.

Hjelmslev, L. 1948-49. Le système d'expression du français moderne (résumé). *Bulletin du Cercle Linguistique de Copenhague 1941-1965.* Copenhague: Akademisk Forlag, 1970.

Hooper, J. 1972. The syllable in phonological theory. *Language* 48: 525-540.

———. 1975. The archi-segment in natural generative phonology. *Language* 51: 536-560.

———. 1976. *An introduction to natural generative phonology.* New York: Academic Press.

Howard, I. 1972. A directional theory of rule application in phonology. Ph.D. dissertation, MIT. Distributed by Indiana University Linguistics Club.

Hyman, L. 1970. The role of borrowing in the justification of phonological grammars. *Studies in African Linguistics* 1:1-48.

Jackendoff, R. 1975. Morphological and semantic regularities in the lexicon. *Language* 51:639-671.

Johnson, C. D. 1970. *Formal aspects of phonological description.* Project on Linguistic Analysis, second series, no. 11, Phonology Laboratory, Department of Linguistics, University of California, Berkeley.

Kammans, L. P. 1956. *La prononciation française d'aujourd'hui.* Amiens: Les Editions Scientifiques et Littéraires; Bruxelles: Baude.

Kaye, J. 1974. Morpheme structure constraints live! *Recherches Linguistiques à Montréal* 3:55-62.

———. 1975. Contraintes profondes en phonologie: les emprunts. *Les Cahiers de Linguistique* 5:87-101. Montreal: Les Presses de l'Université du Québec.

Kaye, J., and Y. Morin. 1977. Il n'y a pas de règle de troncation, voyons! MS, Université du Québec à Montréal and Université de Montréal.

Kayne, R. 1975. *French syntax: the transformational cycle.* Cambridge, MA: MIT Press.

Kenstowicz, M., and C. Kisseberth. 1977. *Topics in phonological theory.* New York: Academic Press.

King, R. 1969. *Historical linguistics and generative grammar.* Englewood Cliffs, NJ: Prentice-Hall.

Kiparsky, P. 1968a. How abstract is phonology? Paper distributed by Indiana University Linguistics Club. Reproduced in Kiparsky 1973b.

———. 1968b. Linguistic universals and linguistic change. In *Universals in linguistic theory,* ed. E. Bach and R. Harms, 170-202. New York: Holt, Rinehart and Winston.

———. 1971. Historical linguistics. In *A survey of linguistic science,* ed. W. O. Dingwall, 576-649. College Park: Linguistics Program, University of Maryland.

———. 1972. Explanations in phonology. In *Goals in linguistic theory,* ed. S. Peters, 189-225. Englewood Cliffs, NJ: Prentice-Hall.

———. 1973a. "Elsewhere" in phonology. In *A Festschrift for Morris Halle,* ed. S. Anderson and P. Kiparsky, 93-106. New York: Holt, Rinehart and Winston.

———. 1973b. Phonological representations. In *Three dimensions of linguistic theory,* ed. O. Fujimura, 1-136. Tokyo: TEC Company.

Kisseberth, C. 1970a. On the functional unity of phonological rules. *Linguistic Inquiry* 1:291-306.

———. 1970b. The treatment of exceptions. *Papers in Linguistics* 2:44-58.

————. 1970c. Vowel elision in Tonkawa and derivational constraints. In *Studies presented to Robert B. Lees by his students,* ed. J. Sadock and A. Vanek, 109–137. Edmonton: Linguistic Research Inc.

Klausenburger, J. 1974. Rule inversion, opacity, conspiracies: French liaison and elision. *Lingua* 34:167–179.

————. 1977. A non-rule of French: h-aspiré. *Linguistics* 192:45–52.

————. 1978a. French linking phenomena: a natural generative analysis. *Language* 54:21–40.

————. 1978b. Liaison 1977: the case for epenthesis. *Studies in French Linguistics* 1-2:1–20.

Koutsoudas, A., G. Sanders, and C. Noll. 1974. The application of phonological rules. *Language* 50:1–28.

Landais, N. 1850. *Grammaire générale des grammaires françaises.* Sixième édition revue et corrigée. Paris: Didier.

Langlard, H. 1928. *La liaison dans le français.* Paris: Champion.

Laveaux, J.-Ch.-T. 1847. *Dictionnaire raisonné des difficultés grammaticales et littéraires de la langue française.* 3d ed. Paris: Hachette. 1st ed., 1818.

Leben, W., and O. Robinson. 1977. "Upside-down" phonology. *Language* 53:1–20.

Léon, P. 1966. *Prononciation du français standard.* Paris: Didier.

Lesaint, M.-A. 1871. *Traité complet de la prononciation française dans la seconde moitié du XIXe siècle.* Seconde édition entièrement neuve. Hambourg: Wilhelm Mauke.

Levitt, J. 1968. *The grammaire des grammaires of Girault-Duvivier.* The Hague: Mouton.

Lévizac, J.P.V. de. 1797. *L'art de parler et d'écrire correctement la langue françoise.* Cited after Lévizac. 1853. *A theoretical and practical grammar of the French tongue.* 26th ed. London: Dulau and Co.

Lightner, T. 1970. Why and how does vowel nasalization take place? *Papers in Linguistics* 2:179–226.

Littré, E. 1881. *Dictionnaire de la langue française.* Paris: Hachette.

Love, N., and R. Harris. 1974. A note on French nasal vowels. *Linguistics* 126:63–69.

Malécot, A. 1975a. French liaison as a function of grammatical, phonetic, and paralinguistic variables. *Phonetica* 32:161–179.

————. 1975b. The glottal stop in French. *Phonetica* 31:51–63.

Malécot, A., and M. Richman. 1972. Optional word-final consonants in French. *Phonetica* 26:65–88.

Malmberg, B. 1975. *Phonétique française.* Troisième édition revue. Malmö, Suède: Hermods.

Malone, J. 1970. In defense of the non-uniqueness of phonological representations. *Language* 46:328–335.

Malvin-Cazal, J. de. 1846. *Prononciation de la langue française au XIXe siècle.* Paris: Imprimerie Royale.

Martinet, A. 1965. De la morphonologie. *La Linguistique* 1:15–30.

————. 1969. *Le français sans fard.* Paris: Presses Universitaires de France.

————. 1971. *La prononciation du français contemporain.* 2d ed. Genève-Paris: Droz. 1st ed., 1945.

Martinon, P. 1913. *Comment on prononce le français.* Paris: Larousse.

Mauvillon, E. 1754. *Cours complet de la langue françoise.* Dresde. See Thurot I:lxxxii.

Meigret, L. 1550. *Le tretté de la grammère françoèze.* Paris. See Thurot I:xxvii–xxviii.

Milner, J.-C. 1967. French truncation rule. *Quarterly Progress Report* no. 86, Research Laboratory of Electronics, MIT, 273–283.

———. 1973. *Arguments linguistiques.* Paris: Mame.

Monod, J. 1968. *Les Barjots.* Paris: Julliard.

Morin, Y. 1971. *Computer experiments in generative phonology: low-level French phonology.* Natural Language Studies no. 11, Phonetics Laboratory, University of Michigan, Ann Arbor.

———. 1972. The phonology of echo-words in French. *Language* 48:97–108.

———. 1974. Règles phonologiques à domaine indéterminé: chute du cheva en français. *Les Cahiers de Linguistique* 4:69–88. Montreal: Les Presses de l'Université du Québec.

———. 1978. The status of mute "e." *Studies in French Linguistics* 1-2:79–140.

Morin, Y., and J. Friedman. 1971. *Phonological grammar tester: underlying theory.* Natural Language Studies no. 10, Phonetics Laboratory, University of Michigan, Ann Arbor.

Nyrop, K. 1914. *Manuel phonétique du français parlé.* Traduit et remanié par E. Philipot. Troisième édition revue et corrigée. Paris: Alphonse Picard et Fils.

———. 1936. *Grammaire historique de la langue française. Tome troisième. Formation des mots.* Deuxième édition revue. Paris: Alphonse Picard et Fils.

———. 1968. *Grammaire historique de la langue française. Tome deuxième. Morphologie.* 5th ed. Gyldendal.

Ohala, M. 1974. The abstractness controversy: experimental input from Hindi. *Language* 50:225–235.

Orr, J. 1951. Les oeufs de Pâques . . . et d'été. *Le Français Moderne* 19:10–12.

Oudin, A. 1640. *Grammaire françoise rapportée au langage du temps.* 2d ed. "revue et augmentée de beaucoup." Paris. 1st ed., 1633.

Passy, P. 1899. *Les sons du français.* Paris: Firmin Didot.

Pernot, H. 1929. L'e muet. *Revue de Phonétique* 6:64–151.

Peyrollaz, M. 1954. *Manuel de phonétique et de diction françaises.* Paris: Larousse.

Picard, M. 1974. Re-examining phonological rules: examples from French. *Recherches Linguistiques à Montréal* 1:123–132.

Pichon, E. 1942. *Les principes de la suffixation en français.* Paris: d'Artrey.

Pope, M. 1934. *From Latin to Modern French with especial consideration of Anglo-Norman.* Manchester: Manchester University Press.

Postal, P., and G. Pullum. 1978. Traces and the description of English complementizer contraction. *Linguistic Inquiry* 9:1–29.

Pupier, P., and L. Drapeau. 1973. La réduction des groupes de consonnes finales en français de Montréal. *Les Cahiers de Linguistique* 3:127–144. Montreal: Les Presses de l'Université du Québec.

Restaut, P. 1763. *Principes généraux et raisonnés de la grammaire françoise.* 10th ed., "revue, corrigée et augmentée par l'Auteur." Paris. 1st ed., 1730.

Roche, J. B. 1777. *Entretiens sur l'orthographe françoise et autres objets analogues.* Nantes. See Thurot I:lxxxv.

Rochet, B. 1976. *The formation and evolution of the French nasal vowels.* Tübingen: Max Niemeyer Verlag.

Rosset, T. 1905. *Exercices pratiques d'articulation et de diction.* Grenoble: Gratier.

──────. 1911. *Les origines de la prononciation moderne.* Paris: Colin.

Rousselot, P. J., and F. Laclotte. 1902. *Précis de prononciation française.* Paris: Welter.

Roux, S. 1694. *Methode nouvelle pour apprendre aux enfants à lire parfaitement bien le latin et le françois.* See Thurot I:lxix.

Ruhlen, M. 1978. Nasal vowels. In *Universals of Human Language,* ed. J. Greenberg, C. Ferguson, and E. Moravcsik, 203–241. Stanford, CA: Stanford University Press.

──────. 1979. On the origin and evolution of French nasal vowels. *Romance Philology* 32:321–335.

Saint-Liens, C. 1580. *De pronuntiatione linguae gallicae libri duo.* London. See Thurot I:xxxvii–xxxviii.

Sauvageot, A. 1972. *Analyse du français parlé.* Paris: Hachette.

Schane, S. 1968a. *French phonology and morphology.* Cambridge, MA: MIT Press.

──────. 1968b. On the abstract character of French "e muet." *Glossa* 2:150–163.

──────. 1968c. On the non-uniqueness of phonological representations. *Language* 44:709–716.

──────. 1971. The phoneme revisited. *Language* 47:503–521.

──────. 1972. The hierarchy for the deletion of French "e muet." *Linguistics* 82: 63–69.

──────. 1973a. Sur le degré d'abstraction de la phonologie du français. *Langages* 32:27–38. English version: How abstract is phonology? In *Generative studies in Romance languages,* ed. J. Casagrande and B. Saciuk, 340–352. Rowley, MA: Newbury House, 1972.

──────. 1973b. The treatment of phonological exceptions: the evidence from French. In *Issues in Linguistics,* ed. B. Kachru et al., 822–835. Urbana: University of Illinois Press.

──────. 1974. There is no French truncation rule. In *Linguistic studies in Romance languages,* ed. R. Campbell et al., 89–99. Washington: Georgetown University Press.

──────. 1978a. Deletion versus epenthesis: a pseudo-controversy. *Studies in French Linguistics* 1-2:71–78.

──────. 1978b. L'emploi des frontières de mot en français. In *Etudes de phonologie française,* ed. B. de Cornulier and F. Dell, 133–147. Paris: Editions du CNRS.

──────. 1978c. Syllable versus word boundary in French. In *Contemporary studies in Romance linguistics,* ed. M. Suñer, 302–315. Washington: Georgetown University Press.

Selkirk, E. 1972. The phrase phonology of English and French. Ph.D. dissertation, MIT.

──────. 1974. French liaison and the X̄ notation. *Linguistic Inquiry* 5:573–590.

Selkirk, E., and J.-R. Vergnaud. 1973. How abstract is French phonology? *Foundations of Language* 10:249–254.

Serreius, J. 1598. *Grammatica gallica.* See Thurot I:xliv.

Shibatani, M. 1973. The role of surface phonetic constraints in generative phonology. *Language* 49:87–106.

Skousen, R. 1975. *Substantive evidence in phonology.* The Hague: Mouton.

Stampe, D. 1969. The acquisition of phonetic representation. *Papers from the Fifth Regional Meeting of the Chicago Linguistic Society,* 443–454.

———. 1973. A dissertation on natural phonology. Ph.D. dissertation, University of Chicago.

Straka, G. 1950. Système des voyelles du français moderne. *Bulletin de la Faculté des Lettres de Strasbourg* 28:172–179, 220–223, 275–284, 368–375.

———. 1955. Remarques sur les voyelles nasales, leur origine et leur évolution en français. *Revue de Linguistique Romane* 19:245–274.

Syllabaire de Bouillon. 1777. *Syllabaire prosodique ou la vraie prononciation françoise.* Bouillon. See Thurot I:lxxxv.

Thurot, C. 1881–1883. *De la prononciation française depuis le commencement du XVIᵉ siècle d'après les témoignages des grammairiens.* 2 vols. Paris: Imprimerie Nationale. Cited after 1966 ed. Genève: Slatkine Reprints.

Togeby, K. 1951. *Structure immanente de la langue française.* Travaux du Cercle Linguistique de Copenhague, Vol. VI. Copenhague: Nordisk Sprog-og Kulturforlag.

Trager, G. 1944. The verb morphology of spoken French. *Language* 20:131–141.

———. 1955. French morphology: verb inflection. *Language* 31:511–529.

Tranel, B. 1972. L'effacement du schwa au futur et au conditionnel des verbes du premier groupe en français moderne. Unpublished MS, University of California, San Diego.

———. 1974a. Le cas de l'effacement facultatif du schwa en français: quelques implications théoriques. *Recherches Linguistiques à Montréal* 1:1–11.

———. 1974b. The phonology of nasal vowels in Modern French. Ph.D. dissertation, University of California, San Diego.

———. 1976a. A generative treatment of the prefix *in-* of Modern French. *Language* 52:345–369.

———. 1976b. A note on final consonant deletion in Modern French. *Lingua* 39: 53–68.

———. 1977a. On the source of non-alternating nasal vowels in Modern French. *Glossa* 11:74–105.

———. 1977b. Review of *Aspects de la phonologie générative du français contemporain,* by M. Francard. *Language* 53:692–697.

———. 1977c. The [al] ~ [o] alternation in Modern French. To appear in *Juncture,* ed. M. Aronoff and M.-L. Kean.

———. 1978a. On the elision of [i] in French *qui. Studies in French Linguistics* 1-1:53–74.

———. 1978b. The status of nasal vowels in Modern French. *Studies in French Linguistics* 1-2:27–70.

———. 1979. Review of *Etudes de phonologie française,* ed. B. de Cornulier and F. Dell. *Language,* to appear.

Trubetzkoy, N. S. 1967. *Principes de phonologie.* Paris: Klincksieck.

Valdman, A. 1976. *Introduction to French phonology and morphology.* Rowley, MA: Newbury House.

Vaudelin, G. 1713. *Nouvelle maniere d'ecrire comme on parle en France.* Paris. See Cohen 1946:1.

———. 1715. *Instructions cretiennes mises en orthografe naturelle pour faciliter au peuple la lecture de la Sience du salut.* Paris. See Cohen 1946:1.

Vaugelas, C. de. 1647. *Remarques sur la langue françoise*. Paris: Chez la Veuve Jean Camusat et Pierre le Petit.

Vennemann, T. 1971. Natural generative phonology. Paper presented at winter meeting of Linguistic Society of America, St. Louis, MO.

———. 1972*a*. Phonetic analogy and conceptual analogy. In *Schuchardt, the Neogrammarians, and the transformational theory of phonological change: four essays*, ed. T. Vennemann and T. Wilbur, 181–204. Frankfurt am Main: Athenäum.

———. 1972*b*. Phonological uniqueness in natural generative grammar. *Glossa* 6: 105–116.

———. 1972*c*. Rule inversion. *Lingua* 29:209–242.

Walker, D. 1973. Syllabification and French phonology. *Cahiers Linguistiques d'Ottawa* 3:25–41.

———. 1975*a*. Contraintes profondes en phonologie française. *Les Cahiers de Linguistique* 5:77–86. Montreal: Les Presses de l'Université du Québec.

———. 1975*b*. Word stress in French. *Language* 51:887–900.

Wang, W. 1969. Competing changes as a cause of residue. *Language* 45:9–25.

Whitney, W. 1971. *Sanskrit grammar*. Cambridge, MA: Harvard University Press.